ART DECO SCOTLAND

DESIGN
AND
ARCHITECTURE
IN
THE
JAZZ
AGE

BRUCE PETER

ART DECO
SCOTLAND

Published in 2025 by
Historic Environment Scotland
Enterprises Limited SC510997

HISTORIC ENVIRONMENT SCOTLAND | ÀRAINNEACHD EACHDRAIDHEIL ALBA

Historic Environment Scotland
Longmore House
Salisbury Place
Edinburgh EH9 1SH

Historic Environment Scotland
Scottish Charity SC045925

British Library Cataloguing-in-Publication Data.
A catalogue record for this book is available from
the British Library.

ISBN 978 1 84917 344 5

Typeset in Acier, Futura and Garamond
Printed and bound by Short Run Press, Exeter, UK

FSC
www.fsc.org
MIX
Paper | Supporting
responsible forestry
FSC® C014540

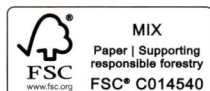

COVER
Tower of Empire, Empire Exhibition, Glasgow
Thomas S Tait of Sir John Burnet, Tait & Lorne
and Launcelot Ross, 1938

FRONTISPIECE
Scotland Pavilion, Empire Exhibition, Glasgow
Thomas S Tait of Sir John Burnet, Tait & Lorne, 1938
Courtesy of Ian Johnston

ENDPAPERS
**Lighting designs for Regal Cinemas and
Menzies & Sons, Aberdeen**
Claudgen Neon Signs, c1936
HES DP061451, SC1450655

CONTENTS

INTRODUCTION

Glamorous super-cinemas, flat-roofed villas, luxurious ocean liners, fashion boutiques, railway posters, tramcars, hydro-electric power stations, patterned linoleum, pithead baths and an Empire Exhibition: these were just some of the many diverse Scottish manifestations of the interwar modern design styles that since the late 1960s have been collectively defined as representing Art Deco. With a northerly maritime climate, Scotland may have seemed an unlikely place for large numbers of buildings and instances of design and visual culture exhibiting elements reflective of the sunny south and of smart metropolises such as Paris and New York to have materialised. Yet, the style was very influential among Scots, and during the 1920s and 1930s a remarkably large and diverse variety of Art Deco objects, structures and images were created. The production and experience of Art Deco in Scotland raises issues of how in the interwar era fashionable design spread through the expanding media from cultural centres to relatively small and unlikely places such as Peterhead, Tobermory and Stornoway.

It was the publication in 1968 of *Art Deco of the 20s and 30s* by Bevis Hillier, a young Oxford-educated historian and aesthete, that first provided a definitive guide to this highly appealing but hitherto critically neglected aspect of interwar visual culture.[1] Since

Hillier's identification of Art Deco, which he argued to have been the last 'total design style', interest in it has grown greatly and, where once buildings in the style were demolished with nary a backward glance, they are now usually listed, while Art Deco objects are sought by an international market of collectors.

The term 'Art Déco' had first been used by the Swiss-French architect, artist and theoretician Le Corbusier (1887–1965) in a review he wrote of the Exposition Internationale des Arts Décoratifs et Industries Modernes, a great exhibition of the decorative arts held in central Paris in 1925; this was published in the journal *L'Esprit Nouveau*.[2] His diminution of 'Arts Décoratifs' was reflective of his disdain for the majority of the exhibits shown within the Exposition, which he felt to be inappropriately ornate distractions from the more fundamental modernist design and cultural reform that he and his acolytes were seeking to achieve.[3] Thereafter, the term did not again appear significantly within architecture and design discourse until 1966 when, also in Paris, a retrospective exhibition of modern interwar design, entitled 'Les Années "25" Art Déco/Bauhaus/Stijl/Esprit Nouveau' took place at the Musée des Arts Décoratifs. It was the catalogue for this exhibition that probably inspired Hillier's work.[4] With hindsight, 'Art Deco' was an ideal moniker, being short, slick and indicative of sophisticated, fast-moving and up-to-date glamour and stylishness.

The content of the Exposition Internationale des Arts Décoratifs et Industries Modernes was highly diverse in character, encompassing pavilions that harked back

The Regal, Bathgate
Andrew D Haxton, 1938
Bruce Peter

to the ancient world and many more that sought to evoke colonial exoticism, plus a small number that were radically avant-garde. Britain's (and Scotland's) displays there were worthy but unexceptional. Whereas the Turin International Exhibition (Esposizione internazionale delle industrie e del lavoro) of 1911 had featured three rooms designed by Charles Rennie Mackintosh (1868–1928) and Margaret Macdonald Mackintosh (1864–1933), the Scottish exhibits in Paris were comparatively paltry. This reflected changed circumstances in the wake of the First World War which led to a more conservative vision of an imperial Britain centred upon London, rather than the design novelties from regional industrial centres such as Glasgow that were shown in Turin. The British displays at the Paris Exposition were influenced by the approach applied at the British Empire Exhibition at Wembley the previous year. As staging that event had used up most of the British government's exhibition budget, the UK's presence at the Paris Exposition was smaller than might have been expected of one of the major manufacturing nations. Nonetheless, its contribution comprised three elements. One was a pavilion that somewhat resembled a church on the Esplanade des Invalides by the River Seine designed by the American-born, English-educated, École des Beaux Arts-trained Howard Robertson (1888–1963) of Easton & Robertson. The others were a restaurant with a festively painted tented roof by the main entrance to the entire exhibition at the Pont Alexandre III, and display rooms within the Grand Palais, which was an existing structure containing exhibits from various participating nations.

The preparation of the British exhibits was overseen by HRH Prince Arthur of Connaught, President of the Council of the British Section, while their installation was arranged by Colonel Henry Cole. A relative and namesake of Sir Henry Cole, co-organiser of the 1851 Great Exhibition of the Works of Industry of All Nations, he was a veteran of the Indian Army who in 1921 was made Director of the Exhibitions Division of the Department of Overseas Trade and thereafter had a central role in organising the exhibits at the British Empire Exhibition.[5] Neither Prince Arthur nor Colonel Cole was of progressive persuasion, their desire being to express British tradition and to avoid at all cost any risk of the nation appearing insufficiently dignified. In these aims at least, they apparently succeeded. The *Glasgow Herald* reported somewhat fawningly that the British Pavilion was 'a monument of dignity, not without an ornate note, which gives it distinctness. The building,

graceful in its architecture, is symbolic of the country and the Empire it represents. There is a stateliness, a grandeur about it which differentiates it from other pavilions in the exhibition'.[6]

The Scottish contribution comprised works by nine students and staff members of Glasgow School of Art in textiles, jewellery and metalwork, there being four framed samplers, a silver brooch and items such as a candle-holder and a decorative plaque in brass.[7] These creations were undoubtedly virtuous, but their Arts and Crafts-inflected design reflected safely established approaches to aesthetics and making. In contrast with Britain, several of the other countries participating used the opportunity to assert boldly visionary identities that looked optimistically towards the future. Soviet Russia's contribution, designed by Konstantin Melnikov (1890–1974), was perhaps the most daring, its dramatic constructivist forms unambiguously portraying the aim of giving rise to a new kind of society. Largest in number, scale and ostentation were the French pavilions and displays; indeed, although the Exposition was promoted as 'international', a very large proportion was provided by the home nation, which used the opportunity to re-assert itself as the world's leading creator of all that was chic and luxurious. Germany was not invited to attend as Franco-German relations remained at a low ebb as a result of the recent war and post-war settlement, while America, which was invited, refused to exhibit, claiming that as it copied all of its 'high end' design from Europe, it would have nothing original to show.[8] This position, however, merely reflects the reactionary conservatism of its established arbiters of taste who would not have considered such quintessentially American cultural innovations as skyscrapers or jazz music as worthy of consideration.

In the years following the Paris Exposition, Art Deco forms and imagery spread around the world, manifesting in objects and edifices ranging in scale and complexity from tiny trinkets to the giant skyscrapers and trans-Atlantic liners that were among the largest human-made objects yet conceived. Art Deco appeared in quantity throughout the Americas, in the British, French and Dutch colonies and in China, Japan and elsewhere in the East. In such contexts, it combined with vernacular elements.[9]

For many, Art Deco is the luxurious-looking and stylistically exaggerated yet highly mannered aesthetic of a majority of the French exhibits and of decorative craft work in this style created in the exhibition's wake. Some

British Pavilion, Paris Exposition
Howard Robertson of Easton & Robertson, 1925
Bruce Peter collection

have suggested that, owing to its having been applied retrospectively by Hiller in *Art Deco of the 20s and 30s* as an 'umbrella' term, encompassing very broad diversities of decorative work with points of origination all over the world, Art Deco is more a 'tendency' than a 'style'. The American cultural critic Susan Sontag argues that style is omnipresent in human cultural production and that what often distinguishes early twentieth-century decorative work is its sense of artifice, which she terms 'stylishness'. She also notes that such theatricality is an essential ingredient of camp.[10] Art Deco imagery and ornamentation could indeed appear effeminate or exaggeratedly masculine and its concentration as surface rather than substance provoked and reflected desire. In terms of the framing of design debates in the mid-twentieth century, however, none of these characteristics was considered meritorious. Since then, revisionist stances have led opinion to shift, with the result that the style's qualities have come to be better appreciated.

Nowadays, Art Deco usually has a broad definition, encompassing all essentially modern interwar design that was inexplicable within the functional and rational terms of modernism, as defined by architects and theorists such as Le Corbusier, Walter Gropius (1883–1969) and Ludwig Mies van der Rohe (1886–1969) and by the American art critic Clement Greenberg. (The latter promoted the concept of 'medium-specific purity', through which each art form would focus only upon its own unique characteristic.) A consequence was the marginalisation of mixed approaches typically found within the mainstream of decorative arts output.[11] For many, modernism in architecture and design was characterised by three principles – the use of advanced technology, futuristically minimalist or highly abstracted aesthetics and a desire to use architecture, design and visual culture to achieve positive social transformation.[12] By contrast, Art Deco elements were often applied as embellishment upon underlying structures that used well-established technologies and on products and in environments that were primarily commercial in aim and aspiration. But such distinctions are clearer in theory than in practice. Particularly in the Francophone world, the term 'art moderne' was often used for hybrid work, which in any case represented the great majority of broadly 'modern' architecture and design output. (This combined the first and last words of the Paris Exposition's name but could also be interpreted as a successor term to Art Nouveau.)

The Art Deco style's architectural roots long predated the 1925 Paris Exposition, however. They were well established in existing decorative variations of European neoclassicism that were embellished with baroque and rococo-derived naturalistic ornamentation – and it was classical proportions and symmetry, rather than modernist abstract formalism, that initially usually governed Art Deco composition. The mannered design forms evident in Art Deco had a key point of origin in the wake of a different famous exhibition of the past – The Great Exhibition of 1851, which was housed in a vast iron and glass temporary pavilion erected in London's Hyde Park (which would become known as the Crystal Palace). Five years later, one of its organisers, the architect, designer, curator and critic Owen Jones (1809–1874), published a folio of patterns for decoration entitled *The Grammar of Ornament*.[13] Jones and his followers argued that all peoples and cultures produced patterning and that there was a universal grammar underpinning these forms that involved flattening out and abstracting imagery inspired by nature into simplified, repetitive forms. Only in Europe in the wake of Raphael's use of single-point perspective had this universal grammar been broken. Furthermore, for industrial manufacture, the universal grammar was ideal and it was morally wrong – indeed, a visual lie – to print three-dimensional perspective on flat surfaces. The content of Jones' *Grammar of Ornament* was eagerly imbibed by British manufacturers of wall finishes, tilework and textiles. Designs derived from the exemplars of patterning it contained came to feature heavily in British and foreign interiors of the latter Victorian era and thereafter.

In the years leading up to and after the Great Exhibition, Government Schools of Design were formed in response to increasing competition between the industrialised nations, the intention being that their graduates would work in industry to improve the appearance of British manufactured output. Glasgow's began in 1845, and eight years later was renamed Glasgow School of Art – a decision underscoring design's relatively lowly status in the cultural hierarchy at that time.[14] In the latter nineteenth century, one especially influential graduate of the Government

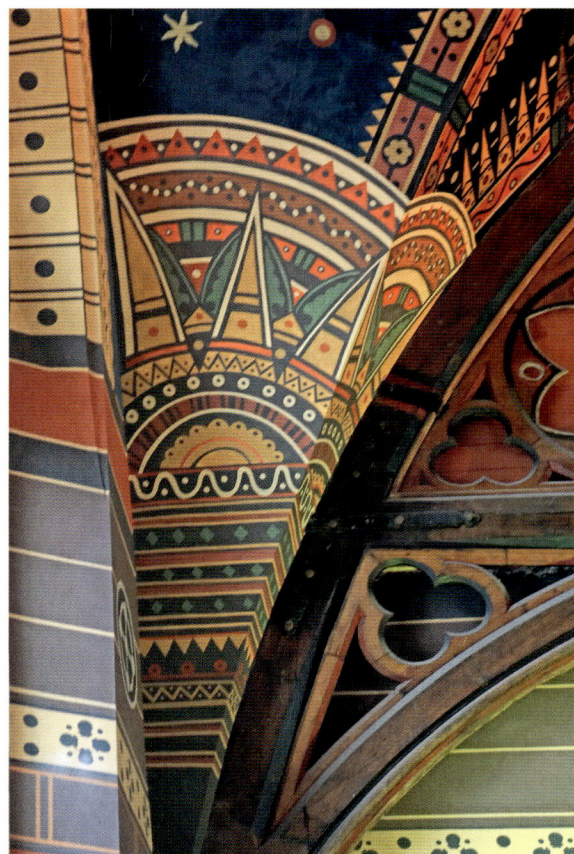

Dowanhill Church, Glasgow
William Leiper and Daniel Cottier, 1866
Bruce Peter

School of Design in London was Christopher Dresser (1834–1904). A Glaswegian by birth, he used heavily abstracted and aestheticised forms derived from plants to shape strikingly novel tableware and household ornaments, such as 'Clutha' glass, created in the 1880s for the Glasgow manufacturer James Couper & Sons.[15] With hindsight, many of Dresser's designs appear to have exemplified what would become characteristics of Art Deco and his approach continued to be influential in the interwar era and subsequently.

As Scotland saw itself as a forward-looking industrialised nation with a strong engineering culture, there was a well-established interest in whatever was up to date or emergent in visual culture. In the mid-Victorian period, the United Presbyterian Church

St Vincent Street Church, Glasgow
Alexander Thomson, 1859
HES SC777202

Guthrie & Wells brochure
Guthrie & Wells, 1925
Bruce Peter Collection

became a major patron of the decorative arts, using coloured, textured and patterned surfaces in its churches as a means of encouraging congregations to transcend their thinking from the earthly to the spiritual. For example, in Dowanhill Church in Glasgow, completed in 1866 to a design by the highly imaginative William Leiper (1839–1916), the entire interior was painted in a vividly ornate decorative scheme, embellished with equally vivid stained glass by Daniel Cottier (1838–1891). One of Cottier's pupils was Andrew Wells (1845–1918), who subsequently went into partnership with William Guthrie (1851–1939) in 1897, forming the major Glasgow interior designers and furnishing manufacturers, Guthrie & Wells. In 1913, Guthrie headhunted his successor John Alexander

Christie (1879–1964) from the London wallpaper manufacturers, John Line & Sons.[16] With Christie as managing director and principal designer, in the 1930s Guthrie & Wells produced colourful Art Deco interiors for restaurants, hotels, cinemas and other commercial premises for hospitality and entertainment. Their designs varied widely between boldly coherent schemes and ones that were merely twee.[17]

Mid-nineteenth-century church interiors and those of private homes and commercial premises designed by Alexander 'Greek' Thomson (1817–1875) likewise were highly coloured and patterned in a manner that would not look significantly out of place in the Art Deco era. His Egyptian Halls of 1870–72 in central Glasgow were to prove especially prescient as they deployed decorative forms that were not only favoured by Owen Jones but would experience a further revival in the interwar period as a result of the discovery of the intact tomb of the ancient pharaoh Tutankhamun in 1922.[18] The stylised forms and polychromatic ornamentation of ancient Egyptian architecture and visual culture were highly influential in Art Deco's initial development.

The prosperous industrialists of west central Scotland whose wealth enabled the patronage of art, design and architecture may have usually appeared outwardly conservative – but even in the latter nineteen century, several exhibited progressive taste tendencies. For a few, commissioning grand villas in Arts and Crafts or Art Nouveau styles signalled being up to date. For others, modernity was expressed by collecting French and Dutch art of the Impressionist school. So popular did this become among Glasgow's wealthy elite than a picture-framer and gallery owner Alex Reid came to specialise in its sale. The Scottish Colourists, a group of painters whom Reid also represented, followed a similarly Frenchified approach.[19] Around 1908–1909, John Duncan Fergusson (1874–1961) painted the scene on the terrace of the Café D'Harcourt in Paris, which was a popular meeting place for employees of the city's fashion studios. There, he captured models, dressed in the latest and most audacious styles, who had come to dine and socialise. Fergusson's treatment of the scene, with sharp black and white contrasts, pastel hues and bright floral flourishes, accords with a Francophile Scottish appreciation the fin-de-siècle Parisian aesthetic culture from which Art Deco would subsequently emerge.[20] In the first half of the 1920s, Reid exhibited works in Glasgow by Paul Gauguin (1848–1903) and Henri Matisse (1869–1954), among others, their combination of modern sophistication and tropical exoticism being an escapist antidote to the dark and often cold and wet industrial city to which they were transposed. In addition, he dealt in Japanese art, which since the mid-nineteenth century had been admired and increasingly sought by European aesthetes. Such exotic and orientalist imagery also influenced aspects of Art Deco ornamentation.

Derngate, Northampton
Charles Rennie Mackintosh, 1916
Bruce Peter

'The Dug-Out' design, Cranston's Willow Tearoom, Glasgow
Charles Rennie Mackintosh, 1917

The Edwardian era witnessed an economic boom, during which much new construction occurred. Buildings in the Glasgow Style of Art Nouveau were small in number but aesthetically significant, finding popularity especially among the more prosperous of the era's young adults. The daughters and sons of the mid-Victorian entrepreneurs and industrialists, they sought out such fresh visual culture, symbolising youth and beauty, and made it distinct to their own generation.[21] In Glasgow, the tearooms designed by the Mackintoshes for Catherine Cranston's successful chain were fine Scottish examples of a phenomenon that spread Europe-wide wherever significant industrial wealth and the craving for the novelty it enabled were found. They were forerunners of the many Art Deco catering outlets added in the 1920s and 1930s.

In the years preceding the First World War, the leading members of the Vienna Secession, founded in 1897 to encourage novel artistic and decorative work, and of the subsequent Deutscher Werkbund, established in 1907 to enhance German industrial design, developed new geometric forms of decoration. These were to an extent reflected in the boldly stepped door architrave and vertical fenestration of Glasgow School of Art's western elevation, designed by Mackintosh. They could also be seen in the hallway and bedroom he designed for the home of W J Basset-Lowke at 78 Derngate in Northampton in 1916, as well as in a striking scheme for a small space added to Cranston's Willow Tearoom on Glasgow's Sauchiehall Street, known as 'The Dug-Out'.[22] In ensuing years, Mackintosh produced numerous designs for textiles

and ceramics with geometric, wave and floral patterns and imagery, but no further designs by him for buildings or interiors were realised.[23] In the German-speaking world, where his inventiveness had been much admired, a new generation continued to develop similar forms into the dynamic modes of visual and spatial expression collectively known as Expressionism. In its early iterations, this often tended towards a modernised and greatly simplified version of the neo-gothic, involving the dramatic repetition of spiky, angular, slightly sinister shapes, which may in part have reflected their designers' wartime experiences. A similarly disturbing visual language was apparent in German film sets of the early-to-mid 1920s.[24] Exaggerated vertical and horizontal forms and interplay between them, as found in some expressionist imagery, would become a frequent characteristic of Art Deco composition. The former were perhaps suggestive of strength and levity while the latter could imply fast horizontal movement. Repetitive patterns of columns and bays, though a motif rooted in the Ancient World, were in modern contexts also relatable to ideas of mass production and consumption.

Much greater in quantity than Glasgow Style Art Nouveau buildings – but attracting far less retrospective interest – were large commercial edifices in the manner

of the École des Beaux Arts, the facades of which were composed of giant pilasters interspersed with window bays featuring restrained baroque enrichment and with deep cornicing around the roof edge. The appointment in 1904 of the Parisian architect Eugène Bourdon (1870–1916) as head of the Glasgow School of Architecture, the new joint programme of the city's School of Art and Royal Technical College, influenced the subsequent trajectory of the Beaux Arts style in Scotland. Beforehand, Bourdon had worked in New York, where he had been involved in the design of a skyscraper and so he had an appreciation for American monumentality and repetitive detailing, as well as a decorative sensibility gained through his French training.[25] Commercial blocks in the Beaux Art style continued to be built in Scottish cities well into the 1930s, albeit with Art Deco detailing appended where earlier the enrichments had been either conventionally neoclassical or baroque-inspired.

As Anthony Jackson showed in *The Politics of Architecture: A History of Modern Architecture in Britain*, published in 1970, only a couple of years after Hillier's work on Art Deco had appeared and making a comparably revisionist analysis, in 1930s Europe, attitudes to matters of architectural style were often the subject of factious debates. Arguments between British advocates of modern architecture and of the neoclassical occurred against a background of the extreme politics of Soviet Russia and Germany, in both of which avant-garde modernism had been suppressed in favour of state-approved neoclassicism. While there were fundamental theoretical differences underpinning these polarities of visual expression, in actuality there was often a remarkable similarity of appearance in what was built, elements of the two frequently appearing in hybridised form. Even so, whether a facade composition was symmetrical or asymmetrical, had vertically or horizontally arranged fenestration, used a modern or classical font for signage and had either a cornice or curved corners apparently counted for a great deal with regard to whether it was likely to

be well-received or disparaged by particular critics. Neoclassicism was regarded as a safe choice while too many modern decorative flourishes risked signifying adherence to current fashion with a commercial intent, which was thought unworthy by arbiters of architectural taste in both the classical and modern schools of thought.[26]

Particularly in its earlier manifestations of the latter 1920s and early 1930s, Art Deco building facades in Britain were essentially neoclassical, neo-Georgian or Beaux Arts in basic composition, which tended to favour symmetry. Usually, but not always, stripped-back versions of the neoclassical were preferred, with the exclusion of cornicing and columns in favour of flattened surfaces and with stepped rectangular pediments and architraves, rather than triangular-headed ones. In the 1920s, a distinctly monumental school of design emerged on both sides of the Atlantic and this was used for some government buildings and many commercial ones too, the aim being to project images of order and power as well as modernity. More generally, detailing tended either to be reflective of ancient patterning originating in the Near East, or abstract wave and zig-zag shapes that might also have had Mayan or Egyptian overtones, or could equally have been inspired by elements of continental avant-garde art, such as Cubism and Futurism, or even the rhythms of jazz music. In the USA, comparable architectural composition and decorative forms were found in designs by Frank Lloyd Wright (1857–1959), who was admired in the 1920s by British architects of progressive persuasion. Following the Paris Exposition, French-influenced Art Deco adornment began to be applied on New York skyscrapers, such as the 56-storey Chanin Building, constructed between 1927 and 1929 to a design by Sloan & Robertson.[27] Skyscraper imagery was thereafter emulated at much smaller scales as external and interior decoration on Scottish commercial buildings, especially when American references were thought appropriate.

Significant public, educational, commercial and exhibition buildings were occasionally adorned with Art Deco architectural sculpture, which was usually in essence neoclassical. The desire to represent handsome and heroic bodies on the one hand reflected British imperialist mythologising and on the other, ideals of health and youthful beauty that came to be emulated right across the 1930s European ideological spectrum. This ranged from communism at one extreme, via

Glasgow School of Art
Charles Rennie Mackintosh, 1909
HES SC1427928

various more moderate political shades, to fascism at the other. God-like and Goddess-like figures with unblemished skin and stylised hair were moreover a leitmotif of interwar figurative painting and commercial art. These were in some senses relatable to the realist tradition, while also referencing the countering tendency towards greater abstraction, the latter particularly apparent in background treatments that often were reduced to patterns of parallel lines and curves.[28]

At the popular end of the commercial spectrum, meanwhile, entrepreneurs realised that decorating their premises with jazz-inspired forms and patterning was an inexpensive way of signalling to a youthful clientele that they were fashionably up to date. Jazz had first arrived in Scotland in the late Edwardian period, heralding an increasing American cultural influence. 'Alexander's Ragtime Band', composed by Irving Berlin and released in March 1911, was a bandstand favourite with attendees of the Scottish Exhibition of National History, Art and Industry, which opened two months thereafter in Glasgow's Kelvingrove Park.[29] After the hiatus caused by the First World War, in December 1919, the 50-strong Southern Syncopated Orchestra, led by Will Marion Cook, arrived from the USA to perform a wide repertoire of jazz, ragtime and spirituals in the city's Kelvin Hall.[30] In 1932, Louis Armstrong performed in Glasgow, followed in 1933 by Duke Ellington.[31] (On a subsequent visit, Armstrong noted that his surname came from the Scottish managers of a plantation on which his forebears had been enslaved.[32]) Jazz brought a style of dancing that was distinct from European ballroom conventions and this, in turn, encouraged the wearing of novel styles of fashion and jewellery for easier movement and to complement the music's form. Syncopated jazz rhythms, moreover, seemed to express musically what were already emergent trends in progressive European visual culture, which in the twentieth century's first decades veered increasingly in favour of bold, contrasting colours and abstraction. Partly these trends reflected a desire to capture the speed and ephemerality of contemporary urban life, but they may also have been a reaction against the strictly formal neoclassical grandeur of the public buildings and monuments commissioned by the great powers. For many of the still-young veterans of the trenches, informality reflected a modern cosmopolitanism that was more attractive than expressions of nationalist pomposity and jingoism. British architectural and cultural critics were unenamoured with what became known as the

jazz moderne style, which from their perspective seemed to epitomise the worst aspects of commercial expediency and, worse still, Americanisation. (Though rarely directly expressed, such positions perhaps also reflected a latent racial prejudice against a visual culture arising from a predominantly black musical origin.) Although particularly notable in interior decoration, jazz moderne patterning adorned objects of many kinds, ranging from commercial art and printed textiles to furniture and tableware, the output of the British ceramicist Clarice Cliff (1899–1972) being particularly emblematic of the style's distinctive characteristics of colour and form.

Later in the 1930s, the size, splendour and style of ocean liners, some of the biggest and most technologically advanced of which were constructed in Clyde shipyards, helped to make internationally fashionable a nautical aesthetic of elongated horizontals with portholes or narrow glazing strips and walls with curved and chamfered corners. In Britain, North America and elsewhere in the English-speaking world, this tended to be described as 'streamline moderne' and, on account of the somewhat improved economic conditions, a greater amount of it was built in Britain than of the earlier, angular variety of Art Deco. Although, for some, Art Deco and streamline moderne are distinct styles, each with its own characteristics, they often manifested in hybridised form and so in the present work they will be considered within a broader understanding of Art Deco. There were also stylistic lags as some architects, designers and their clients who were less conscious of the latest aesthetic developments continued to design in the earlier manner.

A simple distinction between a building or object that was 'moderne' and one that was 'modernist' would be that the former would be designed in the established way from the outside in, beginning with the composition of the exterior, whereas the latter would be designed from the inside out with the facades merely a skin over whatever arrangement of internal content would best fulfil the programme. The moderne thus usually appeared to be formally relatively conventional, but with up-to-date detailing, whereas 'true' modernism aspired to achieve outcomes that were spatially, structurally and technologically more daring. In actuality, and not least in Scotland, as we shall see, it was usual that architects and designers of progressive persuasion fused together a range of what they considered to be modern elements. Reflecting this

Hilversum Town Hall, the Netherlands
Willem Marinus Dudok, 1931
Bruce Peter

hybridity, in the present work, the terms Art Deco and moderne are often used in combination.

Moderne building frontages are often composed of primary forms, such as horizontal and vertical cuboids, vertical projecting triangular sections and half-cylinders, used either symmetrically or as asymmetrical abstract formalist compositions. The earliest points of origin of this approach predated its widespread application in Britain and the USA by a couple of decades. In Germany, a pavilion designed by Walter Gropius for the 1914 Deutscher Werkbund exhibition in Cologne featured entirely glazed cylindrical stair towers at either end. Later, in the 1920s, Erich Mendelsohn (1887–1953) was the most prominent of a number of German commercial architects, mainly located in Berlin, who sought by similar means to reflect the dynamism of modern conditions in their designs for department stores and other new city-centre premises. Mendelsohn's approach had been inspired by a trip he had made to the USA in 1924 in the company of his friend, the film director Fritz Lang. The forms of the German ocean liner *Columbus*, on which Mendelsohn travelled, were translated into his subsequent building compositions.[33] Whereas Le Corbusier, who also greatly admired liners, advocated emulating their functional, technological and organisational aspects, Mendelsohn was more interested in their symbolism, using in his buildings features such as sundecks with ship-like railings and porthole windows.

In the Netherlands, meanwhile, the revolutionary De Stijl movement advocated the creation of a new universal visual culture using only such primary forms, along with primary colours, that would be equally comprehensible by everyone, transcending all existing cultural boundaries. It was a kind of Esperanto in art, design and architecture and was manifested in works in various disciplines by, for example, the artist Piet Mondrian (1872–1944) and the architects and designers Gerrit Rietveld (1888–1964) and J J P Oud (1890–1963), the latter of whom was the City Architect responsible for housing in Rotterdam.[34] Elsewhere in the Netherlands, Willem Marinus Dudok (1884–1974) designed a town hall for the new town of Hilversum as a series of rectilinear brick volumes.[35] Its clean-lined appearance, achieved through the use of a traditional material, proved inspirational for British architects when similarly faced with the task of lending dignity to large free-standing structures with relatively few windows.[36]

In Scandinavia, the Stockholm Exhibition of 1930 comprised nautical-looking curving pavilions in white with extensive glazing, sun terraces, coloured banners and bold graphics outlined in neon. Designed by a team of young Swedish architects led by Erik Gunnar Asplund (1885–1940), who was already well-established, it looked positively utopian under Nordic summer skies and attracted international admiration.[37]

Similar forms to those used by Mendelsohn in Berlin, Oud in Rotterdam, and Asplund and his colleagues in Stockholm were even found in new buildings in Moscow and elsewhere in 1920s Soviet Russia, where the communist government was the ideological antithesis of Mendelsohn's entrepreneurial clients.[38] In Russia and Germany, the subsequent rises of Stalin and Hitler mostly snuffed out such approaches in favour of monumental neoclassicism expressive of order, hierarchy and state dominance. Mendelsohn

Stockholm Exhibition

Erik Gunnar Asplund *et al*, 1930

escaped to Britain, where his work was greatly admired by influential RIBA members.

Art Deco and moderne thus spanned a wide hinterland, ranging from high Parisian sophistication at one extreme, through adaptations and combinations of various European modern aesthetics, to American mass culture at the other. While their characteristic forms are recognisable across these contexts, there is great variation in their scaling, in the complexity of their detailing, in the methods of making and in the quality of materials employed in their execution.

By the mid-1930s, when new buildings exhibiting Art Deco and moderne characteristics began to appear throughout Britain, the range of proprietary framing systems and off-the-shelf componentry for cladding and fenestration had proliferated. While reinforced concrete or steel framework could potentially be faced in a wide variety of design styles, certain facade finishes and types of windows were either specifically intended to assist in achieving Art Deco and moderne aesthetics, or were capable of adaptation. Since the latter Victorian era, faience ceramic tiles and blocks for facades and interiors had been made in Staffordshire. Architects arranged designs with reference to the dimensions and shapes listed in the manufacturers' catalogues, then submitted them for making, the finished kits being delivered to construction sites nationwide by road and rail. Although faience blocks could be moulded in a broad range of styles, the material particularly lent itself to smooth or fluted Art Deco or moderne treatments. Faience was most often in cream, biscuit brown or white, though it could also be coloured light green, orange-red or blue, the latter shades usually sparingly used, presumably on account of their greater cost. An alternative to faience was reconstructed stone which, similarly to terrazzo, comprised cement mixed with coloured granite chips, albeit formed into blocks, the outer facings of which were mechanically polished to achieve a slightly shiny, grime-resistant surface.

A third option, popular for Art Deco and moderne shop, pub, cafe and restaurant fascias, was Vitrolite coloured glass panelling. The Vitrolite company of Chicago was the leading maker and in 1932 the British glass manufacturer Pilkington of St Helens bought a licence to produce and sell its products in the UK. On both sides of the Atlantic, re-facing in Vitrolite became a common and successful way of modernising high-street premises and thereby hopefully boosting trade. Vitrolite could have graphics and patterns etched into its surface and enamel paint could also be applied. Other than stark black and white, its colours are usually soft – mint green, buttermilk yellow, pale pink or light blue being typical. A derivative of Vitrolite was Vitroflex, made from coloured or mirrored glass strips that could be wrapped round circular columns or used to line curved niches, giving them a faceted appearance with glinting highlights. Vitrolite is, however, very prone to breakage and, although once widely used, few completely intact installations survive. Faience, reconstructed stone and Vitrolite could all be washed clean, enabling frontages to stand out from neighbouring buildings clad in sooty sandstone.

The cheapest – and, with hindsight, the most problematic cladding material – was asbestos cement sheeting. An Empire product mined in Canada, asbestos was considered almost a magical material, being light, fireproof and, when mixed with cement or plaster, capable of being moulded and painted. It was only later that its fibres were realised to be carcinogenic. In the 1930s, it was used to clad factories, ice rinks, cinema auditoria, ballrooms and pretty much the entirety of the 1938 Empire Exhibition. No doubt it allowed projects to be achieved that would otherwise have been deemed too expensive – but at great health cost to those involved in making and installing the panels.

Perhaps the most style-specific factory-made components of Art Deco and moderne buildings were metal-framed windows with horizontal bars and curving corner units, mostly associated with the Crittall company of Braintree in Essex, but also produced by other manufacturers. During the 1930s, these became an almost indispensable feature of edifices of many types and their specification could lend a property a hint of the moderne look without need for much further effort.

The use of bright, coordinated colours is a characteristic of the Art Deco and moderne styles internationally – though in Scotland this was usually most evident in interiors. Legacies of nineteenth-century and early twentieth-century decorative arts styles, plus the discovery of the polychromatic treasures on Tutankhamun's tomb, gave architects, designers and decorators much to emulate. The boldest designs

by leading French decorators shown at the Paris Exposition were distinguished by strong contrasts, for example the juxtaposition of black and saturated red with soft pastel tones. Gilded enrichment was passé, with silver – the colour of the future – preferred for embellishment. Such palettes were considered daring and sophisticated and were replicated in Britain in exclusive Mayfair hotel and apartment interiors – spaces occupied by relatively small, exceedingly wealthy and cosmopolitan elites. By contrast, those designing mainstream commercial venues aiming to attract popular audiences usually sought to achieve a welcoming sense of warmth and so orange, apricot, tan and gold tones were more likely to be used. More often than is perhaps imagined looking back, British Art Deco and moderne commercial interiors also often featured dark shades of green, mustard and especially chocolate brown, which while relatively effective at concealing dirt were neither uplifting nor distinctly up-to-date looking.

A Scottish Art Deco?

Art Deco in Scotland raises issues and themes concerning Scotland's architecture, design and manufacturing roles within Britain as a whole and within the British Empire, as well as its relationships with continental Europe and the USA. There was a long-standing French influence upon Scottish culture and since the eighteenth-century merchants in Glasgow had developed close business ties with America. In the interwar period, as we have already seen, the impacts and effects of American popular culture came to be increasingly keenly felt in Scotland. The large Scottish diaspora, scattered across the Empire, included architects who migrated during the Great Depression, seeking better employment opportunities than at home. Art Deco in Scotland resulted from Scottish architects and designers discovering and adopting European and American practices.

With regard to the initial rise of Art Deco and moderne in the interwar era, the most important centre was of course Paris, followed later on by New York and with London as the first significant British location where the smart set sought to emulate the latest in continental style. In such a context, Scotland arguably represented a series of increasingly remote peripheries. The Canadian geographer and sociologist Rob Shields has shown how modern conditions have a hierarchical spatiality. In *Places on the Margin: Alternative Geographies of Modernity*, he observes that 'marginal status may come from out-of-the-way geographical locations… being the Other pole to a great cultural centre. In all cases … geographic marginality… is a mark of being… placed on the periphery of cultural systems of space in which places are ranked relative to each other'.[39] In the British national consciousness, the northern conurbations were framed primarily as sites of engineering and manufacture. This was particularly true of how Glasgow was represented, the large passenger ships built by Clyde shipyards being world-famous symbols of Scottish pre-eminence in engineering and skilled making on a very large scale. The farming hinterlands with their villages and market towns as well as the Highlands and islands, were seen as further removed and increasingly remote Scottish peripheries to be made desirable through promotion for tourist visitors – yet, in all these diverse contexts, examples of the Art Deco and moderne styles appeared. There were, of course, very lengthy physical, economic, cultural and perceptual distances between Paris, London, Glasgow and such small and far-flung communities. The ways in which the style manifested and was experienced in these locations were commensurately different too.

The idea of there possibly being a distinctly Scottish Art Deco implies that there were particular approaches north of the border that were recognisably different from those to the south and, that to achieve such a unique design culture would have required separate design educational traditions, trajectories of practice and professional infrastructures. In architecture, a prime discipline through which Art Deco was manifested in Scotland, these prerequisites were well established. The Scottish profession has its own organisation, separate from the Royal Institute of British Architects in London (RIBA), though with much cross-fertilisation of members and thinking between the two. The Royal Incorporation of Architects in Scotland (RIAS) can trace its origins back to 1840 in Edinburgh but became a national body in 1916 through the diplomacy of the distinguished Edinburgh-based architect Robert Rowand Anderson (1834–1921). Towards the end of his life he encouraged a merger of the Edinburgh Architectural Association and the Glasgow Institute of Architects to form the RIAS and donated his home to house its headquarters; it first gained its Royal Charter in 1922.[40] Scottish architecture and building had over time absorbed various continental influences,

and more recently colonial and American ones were integrated too. In the interwar era, the new RIAS and its *Quarterly Illustrated* journal provided channels for vigorous debates with regard to how modern Scottish architecture and urban planning should proceed. Irrespective of style, Scottish stone and harling lent many buildings a distinctly local character while, for some observers, modern asymmetrical architectural composition apparently could be interpreted as being a continuation of the Scots vernacular, shorn of period details. This was, however, a tenuous line of argument which possibly illustrated above all that one could see in modernism whatever one chose to see.[41] With regard to architectural embellishment, the revival of Celtic symbolism, which had gathered momentum since the latter nineteenth century as part of a wider European national romanticism, was occasionally reflected in sculpture, decorative glasswork and murals. Yet, in most instances, Art Deco in Scotland involved transposing, without much modification, forms, typologies and details originating in the sunny south or in the USA or both. There was often a striking disjunction between boldly novel insertions into the Scottish public realm, such as flat-roofed villas with extruded balconies, outdoor lidos with floodlighting, and cinemas with Hollywood-style signage, and their often couthy and sometimes dreich surroundings. What there was not in any significant amount in Scotland was the highly ornamental Art Deco found in France and the Americas. This lack in part reflected a desire among progressive Scottish practitioners to be aligned with reputable opinion about 'good' design exhibiting restraint, but it was also a reflection of economic necessity.

If architecture represented the respectable end of the Scottish creative spectrum, commercial art, another area where distinctly Scottish approaches may be identified, generally reflected modern taste in populist form. Poster advertising and product packaging directly addressed the consumer and, in many instances, up-to-date fonts, images and references were fused with ones that evoked nostalgia for much older Scottish traditions. Scotland already had its own abstract, geometric, boldly coloured national pattern in the form of tartan, which – contrary to what one might suppose – actually lent itself rather well to modern graphic, fashion and interior contexts. This was widely employed in travel and tourist imagery, as well as for the packaging of Scottish-made food and drink, among a wide variety of other situations. More prosaically, at the demotic extreme, what might be termed 'Scotchity' – naively romantic or downright banal Scottish imagery – was endemic in the interwar era: even the slickly futuristic Glasgow Empire Exhibition of 1938 included a Highland Clachan, a recreation of a small village which proved to be among its most popular exhibits.

Art Deco and moderne objects, edifices and images were inserted into a Scottish urban scene very different from that of the present day. Scotland was a coal economy and it was from the coalfields of Fife, the Lothians, Lanarkshire and Ayrshire that modest six-coupled steam locomotives of late-Victorian era design hauled unfitted trains of wagons to the towns and cities, where the coal was used for heating, industry and transport. Practically every room in every household had a coal fire and the belching chimneys of factories ensured that air in industrial areas was usually filthy with sooty smoke and, in autumn and winter, thick smogs enveloped the cities. The porous sandstone from which most of central Scotland's buildings were constructed was consequentially uniformly black with absorbed pollution. People smoked everywhere – at home, at work, on transport, in cafes, bars and restaurants and even at their seats in the cinema. Clothing became saturated in smoke from coal and tobacco alike and so, for housewives, doing the washing was a constant burden.

The Scots in the interwar years – and the British as a whole – were far more insular than they have since become. The social classes were more stratified with manual workers and their dependants forming a large majority of the population of the Central Belt. For men, the type of hat worn signified one's position in the hierarchy; 'bunnets' for the blue-collar labouring masses and bowlers for those of managerial rank. The rural lives of the substantial but widely spread farming communities were often separate again, though the rural and industrial mixed on the expanding urban fringes and in mining districts. The Scottish aristocracy led existences that were also distinct, though many were involved in farming through land ownership, or in industry as company directors and investors, so they, like most others, were buffeted by the era's strong economic, cultural and social winds of change. Only

the wealthy could afford cars and so public transport was the main means of getting about. Scotland was largely ethnically homogeneous too, though urban communities tended to be either overwhelmingly Protestant or Roman Catholic. Although mass-immigration was yet to begin, in port cities, the Indian seafarers who formed the crews of many British ships were part of the urban scene as they took brief shore-leave from their vessels. Scottish universities also taught relatively small numbers of students from all over the British Empire. The radio (or 'the wireless', as most would have referred to it) was a prime source of information and stimulation and a much greater variety of newspapers were read than today, while the cinema, following the invention of films with soundtracks in the late 1920s, soon gained crucial importance as a source of both news and entertainment.[42]

Glasgow, in particular, was far busier and much more densely populated than today, having approximately double the current population with very large numbers packed into inner city areas peripheral to the central business district. One did not have to walk far from the main city centre shopping streets with their grand department stores to encounter pockets of grinding poverty with slum housing and dishevelled children playing in the streets. Some city traffic remained horse-drawn, horse droppings lying on the granite sets and tramlines. There was little by way of litter, though – but that was because most food was unpackaged and had to be consumed either on the premises where it was purchased, or at home.

The after-effects of childhood malnutrition in the impoverished areas manifested in adults with bone-deformity. During the First World War, the poor physical condition of young men of fighting age became a political matter and across Europe regimes both moderate and radical encouraged investment in new sports and health facilities and, as we shall see, Scottish examples were often fine instances of moderne. Images in the popular press of film stars and the rich and famous enjoying riviera beaches, meanwhile, encouraged a growing popular interest in beautiful bodies. While this was mostly positive, there was also a darker aspect in the parallel growing fascination for the possibilities of eugenics.[43]

For those able to afford to escape, the great interwar expansion of suburbia offered a different way of living amid relatively clean air and green space. Municipal and private developers alike took degrees of inspiration from the pre-war Garden City concepts of Ebenezer Howard (1850–1928) to expand conurbations into the adjacent countryside. However, as suburbia grew, increasing numbers within the architectural profession tended towards agreement with the Welsh-born architectural romantic Clough Williams-Ellis (1883–1978) that an untamed 'octopus' of new arterial roads and urban sprawl was threatening to destroy the countryside. Others, meanwhile, were merely delighted by the amount of new building work this expansion was generating.[44] In the suburbs, light manufacturing provided new employment possibilities and transport was largely dependent on internal combustion engines.

Looking back, part of the fascination of the interwar period derives from its financial and political turbulence, involving great economic swings and radical politics with the rise of communism at one extreme and of fascism at the other. The effects of the post-war Treaty of Versailles of 1918, the stringent terms of which the victorious allies imposed upon a reluctant Germany, were to emasculate the economy of what, pre-war, had been continental Europe's pre-eminent industrial nation – but the consequent negative effects on international trade, coupled with Germany's size and central geographical position, caused stagnation across much of the continent. Scotland had in any case lost between 100,000 and 135,000 young men in the war and a far greater number were badly injured physically and mentally.[45] Had they not been cut down in their prime, many would no doubt have gone on to become the inventors, entrepreneurs, managers and skilled workers who would have refreshed Scottish culture, economy and public life, but instead it was an older generation who often perpetuated established ways of doing things while new developments happened elsewhere.

For those who did return from the war, there was anger about rising unemployment and a shortened working week, which led the Trades Union Congress in Glasgow to call a strike in January 1919 with a mass protest in the city's George Square. Fearing a Bolshevist uprising, the Sheriff of Lanarkshire requested military assistance – but it was the Glasgow police who baton-charged the protesters, dispersing them.[46] In the

1922 general election, Scotland returned 29 Labour MPs, signalling a growing adherence to socialism, particularly in the Central Belt. The 1919 strike was the first of a succession of sometimes prolonged and acrimonious disputes to affect central Scotland's industrial base and mining industry in the 1920s, culminating in the nation-wide General Strike of May 1926.[47] In America, meanwhile, fear that dissatisfied German workers might take inspiration from the Russian Revolution of 1917 led the US government to appoint the politician Charles Dawes to devise an economic aid plan, involving loans of $200 million to boost the German economy.[48] The Dawes Plan succeeded as intended and the epithet of 'the roaring twenties' may be thought of as referring to the economic boom that it helped achieve in the decade's second half.

The Wall Street Crash of 1929 and the Great Depression that followed particularly badly affected Scotland's manufacturing economy, as the kinds of large, capital-intensive, heavily engineered outputs it produced were among the first to cease to be ordered when the sharp downturn began and the last for which new orders were placed when confidence returned. Indeed, for the established industries, the decade from 1929 until 1939 was exceptionally challenging and it was their manual workers who suffered most. By contrast, there was some industrial expansion with the development of new, light industries, powered by electricity and making consumer goods, cosmetics and foodstuffs. Their growth in Scotland was less than in central and southern England, however. Service industries also expanded and the rising wages of the administrative class, combined with overall price deflation, gave them extra disposable income.[49]

Disenchantment with the political status quo led initially small numbers of Scots to believe that greater – or complete – national autonomy was in their interest. The National Party of Scotland, established in 1928 through a merger of three existing very small nationalist parties, favoured home rule, while the more moderate Scottish Party, founded in 1932, initially called for Scotland to have Dominion status, akin to Canada. The two merged in 1934 to form the Scottish Nationalist Party, but it remained for the time being a minor political force. The aim of Scotland running more of its own affairs and cultivating a distinct identity as a British nation, however, gained a growing following with tacit support from across the political spectrum and this contributed to the case for the strengthening of the Scottish Office as a department of the British government.[50] The consequently expanded bureaucracy would need a new headquarters in Edinburgh, providing an architectural opportunity to reflect a modern Scottish identity.

The Great Depression had mostly negative consequences both for the architectural profession and for the construction industry, in both of which work became suddenly scarce. There were a few years of recovery between the mid-1930s and 1939, the peak year for building being 1937, after which political instability in Europe meant that finance for new projects became harder to obtain. Towards the end of the decade, the rearmament programme made inroads into steel supplies, meaning that its price rose and less was available. Britain's declaration of war on 3 September 1939 brought an abrupt end to all new non-essential building while permission needed to be sought for the completion of projects already under way.[51] It was not until the 1950s that new construction projects began once more on an appreciable scale.

CHAPTER 1
THE ARCHITECTURE AND DESIGN PROFESSIONS

The interwar era is a fascinating period of intellectual and aesthetic ferment across the arts – and, as Charles McKean showed in the landmark publication *The Scottish Thirties*, the architecture scene in Scotland to a significant extent reflected this uncertain situation.[1] Neoclassicism – the established aesthetic of order and authority from the ancient world via the Renaissance and the Enlightenment – was one eminently respectable design approach at that time; a national romantic aesthetic inspired by regional vernaculars and given fresh impetus by the Arts and Crafts Movement was another, and new forms of architecture that sought in some way to reflect present conditions and to foresee those of the future formed a third. In reality, many of the Scottish buildings definable under the loose umbrella of 'Art Deco' to a greater or lesser extent reflected all of these broad approaches, quite often in hybridised form.

Another factor impacting upon architectural debates was that the profession's sense of authority as a maintainer of high culture and arbiter of cultivated taste was appearing increasingly threatened by entrepreneurial newcomers who seemed content to choose commercial expediency over artistic virtue. To an extent, the different outlooks within the Scottish profession related to the differences between

the generations and even cultural and contextual differences between, for example, Edinburgh-based practitioners who aspired to perpetuate its grand architectural traditions and some in Glasgow who were more used to serving the needs of commerce and industry, while necessity led firms based outwith the largest cities to be flexible.

As far as the *Quarterly Illustrated* journal, the official organ of RIAS, was concerned, the Paris Exposition might as well have been taking place on a different planet; no mention of it whatsoever was made in 1925 or thereafter. Instead, the *Quarterly Illustrated*'s prime focus was on what could be learned from the great Scottish architecture of the past, which mostly meant eighteenth-century neoclassicism, explained in a series of scholarly articles by the architect and educator, T Harold Hughes (1887–1949). However, even the erudite but traditionalist Hughes would occasionally create moderne design when he felt that a building's programme merited such treatment, or a client demanded it. In the autumn of 1926 the 'modern' and 'commercial' asserted themselves in the *Quarterly Illustrated* when an article concerning the design of skyscrapers entitled 'The Quest of Maximum Efficiency' by Earle Schultz was reproduced from the *Journal of the American Institute of Architects*. The editor's foreword noted caustically that an architect whose focus was on the optimisation of efficiency 'may not receive the Royal Gold Medal but he will have the blessings of his clients'.[2]

'Modern Fenestration', student drawing
Antony Wolffe, c1938
HES DP200484

In the summer of 1929, the *Quarterly Illustrated* published a series of three articles by Francis Orr Templeton (1904–1972), entitled 'Notes on the Work of Contemporary French Architects'; these were its first to reflect upon the emergent Modern Movement, for which Templeton was enthusiastic. A recent Glasgow School of Architecture graduate and winner of the Rutland Prize for architectural design who had briefly been employed in the Glasgow office of Sir John Burnet (1857–1938), later in 1929 he emigrated to Montreal. There, he worked for the Inverness-born John S Archibald (1872–1934) who was a traditionalist, favouring Arts and Crafts approaches for housing and the neoclassical for public buildings. The *Quarterly Illustrated* articles were thus Templeton's only contribution to the emergent debate concerning what forms modern architecture in Scotland might subsequently take.

Templeton's first article began with a report of his visits to buildings by Auguste Perret (1874–1954) and Gustave Perret (1876–1952). Their Théâtre des Champs-Élysées of 1913 in central Paris, clad in large marble slabs with three bas relief sculptures beneath a deep cornice, impressed him on account of its 'simple and direct' decoration, the effect of which was 'rich but unostentatious'.[3] The second article focused on works by Rob Mallet-Stevens (1886–1945) and Le Corbusier, whose revolutionary ideas evidently fascinated Templeton as they did many another young architect of his generation. The final instalment of the series described apartment blocks by Henri Sauvage (1873–1932) and Michel Roux-Spitz (1924–1932), Templeton reporting on his visit to Roux-Spitz's own apartment on Rue Guynemer that the living room was panelled in marble while the bedroom was finished in 'grey wood with large mirror panels'.[4] He concluded that 'the work of these eminent French architects gives us a very good standard… We find in the forefront the extremists [who] tend to stimulate the imagination of the timid and the conservative'.[5]

It is worth noting for strict accuracy that, far from all being French, the Perrets were Belgian-born while Le Corbusier was Swiss, though all were, of course, French-speaking. Furthermore, all had designed buildings for the Paris Exposition: the Perrets were responsible for the Théâtre Moderne, while Mallet-Stevens had created the Pavillon du Tourisme with a slender tower feature and horizontal accents, much like the ones earlier proposed by Walter Gropius as adornments on the upper storeys of his design submitted for the Chicago Tribune international architectural competition. Sauvage produced the Pavillon Primavera; Michel Roux-Spitz wrote a book about the exhibition's architecture and landscaping entitled *Batiments et Jardins* and Le Corbusier – perhaps unsurprisingly – was responsible for the Exposition's *succès de scandale*, the Pavillon de l'Esprit Nouveau.[6] The exhibit within, entitled *Plan Voisin*, envisaged the complete demolition of central Paris on the left bank of the River Seine and its replacement by a new 'radiant city', comprising identical high-rise point-blocks, interspersed with open spaces and elevated motorways. This iconoclastic vision would have profound implications in the longer term, not least in the planning of post-war Scotland.

Over the course of the ensuing decade, the more stylish of the architecture examined by Templeton – particularly the outputs of Mallet-Stevens and Roux-Spitz – would influence Art Deco and moderne as they developed in Britain and elsewhere.

The significant Scottish practitioners of architecture

Of Scotland's major established architectural practices, before the First World War, the Glasgow-based Honeyman & Keppie had been most progressive on account of its employment of Charles Rennie Mackintosh, whose partnership there ended somewhat acrimoniously in 1913. Post-war, the firm, which was

Théâtre des Champs-Elysées, Paris
Auguste and Gustave Perret, 1913
Bruce Peter

Flats, Rue Guynemer, Paris
Michel Roux-Spitz, 1925
Bruce Peter

**Pavillon du Tourisme,
Paris Exposition**
Rob Mallet-Stevens, 1925
Bruce Peter collection

**Architectural competition entry
for the *Chicago Tribune***
Walter Gropius, 1922
HES

renamed Keppie & Henderson, with Andrew Graham Henderson (1882–1963) as a partner, distanced itself from the Mackintosh legacy. Its output, though of fine quality, was thereafter not notable for any particular distinguishing style. Another forward-looking Glasgow-based practice was that of the versatile and prolific James Miller (1860–1947), who in the late-Victorian and Edwardian eras had designed buildings of many kinds, ranging from railway stations to hotels, theatres and exhibition pavilions. In the interwar period, Miller's senior assistant Richard Gunn (1899–1933), whom he had first employed in around 1910 and who specialised in applying an American-influenced Beaux Arts approach to the design of city commercial blocks, incorporated Art Deco detailing into the later examples of these. Miller's son, George

James Miller (1902–1940), who had attended St John's College, Cambridge and in the first half of the 1930s was an employee of Herbert Baker (1862–1946) in London, joined his father's practice in 1936 and also applied variations of Art Deco and moderne aesthetics whenever a client desired an up-to-date-looking solution.

Standing head-and-shoulders above these, however, was the firm of Sir John Burnet, Tait & Lorne, which had a distinguished history stretching back the best part of 80 years and had been run by two generations of Burnets by the time it began to produce designs in the Art Deco and moderne styles from the mid-1920s onwards. The senior partner, Sir John James Burnet (1857–1938) was the son of the founder, John Burnet Snr (1814–1901) and both were primarily known for their scholarly neoclassical designs for churches, civic buildings and commercial premises. Between them, they had created many of the finest edifices of Glasgow's latter nineteenth and early twentieth-century cityscape. The younger Burnet, who had trained in Paris, aspired to win national architectural competitions and to realise significant works in London. In 1903, after several unsuccessful attempts at winning London competitions, Burnet was invited to design a new wing for the British Museum, the Edward VII Galleries, which was a most prestigious commission. (The eventual project was, however, smaller than Burnet's original proposal, which would have greatly extended the complex around a new central boulevard.) To carry out this work, a London office was established, Burnet purchasing a terraced townhouse in Montague Place to contain both this and his own home, which he employed the Glasgow-based Guthrie & Wells to decorate.[7] Burnet brought with him to London Thomas S Tait, a Glasgow School of Art graduate whom he had recently appointed as an assistant. Born in Paisley, Tait would later become a significant figure in the development of Art Deco in Scotland. Burnet's Glasgow office meanwhile operated as Burnet, Son & Dick, the latter partner being Norman Aitken Dick (1883–1948), a draughtsman who had been put in charge in 1907 with Burnet making monthly visits to direct the design work. Burnet, Son & Dick practised only in Scotland while the London office refrained from working north of the Border.

Burnet was knighted for his British Museum design and was soon in receipt of commercial commissions for new office blocks, such as the General Buildings in Aldwych and Kodak House on Kingsway. Built in the 1909–1911 period, the latter was notable for the American-style modernity of its frontages, while the interiors were again by Guthrie & Wells.[8] Burnet and Tait had an occasionally fraught relationship, however: Tait was driven and ambitious, prone to 'moonlighting' in rival London practices after working in Burnet's office during the day, much to the latter's annoyance. Notwithstanding their occasional tensions, Burnet admired Tait's ability and so his status grew within the firm.

In 1925 the imposing Adelaide House was completed on a prominent site by the Thames next to London Bridge. Tait was the lead designer. As a starting point he used pre-war drawings by Burnet with input also from Joseph Emberton (1889–1956), another progressively minded assistant in the Burnet London office at that

Adelaide House, London
Sir John Burnet, Tait & Lorne, 1924
Bruce Peter

time. Steel-framed and clad in Portland stone, Adelaide House was London's tallest office block and, with its soaring mullions, Egyptian cornices and Art Deco sculpture by the Glasgow School of Art-trained William Reid Dick (1878–1961), it attracted considerable critical acclaim.[9] Tait was next involved in designing a new headquarters for the *Daily Telegraph* in Fleet Street, working with the Belfast-born but London-based Charles Ernest Elcock (1878–1944) of Elcock and Sutcliffe and the progressive and innovative architect-engineer Sir Owen Williams (1890–1969). Tait – who was a superb draughtsman – produced various atmospheric sketch suggestions for the facade treatment. One option had a dramatically expressionistic vertical emphasis, but the *Telegraph* – true to form – preferred his more conventional columned solution.[10] The end result was another monumental edifice faced in Portland stone with Egyptian embellishment and a projecting Art Deco clock. The upper stories are stepped in and the entrance is beneath a bas relief panel depicting two Mercuries by Alfred Oakley (1878–1959).[11]

The Daily Telegraph building, design proposal
Thomas S Tait, c1928
Bruce Peter collection

The Daily Telegraph building, London
Thomas S Tait with Elcock and Sutcliffe, 1931
Bruce Peter

In the mid-1920s, Burnet's firm was employed to complete the very large Selfridge's department store on London's Oxford Street, the original architect of which was the American David Burnham (1846–1912). He had produced a giant columned frontage, somewhat reminiscent of Burnet's own British Museum facade. Perhaps realising that in such grand retail premises, it would be advisable to reflect the latest in style, Burnet and Tait added internally illuminated Art Deco canopies above the entrances while the lift and its lobby were decorated with highly intricate designs in bronze and marquetry. Screens with figures representing the signs of the zodiac were by Walter Gilbert (1871–1946), a significant Art Deco craftsman, while the panels lining the lift car depicted crane birds and were by Edgar William Brandt (1886–1960). The decorative splendour of this ensemble was at least the equal of the fanciest found in any contemporary New York skyscraper. The new section of the store was opened in 1928.[12]

Some of the influences on Tait which manifested in these and other projects were a result of visiting the USA before the First World War and travelling to continental Europe in the mid-1920s, where he familiarised himself with designs by Mallet-Stevens and Le Corbusier in France and by Oud and Dudok in the Netherlands. In a British context, he was very early in producing flat-roofed moderne housing, inspired by such continental precedents and also by the recent work of Peter Behrens (1868–1940), whose villa New Ways in Northampton, completed in 1926 for W J Bassett-Lowke, was arguably the first such residence in the UK.

Entrance canopy, Selfridge's, London
Sir John Burnet, Tait & Lorne with sculpture by Gilbert Bayes, 1928
Bruce Peter

Elevators, Selfridge's
Sculptural decoration by Walter Gilbert and Edgar William Brandt, 1928
Bruce Peter collection

Tait's housing commissions were almost exclusively in the south-east of England. The Crittall company, which made metal-framed window units and was expanding rapidly in the 1920s in response to a significant upswing in demand for its products, commissioned a design from Tait for housing in one area of a new factory village in Essex named Silver End. It was in part a philanthropic venture on the part of the company founder, Francis Henry Crittall, to house and employ war-wounded men to make window and door furniture, feeding the company's main factory in nearby Braintree.[13] Constructed between 1927 and 1930, the Silver End villas and terraces contributed by Tait repeat Behrens' vertical triangular projecting window leitmotif. Others by his assistant Frederick McManus (1903–1985) are detailed with a horizontal emphasis. Also involved in the project were other young members of Burnet's London staff, Clifford Strange (1902–1995) and the German-born Franz Stengelhofen (1901–1977).

Silver End, Essex
Thomas S Tait of Sir John Burnet, Tait & Lorne, 1927
Bruce Peter

Crittall additionally commissioned terraces of smaller houses for Silver End from James Miller in Glasgow which feature projecting roof eves, rather than the flat parapets favoured by Tait and McManus. These were for ordinary workers – the type of housing in which one was allowed to live in was decided by one's position in the employment hierarchy.[14]

Tait, who became wealthy as a result of his hard work, purchased an Arts and Crafts-style villa in Hampstead named Gates House, the interior of which he renovated in Art Deco style with bespoke and built-in furniture, marble fireplaces and abstractly patterned rugs, all of his own design. He then went on to produce further villas in the idiom of those at Silver End, The Haven in Newbury and West Leaze in Aldbourne being notable examples.[15]

Burnet's health declined in the late 1920s and he was no longer able to design. In 1930 Tait became a partner, but, rather than allowing him to take full control, Burnet also gave a partnership position to a Scottish-born and Glasgow-trained American-based architect, Francis Lorne (1889–1963), who was the brother of Burnet's secretary and had earlier worked briefly in his Glasgow office while studying at the Glasgow School of Architecture. Before the First World War, Lorne had gone to New York, where he had worked for Cross & Cross, then to Canada, returning to the USA in 1924. There, he had joined the New York office of Bertram Grosvenor Goodhue (1869–1924), whose firm also had a California branch and who designed large commercial buildings in a variety of thematic styles, ranging from Spanish colonial to Egyptian Revival. Goodhue died shortly after Lorne arrived, though the business continued until the Wall Street Crash left it without any new projects, at which point Lorne fortunately received Burnet's partnership offer in London and moved there.

Tait and Lorne knew each other from Glasgow days and from a sojourn Tait had spent in New York in 1914. They were, however, very different types of character: the former was rather formal and, like Burnet, wore the established professional attire of a stiff-collared shirt and morning coat, whereas Lorne was thoroughly Americanised, dressing in the latest snappy men's fashions and peppering his speech with up-to-date Americanisms. He also had an American approach to practice, being an avid publicist who was not averse to touting possible projects to potential clients. Lorne recruited acquaintances from the USA to supersede existing Burnet office staff. One was his brother-in-law Ludovic Gordon Farquhar (1899–1945), who was Scots-American and had worked in New York for the firm of Raymond M Hood (1881–1934) on the design of the spectacular Art Deco Rockefeller Center; others were the Australian-born Oscar Bayne (1905–1964) and Henry Pynor (1901–1946), the latter of whom had previously been employed by Frank Lloyd Wright and brought with him drawings from Wright's office for inspiration.[16] Other recruits were young and politically progressive assistants from New Zealand. Tait and Lorne each had his own preferred team of collaborators, Lorne adding Stengelhofen to his highly cosmopolitan group, while Tait preferred to work with older long-term colleagues whom he had known since his days in Glasgow.

Royal Masonic Hospital, London
Thomas S Tait of Sir John Burnet, Tait & Lorne, 1933
Bruce Peter

Mossehaus, Berlin
Erich Mendelsohn, 1923
Bruce Peter

In 1929, Tait won the competition for a new Royal Masonic Hospital at Ravenscourt Park in West London, his successful submission being in a modernised Georgian idiom with symmetrical elevations and steep dormer roofs. Possibly with Lorne's encouragement, he thereafter redesigned it in a Dutch-inflected moderne manner with flat parapets, horizontal fenestration, elongated sills and rounded corners. Above the main entrance, two square concrete pilasters are topped with sculptures by Gilbert Bayes (1872–1953) depicting Hebe and Aesculapius. Within, Tait designed a grand marble-lined hallway with a monumental Art Deco stairway and a bas relief panel by Charles Doman (1884–1944), a splendidly appointed office for the director and an equally elegant boardroom, all lined in hardwood and furnished with items of Tait's bespoke design.[17] The hospital won the RIBA's Gold Medal for the best new building in 1933. Lorne and his colleagues, meanwhile, made an unsuccessful competition entry for a new Co-operative Society (Centrosoyuz) headquarters in Moscow; this featured parallel vertical fins over the central entranceway with contrastingly horizontal ribbon windows in the symmetrical flanking wings, the corners of which were curved in the manner of Erich Mendelsohn's 1920s work in Berlin, such as the Mossehaus building.[18] In London, meanwhile, Lorne was lead designer of the Dudok-influenced Curzon cinema in Mayfair, opened in 1934, and of a nine-storey combined hotel and serviced apartment block named the Mount Royal which was completed in 1935 and fills an entire block at the Marble Arch end of Oxford Street.[19] Lorne's expressionistic design solution with a strongly horizontal emphasis was reminiscent of his earlier proposal for the Centrsoyuz in Moscow but with stepped-in upper storeys to lessen the apparent mass.[20]

Tait and Lorne both produced significant works in the colonies and dominions too. Tait was responsible for the portals of the Sydney Harbour Bridge, completed in 1932, and in 1935 drew up the initial design for a monumental Art Deco headquarters for the Anglo-American Corporation in Johannesburg, South Africa, owned by the British businessman Ernest Oppenheimer.

After Burnet's retirement, the exclusive right of Burnet, Son & Dick to carry out all Scottish work had ended. In 1932 Tait won the competition for a new Infectious Diseases Hospital at Hawkhead, near Paisley and in the following year he was commissioned

Mount Royal flats, London
Francis Lorne of Sir John Burnet, Tait & Lorne, 1935
Bruce Peter

Centrosoyuz design, Moscow
Francis Lorne of Sir John Burnet, Tait & Lorne, c1933
Bruce Peter collection

Anglo-American Corporation, Johannesburg
Sir John Burnet, Tait & Lorne, 1937
Alamy

De La Warr Pavilion, Bexhill-on-Sea
Erich Mendelsohn and Serge Chermayeff, 1935
Bruce Peter

to design the new Scottish Office headquarters, St Andrew's House, in Edinburgh. He was also appointed assessor of the De La Warr Pavilion architectural competition – the first British architectural contest to demand modern designs from the entrants. Tait chose as winner the submission by Erich Mendelsohn and his British design partner Serge Chermayeff (1900–1996), and the resultant building, completed in 1935, was structurally innovative, having a welded steel frame, and also aesthetically striking. In 1936, Tait was appointed as Architect-in-Chief of the Glasgow Empire Exhibition, but as the building of St Andrew's House was delayed, these two large and prestigious Scottish projects were executed concurrently (see Chapters 4 and 5). In the 1930s, therefore, Sir John Burnet, Tait & Lorne had a good claim to be Britain's most important architectural practice and its position was emphasised by Francis Lorne's compilation of a design and detailing manual entitled *The Information Book of Sir John Burnet, Tait & Lorne*, published in 1938. As the London office numbered only around 20 staff, this book was clearly intended for far wider distribution.[21]

Tait and Lorne were far from being the only Scottish architects working between the wars who had experience of practice in North America. Another was

James Steel Maitland (1887–1982), who was likewise Glasgow School of Art-educated and who had sought employment with Burnet on the British Museum project, but had been too late as the positions had already been filled. Maitland therefore left for Canada, where he worked in Montreal for Brown & Vallance. After war service in the RAF, he joined Thomas Abercrombie (1862–1926) in Paisley, becoming a partner in 1923 and designing the remarkable Russell Institute building, which was completed in 1927. A confidently up-to-date essay in the Beaux Arts manner, it housed a clinic for children. The exterior features Art Deco sculpture and embellishments by Archibald Dawson (1892–1938), the Head of Sculpture at Glasgow School of Art, and within there is an impressive two-storey hallway in various shades of grey marble. The project was financed by a local woman, Agnes Russell, using the legacies of her late brothers, both Paisley solicitors.[22] For the remainder of a long career, Maitland was a Paisley architect – but had he been employed by Burnet's firm, his trajectory could have been very different; in the architectural profession, luck and timing are often as important as talent in achieving success.

Russell Institute, Paisley
James Steel Maitland of Abercrombie & Maitland, 1927
Bruce Peter

Nor was Sir John Burnet, Tait & Lorne the only significant Scottish architectural presence in London. Another, which might have rivalled it had events unfolded differently, was that of the Aberdeen-born A G R Mackenzie (1879–1963), who was the third generation of architect in his family. His father, Alexander Marshall Mackenzie (1848–1933) had run Aberdeen's leading architectural practice, having taken over that of James Matthews (1819–1898), under whom he had earlier trained, in 1893.

A G R Mackenzie had initially studied at Robert Gordon's Technical College, then at the Architectural Association School of Architecture in London and in Paris before finding employment in London with Niven & Wigglesworth. Having worked briefly with his father on an extension to Aberdeen's Marischal College, he returned to London in 1902 to found a branch office, which designed the Waldorf Astoria Hotel in Aldwych, completed in 1908. The office then won a competition for Canada House, followed by another for Australia House. The former was never built, but the latter was constructed between 1913 and 1918 and, along with the hotel, is another significant Aldwych landmark, both being grand edifices in the imperial baroque manner. A G R Mackenzie's firm might have continued at the same pitch as Burnet's, but the ill-luck of the Canada House cancellation and the post-war slump meant that in the 1920s it struggled to maintain momentum. It merged with the remnants of Niven & Wigglesworth's practice in 1927 and in the early 1930s Mackenzie and his assistants there were often assigned work from Aberdeen.

The Mackenzie Aberdeen office's embrace of Art Deco occurred in the wake of the death of Alexander Marshall Mackenzie in 1933, at which point A G R Mackenzie invited David Stokes (1908–1990), the talented but temporarily unemployed son of a London architect friend, Leonard Stokes (1858–1925), to take over there. The young Stokes had graduated from the Architectural Association in 1930, where Erich Mendelsohn had been among the visiting lecturers. He may also have been inspired by a former employee of his father's, Basil Ionides (1884–1950), who, though London-born, was Glasgow-trained and in the latter 1920s designed striking Art Deco interiors for the hotelier and impresario Rupert D'Oyly Carte. Ionides was from a prosperous and well-connected London family of Greek origin who used their mercantile wealth as patrons of the Arts and Crafts Movement. Having visited the Paris Exposition, Ionides was commissioned by D'Oyly Carte to redecorate suites at his Claridge's Hotel and also to modernise its restaurant.[23] His next task was to thoroughly rebuild the Savoy Theatre, which is an adjunct of the Savoy Hotel, and the outcome was spectacular; new fluted wall linings were entirely swathed in shiny aluminium leaf and the splayed walls of the proscenium arch feature a grid of recessed decorative panels inspired by a Ming-dynasty screen. The entrance, in a small courtyard off the Strand, features stainless steel Art Deco canopies and black-framed doors with silvered embellishments.[24] Up in Aberdeen, Stokes attempted to deliver similarly up-to-date glamour, but he found the whole experience to be a severe culture shock and so when A G R Mackenzie returned north, relieving him, he was glad to get back to London.[25] Thereafter, Mackenzie perpetuated Stokes' progressive approach, albeit often producing outcomes of remarkably austere appearance. The four-square, undressed granite exterior of St Mary's Parish Church in King Street, completed in 1938, is an extreme example, though enlivened with unusual ecclesiastical Art Deco stained glass by the Gray's School of Art-trained James Steedman Hamilton (1890–1950), including a crucifixion triptych – a bleak subject for which the style arguably was not best suited.[26]

Owing to the attrition of young men in the First World War, there were fewer graduates entering the architectural profession in the 1920s than in pre-war days. This doubtless enabled those who were better placed financially and socially to make early positive impressions. Two such bright talents were the Edinburgh College of Art-trained William Kininmonth (1904–1988) and his friend Basil Spence (1907–1976), both of whom were ambitious and from prosperous backgrounds. In 1929–30, the two were employed in London by the distinguished traditionalist Sir Edwin Lutyens (1869–1944), who was admired for his country houses and major public buildings and was at that time working on the Viceroy's House in New Delhi. They also attended evening classes at the Bartlett School of Architecture where Professor Sir Alfred Richardson (1880–1964) advocated a modern architecture derived from the classical tradition. At the Edinburgh College of Art, meanwhile, a historically informed advocate of the Modern Movement from London, John Summerson (1904–1992), was briefly appointed as a tutor in 1929 and also made editor of the RIAS *Quarterly Illustrated*.[27]

In 1930 Kininmonth was given a workspace in the office of A F Balfour Paul (1875–1938), perpetuator

Savoy Theatre, London
Basil Ionides and Frank A Tugwell, 1929
Mickey Lee / Alamy Stock Photo

of Robert Rowand Anderson's famous practice, which would become Rowand Anderson and Paul. Spence subsequently joined him there to form Kininmonth & Spence, which was effectively a practice within a practice. The reason for this unusual arrangement was that, owing to the uncertain economic climate, Paul could not afford to employ them directly.[28] The two had very different personalities; Kininmonth was quietly pensive, whereas Spence was an extrovert whose swagger eventually brought him national and international recognition. In long careers that stretched from the 1930s until the 1970s, both proved themselves highly adaptable in designing with equal finesse in the neoclassical manner of Adam, in 1930s moderne, in 1950s contemporary and, in the 1960s, even Corbusian brutalism. Kininmonth later remarked to architectural historian Charles McKean that 'I suppose we rather prided ourselves in being able to work in any style'.[29] Typical of the Scottish young generation, they sought to embrace the architectural profession's established values, requiring a cultivated respect for, and deep knowledge of, its history. In the London architectural scene, by contrast, youthful architects were rebelling against tradition, equating modernist aesthetics with a superior morality. The surrounding Scottish architectural culture at that time, particularly in stately Edinburgh, understandably preferred gradual, rather than radical, modernisation – or none at all.

Reflecting this equivocal position, the Glasgow-born and trained Ninian Johnston (1912–1990) – most likely aware of adulation among some of the younger generation in the south for the London-based Russian émigré architectural and political revolutionary Berthold Lubetkin (1901–1990) – wrote in the *Quarterly Illustrated* in 1934 that 'a functionalist is a man who writes to the architectural papers that several foreign architects with unpronounceable names were sent by God to show us how architecture should be done. They weren't of course'. [30] Yet Johnston also wrote metaphorically of the possible sensual pleasures which modern architecture could bring about, asking rhetorically of the architectural traditionalist: 'Does he not envy me my naked body glistening in the water and the sunlight, clean, fresh, invigorating, rhythmic, alive, gloriously white and shining silver?'[31] The sentiment might have come from Le Corbusier himself.

Surviving drawings from Edinburgh College of Art students who were training to be architects show a desire to engage with up-to-date building types, interiors and technologies. For example, Basil Spence, Jean Payton Reid (1917–1997) and Antony Wolffe (1920–2016) produced schemes for cinemas, cocktail bars, boutique shops and department stores in Art Deco and moderne styles. This suggests ambitions to become involved in producing buildings and spaces of these types and styles upon entering practice between the late 1920s and latter 1930s.[32]

The architectural practitioners and Scottish-owned practices described above were characterised by images that appeared solid and dignified. Their outputs sought to bring order and improvement to the urban environment, based on cultivated interpretations of historic and recent precedents and on logical interpretations and responses to modern requirements. The seniors were usually well-travelled relative to what was typical of the era, with consequently wide fields of cultural vision, encompassing lived experiences in the sophisticated centres on the continent and in North America.

Entrepreneurship and expediency

There were, of course, other sides to the Scottish profession. Many architectural practices, particularly those located outwith the major cities, by necessity designed everything and anything their clients requested. Examples of firms in Scottish regional towns that embraced Art Deco and moderne during the 1930s include those of James G Callander (1881–1942) of Falkirk, William Williamson (1871–1952) of Kirkcaldy, Alexander Mair (1883–1943) of Ayr, Andrew D Haxton (1878–1961) of Leven, Matthew Steele (1878–1937) of Bo'ness, Alexander Cattanach (1895–1977) of Kingussie and Roy Caruthers-Ballantyne (1891–1981) of Inverness. The first five were all in their fifties by the time they began designing in these styles.[33] Although the latter two were younger, both inherited established practices from architect fathers. Williamson, Mair, Haxton and Callander all learned as apprentices in the established firms of, respectively, James Bow Dunn (1861–1930) in Edinburgh, Cullen, Lochhead and Brown in Hamilton, Gillespie & Scott in St Andrews and Alexander Gauld (1867–1929) in Falkirk.[34] Steele, however, attended the Glasgow and West of Scotland Technical College and Carruthers-Ballantyne, who was of wealthy parentage, went to the Architectural Association in London. These architects' typical outputs consisted of local housing, shops and bank

Student renderings for a cocktail bar and a fashion boutique
Jean Payton Reid; Antony Wolffe, late 1930s
HES DP266265, DP203038

ESQUISSE COLOUR FOR A BAR

LADIES - FASHIONS

buildings in a range of styles dependent on context and client. Their Art Deco or moderne projects were usually for transport, leisure or hospitality, Mair's firm designing airport buildings, Williamson's producing an ice rink and Carruthers-Ballantyne's devising a roadhouse hotel. In the 1930s, cinemas came to form the greater parts of the outputs of Haxton and Cattanach, though these were produced alongside other types of building. Providing satisfactory solutions to initial commissions resulted in welcome repeat business. Prominent, well connected and admired figures in their communities, all of these architects evidently took great pride in designing to make these places appear as distinguished and attractive as budgetary constraints would allow. Depression conditions however meant that a majority of their outputs in the first half of the 1930s consisted of minor conversion projects, while large commissions were relatively few and far between.

Another category of practitioners, some no doubt forced by the period's economic realities, unapologetically embraced commerce, combining the design of buildings with property development and other business initiatives. The wide conceptual gap regarding what being an architect meant almost risked creating a schism within the Royal Institute of British Architects. The institute's mandate was felt by existing influential members to be one of defending the idea of architecture as an art against any threat of excess entrepreneurship by possibly less scrupulous fellow members. To deal with the profession's entrepreneurial extreme, the introduction of a professional Code of Conduct in the wake of the Architects Registration Acts of 1931 and 1938 gave the RIBA powers to strike off members whose approaches it deemed to have too flagrantly crossed its fuzzily policed lines of demarcation between architectural practice and property speculation.

In Scotland, the RIAS, by contrast, appears to have been pragmatically more tolerant, there having been several quite prominent architects who were also entrepreneurs and developers. Perhaps the most high-profile was the Aberdonian Thomas Scott Sutherland (1899–1963), who was a member of both the RIBA and the RIAS. His property company Modern Homes (Aberdeen) Ltd sold new bungalows and villas directly from his architectural office and he was otherwise a director of around 39 diverse local businesses, many entirely unlinked to his core

architectural practice. McKean records that at slack times, his office assistants were redeployed packing pills for one of these concerns.[35] Sutherland endowed the Scott Sutherland School of Architecture at Gray's School of Art, thereby gaining an enduring legacy.[36] In Glasgow, meanwhile, William Beresford Inglis (1884–1967) was an architect and operator of cinemas and, subsequently, of the eponymous hotel in the city's Sauchiehall Street, again without falling foul of the RIBA's Code of Conduct. By contrast, the Edinburgh architects and housing developers William Patterson (1891–1963) and James Broom (1890–1967) were not so fortunate as they were forced to resign from the RIAS for both building and selling houses.[37] Incomers to the city from modest backgrounds in Perth and Bathgate respectively, perhaps their greater sins were to have been insufficiently well-connected within the architectural hierarchy and to have enriched themselves designing occasionally prominent and brash buildings which some fellow members would have considered unforgivably vulgar.

Design and craft

Neither in the interwar era nor in the period directly after were there any Scottish design firms of a calibre equivalent to its best and most prominent architectural practices. Furthermore, young and emergent designers with talents and connections comparable to architects such as Spence or Kininmonth were conspicuous by their absence. Britain's design scene and infrastructure at that time and thereafter was very much centred upon London, whereas Scotland's reputation remained primarily concentrated on heavy industry, meaning that engineering disciplines had greater prominence. This situation notwithstanding, there were nonetheless many designers, professionally trained and otherwise, at work there.

In contrast with architecture, the history of which stretched back to the ancient world, design was a modern and emergent discipline of the industrial age. Unlike the more high-profile Scottish architects, nearly all Scottish designers in the interwar era were anonymous handmaidens of industry on the payrolls of the significant fabric, furniture and homeware manufacturers. Whereas architects took their high cultural status as a given and a right upon joining the profession, designers still needed to argue for their usefulness and in Scotland had neither a professional body equivalent to the RIAS to speak on their behalf nor a published forum for debate of equivalence to its *Quarterly Illustrated* journal.

The formation of the Design and Industries Association (DIA) in 1915 was inspired by the apparent success in Germany of the Deutscher Werkbund and, in the interwar era, the DIA gradually gained some influence. Occasionally it even succeeded in its aim of achieving cooperation between industrialists, bureaucrats and creatives.[38] In 1930s Scotland it was an all too frequent criticism of industry that not enough attention was being paid to design and that there was a consequent danger of Scottish output in the light industries looking less appealing than competing items made elsewhere – with negative economic consequences. In certain industries – for example, coachbuilding – rather than involving trained designers, it was instead draughtsmen or engineers who had shown a flair for design who made suggestions for what might be attempted by way of styling. It was not until after the Second World War that Industrial Design began to be taught in Scottish art schools as a distinct professional discipline.

Commercial art sat uncomfortably between the worlds of art and design. Advertising imagery promoting travel and tourism to Scotland included some of the interwar period's most iconic Art Deco images, as coastal and mountain scenery lent themselves to dramatised graphic treatments with bold forms and contrasting colours. Although commercial art undoubtedly provided lucrative employment to artists who were willing to produce suitable material, its aim of serving the needs of business appeared much less noble than that of modernist fine art, which claimed instead to provide a cultural lead.

For different reasons, the broad category of craft had complex relationships with both art and design. In the interwar era, there were arguably two overlapping conceptions of craft in Scotland. One was of quaint and vernacular small-scale hand-making, such as Harris Tweed, which was considered an important aspect of Scottish identity. The other occurred within certain branches of industry, such as textiles or cabinetmaking, where ideals of craft involvement – derived from the Arts and Crafts Movement or even the Bauhaus – were to add an aura of quality and distinctiveness to what were otherwise modern machine-based production processes. Scottish craft makers were usually anonymous. Scottish manufacturers of fabrics would, however, occasionally commission patterns from high-profile celebrity designers in London, such as the American-born rug and textile specialist Marion Dorn (1896–1964), who had society connections and was known for her daringly modern abstract compositions. In subsequent advertising, virtue would be made of their involvement.

The types of authorship of Art Deco and moderne architecture and design in Scotland were thus highly diverse, while the degree of 'Scottishness' of what was produced was in terms of source and style equally varied and sometimes rather nebulous. Scottish architects who were attracted to experiment with modern approaches tended mostly to adapt elements from continental and American precedents. Manufacturers commissioning up-to-date designs meanwhile usually aspired to sell to British, Empire and international customers for whom appearances of cosmopolitan modernity were apparently believed to be of greater value. Yet, as we shall see, items ranging in scale and complexity from homewares to the giant outputs of heavy engineering were promoted and recognised for their qualities of robustness and precision, which were regarded as being among the prime virtues of Scottish designing and making.

CHAPTER 2
HOUSING AND FURNISHING

In the interwar era, the provision of more and better housing appeared as a pressing matter, not only in Scotland but across much of industrialised Europe and beyond. On the continent, alongside the perpetuation of established solutions, a wide variety of novel concepts were proposed, ranging from avant-garde villas to experimental blocks of flats. In Britain, meanwhile, municipal and private developers alike built new housing estates on the fringes of pretty much every town and city. Amid the douce bungalows and villas erected in suburban Scotland, some bold individuals bravely asserted their progressive beliefs by commissioning architect-designed moderne examples, risking chills, leaks and the wrath or mere incomprehension of conservatively minded neighbours to achieve the image of a modern Mediterranean lifestyle. Such houses often were patron-led small architectural commissions for emergent practitioners, enabling them to prove themselves before moving on to tackle bigger public and commercial projects.

Scottish Art Deco and moderne villas represented both a continuation of, and divergences from, established ideas about the design of such properties. Lower ceilings, sunrooms with corner windows, balconies and flat roofs (sometimes with outdoor terraces), were novel features rarely or never found in their late-Victorian and Edwardian equivalents. Other less daring clients aspired instead to live in relatively conventional-looking houses with only superficially moderne detailing superimposed – perhaps a curved corner, a raised parapet to conceal part of the sloping roof, a porthole window by the door and, frequently, Crittall metal-framed glazing. Such hybridised designs combined some or all of these moderne elements with ones also typical of comparably scaled Arts and Crafts and neo-Georgian-style examples. With the economy in the depth of the doldrums in the early 1930s it was mainly the professional class who could afford the risk of stylistically daring and lavishly scaled architectural statements of domestic modernity, whereas hybridised designs were appealing to a broader clientele and therefore constructed in larger numbers.

Certain Scottish architectural commentators with romantic nationalist sympathies even sought to argue that moderne was merely a radical updating of a long-established Scottish housing design tradition; the Edinburgh and Cambridge-educated Ian G Lindsay (1906–1966), for example, pointed to the L-shaped plans of some recent examples which he claimed were reminiscent of those of seventeenth-century lairds' houses. In the RIAS *Quarterly Illustrated* in 1936, Lindsay highlighted the Scottish romanticism of the Art Deco interior of a Cambridge villa named Finella, which had been transformed in the late 1920s by a reformist don of Scots descent, Mansfield Forbes of Clare College, who had employed a young Australian émigré architect as a designer, Raymond McGrath (1903–1977).[1]

Hallway design for Gribloch, Kippen
Basil Spence and John Hill of Green & Abbott, c1938
HES DP012214

McGrath wrote that the decorative theme was inspired by the fable of Finella, a Scottish queen who had drowned herself and 'to whom the honour of discovering glass was attributed'.[2] This gave him the excuse to make extensive decorative use of the material in his design, as well as Pictish-inspired abstract patterning.[3] Back in Scotland itself, apart from the greater prevalence of painted harling rather than stucco as a wall finish, there was little that made moderne villas significantly different from their southern English counterparts. Nonetheless, the idea that being modern and being Scottish were synonymous perhaps helped give some architects and their clients greater confidence when considering the more audacious of possible design options.

In the vanguard of designing moderne houses in Scotland were William Kininmonth and Basil Spence. From their desks within Rowand Anderson and Paul's long-established and socially well-connected but eclectic practice, they gained their first commissions for suburban villas through Kininmonth's brother, a radiologist who introduced them to wealthy members of the Edinburgh medical profession in his circle of acquaintances. Their initial effort, completed in 1933, was at Craiglockhart for Dr G Grant Allan and was heavily influenced by the work of Sir Edwin Lutyens, having ogee roofs and monumental chimney breasts.[4] Their next, for Dr John King, located on exclusive Easter Belmont Road, a private street on the edge of Murrayfield Golf Course, is a moderne 'cubist' composition with flat roofs and Crittall window frames. On a sloping site, most of the accommodation is on the ground floor, above which are sun terraces and a guest bedroom with corner windows. The garage is integrated, tucked beneath at the site's lowest point. Finished in 1934, it was later published in *The Architect and Building News* – but the client soon discovered that the roof leaked.[5] (Kininmonth later in life recalled to McKean that 'King was decent about it'.[6]) A further commission in the same street from sisters named Reid marries typically moderne elements to picturesque Lutyens-esque ones; it has a hipped roof and a Romanesque arched entrance as well as a V-shaped projecting vertical window strip to illuminate the staircase and Crittall glazing.[7]

Kininmonth, meanwhile, designed a home for himself and his wife, the artist Caroline Sutherland (1907–1978), whom he had met at Edinburgh College of Art. Completed in 1933, it occupies a strip of land

Hallway of Finella, Cambridge
Raymond McGrath, late 1920s
Bruce Peter

he purchased from the owner of Grange Park House, a nineteenth-century neo-gothic mansion designed by Frederick Pilkington (1832–1898), located off Dick Place on Edinburgh's south side. Kininmonth found the site when a developer commissioned him to design two other houses of more traditional design elsewhere on the grounds. From the street, there is little to see, save for a nondescript gravel driveway but, making good use of a falling south-facing slope, he produced a bold composition to the rear. This comprises a semi-circular glazed volume containing the living room with an open terrace above, projecting from a two-storey main block that was originally L-shaped in plan (but has since been enlarged). The composition is highly reminiscent of another architect's home – the considerably bigger Villa Markelius of 1930 by the Swedish Sven Markelius (1889–1972) at Bromma to the west of Stockholm. Originally of white-painted brick but subsequently harled, Kininmonth's house

Easter Belmont Road, Edinburgh
Basil Spence, 1932;
William Kininmonth, 1934
HES DP010912, SC2602053

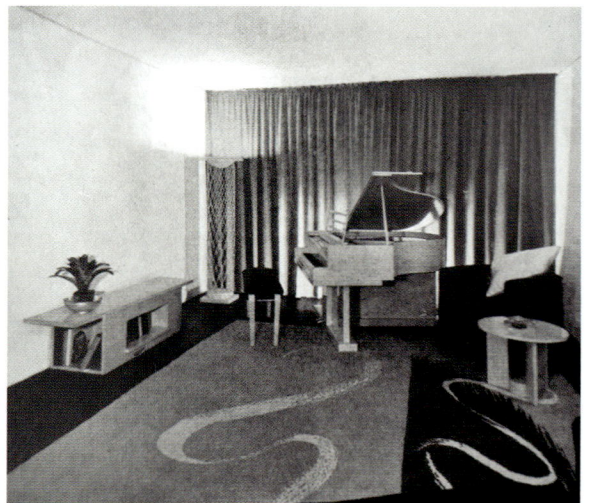

has an open-plan ground floor with two bedrooms above, in front of which is the terrace. Many of the interior fitments, and even the armchairs, were of his own design. Working to a tight £1,500 budget, he chose square plywood tiles rather than solid wood for flooring.[8] In an article for *SMT Magazine and Scottish Country Life* in October 1937, Kininmonth used the house to illustrate modernist thinking, arguing that:

> Vertical lines produce a feeling of aspiration and long horizontal lines a sense of rest. Sloping lines, heavy projections, blank wall surfaces, ornament; each produce their own reactions. The sensitive architect will shape his buildings out of the forms and materials of his own time and imbue them with the personality of his own age.[9]

Such rhetoric typified the era's teleological approach to understandings of visual culture; the contrary argument that many other practitioners used repetitive, exaggerated horizontal lines instead of static vertical ones to capture speed and dynamism in buildings and interiors was evidently not considered. The article did, however, record for posterity the house's elegant original interiors, with chromed metal-framed dining chairs, abstractly patterned rugs and uplighters providing indirect illumination.[10]

In 1934, Spence too got married and his honeymoon was in Germany, which was less than one year into National Socialist rule. He took his new wife to inspect the Weissenhofsiedlung in Stuttgart – a model modernist housing estate built for the 1927 Deutscher Werkbund exhibition, containing villas by Ludwig Mies van der Rohe, Le Corbusier, Walter Gropius, Hans Scharoun (1893–1972) and others, but whereas these were constructed in concrete, Kininmonth and Spence's own designs were of brick with rendering to lend a concrete-like appearance. At this point, A F Balfour Paul not only at last directly employed the two but also made them partners.[11]

Spence was not the only Scottish designer of houses to visit the Weissenhofsiedlung in the early 1930s:

Dick Place, Edinburgh
William Kininmonth, 1933
Courtesy of Thelma Ewing (top); Bruce Peter (bottom left);
Bruce Peter collection (bottom right)

another who inspected it was the Glasgow house-builder and property developer John Robert Harrison McDonald (1907–1996), who was a civil engineer by training and was both enthusiastic and remarkably well-informed about modern architecture. His father, John McDonald senior, had become wealthy as a builder in the Edwardian era and in 1917 had founded the Sunlit Building Company. It constructed many of the houses for Glasgow's new municipal housing schemes created under the Housing and Town Planning act of 1919, often known as the 'Addison Act', and the Housing Act of 1930, sometimes referred to as the 'Greenwood Act'. The company's sunburst logo was introduced a decade in advance of the widespread use of such imagery; the inspiration was biblical, however, as 'Let There be Light' was God's first commandment. Both McDonalds had an aversion to pitched roofs which they viewed as inefficient and costly to build, notwithstanding their very obvious benefits in a wet climate.[12]

In 1931 McDonald junior wrote and had published a substantial and well-illustrated polemical book entitled *Modern Housing: A Review of Present Housing Requirements in Gt. Britain, a Resume of Post-War Housing at Home and Abroad, and Some Practical Suggestions for Future Housing*.[13] Continuing the biblical theme, its first chapter on the origins of the Modern Movement was entitled 'Genesis'. Its scope was wide and, five years before Nikolaus Pevsner wrote *Pioneers of Modern Design*, it included, among others, works by the Vienna Secession architect and designer Josef Hoffmann (1870–1956) and Charles Rennie Mackintosh (which neatly linked the narrative to an earlier phase of Glaswegian design innovation). Continental modernists who had emerged more recently, such as Mallet-Stevens, Dudok and Le Corbusier himself, and Americans such as Richard Neutra (1892–1970) and R M Schindler (1887–1953) were also featured.[14] The second half of the book, which focused on the McDonalds' own building methods, revealed its true purpose: to stimulate additional business for their construction company, the intention being that more clients in the west of Scotland might be persuaded to want approximations of the continental flat-roofed houses it illustrated.

As an example of this, a McDonald Sunlit house was erected at the 1931 Scottish Ideal Home Exhibition in Glasgow's Kelvin Hall; it predated by almost three years the better-known Art Deco Sunspan

Carse View Drive, Bearsden
J H McDonald, 1933–1936
Bruce Peter

Old Kirk Road, Edinburgh
George James Miller of James Miller & Son, 1936
Bruce Peter

house devised by the London-based modern architects David Pleydell-Bouverie (1911–1994) and Wells Coates (1895–1958) for the 1934 Ideal Home exhibition at the Olympia exhibition hall in Kensington.

Towards the end of 1932, McDonald senior bought the Kilmardinny Estate and mansion near Bearsden, an upmarket suburb on Glasgow's north-western fringe. There, McDonald junior designed and had built six moderne villas. The largest, White Lodge on Kilmardinny Crescent, was for him to occupy with his American wife, Dorcas Hutcheson, and the house was later featured in *Country Life* magazine.[15] The remaining five were along Carse View Drive, from which there was a fine vista towards the Campsie Hills. The houses were essentially variations on cube-shapes with one curved corner, built of brick in the conventional way and finished in painted render. There was none of the radical experimentation evident in the more avant-garde of the houses illustrated in McDonald's book. In 1939, the McDonalds were sued by one disgruntled occupant who complained of serious damp penetration, spongy cracks and fungal growth inside owing to faults in the roof construction; £350 in damages were awarded.[16] Fortunately, at present, the houses are all in very good condition and are objects of pride for their occupants.

Concurrently with the building of the Carse View Drive villas, the McDonalds were engaged in building Glasgow's largest municipal housing scheme to date at Cardonald, with 2,512 dwellings of conventional pitched roof design; the contract was worth around a million pounds. John R H McDonald and his wife subsequently emigrated to the USA, where they remained for the rest of their lives and became significant philanthropists.[17]

Back in Scotland, in addition to the work of Spence, Kininmonth and the McDonalds, moderne housing was making an appearance across the country. George James Miller joined the established Glasgow firm of his father James Miller in 1936, thereafter designing a small number of moderne houses for clients in Edinburgh, projects which probably resulted from acquaintances he had made when he attended Fettes College there. 32 Old Kirk Road in Corstorphine somewhat resembles Thomas S Tait's Silver End villas in England, while another overlooking the River Forth at Cramond is more akin to the McDonald's Carse View Drive houses; both were built in 1936.

In Inverness, the local practice of Caruthers-Ballantyne, Cox and Taylor was responsible for a handful of flat-roofed villas, several of notably handsome proportions, located at intervals in the vicinity of Culduthel Road, where they interspersed grand Victorian and Edwardian properties in local stone. The moderne interlopers were largely the work of one of the firm's younger assistants, Donald Fowler (1904–1975), who was an Aberdeen School of Architecture graduate, recently returned from Shanghai, where he had worked through the Great Depression in the Public Works Department. Fowler's employer, the Architectural Association-trained Roy Caruthers-Ballantyne, found flat roofs impractical and so directed clients who wanted these to Fowler, who greatly admired Dudok's buildings in Hilversum and evidently took inspiration from their volumetric compositions.

This work was followed in 1936 by Fowler's own home, Over and Above, in Culduthel Road. Its name was reminiscent of a well-publicised southern English villa of considerably more radical design, High and Over in Amersham, Buckinghamshire by

Culduthel Road, Inverness
Donald Fowler, 1937
Bruce Peter

Culduthel Road, Inverness
Roy Caruthers-Ballantyne of Caruthers-Ballantyne & Cox, 1937
Bruce Peter

Connell, Ward & Lucas. Fowler, however, actually chose it because every time he added extra features, the builder told him that these would cost 'over and above' what had been agreed.[18] Caruthers-Ballantyne himself designed one moderne villa nearby, but this has a pitched and tiled main roof with a mix of facing brick and stucco wall finishes, making it appear more as though transplanted from Surrey than from the Continent.

In Kirkcaldy, William Williamson, who since the latter 1890s had designed most of the town's prominent buildings in styles ranging from Beaux Arts to Arts and Crafts, took into partnership the Glaswegian-born Harry Hubbard (1888–1959), a former employee of Burnet and of Sir Robert Lorimer. Shortly thereafter, Williamson and Hubbard were commissioned by a local builder, R Ritchie Fraser, to design a moderne villa on Bennochy Avenue. This was completed in 1934 and was the first of a number of their designs in the style.[19] Elsewhere in Kirkcaldy, another local building firm, Balfour & Co, included a handful of flat-roofed semi-detached moderne villas in their development of Lady Nairn Avenue, which otherwise comprised bungalows and villas of more conventional design. In nearby Leven, a third builder, Andrew Cook, erected a similarly mixed row on Largo Road, the architect of which was Lawrence Rolland (1894–1959), a former employee of Andrew D Haxton. Further along the Fife coast in St Andrews, the architectural practice of Gillespie & Scott, in which the sole partner in the interwar era was James Scott (1861–1944), assisted by his son, James Hoey Scott (1892–1981), designed a small number of moderne villas. Many more individual examples, designed by various others, appeared elsewhere in mid-1930s regional Scotland.

Catering to the growing middle-class were the mass house builders, of which Mactaggart & Mickel of Glasgow was among the most prolific, being responsible for expansive new suburbs comprising bungalows and villas at Whitecraigs, Giffnock and King's Park on the city's Southside and at Silverknowes and Hillpark in Edinburgh, plus other smaller developments elsewhere in the Central Belt. John Auld Mactaggart was an established Glasgow housebuilder who in 1925 joined forces with the Glasgow School of Art-trained architect and builder Andrew Mickel (1877–1962). The latter had visited North America in the 1900s to examine mass house construction methods there.[20] With keen eyes for a broad market, including potential buyers whose tastes spanned from conservatism to moderate progressiveness, Mactaggart & Mickel's designs were suitably varied and often hybridised with a few tokenistic moderne elements, such as triangular staircase windows, portholes or entrance porches with exaggerated lintels to give a hint of streamlining, superimposed upon what were otherwise conventional designs. They were also imaginative marketers, for example building a full-size plywood mock-up of

Largo Road, Leven
Lawrence Rolland, mid-1930s
Bruce Peter

Benochy Avenue, Kirkcaldy
Harry Hubbard and William Williamson, 1934
Bruce Peter

a semi-detached villa on the concourse of Glasgow Central Station in 1934 – the gateway to London for some but to Glasgow's Southside for many more.[21]

Having brought the Broom Estate land at Whitecraigs near Newton Mearns for housing development, Mactaggart & Mickel planned to contrive their own version of Bearsden. The Broom site would be split into two zones, one for their standard villas and bungalows and the other for larger, architect-designed examples for wealthier residents. These would be devised by James Taylor (1890–1977), who had

Mactaggart & Mickel advertising artwork
Mactaggart & Mickel, 1937
HES SC420817

trained at the Glasgow School of Architecture and with whom Andrew Mickel had worked prior to beginning his business relationship with Mactaggart. To entice buyers, a full-page advertisement was placed in the *Glasgow Herald* in April 1935 showing a model of a Taylor design for a flat-roofed villa with balconies, below which was a text that began with 'The adoption of modernism does not always bid goodbye to beauty…'.[22] The equivocal tone doubtless anticipated the scepticism of the intended clientele and, indeed, Taylor's design was never commissioned, though he was responsible for several of the less daringly moderne villas with pitched roofs that were subsequently built on the Broom Estate.

Mactaggart & Mickel advertisement
Glasgow Herald, 1935
Bruce Peter collection

Broom Estate, Newton Mearns, Glasgow
Mactaggart & Mickel, mid-1930s
Bruce Peter

Mansion flats

Marketed to retirees and cash-rich urban professionals without children, so-called 'mansion flats' or 'serviced apartments' provided an alternative housing solution tailored to their comfortable lifestyles. The type of accommodation was constructed by developers in large amounts in southern England, not only in and around London but in Brighton and Bournemouth too. In popular fiction, Agatha Christie's Hercule Poirot and P G Wodehouse's Bertie Wooster lived in such flats. An early Scottish example with Art Deco detailing is a five-storey block on Napier Road in Edinburgh, completed in 1935 by to a design by John Jerdan (1875–1947), the horizontally banded brick and stucco treatment of which emulated equivalent developments in the South. The subsequent four-storey Ravelston flats designed by Robert Hurd (1905–1963) and Norman Neil (1899–1972) use an ingenious 'butterfly' plan with servants' stairs and quarters at the core and, in each of the four wings, a flat consisting of a dining room and sitting room with balcony plus three bedrooms, two bathrooms and a kitchen. At both ends of the ground floor are long single-storey garage wings.[23] Hurd, who was English-born to a mother from Dundee, studied at Cambridge, where he befriended Mansfield Forbes

Ravelston flats, Edinburgh
Neil & Hurd, 1936–1937
HES DP215716, SC453895

and his architect-friend Raymond McGrath, whose ideas about Scottish symbolism in modern form perhaps influenced his thinking. Although the flats' white-painted stucco exteriors with extruded balconies and curved corners are indistinguishable from their English contemporaries, Hurd argued that such forms were related to traditional Scottish building, shorn of historicist details. Managed by the upmarket Jenners department store, the flats accommodated the type and class of resident who doubtless would also have shopped there.

On Mactaggart & Mickel's Broom Estate development on Glasgow's Southside, another of their architects, William A Gladstone (1890–1949), designed two three-storey blocks named Sandringham Court. These were intended to enable retirees and the widowed to downsize by renting flats in lieu of the large villas they would have owned hitherto. Typical of the developer's hybridised design approach, their frontages combine brick and stucco with bulging protrusions of glass bricks on the rear elevations where the servants' quarters were located. The roofs were originally pitched and tiled, though in recent times an extra storey with flat roofing has been added to each block, resulting in their more uniformly moderne current appearance.

Most impressive of all the Scottish mansion flats in terms of scale and ambition is the Kelvin Court development at Anniesland, completed in 1938 and consisting of two mighty six-storey blocks, H-shaped in plan, together containing over 100 flats with parking. Commissioned by a Newcastle property entrepreneur, Alec Woolf, they were designed by James Newton Fatkin (1882–1940), also from Newcastle, whose specialisms were flats and cinemas.[24] Making no concessions to the Glaswegian context, he specified blown-red facing brick with white-painted concrete continuous sills and lintels, making the development appear as though an area of modern urban England had miraculously been transposed to the city's West End.

Sandringham Court, Broom Estate, Newton Mearns
Mactaggart & Mickel, 1938
Bruce Peter

Kelvin Court, Great Western Road, Glasgow
James Newton Fatkin, 1938
Bruce Peter, HES DP029739

A moderne country mansion

Beyond bourgeois suburbia, the few exceptionally
wealthy Scottish families who commissioned
new country houses preferred national romantic
styles. The exception is Gribloch near Kippen in
Stirlingshire, which Basil Spence largely designed
for the wealthy industrialist John Colville, chairman
of the Motherwell iron and steel makers David
Colville & Co. Between drawing up moderne villas in
Edinburgh and tackling the Gribloch project, Spence
had designed two country houses which, at the behest
of his clients, were in historicist styles. Broughton
Place near Biggar resembles similarly castle-like works
by Robert Lorimer (1864–1929) while Quothquan
in Lanarkshire, the client for which was married to
Colville's cousin, is a neo-Georgian-style hunting
lodge. In terms of programme, if not aesthetic, these
widely diverse designs actually have much in common
with Gribloch, all containing the traditional Scottish
country house elements. Spence was nothing if not
stylistically versatile. [25]

Gribloch's site is the flat top of a drumlin, giving
a commanding panoramic view over the Carse of
Stirling. The Colvilles were engaged and demanding
clients; following extensive consultation, during which
numerous sketch layouts were suggested and modified,
Spence completed the initial design in August 1937.[26]
This was L-shaped with two storeys around a courtyard,
one wing being the main house and the other
containing servants' quarters. In Spence's elevations, the
detailing of the fenestration, the suggestion of low-
relief sculpture and the copper-clad pitched roof were
reminiscent of recent Swedish architecture. However,
Colville's wife, Agnes Anne (née Bilsland), who took
a very keen interest in the design process, had another

Gribloch, Kippen
Basil Spence, 1939
Bruce Peter

Gribloch design proposals
Basil Spence, 1937
HES DP011988, DP020033

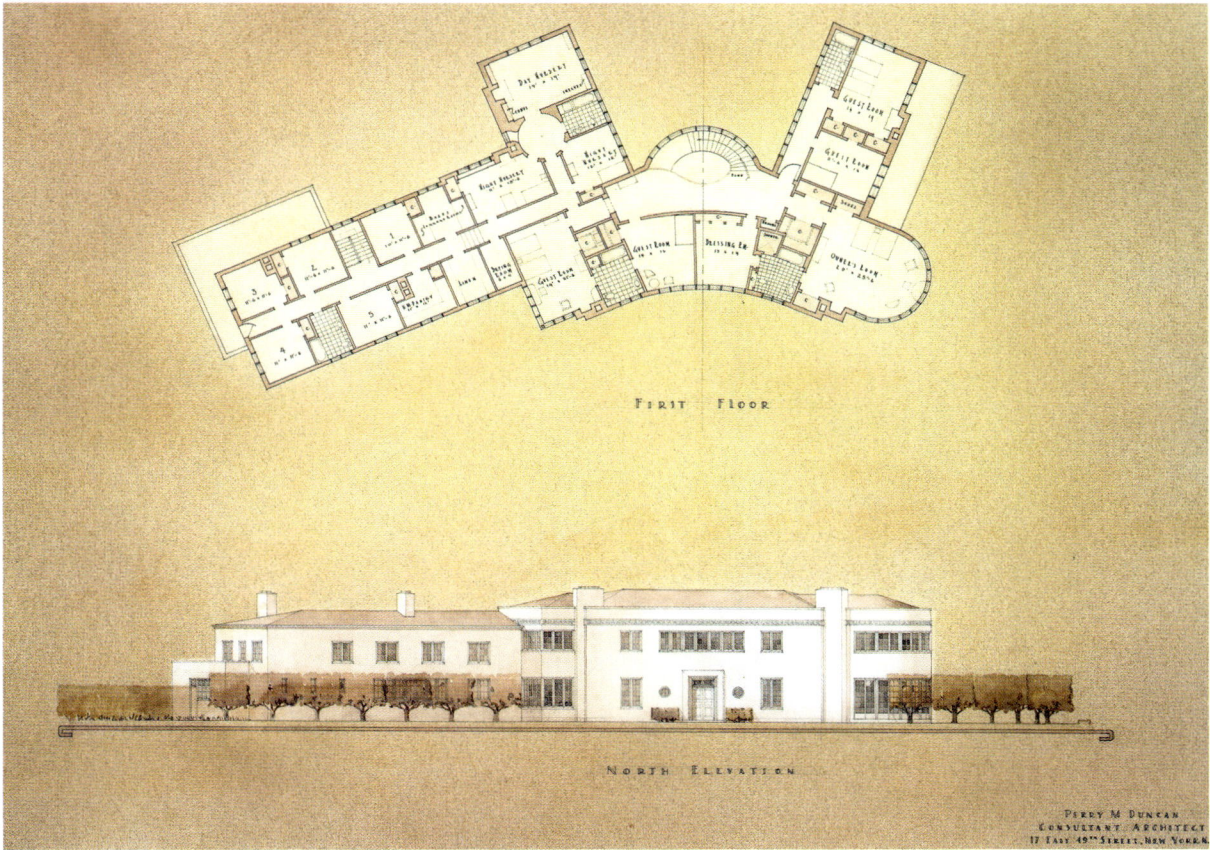

FIRST FLOOR

NORTH ELEVATION

PERRY M DUNCAN
CONSULTANT ARCHITECT
17 EAST 49TH STREET, NEW YORK, N.

recent country house in mind as her preferred model, Joldwynds at Holmbury St Mary in Surrey by Oliver Hill (1887–1968). Spence was therefore asked to re-draw Gribloch with a concave north facade in which the entrance was located.[27] Fortunately for Spence, Mrs Colville liked his proposed circular hallway containing a grand curving stairway behind a two-storey projecting south-facing window and also his adjacent bow-shaped living room, which were to be the house's principal spatial features. They were thus retained in the next iteration, which had two wings projecting from the south elevation and a third facing east for servants' quarters. The roof-pitch was lowered and the parapet slightly raised to give a flat-roofed impression.[28] Yet, the Colvilles still were not entirely satisfied – and they also perhaps thought Spence was devoting insufficient energy to the project, which would have been unsurprising when the client was driving the design to such an extent. They therefore

sought the advice of another architect, the New York-based Perry M Duncan (b 1902), who suggested to Spence splaying the walls further and thereby compressing the hallway with its curving stairway into an oval-shape. Duncan also criticised the exterior detailing as 'a little light and … fussy', noting that the ironwork looked 'slightly Spanish which is a curse on a modern house'.[29] Outside, a swimming pool was added, taking advantage of the shelter that the splayed wings created.[30]

To design the interiors, the Colvilles contacted Gordon Russell Ltd in London, who supplied three different proposals for the entrance hall plus one for the gun room; the correspondence with them was written by and signed by Nikolaus Pevsner, who at that time was an employee of Russell.[31] The Russell-Pevsner schemes were probably insufficiently fancy for the Colvilles' taste and so they instead hired John Hill (1900–1957) of the London decorators Green & Abbott to design all of the interiors.[32] His schemes feature Art Deco fireplaces and door surrounds, Georgian revival rope mouldings, arched doorways and chandeliers. The design of the hall stairway, with its sweeping curve and swirling Art Deco balustrade, appears as though straight from Hollywood.[33] Colville even contacted the Parisian decorative metalworker, Raymond Subes, as a possible supplier of this.[34] Osbert Lancaster's gently satirical identification of 'Vogue Regency' in *Homes Sweet Homes*, published in 1939 almost concurrently with the completion of Gribloch, accurately described the effect achieved.[35] For a nouveau riche Lanarkshire industrialist, all of this must have felt like a dream come true.

Gribloch stair balustrade design
Raymond Subes, 1938
HES DP011990

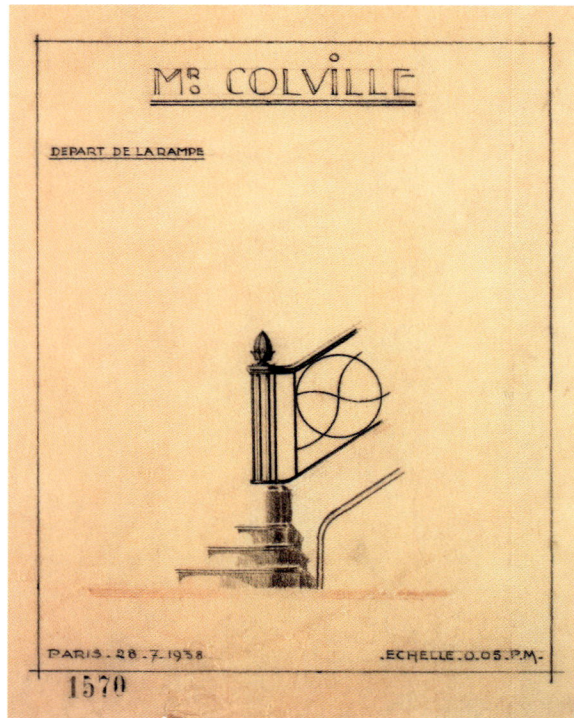

Gribloch hallway
Basil Spence and John Hill of Green & Abbott, 1939
Bruce Peter

Municipal housing

Interwar municipal housing initially followed the garden suburb model, the so-called 'Homes for Heroes' built in the wake of the Addison Act of 1919 becoming highly sought-after. This was not least because great numbers of the working-class were struggling to eke out existences in properties that were squalid and overcrowded, while far too few new homes for rent were being built. In 1930, Ramsay MacDonald's Labour government passed the Housing Act and Housing (Scotland) Act, often known as the Greenwood Acts, providing subsidies for municipalities to build many more homes to supersede slum properties. In Scotland, owing to the challenging economic climate, this resulted in only around 3,000 new homes being erected – far from sufficient.

A 1935 report by the Scottish Architectural Advisory Committee, which comprised such heavyweights as Thomas S Tait, James Miller, Frank Mears (1880–1953) and John Begg (1866–1937), to the Department of Health for Scotland regretted that those commissioning Scottish municipal housing appeared to measure success only in terms of quantity, rather than aesthetic and environmental quality.[36] They were not wrong in their assessment; the new homes were almost all of plain brick swathed in porridge-like brown or grey harling, which quickly stained with soot from coal fires. Yet, the minority of new housing schemes which did feature moderne elements such as flat roofs and Crittall windows – for example parts of the Pilton and Saughton estates around Edinburgh – appeared much more austere than private developments with similar features. Partly this was a consequence of their dull facings and less luxuriantly foliated environs and partly it was one of culture and perception. As the future professor Charles McKean astutely observed, had these been the homes of professors, the situation would have been different.[37] Gazing outward between the same type of horizontal metal window bars was perhaps a social leveller of sorts.

In Bo'ness, an old coal port on the south bank of the River Forth, the local architect Matthew Steele designed three sets of tenement-style municipal flats that were striking exceptions to this situation. Born in Bo'ness, he graduated from the Glasgow and West of Scotland Technical College, then worked for the city's telephone company in the 1890s before marriage to a relative of the Bo'ness burgh surveyor brought him back to the town. Over a 20-year span from 1905, he designed nearly every new building there, but produced little or

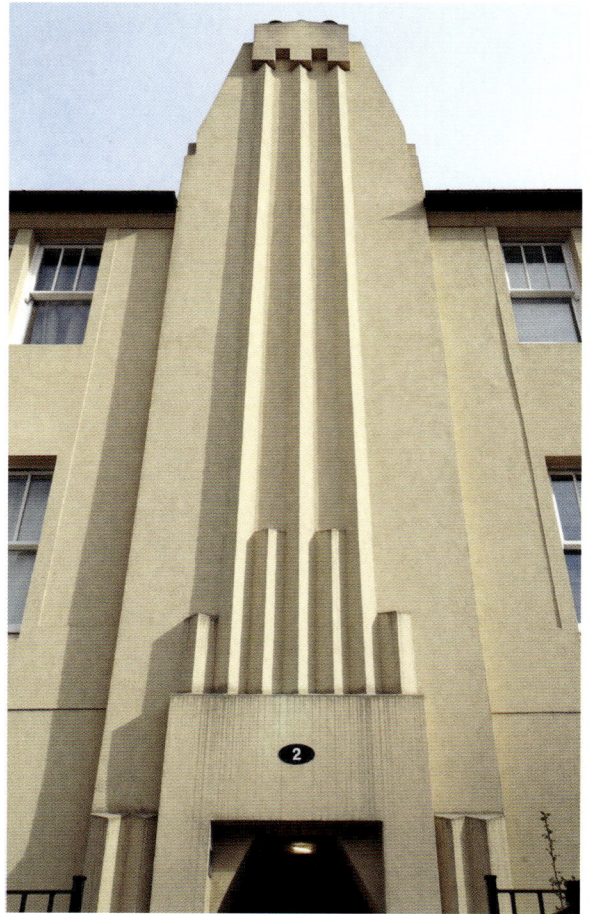

Chimneybreast of flats, Bo'ness
Matthew Steele, 1932
Bruce Peter

nothing elsewhere. Steele may have been influenced by early twentieth-century architectural trends in the Scandinavian nations and Germany – countries where the Glasgow Corporation had sought advice for its telephone services, possibly enabling him to familiarise himself with modern designs for buildings too. Several of his initial projects in Bo'ness had Art Nouveau detailing but in the 1930s, he embraced Art Deco, albeit of a peculiarly Germanic or Nordic variety. Some of the flats he designed are notable for their dramatically expressionistic chimney stacks, the bottoms of which contain the entrance doors with striking fluted patterning above.[38]

Rosemount Square flats, Aberdeen
Leo Durmin of Aberdeen City Architects'
Department, 1938–1946

While initial Scottish interwar municipal housing was of relatively low density, a radical and compelling alternative had appeared at the Paris Exposition in the form of Le Corbusier's *Plan Voisin*, shown in the Pavillon de L'Esprit Nouveau. This plan proposed a high-rise future Paris which he insisted would be the best way of providing space, light and urbanity there and elsewhere. In Britain, the planner Elizabeth Denby (1894–1965), who in the 1930s became a go-to expert on municipal housing matters, argued with sound evidence that the best solutions were of medium-density.[39] This echoed the established Scottish preference for urban tenement housing.

Denby particularly admired recent Viennese estates, especially the Karl-Marx-Hof, a model development containing 1,382 apartments and many diverse social amenities, built between 1927 and 1930 to a design by the city architect and planner Karl Ehn (1884–1959). In Britain, the municipal architects in Liverpool and Sheffield produced their own approximations of its layout, which comprised a massive continuous, repetitively detailed accommodation block around the perimeter with communal central gardens accessed via wide archways through the lower storeys. In 1935, the RIAS *Quarterly Illustrated* published an article titled 'Continental Housing', which highlighted the Karl-Marx-Hof.[40] Shortly before, the Edinburgh Architectural Association had invited Liverpool Corporation's Director of Housing, Lancelot Keay (1883–1974), to address its members about his recent similar designs for municipal housing there.[41]

The closest Scottish homage to the Karl-Marx-Hof and to Keay's housing schemes in Liverpool is the Rosemount Square flats in Aberdeen. Their design was by Leo Durmin (1902–1988) who had first joined the City Architect's Department in 1926 having trained at Robert Gordon's Technical College and who had visited the Netherlands in the mid-1930s to study works by Dudok. D-shaped in plan and of four-storeys in granite, the flats form a bold, sweeping curve among the surrounding nineteenth-century blocks. Above the main entrance arch is an Art Deco bas relief of Lady Godiva by T B Huxley-Jones (1908–1968), the Head of the Sculpture Department of Gray's School of Art. Designed in 1938, their completion was delayed until 1946 by the Second World War.

Rosemount Square flats, Aberdeen
Leo Durmin with sculpture by T B Huxley-Jones, 1938–1946
Bruce Peter

Furniture and furnishing

Once they had acquired a house in the moderne style, one might assume that its occupants would have felt obliged to decorate its interiors in the same idiom. In reality this rarely happened because those who could afford the most convincingly up-to-date-looking houses also were likely to be the inheritors of good-quality furnishings of older vintage, meaning that a bricolage of the old and new was usually what was achieved. Wholly Art Deco or moderne domestic interiors were thus rare – though it was possible to buy Scottish-made furniture and furnishings to decorate in these styles.

Although London's East End was established as the global epicentre of furniture production, Scotland had a significant and respected cabinetmaking industry too. There were several notable manufacturers in Glasgow, while the towns of Beith and Lochwinnoch to the south-west were almost entirely dedicated to the industry. In Beith, cabinetmaking had begun in the mid-1850s. By the 1930s, the principal manufacturers were McNeil Bros, Matthew Pollock Ltd, Stevenson & Co, Higgins & Co and the West of Scotland Furniture Manufacturing Co, while in Lochwinnoch, they were Hamilton & Crawford, James Hunter Ltd and Joseph Johnstone Ltd. [42]

Although Scottish cabinetmaking was noted for its traditional solidity, there was also an established interest in producing up-to-date designs. In the 1880s–1900s period, upmarket manufacturers, such as the firms of Daniel Cottier and Wylie & Lochhead in Glasgow and Scott Morton & Co and Whytock, Reid & Co in Edinburgh, had embraced the latest Aesthetic, Arts and Crafts and Art Nouveau styles. [43] Designs by Charles Rennie Mackintosh and George Walton (1867–1933), which drew inspiration from progressive developments in Germany and Austro-Hungary, were exhibited on the continent and were greatly admired there. But the First World War changed everything and, in its wake, Scottish cabinetmakers initially reverted to neo-Georgian styles before some tentatively began producing somewhat diluted versions of Art Deco and moderne.

In April 1935 *The Cabinet Maker and Complete House Furnisher* dedicated nearly a whole edition to an analysis of the Scottish furniture industry. The editorial characterised the Scots as 'a race of workmen, competent, tenacious and ambitious to become masters of their craft… Hand-made furniture is the speciality

Bedroom suite
A H McIntosh Ltd, 1936
The Cabinet Maker

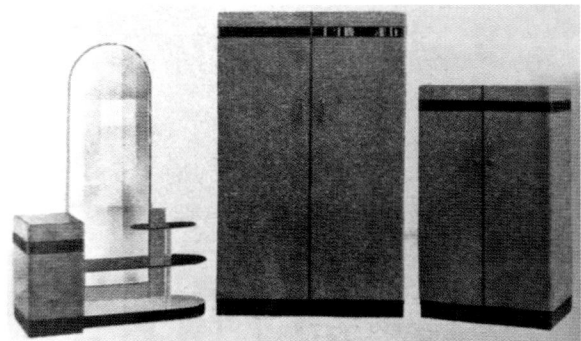

Bedroom suite
McNeil Bros, 1937
The Cabinet Maker

of many Scottish factories'. Distinguishing traits were 'solidity and soundness of construction' though 'products lack something from the point of view of design'.[44] Representing the industry's management was the Scottish Furniture Manufacturers' Association, the head of which was Neil McNeil of McNeil Bros of Beith. *The Cabinet Maker* reported that the Scottish industry was fully unionised but that labour relations were harmonious (though that was about to change). In London, by contrast, union membership was lower, several firms being family affairs in the craft tradition while others used casual workers. In Scotland, associations with retailers were close and consumers tended to prefer pieces that were locally made. Although fashion was followed, this happened at a slower pace than in the south and because 'a new vogue [might] not immediately become popular north of the Tweed, the retailer hesitates to stock until he is certain that the vogue is assured some degree of permanence. In the ordinary way, a period of six months will elapse from the launching of the fashion before it really shows signs of popularity among Scottish retailers'.[45] Exemplifying this situation, the upmarket Kirkcaldy cabinetmakers A H McIntosh, which had been founded in 1869 by Alexander Henry McIntosh, continued to follow an Arts and Crafts approach in the 1930s, its management and their retailer clients believing that the public would get better value from traditionally made pieces that would become heirlooms than ones that were merely reflective of ephemeral passing trends.[46]

To encourage growth, in the mid-1930s, a succession of home furnishing exhibitions were staged in Glasgow's Kelvin Hall. The latest outputs of Scotland's cabinetmakers were showcased and it was for these that some of the manufacturers tried to stimulate fresh demand with novel designs. Reporting on the Century of Progress Exhibition in April 1935, *The Cabinet Maker* records that Wylie & Lochhead had embraced Art Deco, presenting 'one of the largest and most interesting displays, which included a bedroom suite in smoky sycamore, with interiors of natural polished sycamore, a dining set in mahogany and ash-root veneers, with Macassar ebony bandings and bases, and a dining-room set in toned nut-brown oak'.[47] For the subsequent Housing and Health Exhibition in October, the Scottish National Development Council, Glasgow Corporation and the Scottish Furniture Manufacturers' Association sponsored an 'All-Scottish Home' at a cost of £2,000. Its lounge was designed by James Dunlop, principal of the furniture department of Bow's Emporium in Glasgow, using furniture made by John Walker and Sons, also of Glasgow. *The Cabinet Maker* illustrated this alongside a recent interior in Paris by the decorator Pierre Montagne and one in London by the architect John Grey (1890–1966) of the Design and Industries Association (DIA). With its horizontally banded wall lining, the Glasgow room was perhaps a little more overtly 'modernistic' than the others, but the design of the furniture was highly comparable with that of the Parisian apartment (while that in the Grey/DIA design was, as might have been expected, considerably less stylised).[48] A key feature of the lounge in the All-Scottish Home was a built-in settee with curved ends and storage cupboards to the rear, which split the space into two sections. The bedrooms had walnut-veneered furniture by Wylie & Lochhead, Matthew Pollock Ltd and West of Scotland Furniture Manufacturing Co, carpets by James Templeton & Co, curtains by John Brown and Son and William Strang and Son (both of Bridgeton, Glasgow) and by Morton & Co of Darvel in Ayrshire.[49] These suppliers would no doubt have felt highly satisfied upon seeing *The Cabinet Maker*'s comparison of their work with the latest in luxury domesticity in the French capital. That 100,000 visitors passed through the spaces would also have given them cause for cheer.[50]

Shortly thereafter, at the Scottish Manufacturers' Exhibition, John McGregor and Sons of Renfrew displayed 'an unusual three-piece suite in pink and black covering', Joseph Johnstone of Lochwinnoch showed a walnut sideboard with rounded ends and also a 'very modern' sideboard with swing-out cutlery boxes, while McNeil Bros of Beith presented a bedroom suite 'in African rosewood on modern lines'. A three-piece lounge suite by East Brothers of Dundee, meanwhile,

All-Scottish Home, Housing and Health Exhibition, Glasgow
James Dunlop and John Walker and Sons, 1935
The Cabinet Maker

had a 'streamline effect' and was upholstered in green velvet.[51] Even the traditionalist A H McIntosh began producing compact bedroom suites in comparatively racy moderne styles in the hope attracting the custom of young professionals with money to spend.

In the spring of 1936, the Scottish furniture industry experienced an unusually acrimonious three-month-long strike as, against a backdrop of tentative economic recovery, workers sought to make up for years of lowered earnings while management remained cautious.[52] Nonetheless, *The Cabinet Maker* reported optimistically that:

> in Scotland generally there is less unemployment… Money is more plentiful… Design and quality are now being taken more into account… In model houses built by local authorities in connection with housing and health exhibitions there is keen competition for the privilege of furnishing the various rooms; Scottish-made furniture is regularly on view at the British Industries Fair… The continuation

of the building boom and the increased spending power of the public caused a gradual but steady expansion in retail sales throughout the year, the trade in fabrics and furnishings being particularly bright…[53]

With regard to soft furnishings, Scotland had a substantial fabric industry, which in its industrialised form mainly dated back to the mid-nineteenth century, but had much longer origins as a cottage-based craft tradition. Glasgow's Bridgeton district was home to the factories of John Brown and Son, Holmes and Allan Ltd and William Strang and Son, while David Barbour & Co was located in Pollokshaws. Other makers were in Strathaven, the Irvine valley and Newmilns and Darvel in Ayrshire. James Finlay of Catrine in Ayrshire produced sheets, towels and embroidery, much of which was exported, while Hay and Robertson of Dunfermline were highly regarded for their silk products.[54]

In May 1935, *The Cabinet Maker* noted a shift in Scottish taste in the patterning of soft furnishings. Interviews with Glaswegian retailers revealed that 'older fabrics, such as heavy silk brocades, are being produced today with futuristic designs' but that they 'do not sell many light [back]grounds in Glasgow. This is easily understood when one considers that the atmosphere is heavily impregnated with soot and chemicals. The most popular colours today are gold, brown, rose and green. The latter is growing in favour, and the superstitious reluctance to use it is apparently dying out.'[55]

Leading the way in Scotland with Art Deco and moderne fabric designs was the Dundee-based Donald Brothers Ltd, *The Cabinet Maker* illustrating its 'Kintore' linen with moderne-style foliage and wave patterns by way of example. The company's origins could be traced back to 1780 when James Donald, a tailor from Kirkton of Lundie, opened a spinning and weaving business in the city's Lochee area. His son, also James, subsequently built a factory to produce coarse industrial textiles using jute and hemp, but in the 1890s diversified into the weaving of fabrics for domestic settings. The third generation, Francis James Donald, introduced high-quality art textiles in the 1900s, including designs by William Morris (1834–1896), the American designer Gustav Stickley (1858–1942) and Silver Studios. In 1924 production moved to new premises in Dundee's Glamis Road and,

shortly after, the trademark Old Glamis Fabrics was introduced. The marriage in 1923 of Lady Elizabeth Bowes-Lyon of Glamis to HRH Prince Albert, Duke of York gave the Glamis name considerable caché, especially when in 1937, following the abdication crisis, the prince was crowned as King George VI. Although there was no connection between the textiles business and Glamis itself, it was usually promoted in the 1930s as 'Donald Bros of Glamis'. In 1934, it received a Royal Warrant in recognition of the high quality of its output, a significant proportion of which was for export with the USA, a prime market.

Mid-decade, Donald Bros introduced textured weaves, jacquard-woven tapestries and prints on linen, canvas, chintz and rayon 'art silk' designed by, among others, Marion Dorn, Bernard Adeney (1878–1966), Eva Crofts (1875–1945), Riette Sturge-Moore (1907–1995) and Ernst Aufseeser (1880–1940).[56] These attracted an expanded range of retail clients – including, in London, Peter Jones, John Lewis, Heal & Co, Fortnum & Mason and Gordon Russell. In New York, where earlier Arts and Crafts fabrics by Donald Bros already had sold well, the fashionable retailer Dan Cooper became a prime importer. The designs were also sold in Chicago by Seeley & Co and in Sydney, Australia by Margaret Jaye.[57]

In the 1930s, Francis James Donald presented himself as a design reformer, his starting point – aligning with British reformers since the mid-nineteenth century – being that traditional Middle-Eastern carpet design and making represented the epitome of excellence. In a public lecture given in Dundee in 1934, he observed that the Modern Movement reflected 'a deep-seated desire for a new simplicity, in definite revolt against ostentation, over-ornamentation, ignorance and stupidity. It is a movement which … before it loses its impetus, will have revolutionised the whole existing order of things…'. With regard to the domestic realm, he noted that while modernism might have 'roots in tradition, it must be essentially new in thought', adding 'I would not suggest you follow the cult for "glass and steel." Along that ultra-severe line, I think there are too few surprises… Dull houses … should not be allowed to exist.'[58] Donald's position was evidently reflected in the bright, often quirkily patterned printed fabrics produced by his firm.[59]

In the latter 1930s, Donald became greatly interested in the Bauhaus, which by then had been closed in Germany by the Nazis. In February 1938 he presented a lecture to the Dundee Arts Society, entitled 'The Bauhaus in Germany and the New Bauhaus in Chicago'.[60] Having illustrated the work and approaches of Walter Gropius and his colleagues, he observed that:

> For many months of the year, Scotland has not much real sunshine. Why, therefore, should we not let as much of it as we can into our homes and our works? Why do we make so little use of glass? Why not have bigger windows … and … a central heating plant? … In Scotland I sometimes think we are still obsessed by the doctrine of eternal punishment, both in this life and in the world to come. We accept affliction, a dull, drab existence which we imagine has been pre-ordained…[61]

Donald evidently felt that the 'utilitarian' culture of Presbyterianism might be countered by bright, Bauhaus-like abstract forms and materials. He later shared his address with the Scottish-born, though London-based, architecture critic Philip Morton Shand, who three years previously had translated Gropius's *The New Architecture and the Bauhaus* into English.[62] In correspondence, Shand told Donald that he considered the departure of Gropius from Britain to the USA as 'the bitterest failure of my life.'[63] Shand added 'I doubt if I should ever have been brave enough to choose the Bauhaus as a theme for a Scottish audience' and that, in doing so, Donald was carrying out a 'most valuable pioneering effort.'[64] What was pioneering in Dundee, however, happened a decade after Gropius himself had left the Bauhaus in Dessau. Nonetheless, the Old Glamis Fabrics by Donald Bros were of good quality and were widely used in moderne interiors in Britain and overseas.

Whereas Donald Bros targeted a wide international market, another comparably progressive but considerably more niche maker of modern abstractly patterned textiles, Edinburgh Weavers, instead aimed its products specifically at modern architects and interior decorators. Its establishment in 1928 was a pet retirement project by James Morton, who was the second generation to lead a weaving business first established in Darvel in Ayrshire in the 1860s and which initially began as a co-operative of local hand-weavers. Even after switching to power looms, Morton

continued to aspire to Arts and Crafts principles and in the 1880s supplied textiles to William Morris & Co and later commissioned patterns from, among others, Lewis Foreman Day (1845–1910), Christopher Dresser, C F A Voysey (1857–1941), Jessie M King (1875–1949) and George Walton. In 1900 the bulk of production switched to a new and bigger mill in Carlisle where colourfast dyes were introduced, marketed under the curious name of Sundour, 'dour' being a Scots term for unyielding (but also meaning gloomy and humourless). Later, the name of the company itself was changed to Morton Sundour. [65]

Donald Bros Old Glamis fabric samples
Donald Bros, 1934–1939
GSA Archives

The origins of the Edinburgh Weavers were in 1926 when Morton bought a mansion at Craigiehall in Corstorphine, where he planned to retire. Instead, he set up a textile workshop in the grounds to hand-weave exclusive designs, marketed as Scottish Folk Fabrics. He brought in Morton Sundour's in-house designer Ronald Simpson (1890–1960), who was the son of the Kendal-based Arts and Crafts furniture maker Arthur Simpson (1847–1922), to lead the making. *The Cabinet Maker and Complete House Furnisher* records that its output thereafter included quilts, cushions, embroidered hangings, curtains for houses and even cinema curtains.[66]

Having visited the Arts and Crafts-inspired St Edmundsbury Weavers' studio in Letchworth Garden City, run by Edmund Hunter (1866–1937) and his son Alec Hunter (1899–1958), Morton decided to take it over, relocating to Craigiehall as an adjunct to Scottish

Folk Fabrics and with the new name of Edinburgh Weavers.[67] There, the younger Hunter first produced abstract, jazzy patterns with names such as Wave and Aztec, both of which were released in 1930. The after-effects of the Wall Street Crash caused losses and led to a falling out with the Hunters. Morton then decided to move Edinburgh Weavers to Carlisle with his artistically inclined and visionary 21-year-old son, Alastair Morton (1910–1963), as its director. He had recently abandoned the study of mathematics at Balliol College, Oxford, in favour of a hands-on role in the family business. Greatly enamoured with constructivist art,

he also painted and was exhibited in leading London galleries. At Edinburgh Weavers, he commissioned designs from Marion Dorn, Hans Aufseeser, Maxwell Armfield (1881–1972), John Chirnside (1905–1978), Ashley Havinden (1903–1973), Ben Nicholson (1894–1982) and Paul Nash (1889–1946). These and others were shown in London at the Dorland Hall

Edinburgh Weavers fabrics
Edinburgh Weavers, 1936
GSA Archives

domestic design exhibitions, as well as at the Royal Society of the Arts and the Royal Academy. In the mid-1930s, the fabrics were used in upmarket modern interiors of many kinds and even in those of the new RIBA headquarters and BBC Broadcasting House, in the latter augmenting striking moderne spaces designed by Raymond McGrath, Serge Chermayeff and Wells Coates (1895–1958).[68] Outstanding though its outputs were for quality and appearance, Edinburgh Weavers was by then a misnomer, it having had connection with the city of that name only for the first three years of its existence.

One element of soft furnishings that came to the foreground in the 1930s was carpeting. The percolation of smart American taste through the expanding lifestyle media encouraged a belief that modern interior luxury meant having fitted carpets. The growing availability of electric vacuum cleaners and mechanical carpet sweepers enabled carpeted rooms to be kept reasonably clean. Apart from featuring in the interiors of the many new houses constructed during the 1930s, carpets were used in quantity in cinemas and in the First Class saloons of ocean liners, all of which was reflected in a great expansion of the industry. In 1937, *The Cabinet Maker and Complete House Furnisher* reported that:

> Carpet manufacture is one of the most important and flourishing of Scottish industries. It gives direct employment to over 100,000 persons, of whom the majority are women and girls. But, in addition, it utilises the services of mechanics and engineers, dyers and chemists, decorative artists and designers, welfare workers and a host of others engaged in tasks of administration, distribution and selling. In Dundee, the principal trade is in jute-surfaced carpets, and there are carpet factories in Perth, the East of Scotland and in various towns up and down the country. But the centre of the industry is in the West, in Glasgow, where James Templeton & Co have built up a name that is known throughout the world; in Paisley where A F Stoddard and Co, have created in recent years as sound a reputation for their Wilton and Axminster carpets as they enjoyed for their tapestry products; in Ayr, where the factory

of W C Gray and Sons Ltd is situated, and in Kilmarnock, where Blackwood, Morton & Sons Ltd have in the last ten years increased the number of their employees from 400 to 1,400 and have spent hundreds of thousands of pounds on new buildings and machinery.[69]

James Templeton & Co developed into Scotland's largest carpet maker from an initial business, founded in Paisley in the latter 1820s, which made shawls. In the 1830s, knowledge from producing tufted shawls was transferred to carpet-making with an initial factory in Bridgeton. The next generation greatly expanded the company, in the late 1880s commissioning from William Leiper a magnificent factory modelled on the Doge's Palace in Venice to occupy a prominent site adjacent to Glasgow Green. Templeton's output was notably design-conscious, using patterns by, among others, Owen Jones (1809–1874), C F A Voysey and Walter Crane (1845–1918).[70] The interwar expansion of the carpet trade required their premises to be extended to provide sufficient space for the burgeoning production of Axminster and Wilton designs (see Chapter 9).[71]

As with Donald Bros, James Templeton and W C Gray were long-standing advocates of the beauty of designs from the Orient. Since the latter nineteenth century Templeton had made the accurate reproduction of Persian traditional carpets and textiles an important part of its image.[72] In the 1930s, these firms continued to produce such designs as signifiers of craft quality, alongside their modern ranges. The established popularity of oriental abstract patterning among their customers may also have encouraged the embracing of Art Deco forms.

Design histories of abstract modern carpets and rugs tend to emphasise the influence in 1930s Britain of émigré continental avant-garde artists such as Naum Gabo (1890–1977). Already, in advance of such developments, Templeton's large design department, which between 1918 and 1939 was headed by James Kincaid (1876–1965) and staffed mainly with Glasgow School of Art graduates, was imbibing emergent European design trends through a library of up-to-date books about art, applied art and decorating, purchased from France, Germany and Sweden.[73] The company additionally had a design studio in London, where leading British artists, such as Frank Brangwyn

(1867–1956) and Ernest Procter (1885–1935), were consulted. Templeton's carpet designs were in a very wide range of styles and its abstract patterns often were bold and bright.[74] Upon Kincaid's retirement, the *Templetonian* company magazine noted that he had 'maintained a high standard of artistic excellence' and 'could appreciate and interpret any style, and in a happy way he blended the artistic with such an amount of the business outlook as is called for in industrial art'.[75]

Scotland's other significant manufacturer of Art Deco and moderne carpets, W C Gray & Sons of Ayr, was founded in 1876 by the dynamic William Crawford Gray, who developed new carpet manufacturing techniques and used his personal wealth to become a major collector of Asian applied art. When he died in 1918 his eldest son, Andrew Jardine Gray, became chairman with his two younger brothers assisting. By the mid-1930s, the company had showrooms in Glasgow, Manchester, Birmingham, Leeds, Dublin, and Belfast and representatives in the USA, Canada, New Zealand, Australia, South Africa, Scandinavia, and the Netherlands. Boldly abstract

designs by then formed a significant aspect of its output and were emphasised in promotional material.

By 1937, *The Cabinet Maker and Complete House Furnisher* was reporting that 'the demand is for floor coverings of a more luxurious character… a natural sequel to the general rise in the standard of living and to the improvement of machinery and mass production methods'.[76] Sales of Scottish-made carpets were strong in Australia, New Zealand and South Africa. Duties on imports to a large degree protected the UK trade from foreign competition.[77]

For those who perhaps would have found carpet too costly, or impractical to maintain, or for those wanting the appearance of carpet in a kitchen, bathroom or hallway without worrying about its getting damaged, Nairn & Co, the famous Kirkcaldy manufacturer of linoleum, provided what appeared to be an ideal solution – linoleum made in carpet-like Art Deco and moderne patterns. Indeed, viewed as prints in a catalogue, one would not guess that the range of designs, introduced in the mid-1930s, were for anything other than Axminster, especially as the colour gradations from one shade to another

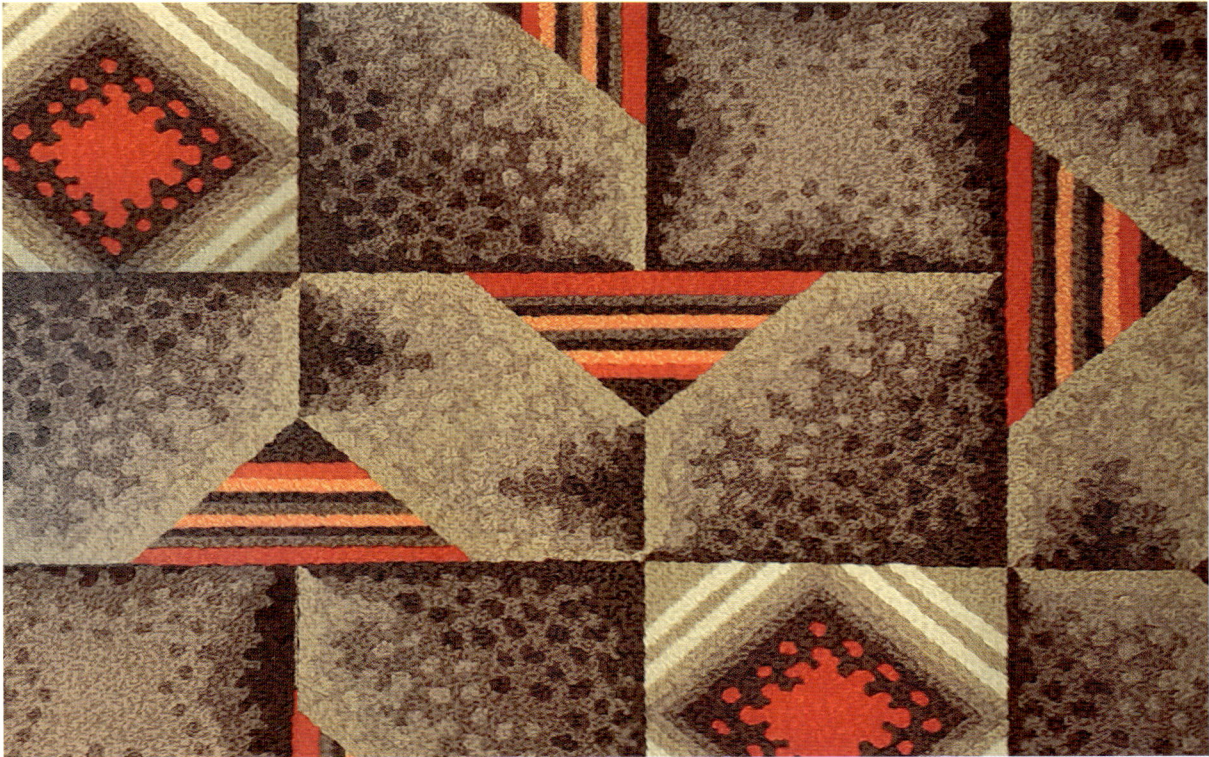

Michael Nairn linoleum designs
Michael Nairn & Co, 1939
Fife Archives

were speckled, just as they would be in a tufted weave. The company had been founded in 1828 by Michael Nairn, an entrepreneur who discovered that a robust floor covering could be made by compressing a paste of linseed oil, wood flour and chalk on a jute backing. Until the early 1930s, Nairn's patterned linoleums had tended towards intricate Arts and Crafts-inspired floral designs, but in the decade's first half, an initially small number of wholly abstract designs appeared on an experimental basis. As these proved popular, more were developed until at least one-third of the range was of this kind. The modest scale of the patterning made them ideal for domestic use.[78]

There were, in addition, Scottish manufacturers of wallpaper and lighting, though these were insignificant in comparison with the main English producers that dominated the UK market. So far as can be ascertained, the Scottish makers all favoured traditionalist designs over Art Deco or moderne ones.

With regard to the furnishing of new municipal housing, in the spring of 1937 *The Cabinet Maker* reported approvingly on the 'innumerable people in Scotland [who] have found themselves in the last few years transplanted from ugly tenements to modern homes built by municipal enterprise. The new surroundings have created a new spirit of pride in the home, reflecting itself in a desire for new furnishings'.[79] For Glaswegians moving out of inner-city slums and into flats in the new peripheral housing schemes, the Corporation introduced a hire-purchase policy to enable fully furnished homes to be afforded, the contents paid for through a down-payment and a levy of one shilling a week added to rent, paid over three years.[80] The designs of the approved furniture, furnishing items and flooring preceded by a couple of years the wartime utility ranges and had similar characteristics of simplicity and solidity. In the domestic realm, unsurprisingly, Art Deco and moderne mainly were reflective of the forward-looking faction of bourgeois taste.

CHAPTER 3
TRANSPORT AND TRAVEL

Of the various areas in which streamlined design forms appeared in the 1930s, transport was the most significant and arguably appropriate. The approach had first been suggested by aerodynamic experiments in the late nineteenth century to reduce the wind resistance and drag of fast-moving airborne objects, the most efficient shape being found to be a teardrop with a bulbous front and a tapering, cone-shaped tail. In the art world prior to the First World War, the Futurists were early to promote the idea of streamlining, admiring the design of Zeppelin airships with their smooth, bulbous forms. Later, during the 1920s, the Italian car designer Ettore Bugatti (1881–1947) produced strikingly horizontally elongated sports cars with bulbous radiator covers, in which even the engine blocks were given streamlined details to look magnificent when the bonnet was opened. Thereafter, on both sides of the Atlantic, streamlined shapes transferred from the worlds of science, technology and advanced engineering into popular culture. During the Great Depression, the French-American industrial designer Raymond Loewy (1893–1986) successfully re-packaged existing mundane products ranging from office copiers to fridges in streamlined encasements, the designs of which were subtly modified at intervals to encourage

consumers to buy the latest model. In Britain, largely as a consequence of American cultural influence and the senses of glamour and modernity with which it was associated, even quite slow-moving modes of public transport came to be given streamlined embellishment so as to appear appealingly up to date. Supporters of the functionalist school of modern design found such symbolic use of form inappropriate or even immoral – and there were also practical arguments that an extra streamlined casing would add weight and make access for maintenance more challenging. This was a minority position, however, especially in a context of strong competition among transport providers to attract custom. Art Deco and moderne futuristic visions of glamour were thus liberally applied to all modes of passenger transport in the 1930s, providers all coming to believe that it was necessary to 'jazz up' travel experiences with bulbous streamlined styling on the exterior and fancy lighting, chrome trimmings and upholstery within.

The most sensational and futuristic vision for transport in interwar Scotland materialised in 1929–1930 to the east of Milngavie, where a short demonstration section of the Bennie Railplane was constructed above the existing commuter railway line. As the name suggested, it was an attempt to hybridise rail and air travel and comprised elevated tracks mounted on a system of gantries and girders, from which was suspended a Zeppelin-like high-speed streamlined capsule, thrust along by an aircraft

Bennie Railplane, Milngavie
George Bennie, 1930
J A Hampton, Hulton Archive

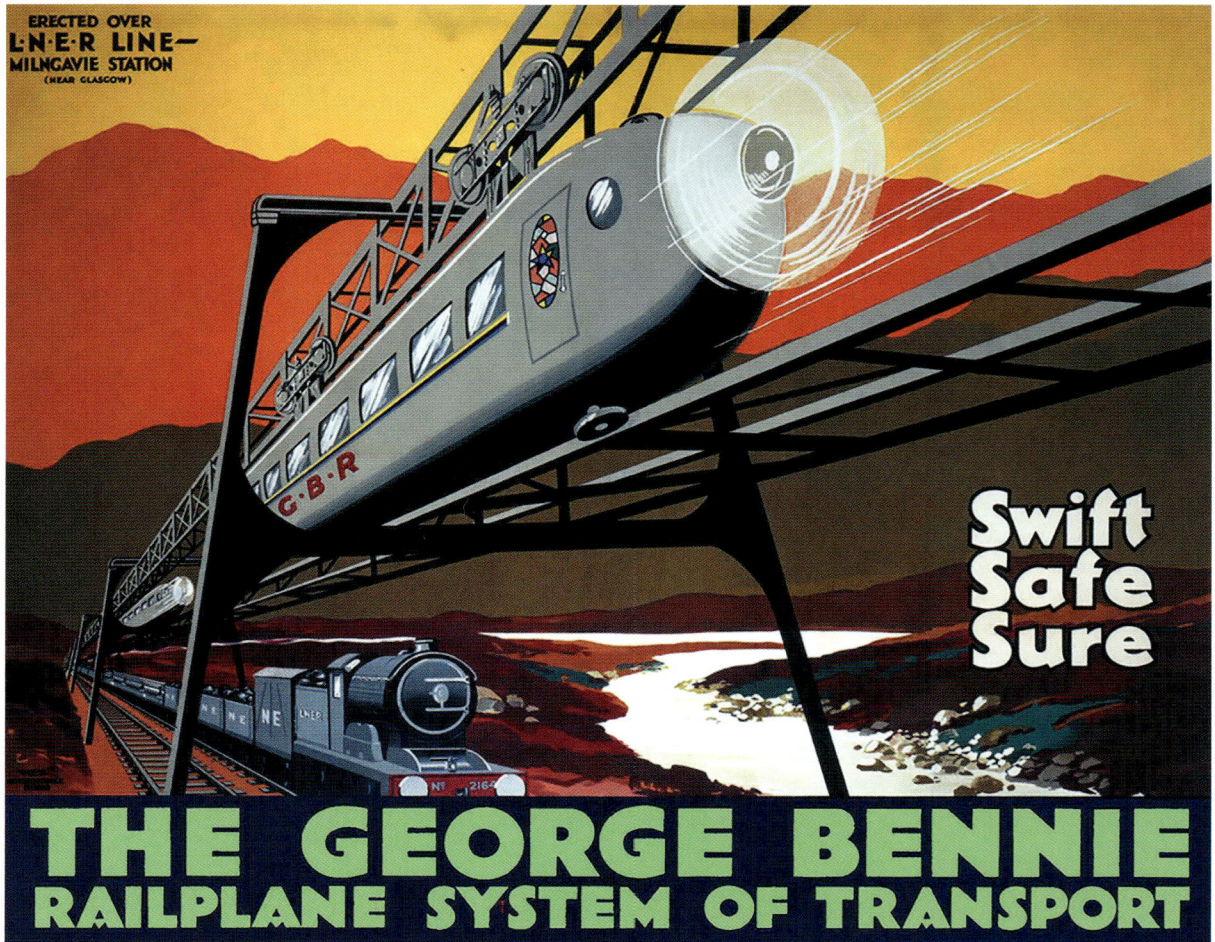

ERECTED OVER
L·N·E·R LINE—
MILNGAVIE STATION
(NEAR GLASGOW)

G·B·R

Swift
Safe
Sure

THE GEORGE BENNIE
RAILPLANE SYSTEM OF TRANSPORT

propeller. All of this was the vision of a Glasgow-born engineer and entrepreneur George Bennie (1892–1957) who, having been interested in transport from a young age, patented an innovative 'System of Aerial Transport' in 1923, which envisaged a vehicle suspended between two guide rails. Upon acceleration, lifting planes positioned on its roof would support some of its weight, reducing friction upon the rails. The elevated track would allow the Railplane to span geographical obstacles and to 'fly' over buildings at speeds of 120 mph or more. The steelwork for the five spans of test track was fabricated on Teesside and the lightweight aluminium test vehicle was assembled in Milngavie using components supplied by William Beardmore & Co. Its rather plush Art Deco interior, with seating for 24, was provided by the London decorators, Waring & Gillow. An anonymous but talented illustrator with the

Bennie Railplane poster
W C N, McCorquodale & Co, 1930
Bruce Peter collection

initials 'W C N', employed in the design studio of the large British printing company McCorquodale & Co, which had a Glasgow office and printworks, produced a striking promotional poster.

Between Bennie's raising of private sponsorship to have the demonstration section and test vehicle built in 1929 and the press inauguration in July 1930, the Wall Street Crash occurred and the ensuing Great Depression made it impossible to find anyone with sufficient capital to develop the concept further. A plan for a Railplane route between east and west London, via Oxford Street, which would more or less

Bennie Railplane above LNER freight train, Milngavie
George Bennie, 1930
Bruce Peter collection

have followed the route of the London Underground Central Line was publicised, but nothing came of the idea. In the spring of 1937, Bennie proposed that his concept be used to provide transport along Paisley Road West to the forthcoming Empire Exhibition. The Administrative Committee liked the idea, but before anything further could happen, Bennie went bankrupt.[1] Remarkably, despite the great and urgent need for steel for wartime production, the experimental structure near Milngavie remained in situ until the early 1950s, when it was demolished.[2]

Railways

By comparison with the Bennie Railplane, all other new Scottish transport innovations during what remained of the interwar period were relatively conventional and pragmatic, being based upon the development of soundly proven existing technologies, albeit usually made to appear more advanced through being packaged in Art Deco and moderne fancy dress. For the railways, the interwar era brought severe economic challenges as they were mandated by law to act as a 'common carrier', transporting anything and anyone requiring moving at limited cost. A lack of money meant that such resources as were available needed to be targeted where they would have the maximum impact. In order to show that the railways were keeping up with the modern spirit of the time, Art Deco and streamlined styles were used for prestige

LNER A4 Pacific locomotive hauling the Coronation train
Sir Nigel Gresley, 1937
Bruce Peter collection

new locomotives and coaches forming their crack express trains.

In 1923, Britain's many private railway companies were restructured (or 'grouped', as the change was described at the time) into four much bigger and hopefully more financially resilient regional organisations, sometimes collectively referred to as the 'Big Four'. The pre-grouping Scottish companies were the Caledonian Railway, the Glasgow & South Western Railway, the Highland Railway, the North British Railway and the Great North of Scotland Railway. As they had long cooperated with their counterparts south of the border to run long-distance expresses, the grouping led to their being merged with two different English-headquartered companies, which were the London, Midland & Scottish Railway (LMS) and the London & North Eastern Railway (LNER). Control of Scotland's rail network – and, to a large extent, also of the design and construction of locomotives and rolling stock – thereafter was moved south. The LMS, whose major source of revenue was operating freight trains in the industrial Midlands, suffered badly during the Great Depression. In the latter 1930s, however, streamlined

express trains entered service on both the LNER and LMS between Edinburgh Waverley and London Kings Cross and from Glasgow Central to London Euston.

The LNER's first Chief Mechanical Engineer, Nigel Gresley (1876–1941) was, by chance, born in Edinburgh, where his mother had been visiting from Derbyshire when she went into labour. Having risen through the engineering ranks of various English pre-grouping railways, in his role at the LNER he was based at its main works in Doncaster. His new A1 class Pacific locomotives were soon impressing for their high-speed performances hauling the Flying Scotsman express, which was introduced in 1924 between London and Edinburgh and, from 1928, was operated non-stop. Gresley followed these in 1935 with his A4 locomotive design, the boiler of which was clad in a wedge-shaped streamlined encasement, inspired by aerodynamic

LNER Coronation observation car interior
Sir Nigel Gresley and White Allom Ltd, 1937
Bruce Peter

LNER Coronation observation car
Sir Nigel Gresley, 1937
Bruce Peter collection

experiments carried out on diesel railcars in France in the early 1930s by the Italian automotive engineer Ettore Bugatti. The first A4-hauled streamlined express was the Silver Jubilee, introduced in 1935 between London and Newcastle – but an equivalent London to Edinburgh train, known as the Coronation, commenced in 1937, named in celebration of the crowning of King George VI. Both had articulated coaches of Gresley's advanced lightweight design with bogies shared between adjoining vehicles to spare further weight, but the Coronation had the added refinement of an American-style observation car at the rear, from which the passing scenery could be viewed. Externally, the whole ensemble was painted in garter blue with Marlborough blue around the coach windows, separated by chrome beading and with matching lettering. Within, there were splendid Art Deco interiors designed by the upmarket decorators White Allom of London. Pressure ventilation and Pullman-style armchairs ensured great comfort.[3]

The LMS, meanwhile, introduced its own streamlined express, the Coronation Scot between London and Glasgow, which was hauled by the new and exceptionally powerful Princess Coronation class locomotives. Designed by William Stanier and built in Crewe, they featured bulbous boiler encasement and a blue livery with a silver chevron on the front from which slim parallel stripes arose, then ran along the sides of the entire length of the train. Stanier's rolling stock was of more conventional design than that devised by Gresley and he relied on the brute power of the locomotives to attain speed, rather than ingenious weight-saving engineering innovations. The Coronation Scot coaches also were notable for their Art Deco interiors, which included a stylish cocktail bar, lined in Bakelite with chrome fixing strips.[4]

For the 1939 World's Fair in New York, a brand-new Coronation Scot train was built and this also toured in North America, where its Princess Coronation locomotive looked decidedly small and behind-the-times when parked adjacent to the latest American streamlined diesels. The outbreak of the Second World War temporarily stranded the train there and it never entered service in Britain as had been intended.

Between them, the dynamic A4 and Princess Coronation locomotives and the trains they hauled created the most memorable images of 1930s British railway modernity. Yet, as the railway historian O S Nock records, even when the A4 *Mallard* had

claimed the world speed record for steam traction, its designer, Gresley, was still far from convinced that their streamlined boiler casings made them any better than his earlier non-streamlined designs. During a meeting, he reputedly was handed the log of a journey by a non-streamlined example, which was deputising for a failed A4. According to Nock, he 'passed the paper over to his visitor, saying "There you are Peter; any of my bloody engines can do the job, whether they have a tin case on them or not!"'[5] Both Gresley and Stanier were knighted for their achievements in 1936 and 1943 respectively.

The most substantive Art Deco and moderne contributions to British railway design by a Scot occurred in southern England where in the 1930s the Glasgow-born but Edinburgh-trained architect James Robb Scott (1882–1965) designed numerous new station buildings for the Southern Railway. There, an extensive programme of electrification required new infrastructure to handle the many commuters. The son of an architect, Andrew Robb Scott (1851–1914), he had moved to London in 1907 where within two years he was employed by one of the Southern's pre-grouping precursor companies, the London & South Western Railway. Promoted to Chief Architectural Assistant for the rebuilding of its Waterloo terminus, after the First World War he designed a memorial to fallen railway employees inside the station. Shortly after the grouping in 1923, he became the Southern's Chief Architect and between the mid-1920s and late 1930s was responsible for designing stations across its network. Having produced a number of handsome neo-Georgian edifices in brick, in the early 1930s he first devised Art Deco and moderne solutions for the newly electrified Sutton Loop commuter line. Elsewhere on the Southern, the most impressive example in this idiom is at Surbiton, which has been elegantly restored to a close approximation of its appearance when new in 1937.[6] Other notable instances are at Bishopstone, Richmond, Malden Manor, Horsham, Chessington North, Chessington South, Woking, Kingston and Southampton Central.[7] Flashier in their detailing than the contemporaneous work of Charles Holden (1875–1960) for London Underground, they are nonetheless notable for their excellent planning and for the continuity of detailing from their street frontages through hallways and stairs to platform shelters and canopies.

During the mid-1920s, one of Scott's assistants was Maxwell Fry (1899–1987), who 50 years later

**LMS Princess Coronation locomotive on the
Coronation Scot express**
William Stanier, 1937
Bruce Peter collection

Surbiton Station, London
James Robb Scott of the Southern Railway Architects'
Department, 1937
Bruce Peter

sought to enhance his own reputation for posterity by writing a self-congratulatory autobiography in which he stated that it was he rather than Scott who had moved the Southern Railway's architectural policy in a progressive direction and, condescendingly, describing his former employer as a 'lumbering Scotsman'.[8] While he may well have had some influence, Scott's Art Deco and moderne designs all post-date Fry's departure from the Southern in 1927.

Promoting rail travel

Following the formation of the LMS and LNER in 1923, fresh attention was paid to advertising. In British transport circles, the abstracted styles of new poster art emanating from the Continent were avidly promoted by Frank Pick of the Underground Electric Railways Company in London, who had previously worked for the North Eastern Railway and was an enthusiastic member of the Design and Industries Association. To depict Scottish destinations, the railways unsurprisingly made no distinction from their wider promotional strategies of commissioning poster artwork from reputable established and emergent mainly English-based fine and commercial artists and illustrators, several of whom also provided comparable imagery for a wide range of British companies and organisations. In any case, in the tourism sector, cultural and geographical distance and an understanding of the perspective of the visitor were advantageous.

The newly engaged LMS Superintendent of Advertising, T C Jeffrey, formerly of the Midland Railway, was keen to enhance its promotional output, and so he appointed the Royal Academician Norman Wilkinson (1878–1971) to design posters; he, in turn, suggested fellow Academicians who were known for producing painterly and picturesque images.[9] Wilkinson himself was a master at capturing the essence of Scottish coastal and Highland tonal palettes, typically rendering seascapes, mountains and cumulous clouds in strips of contrasting sunlight and shadow, as seen in images such as 'Glencoe' and 'Glenariff' from 1923, 'Tobermory', 'Gleneagles Hotel' and 'Inverness' from 1924 and 'The Firth of Clyde' from 1925.[10] Early attempts at more experimental approaches by the LMS included a photograph of a bas relief sculpture of Icarus by the Australian-born, London-based, Sir Edgar Bertram Mackennal (1863–1931). Though this was

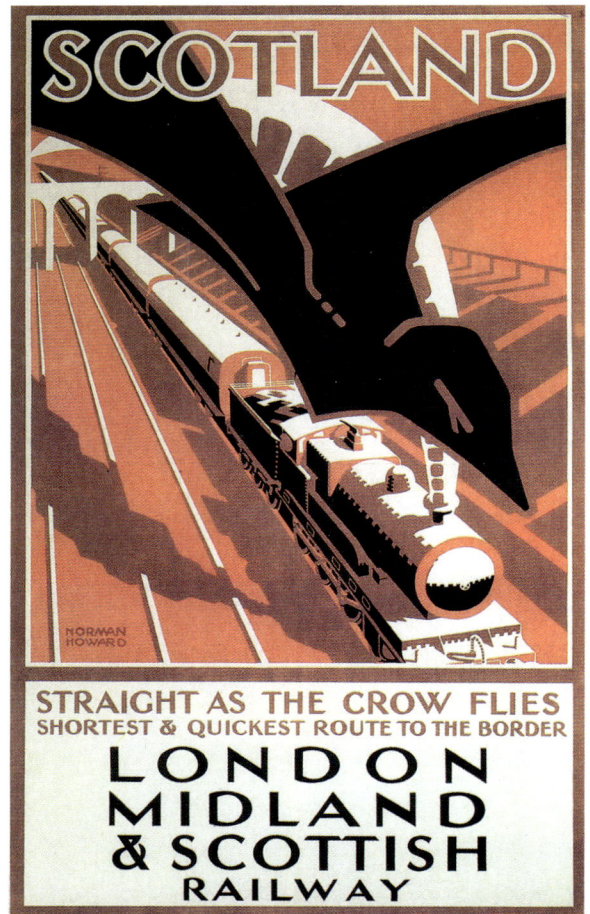

LMS Scotland poster
Norman Howard, 1928
Bruce Peter collection

intended as a metaphor for speed, any viewer with a knowledge of classical myth would have been more likely to associate it with a catastrophic failure ever to reach the intended destination. An early painted LMS poster attempting an Art Deco motif was 'Scotland – Straight as the Crow Flies' from around 1928 by Norman Howard (1899–1955), showing a bird's **eye view** of a rather stylised crow flying above an LMS express, storming northward through the cutting at Tring.[11]

The LNER's advertising manager William Teasdale was considerably more daring, commissioning images that often were more colour compositions than

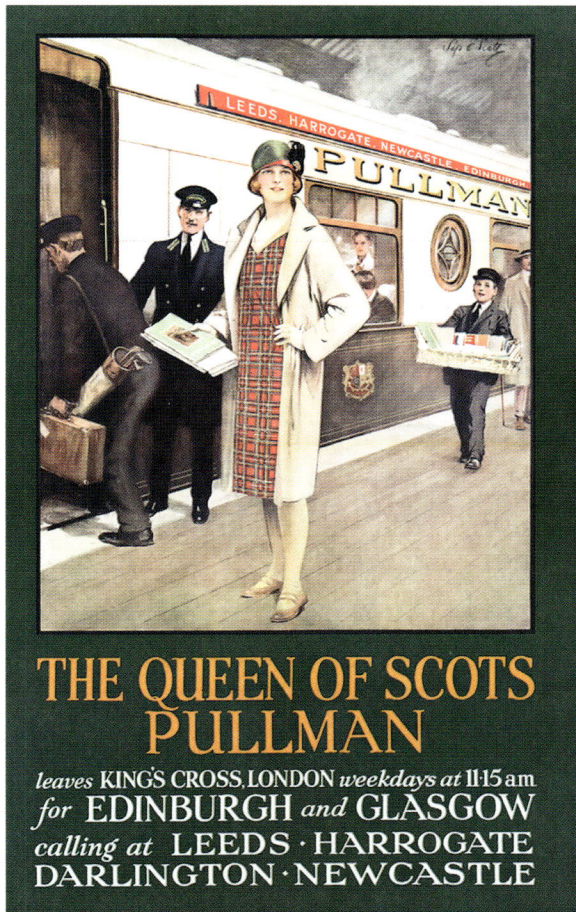

Pullman 'Queen of Scots' poster
Septimus Edwin Scott, 1926

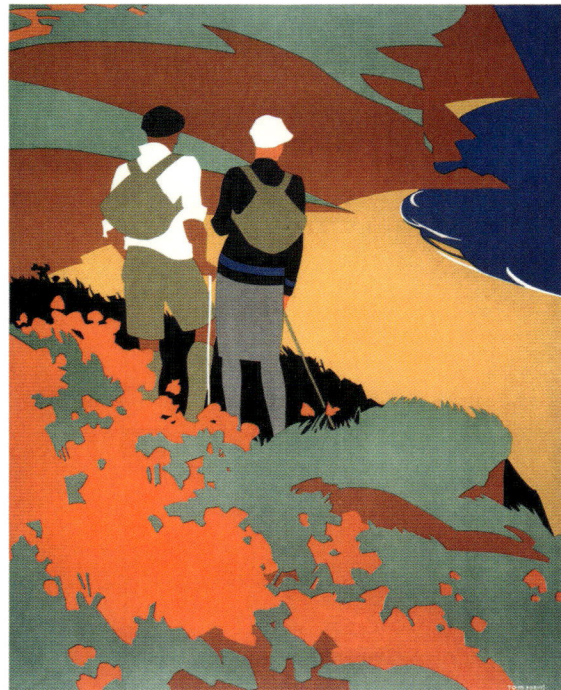

LNER 'East Coast Joys' poster
Tom Purvis, 1931

pictorial and using sans serif lettering even prior to the LNER's adoption of a version of Gill Sans as its standard font in 1929.[12] Up-to-date fashions were also often a common theme. For example, a 1926 poster by Septimus Edwin Scott (1879–1965) promoting The Queen of Scots Pullman featured a young lady in a modern knee-length tartan dress, overcoat and a cloche hat, about to board the train – unaccompanied!

Among the most striking interwar transport posters were those painted for the LNER by Tom Purvis (1888–1959), of which 'The Trossachs by East Coast Route' from 1926 was an early example

of Scottish subject matter. Later, in 1931, Purvis famously painted a set of five strikingly composed and sunnily colour-saturated posters depicting beach pleasures entitled 'East Coast Joys', which emphasised that LNER routes were 'to the drier side of Britain'; these could be co-joined to make a long horizontal panel. In Scotland, however, the LNER also operated the West Highland Line to Fort William and Mallaig, which were among the wettest places in the entire country.

Drier though the East Coast may more often have been, the best thing that could be said about Skegness by the cold North Sea in Lincolnshire was that it

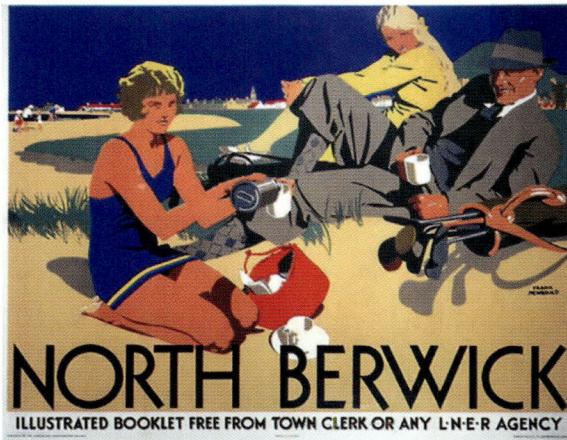

LNER North Berwick poster
Frank Newbould, 1930
Bruce Peter collection

LMS Saltcoats poster
Tom Gilfillan, 1935
Bruce Peter collection

was 'So Bracing' – but this was even more true of St Andrews, Stonehaven or Lossiemouth in Scotland. A poster promoting North Berwick in East Lothian by Frank Newbould (1887–1951) may at a glance have resembled the Mediterranean, but only one of the group of three stylishly dressed people relaxing on the sand was actually in beachwear. Newbould also painted a series focusing on the inhabitants of costal fishing communities entitled 'East Coast Types', of which No. 4 was 'The Scottish Fishwife', whose vernacular layered and wrapped garments with tartan shawl were in contrast with the modern style of the depiction.

For the LMS, in 1935 the Scottish artist Tom Gilfillan (1893–1978) painted the outdoor swimming pool at Saltcoats – one of the less salubrious Clyde resort towns – in a southerly and sunny manner; it might have been Poole or Bournemouth, were it not for the fact that the brooding Arran mountains loomed in the background. As a painter and illustrator, the Glasgow School of Art-trained Gilfillan was highly versatile; much of his wider *oeuvre* was impressionistic and made use of Scottish national romantic imagery, though, in complete contrast, his Saltcoats image appeared inspired by Septimus Scott's similar depictions of lidos and bathers elsewhere around Britain's coasts, while his posters of Hebridean scenery were more in the manner of Wilkinson. In addition he experimented with purely graphic compositions.

In the Edwardian era, the pre-grouping Caledonian Railway had attracted attention for its ongoing series of Golfing Girls posters, depicting fashionable and apparently emancipated women on the fairways and greens of the courses served by its trains; these were regularly updated to keep abreast with the latest in clothing style. After the grouping, some LNER golfing posters were equally notable. St Andrews, home of the Royal and Ancient club and the Old Course, was a frequent subject, usually depicted with emphasis upon the links course and the clothing worn by the golfers, versions being produced by Henry George Gawthorn (1879–1941) and Arthur Michael (1881–1965), while Cruden Bay's course was painted by Tom Purvis and North Berwick's by Andrew Johnson (1893–1973).

Gawthorn, whose initial training had been in architecture, was particularly adept at depicting the essence of large structures and, for the LNER, the Forth Bridge was a favourite motif, which he painted twice in the latter 1920s. His low-angle image of the giant cantilevers in black silhouette in dark blue late-evening light with only the distant orange glow from the firebox in the locomotive cab of a northbound express providing contrast was particularly striking.

Simplified and exaggerated Art Deco treatments particularly lent themselves to the depiction of speed.

**LMS Coronation
Scot poster**
Bryan de Grineau,
1937
Bruce Peter collection

LNER Flying Scotsman poster
Alfred Reginald Thomson, 1932
Bruce Peter collection

The French poster artist A M Cassandre (pseudonym of Adolphe Jean-Marie Mouron, 1901–1968) had provided a prime example with his 'Nord Express' poster of 1925. Alfred Reginald Thomson (1894–1979) similarly emphasised locomotive driving wheels in his LNER 'Take Me by The Flying Scotsman' poster of 1932 but instead of glistening point-work shooting past, as per Cassandre, Thomson borrowed from the Southern Railway the motif of a small boy gazing upward at the giant locomotive (there was even a humorous acknowledgement of this in the bottom corner).[13]

With the advent of the streamlined expresses in the latter 1930s, a veritable avalanche of publicity was produced. Different posters for the LNER Coronation were commissioned from Tom Purvis, Frank Henry Mason and Doris Zinkeisen (1898–1991), while Norman Wilkinson and Bryan de Grineau (1882–1957) painted the LMS 'Coronation Scot'; in 1938 de Grineau additionally produced a poster simultaneously promoting both trains, the railways cooperating to enable travellers to go in one direction on one and back on the other to satisfy curiosity and to enable them to compare and contrast the styles of décor and service provided.[14] This initiative coincided with a sharp upswing in demand for travel to Scotland for the Empire Exhibition, where all of the four major British railways collaborated on a joint exhibit under the name 'British Railways'; it was a foretaste of what was to come by way of post-war nationalisation.

Buses

The streamlined LNER and LMS expresses operated for only a little more than a few years in the latter 1930s and, moreover, were only to be seen in Scotland between Edinburgh or Glasgow and the border. The great majority of Scotland's extensive rail network was run using comparatively utilitarian locomotives and rolling stock, much of which dated from before the First World War, if not the turn of the century. Steam-hauled trains may now be considered romantic by many, but when they were the universal form of traction, their use guaranteed passengers ending up with sooty clothes and faces. Road travel, powered by internal combustion engine, avoided all that.

A Scottish automotive industry had first emerged in the Edwardian era, a number of 'mechanicing' entrepreneurs setting up workshops in West Central

Scotland to build petrol-driven vehicles of various types. While car manufacture gradually fell into decline, the building and operation of buses became a distinct Scottish success and one that continues today. A key reason was that the urban geography of Scotland's Central Belt gave bus operators lucrative opportunities. Many settlements were located where there were mineral deposits to be extracted as the raw materials for industrialisation. In the railway age in the nineteenth century, routes had been established that radiated likes spokes from the big cities of Glasgow and Edinburgh, but connections between the outlying towns and villages were often comparatively poor and so buses were used to fill the gaps in rail provision. As engine, chassis and coachbuilding technologies improved, the industry grew and, by the interwar era, had come to be more regulated. There were by then such well-developed bus service networks that regional tram routes were no longer able to compete and even some local rail passenger services were superseded.

The First World War brought into political focus Britain's growing dependency on oil-based fuels in addition to coal. In 1914, the British government acquired a controlling interest in the Anglo-Persian Oil Company, which had been founded six years previously to exploit the Masjed Soleiman oilfield in Iran; this gave it a source of oil independent from Standard Oil in the USA and Royal Dutch Shell. Having a dependable supply enabled an increased use of internal combustion engines.[15] As the war progressed, a large number of men came to learn how to drive and maintain road vehicles that were built or commandeered to supply the Western Front. When peace returned, their acquired skills enabled the bus industry to expand rapidly.

Early Scottish bus industry entrepreneurs included the mechanical engineers Thomas Murray and Norman Fulton who founded the Albion Motor Car Company in Glasgow in 1899, though its prime focus soon switched from cars to making commercial vehicle chassis. On the operating side, William Thomson established the Scottish Motor Traction Company (SMT) in Edinburgh in 1905, the activities of which were initially centred on the Lothians. The other significant regional Scottish bus operator was W Alexander & Sons, founded in Camelon in 1913, which initially ran local routes but soon developed a wider network encompassing much of central Scotland. In 1924 W Alexander & Sons began a coachbuilding business to supply their own and other fleets. Of the multitude of bus companies that had sprung up all over Scotland in the first decades of the twentieth century, SMT was the first to realise the benefits of 'scaling up' through take-overs and consolidation and in 1920 it began a process of nationwide expansion through the absorption of operators elsewhere in the country.[16] From the mid-1920s onward, the SMT, Alexander and Albion bus businesses grew rapidly; the latter's logo on radiator grilles henceforth being augmented by a sunburst, the rays of which spread across the pediment. This design reflected hope for a bright future and also aligned the company's identity with the advent of the jazz age, which was considered the height of fashionable modernity.[17]

The Road Transport Act of 1928 enabled the two major railway companies operating the Scottish network, the LMS and the LNER, also to run bus services – but rather than doing so on their own account, they instead both bought a large shareholding in SMT, which in 1929 absorbed the bus services of W Alexander & Sons, but not their coachbuilding business.[18] Notwithstanding the negative economic consequences of the Wall Street Crash of 1929, which proved so devastating for other established sectors of the Scottish economy, the Scottish bus industry enjoyed considerable success. Technological advances made buses more reliable than hitherto while returns on investments in bus services were also more satisfactory than those for rural passenger rail services, as buses needed relatively little by way of fixed infrastructure.[19]

Whereas control of the Scottish headquartered railway companies had passed to the LMS and LNER at the time of the 1923 grouping, the headquarters of SMT and W Alexander & Sons remained in Scotland, with the existing managements still in charge. This was crucial for their subsequent development. Although there was some overlap of rail and bus traveller demographics, generally, then as now, the bus operators served different clienteles, many of whom either could not afford or preferred not to spend money on pricier train fares. As buses became more comfortable and sophisticated, women travellers became an important clientele who were less likely to drive themselves and additionally were attracted by the conviviality and feeling of safety in open saloons and with the ever-present conductor surveying the scene.[20]

Albion bus radiator emblem
Albion Motors Ltd, 1931
Bruce Peter

W Alexander & Sons Bluebird logo
W Alexander & Sons, 1934
Bruce Peter

SMT Edinburgh–London Leyland Tiger, beside Scottish Royal Academy, Edinburgh
H V Burlingham and Leyland, 1936
Gavin Booth collection

In 1930 SMT commenced a daily Edinburgh–London coach service with a 15-hour advertised journey time. Within weeks, a summer service between Edinburgh and London taking two days and aimed at tourists was also begun.[21] A further bold new SMT initiative was to enter the aviation industry in 1932 with the intention of fulfilling the wishes of affluent tourists seeking daring new experiences and enabling them to view Highland landscapes from above.[22]

In the same year, W Alexander & Sons introduced its first express coach services within Scotland for which the company's standard bus bodywork was modified with sweeping mouldings, illuminated side destination displays above the saloon windows and, most distinctly, a flying 'bluebird' (fork-tailed swift) emblem that

reflected the aspiration towards streamlined elegance so typical of the period. The coaches had front entrances, rather than the rear platforms of most service buses, and deeply upholstered seats featuring fashionable 'jazzy' patterns, rather than the buses' leather-clad benches. A 1934 article in the *Commercial Motor* reviewing that year's Scottish Motor Show observed that:

One of the most notable impressions gained from an inspection of the bodywork is the decided leaning towards Streamlining. Although most bodybuilders have followed the fashion to this end, there are mixed feelings among them as to its all-round merits. Some regard it as an ultra-modern fetish that will pass, because of the manufacturing and maintenance complications that it introduces, but others hold that the scope it provides for improving appearance, plus the reduction in wind resistance, outweighs any other consideration. Whether or not streamlining is of utilitarian value from the operator's point of view will probably settle its fate for the future. It is certain that controlled streamlining has useful advantages, whilst exaggerated streamlining has definite handicaps.[23]

By the second half of the 1930s, W Alexander & Sons had switched over to all-steel construction for bus and coach bodies, using steel rods, tubes and other types of hollow section and extrusion for body framing, then attaching the panelling using screws. Although not a pioneer of this approach, in the context of wider British coachbuilding that still mostly preferred to use hardwood, it was a relatively early adaptor.[24]

W Alexander & Sons' emulation of the latest style trends continued in 1937 with its Coronation Bluebird coaches, which had large saloon windows with a slight dip towards the rear, aft of which the roof colour and bodyside mouldings swept downward to a curved lip, increasing the sense of sleekness.[25] Two highly innovative Leyland Gnu chassis were also fitted with bodywork made by Alexander & Sons; although these had front-mounted engines, their twin front axles were set back leaving space for the entrance. A 30-foot length helped to engender a striking impression of modernity while the extra wheels eliminated the end-to-end pitching motion of most two-axle vehicles. One example was finished as a bus and the other as a coach. The latter's styling, with tear-drop shaped side mouldings around the wheel arches and a remarkably luxurious interior, represented the height of British coachbuilding modernity.[26] All of this was achieved only a mere 13 years after Walter Alexander and his sons had opened their first coachworks – a remarkable rate of progress indeed.

In contrast with the London-headquartered railways, the Scottish managements of the bus companies almost exclusively employed Scottish-based artists and illustrators to produce their poster and brochure imagery. Promoting SMT's scenic coach tours of the Highlands, the illustrator Jack Peacock painted a particularly dramatic composition of the monument to Prince Charles Edward Stuart at Glenfinnan at the head of Loch Shiel. Another striking poster by an illustrator with the initials 'I N', promoted coach hire through highly aspirational imagery of elegant soirées

W Alexander & Sons Leyland Gnu and Coronation Leyland Tiger Bluebird coaches
W Alexander & Sons, 1937
Gavin Booth collection

SMT coach hire advertisement
I N, McCorquodale & Co, c1936
Gavin Booth collection

**W Alexander & Sons Bluebird coach services
promotional photograph**
W Alexander & Sons, 1934
Gavin Booth collection

**W Alexander & Sons Bluebird coach services
advertisement**
W Alexander & Sons, 1935
Gavin Booth collection

with couples in evening dress, a sunny picnic and sport being played. The by-line promised that 'The "SMT Way" means the finest coaches – finest organisation – complete satisfaction'. SMT additionally published a thick and glossy monthly lifestyle and travel periodical, named *SMT Magazine and Scottish Country Life*, which contained a wide range of newsworthy articles and advice, a fashion column, short stories by popular authors and a great deal of advertising for luxury goods and gifts (and also by coachbuilders and other suppliers to the bus industry, who perhaps wished to curry favour with the company's management to secure orders). As the magazine's main aim was to associate coach travel with a modern and middle-class standard of living, it contained a great deal of Art Deco imagery.

Trams

By comparison with the latest motor buses and coaches, Scotland's urban tramway systems were beginning to be perceived as obsolescent in the interwar era, at which time the regional systems were all replaced with buses, leaving intact only those in the major cities, operated by vehicles of pre-First World War vintage, which had creaking wooden bodywork. Elsewhere in Britain, a new generation of trams incorporating up-to-date technology, construction and styling had begun to enter service. In 1929 Metropolitan Electric Tramways in London had introduced the prototype for what would become a large fleet of modern double-deck trams with rounded ends that came to be known as Felthams. In Scotland, Edinburgh Corporation was in the vanguard, constructing the first of what would be a new fleet of conceptually similar, albeit somewhat shorter, trams in 1932 in its own workshop at Shrubhill. Most stylish of all were the new 'railcoach' trams introduced by Blackpool Corporation in 1933, which had bulbous streamlined ends and roof quarter-lights to enable the autumn illuminations to be viewed as they passed above.

Depression-struck Glasgow held back with regard to the building of new trams and instead renovated its existing fleet as best possible, but when the Empire Exhibition was announced, the Corporation Transport department was spurred into action, designing and building in its workshop at Copelawhill two prototype trams that were far more luxuriously appointed; these entered service in 1936 and 1937.[27] On account of Glasgow's tightly planned city centre street grid, streamlining of the ends was impossible as the consequent overhangs would have fouled the sharp corners, and so the new trams were flat-fronted with tapering sides, giving a faceted appearance (albeit with domed roof ends above). It was in their interiors that they made a bold design impression, having pigskin ceiling soffits inlaid with Art Deco patterns, concealed lighting in chrome encasement, leather wall panelling and, in the lower saloon, jazzy moquette upholstery. Upstairs, where working men in overalls typically travelled and where smoking was allowed, the seating was in leather, cut and stitched in a sunburst pattern. The success of the two prototypes led to the building of a production series at Copelawhill, eventually numbering 150 similar trams, the first of which entered service in 1937 and

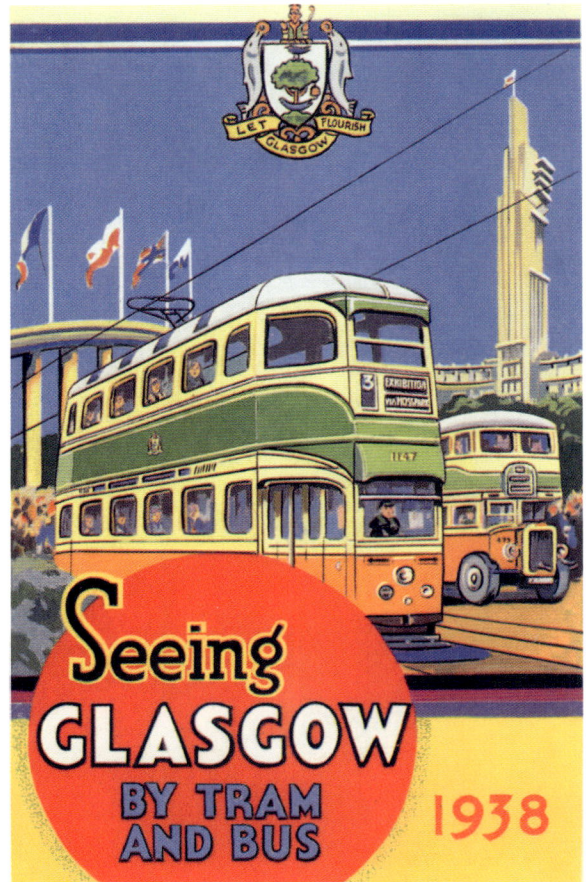

Glasgow by Tram and Bus brochure
Glasgow Corporation Transport, 1938
Chronicle / Alamy Stock Photo

were known as Coronations – yet another example of modern transport named for the crowning of King George VI.[28] The initial examples were deployed on routes towards Bellahouston so that attendees of the Empire Exhibition could experience the latest in public transport design, but eventually they were to be found all over the city's extensive network. They were undoubtedly among the most opulent urban mass-transport vehicles ever built in the UK.[29]

Prior to the opening of the Empire Exhibition, Glasgow Corporation Transport modernised some of the city's Subway stations with faience cladding to give a moderne impression. Copeland Road in Govan, which was closest to Bellahouston Park and occupied

**Lower and upper deck saloons of Glasgow
Corporation Coronation tramcar prototype**
Glasgow Corporation Transport, 1936
Glasgow Life Riverside Museum

a street corner, had the most extensive refaced frontage
with a stepped pediment above the canopy. Others,
such as Bridge Street and Kelvinbridge, which had
small entrances incorporated into larger blocks, received
similar tiling. Meanwhile, a new travel and tourist
information bureau occupying a circular, moderne
pavilion was erected adjacent to the Subway entrance in
St Enoch Square.

After the Second World War, a developed variation
of the Coronation tram design came to be popularly
known as Cunarders as, for ordinary Glaswegians, the
lower saloon décor resembled how they imagined luxury
trans-Atlantic liner interiors might be appointed.[30] By
the latter 1950s, however, what had been considered
state-of-the-art just 20 years before was thought passé
and so Glasgow's tramway system was shut down in
1962; nearly all of the cars were scrapped, though the
newest were not yet a decade old. It was a decision that
many have since bitterly regretted.

Road infrastructure

The great increase in the use of road vehicles that followed the First World War, combined with the ready availability of petrol and diesel, precipitated a nationwide programme of road improvements in the 1920s. In Scotland, the Great North Road from the Central Belt to Inverness, which in 1923 was designated as the A9 as part of the British road designation scheme, was one prime candidate for upgrading. For much of its length, the alignment follows that of a military road built under General Wade's eighteenth-century scheme to pacify the Highlands, improved upon in the early nineteenth century when Thomas Telford carried out extensive bridge construction.[31] In the mid-1920s, the Blair Atholl to Inverness section was widened to give room for dedicated traffic lanes in each direction. The London-based architect-engineer Sir Owen Williams and his architectural partner Maxwell Ayrton (1874–1960) were employed to design new reinforced concrete bridges to span rivers over which the road crossed. Williams and Ayrton were fresh from their great successes in designing Wembley Stadium and pavilions for the 1924 British Empire Exhibition as well as bridges for London's North Circular Road, all of which used mass concrete construction. The appointment of the pair to design the A9 bridges arose from a concern that any new construction in the Scottish Highlands should be of high visual quality and designed to enhance the appearance of the landscape, rather than to risk spoiling it. The pair were, however, rather different in design outlook as

Williams believed that good engineering had its own honest beauty which should always be expressed, rather than concealed, whereas Ayrton, who was a former assistant of Sir Edwin Lutyens, tended towards a more conventional architectural vocabulary. Bridges obviously lent themselves to engineering-led solutions and so for the A9 a wide variety of forms were applied to suit each particular location. Critiquing the new bridges, Christopher Hussey – an astute commentator on all that was up to date in the interwar era – observed in *Country Life* that: 'for structures involving solid mass and tensile strength, concrete has opened up undreamt-of possibilities, while its plastic nature is producing a new constructional art, a cross between architecture, engineering and sculpture'.[32] Whereas the Wembley structures were located amid suburbia, in Scotland, Ayrton and Williams 'had to deal with natural forces rather than with civilisation, and the resulting effect on the design of their Inverness-shire bridges is remarkable'.[33]

Some of the designs have dramatic expressionist characteristics, reminiscent of progressive German architecture following the First World War. One example, the bridge spanning the River Findhorn, has a slightly gothic quality with end pavilions and repetitive pointed openings in its tall parapets.[34] Smaller but even more dramatically formed are the bridges over the Allt Dibheach near Aviemore and the Allt Gheallaidh in Drumochter Pass, the bare concrete sides of which slant inwards and are finished in faceted triangular planes – remarkably futuristic-looking designs for rural Scotland in 1927.[35] Hussey noted approvingly that 'in concrete,

Allt Dibheach bridge, near Aviemore
Owen Williams and Maxwell Ayrton, 1927
Bruce Peter collection

Findhorn Bridge, near Tomatin
Owen Williams and Maxwell Ayrton, 1927
HES SC2559514

Cubism is absolutely justified. A concrete structure is literally built up of plane surfaces … triangular planes that are logical because structural and economical. They are at the same time abstract works of art, designs that stir the imagination solely by their structural form, yet, being so logical, they are under no suspicion of affectation'.[36]

In the Central Belt, meanwhile, work began on the design of a new road bridge across the River Forth at

Kincardine Bridge, Kincardine-on-Forth
Sir Alexander Gibb and James Miller, 1936

Bruce Peter

Kincardine. The design solution was prepared by the engineering firm of Sir Alexander Gibb (1872–1958), a former Admiralty Chief Engineer, born into an engineering family in Broughty Ferry and knighted for his construction work in the First World War. Gibb was an adviser to HM Treasury on transport infrastructure investments and also its representative on the Forth Conservancy Board, as he was as concerned with public amenity and aesthetics. For the Kincardine Bridge project, which was designed from 1930 and built between 1932 and 1936, the Glasgow architect James Miller, in his role as a member of the Royal Fine Art Commission for Scotland, was consulted by Gibb's firm to advise on the structure's appearance to ensure

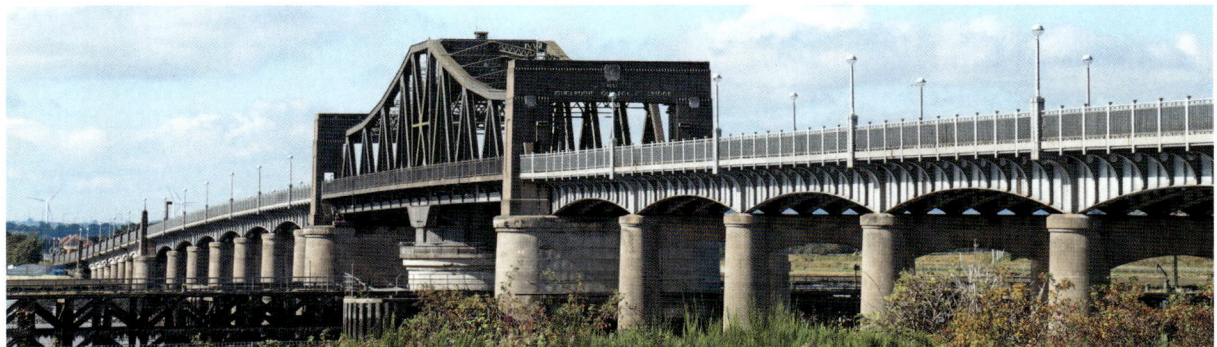

that it would be a notable landmark. It was Gibb's colleague John Guthrie Brown (1892–1976) who was the engineer in charge of the design.[37] Their solution comprises concrete piers, a steel deck and a central box-girder section, which rotated 90 degrees to allow shipping to pass through; it was reputedly the largest swing-bridge yet built.[38] Concrete porticoes at each end of the swing-section and steel balustrades incorporating lampposts with 'Morocco-glass globes' on the fixed deck sections are in the Art Deco idiom and were designed in cooperation with the Miller office.[39] The portals feature 'carved escutcheons of Portland stone, illustrating the arms of the three contributing counties of Fife, Stirling and Clackmannan and have heavy fluting courses'; these contain portcullis-like safety gates, matching the balustrades, which were lowered when the swinging section was to be opened.[40] To ensure an attractive finish to the concrete 'experiments were carried out on various classes of fabric' and 'a wide-mesh hessian canvas similar to that used for backing rugs was selected to line the shuttering'.[41] Aluminium paint 'extensively used for bridges in the United States and Canada' was selected for the steel sections, bright aluminium being applied to the balustrades and swing-section while dull grey was used to coat the underside of the deck.[42] The bridge thus had a shiny, up-to-date appearance, impressive to passing motorists. It still retains its distinctive aura, the design having withstood the test of time remarkably well.

Car showrooms and garages

The growth of private car ownership, initially among the upper and upper-middle classes, was a significant trend of the interwar period and so many new garages and showrooms were built. Their designs had much in common with light industrial premises and other contemporary structures, using simple steel framing and corrugated asbestos cement slabs for roofing, this utilitarian construction concealed behind a suitably up-to-date show facade.

Southern Motors' garage in Edinburgh's Causewayside, an early work by Basil Spence, completed in 1933, is notable for the clean-lined articulation of its first-floor offices, which are cantilevered over a recessed forecourt, infilling a gap between tenements. While its dynamic horizontals and verticals, edge-to-edge glazing and crisp graphics gave a futuristic impression, car repairs took place within a comparatively mundane shed to the rear.

Southern Motors Garage, Causewayside, Edinburgh
Basil Spence, 1933
Bruce Peter, HES SC357577

Many other such premises for motor repairs had a variety of far less refined Art Deco or moderne frontal treatments, often with wings containing office and shop space surrounding a proscenium vehicle entrance. John Jackson's Garage on Bon Accord Street, Aberdeen, was completed in 1937 to a design by A G R Mackenzie. It is architecturally and, in terms of finish, an unusually high-quality example, faced in granite with long bands of horizontal fenestration meeting a recessed vertical section over the entrance.[43] The *Aberdeen Press and Journal*'s correspondent found what was within redolent of science fiction:

> Earlier generations who smiled tolerantly at Wellsian fantasies would find their scepticism swept away by a visit… for here is one of H G's futuristic dreams come true. Motor cars climb by an easy gradient to a car park on the roof of the building, with robot lights controlling the flow of traffic. Turntables whisk round 4-ton motor lorries in a twinkling; hydraulic jacks lift motor cars as though they were toys. The

GARAGE VAUXHALL SOUTHERN MOTORS GARAGE BEDFORD

B.S.

Jackson's Garage, Aberdeen
A G R Mackenzie of A Marshall Mackenzie & Son, 1937
HES SC2518732

SMT Leyland Motors Garage, Tradeston, Glasgow
George James Miller of James Miller & Son, 1936
Glasgow City Archives, HES SC1079980

internal telephone system is automatic, and even the petrol pumps count the gallons and total up the cost… [44]

Apart from appearing excitingly technologically charged, the mechanical installations enabled a highly efficient usage of space. Favourable comment was also made regarding the garage's surprisingly harmonious relationship with its nineteenth-century city-centre environs.[45]

Back in the Central Belt, not only was the Scottish Motor Traction company involved in operating buses and coaches but they also sold and repaired private cars and commercial vehicles. In 1937, a large new SMT garage and showroom for Leyland commercial vehicles was completed on Glasgow's Salkeld Street in Tradeston to a design by George James Miller. Its geometric brick exterior is accented with a U-shaped glazed corner tower with fins in reconstructed stone and, within, the levels are likewise connected with ramps. Another large surviving example is the former Dunlop Motor Co Ford Motor Service garage on Grange Street, Kilmarnock, built for the local cycle and car dealers and repairers Robert and John Dunlop. Probably designed by the firm of Alexander Mair of Ayr, it is a hangar-like building, originally clad in pink-coloured cement render and embellished with flagpoles.[46] There were numerous other examples of lesser distinction, several of which still exist in mutilated condition. In addition, many proud new car owners built private garages with Art Deco pediments and detailing, though the homes to which these were appended were usually comparatively stylistically conventional bungalows or villas.

Air transport

Scotland was pioneering in aviation; in the mid-1890s, Percy Pilcher, an assistant lecturer in Naval and Marine Engineering at Glasgow University who had been born in Bath in Somerset, designed and flew a glider that was record-breaking for duration. An aviation industry grew thereafter and Scotland's geography of mountains and islands invited the use of planes for fast transport and tourism.

By the 1930s, there were numerous small airports and landing strips with regular scheduled flights operating to many destinations, while private plane ownership and flying clubs grew in number as more practical and serviceable models of light aircraft became available. Wealthy and glamorous Scottish celebrity aviators included Lady Elsie Mackay, the daughter of the Earl of Inchcape. A socialite, racing horse jockey, actor and interior designer, who in addition drove her Rolls Royce car at terrifying speed, she epitomised the spirit of the 'Roaring Twenties'. But her short life ended in 1928 when her black and gold monoplane disappeared during a bold but doomed attempt to fly over the Atlantic Ocean.[47] As air travel was relatively high-risk, for commercial passenger-carrying airlines the challenge was to generate images of modern professionalism that would inspire confidence in potential users. Airline poster art was thus very slick with strong, saturated colours and assertive graphics.

In October 1932 SMT made the bold initiative of entering the aviation business, offering an Air Taxi service from Renfrew and also providing sight-seeing tours of the Highlands, using three-seater de Havilland Fox Moth and six-seater Dragon biplanes, smartly painted in silver with a blue waistband. In addition, it ran a flying school in East Lothian. These developments were encouraged by an SMT director, John Sword, who had been appointed when his own Midland bus company in Lanarkshire had been absorbed. Sword quickly grew frustrated that SMT did not run timetabled point-to-point air transport routes (probably to avoid competing directly with its railway shareholders), and so he decided to begin his own aviation business, Midland & Scottish Air Ferries, which from 1933 operated from Renfrew to Campbeltown and Belfast.[48] Notable among its pilots was the pioneering woman aviator, Winifred Drinkwater – the first woman in the world to hold a commercial pilot's licence.[49] Sword's

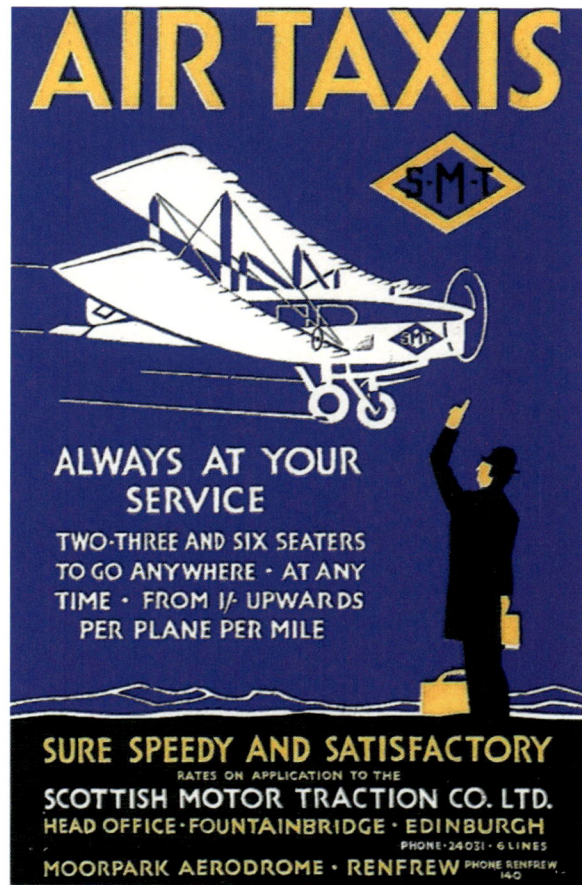

SMT Air Taxis advertisement
Scottish Motor Traction Co, 1933
Bruce Peter collection

fellow SMT directors soon gave him an ultimatum: either cease operations or resign and it appears that in the Depression context, he decided to remain with SMT and so his air venture ended in 1934. SMT also disposed of its Aviation Division at that time, concentrating thereafter on its bus and coach businesses. Later in 1934, Britain's four major railway companies commenced Railway Air Services to operate between Croydon, Birmingham, Manchester, Liverpool and Glasgow. Subsequently, in 1937 the LMS railway was among the financiers of Scottish Airways, alongside Whitehall Securities Ltd of London, which had already made other aviation investments, the purpose being to serve the Western Isles and other destinations which

SMT de Havilland Fox Moth biplane
Arthur Ernest Hogg, 1932
Geoff Collins

were far off the railway network. Both airlines operated fleets of de Havilland Dragon Rapide biplanes, a design which dated from 1934.[50]

New airport architecture materialised in Scotland during the second half of the 1930s. Hitherto, Scotland's aerodromes had resembled modern industrial sites with quite utilitarian hangars and control buildings. The new generation continued to have a design affinity with modern factories, the hangars being fronted with Art Deco and moderne administration blocks, just like the latest premises for other light industries.

New headquarters for the Scottish Flying Club at Renfrew Aerodrome, incorporating a control tower, were designed by Richard Mervyn Noad (1906–1991) of Noad & Wallace in 1934–1935. A Glasgow School of Architecture graduate, Noad had then been offered the chance to study at Clare College, Cambridge, under the reformist don Mansfield Forbes. Having decided instead to remain in Scotland, Noad became editor of the RIAS *Quarterly Illustrated* in 1933 when he took into partnership a slightly younger former

fellow student, Alastair Frew Wallace (1908–1994). Noad's aerodrome was a slick two-storey edifice with a strongly horizontal emphasis, accentuated by bands of brick set in stucco between metal-framed windows and with the control tower in the centre, splitting the main frontage into symmetrical wings.[51]

Along the Clyde Coast at Prestwick, where another aerodrome was located, a new hangar, administration building and air training school complex was drawn up by Alexander Mair's practice, located in nearby Ayr.[52] Having designed farm buildings and industrial premises as well as commercial and residential ones, Mair and his colleagues were well used to addressing a wide variety of briefs and so they rose to the challenge of airport design. The school and offices were contained in a relatively compact corner building of two storeys with its corner at a 45-degree

angle, surmounted by a control tower and all clad in white stucco. This was completed in 1936 and was most likely the work of Mair's senior assistant David Ferguson (1909–1995), who had first been employed by him in 1930. Only two years thereafter, a large extension was built containing a passenger terminal which had a three-storey central section with a curved centrepiece and, at the opposite end from the initial structure, a corner building echoing the style of the air training school and thereby contributing to a more-or-less symmetrical overall composition.[53] The complex was further augmented in 1939 when the former Palace of Engineering from the Empire Exhibition was re-erected adjacent for use by Scottish Aviation Ltd as an aircraft assembly factory; Mair's firm was also responsible for this work.

After the Prestwick project – and having through it become Scotland's de facto airport specialists – Mair's firm was next commissioned to design the hangers and combined passenger terminal, administration and control tower for an entirely new passenger airport to be built on the foreshore of the River Forth at Grangemouth. The Central Scotland Airport, which was largely Ferguson's work, was intended to be a hub for domestic and international flights, easily accessible from across central Scotland. Without having to harmonise with any existing structures, a somewhat more bold-looking solution was achieved than at Prestwick, the centre section of a likewise symmetrical composition presenting a wide sweeping curve towards the apron and the fenestration being interspersed with slenderer mullions, lending a dynamic appearance.[54] The airport operated commercially for just one short summer season between July and September 1939, after which it was taken over by the RAF for war use. In December 1940 Ferguson was appointed as architect and surveyor of Scottish Aviation Ltd.

Prestwick Airport
Alexander Mair and David Ferguson, 1936–1938
Bruce Peter collection

Central Scotland Airport, Grangemouth
Alexander Mair and David Ferguson, 1939
Bruce Peter collection

Renfrew, Prestwick and the other Scottish airports were similarly requisitioned and their bold, bright terminal and administration buildings were urgently repainted with khaki camouflage. All survived the war – but both the Prestwick and Grangemouth terminals were entirely destroyed by fires in the early 1950s and demolished.

Scottish architectural involvement in designing moderne buildings for aviation also included the Glaswegian firm J M Monro and Son. In the mid-1930s they provided designs for the Blackburn aircraft factory at Brough in the East Riding of Yorkshire, but a more significant and enduring contact was for the De Havilland aircraft company site at Hatfield in Hertfordshire.[55] The moderne detailing of the administration block is in a similar vein to several of their industrial and commercial buildings north of the border, notably 1930s stores for Marks & Spencer, who were to become the practice's most lucrative client (see Chapter 6).

Queen Mary
William Denny & Bros, 1933
A Ernest Glen

Coastal shipping

A consequence of the Great Depression was a significant reduction in liner travel during the first half of the 1930s and the repurposing of some liners for leisure cruising. The image of a white-hulled cruise ship in some warm and exotic foreign setting then became the epitome of aspiration – but only a relatively small and wealthy elite could afford such holidays, while the majority who fantasised about them probably would not have enjoyed cruising's cocktail of social one-upmanship and seasickness, even if they had been able to pay. For most Scots, a leisure trip at sea meant taking an excursion steamer from Glasgow, Craigendoran, Greenock or Gourock on a day trip to the Clyde resorts of Dunoon, Rothesay or Brodick.

In 1933 the Clyde excursion operator Williamson Buchanan Ltd introduced the commodious turbine-propelled *Queen Mary* on the popular Glasgow–Dunoon–Rothesay route. It was built by Britain's leading shipyard specialising in vessels of this type, William Denny & Bros of Dumbarton, and had unusually extensive sheltered accommodation for up to 1,500 passengers, the main clientele being Glasgow's working-class, for whom high-density and robust travel environments were the norm. To provide enough deck

space for the multitudes, the *Queen Mary* had long enclosed promenades and a shelter deck extending nearly to the stern. In the forward-facing Observation Lounge, rattan chairs hinted at the glamour of a hotel winter garden, while the Dining Saloon on the deck below provided à la carte service in similarly elegant surroundings. Yet most of the remainder of the interior had the same bare planked decking and painted steel bulkheads as the outdoor boat deck, meaning that it could be hosed clean at the end of each day. The *Queen Mary*'s moderne design features were mostly external, in the form of a plated-in forward bulwark, a cruiser stern and lifeboat davits that were angled aft. The application of the owners' striking black-and-white livery with matching strakes along the upper hull added to the vessel's up-to-date aura of style.[56]

The London, Midland & Scottish Railway meanwhile introduced a series of new paddle steamers for its scheduled Firth of Clyde ferry services; for such use, paddle propulsion using steam expansion engines was preferred by the company, owing to the shallower draught and arguably greater manoeuvrability. The *Caledonia* was built by William Denny & Bros in 1934, but its fleet-mates – the *Mercury*, *Marchioness of Lorne*, *Jupiter* and *Juno*, which took to the water between

Smoking saloon on PS *Caledonia*
McInnes Gardner and William Denny & Bros, 1934
Bruce Peter collection

Tobermory Pier, Isle of Mull
LMS Architects' Department, c1935
Bruce Peter collection

SUMMER TOURS

BY
STEAMER
ROAD
AND
RAIL

In the **WESTERN HIGHLANDS**
and **ISLANDS OF SCOTLAND**
. . . . . by Royal Mail Steamers

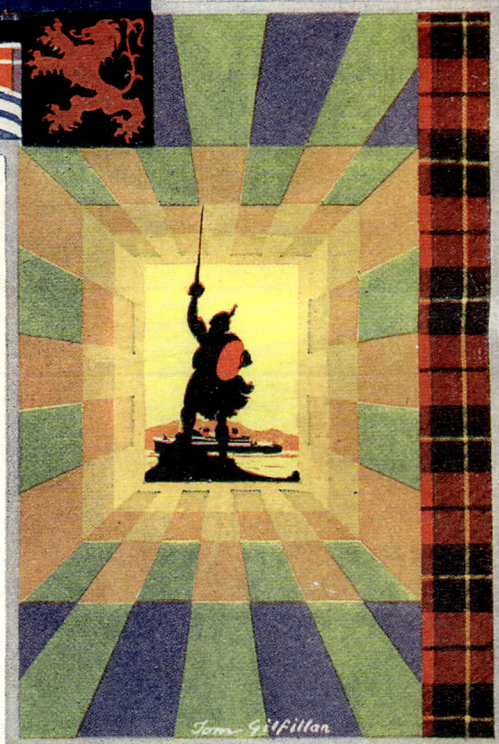

"SEE THIS SCOTLAND FIRST"

DAVID MACBRAYNE LTD., 44 Robertson Street, Glasgow, C.2

1934 and 1937 – were all ordered from Fairfield Shipbuilding & Engineering of Govan. Whereas on earlier paddle steamers, the paddle wheels were emphasised with decorated grilles and scrollwork, these new ones had continuous plating around the paddle boxes to try and disguise their presence as much as possible so that, when viewed side-on, they more closely resembled the newer generations of turbine steamer.[57] Inboard, the vessels' First Class saloons had moderne detailing with curved corners and – on the *Caledonia* – a decorative panel depicting an LMS streamlined Princess Coronation express locomotive rushing towards the viewer, the bow of a futuristic ocean liner, new Glasgow Corporation Coronation trams and an aircraft flying overhead among puffy clouds.

More remarkably, another LMS-controlled Scottish coastal shipping company, David MacBrayne Ltd, whose vessels served the islands of the Hebrides, not only took delivery of new motor ships for these routes, but also built moderne-style pier buildings at Fort William, Mallaig, Tobermory on the Isle of Mull, Port Ellen on Islay and Stornoway on Lewis, all designed by the LMS Architecture Department in Derby under the direction of its Chief Architect, William Hamlyn (1889–1968). They shared a stylistic affinity with new LMS stations on the recently electrified Wirral Peninsula routes south from Liverpool and also with its Prestatyn Holiday Camp in North Wales, the designs for which Hamlyn and his colleagues also had produced. Although existing in one of Europe's wettest climates, MacBrayne's white-painted, flat-roofed edifices with curving balconies were perhaps even reminiscent of recent building on the French Riviera. The company's advertising had traditionally emphasised the rugged romance of West Coast scenery and featured its Highland clan chieftain symbol in various permutations. In the mid-1930s, Tom Gilfillan, who had earlier produced such poster imagery in the style of Norman Wilkinson, experimented with an entirely graphic jazzy Art Deco composition, entitled 'See This Scotland First' with a setting sun projecting coloured rays, a matching strip of tartan and, of course, the obligatory chieftain.

David MacBrayne poster
Tom Gilfillan, c1936
Bruce Peter collection

CHAPTER 4
MUNICIPAL AND GOVERNMENTAL

The Art Deco found in the Paris Exposition's most spectacular pavilions was an expression of the grandeur and wealth of the French State. The subsequent adaptation of the Art Deco and moderne styles by business and industry, particularly in America, tended to cause them to be viewed retrospectively as having been primarily associated with commerce. Yet, in Scotland, alongside many retail applications, they were also widely applied to governmental and municipal properties and services. The social and economic challenges in the wake of the First World War eroded belief in laissez-faire economics while significant tax rises helped enable an expansion of the roles of the public sector. The ongoing negative after-effects of the Wall Street Crash eventually encouraged significant government interventions in the hope of stimulating economic growth. The modern Scottish municipal tradition of ambitious and progressive architectural commissioning was perpetuated in the interwar era. Local worthies who were also councillors bridged the worlds of commerce and public service and, more often than might have been expected, encouraged the deployment of up-to-date design to attract positive attention and pride in their jurisdictions. In industrial areas, Art Deco and moderne public buildings had

St Andrew's House, Edinburgh
Thomas S Tait of Sir John Burnet, Tait & Lorne, 1939
HES SC794219

the potential to signify progressive thinking, while in seaside resort towns, they helped to formulate updated images which were at least useful for advertising to tourists. In some instances, projects commenced in the 1930s only were completed in the 1950s, owing to the Second World War.

In the mid-1920s British architectural opinion regarding the most suitable aesthetic approach for the expression of modern municipal virtue had come to favour elegantly understated neoclassicism with national romantic embellishment known as 'Swedish Grace' – as exemplified by Stockholm's new City Hall, completed in 1923 to a design by Ragnar Östberg (1866–1945). In England, Norwich City Hall, completed after a Depression-induced delay in 1938, was heavily Swedish-inspired, both in its layout by Robert Atkinson (1883–1952) and detailed design by Charles Holloway James (1893–1953) and Stephen Rowland Pierce (1896–1966). In Scotland, on a somewhat smaller scale, the competition-winning design by the Edinburgh-based architect David Carr (1905–1986) and his London-born partner William Howard (1906–1972) for a new municipal headquarters in Kirkcaldy followed the same approach. Construction began in 1937 but the Second World War and post-war material rationing delayed completion until 1950, more than a quarter-of-a-century after the *Architectural Review* had first brought the Swedish style to British architects' attention.[1]

A more frequently applied alternative, especially in southern Britain, was a geometric brick-faced

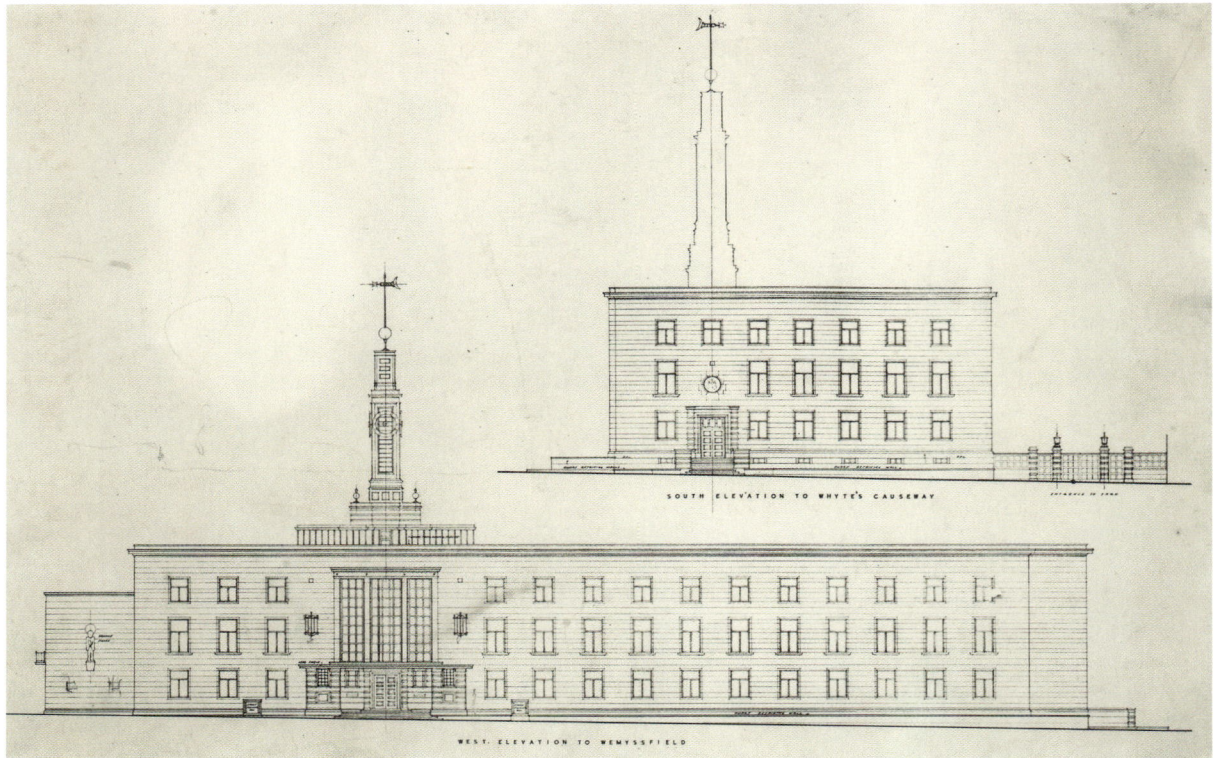

SOUTH ELEVATION TO WHYTE'S CAUSEWAY

WEST ELEVATION TO WEMYSSFIELD

Kirkcaldy Town Hall
Carr & Howard, 1937

neo-Georgian aesthetic with Art Deco elements and occasionally contemporary Dutch influence also in evidence. In 1935, Stirling County Council commissioned James Miller, who was by then living in the town, to design a two-storey extension to its existing headquarters, Viewforth House, a Scots baronial-style mansion by John Hay (1811–1861), dating from 1853. The extension was completed in 1937. Its main frontage, mostly faced in brown brick, has 16 bays with the entrance portico in stone and featuring the municipal crest on a bronze infill panel above the doorway.[2] Flanking statues of William Wallace and Robert the Bruce have since been added, re-sited from elsewhere, and these embellishments are the prime evidence of the building's Scottish location.

Viewforth House, Stirling
James Miller, 1937

Education

New schools, often complementing new housing estates, were necessary municipal investments and therefore constructed in greater quantity. School design was increasingly the subject of debate in the interwar era and this led also to architectural specialism. In Scotland, George Reid (1893–1984) and James Smith Forbes (1894–1976) became leading producers of designs for schools in municipalities as far apart as the Borders and the Highlands. Following apprenticeships in various Edinburgh firms and wartime military service, Reid and Forbes entered joint practice with Reginald Fairlie (1883–1952) in 1919 to design new suburban housing, including the Willowbrae area of Edinburgh. After Fairlie set up alone in the mid-1920s, Reid and Forbes focused on schools, among their early projects being the competition-winning design for Leith Academy, a neo-Georgian brick and stone edifice completed in 1928 that in style could equally have been located almost anywhere in Britain.

In the early 1930s, the typically densely planned and tall archetypal inner-city school layout was superseded by spacious designs of lower density, intended to allow more daylight and healthy fresh air to flow through. Reid and Forbes' Art Deco Inverness High School, completed in 1936, exemplified this new thinking, having long, symmetrical wings with end pavilions

Inverness High School
Reid & Forbes, 1936

Inverness High School
Reid & Forbes, 1936
HES SC1437962

Kelso High School
Reid & Forbes, 1939
Bruce Peter

Chirnside School
Reid & Forbes, 1939
Bruce Peter

extending from a central main entrance.[3] With its stucco-clad rectilinear forms and repetitive large metal-framed windows, it resembles nothing so much as the office block of one of the new light industrial factories built concurrently along the Great Western Road out of London.

Niddrie Marischal Intermediate School, completed in 1938 and serving an Edinburgh peripheral housing scheme, is a more imaginatively detailed example of the same approach by Reid and Forbes, its centrepiece being a tower with carved stone Art Deco embellishments somewhat in the manner of Frank Lloyd Wright.[4] (Currently functioning as business premises, if one did not know that it had earlier been a school, one might easily assume that its present use was the original.) The main building of Kelso High School, designed immediately after, has a similar layout and is notable for its confidently modelled facade with stacked projecting horizontals above the entrance that are even more reminiscent of Wright. At one end is a separate, asymmetrical group of classrooms for the teaching of science, arranged around a quadrangle and with a corner tower, reflecting the central feature of the main block.[5] A comparable design to the Kelso science block with similar detailing was soon after realised for the much smaller Chirnside School, serving a Berwickshire village and its agricultural hinterland, which was Reid and Forbes' final significant school project of the decade. In addition to the architects' favoured decorative stone dressings, the tower has pigeonholes – a charming vernacular detail appropriate for the rural context – and the return elevation, behind which the school hall is located, has plaques depicting the scales of Judgement, the torch of Knowledge and

Tullos Primary School
David John Alexander Ross of John Ogg Allan, 1939
Bruce Peter

a star with laurel leaves for Achievement. Best of all, the school gates feature lightning bolts, suggestive of education's potential for sudden and transformative 'eureka!' moments.

In Aberdeen, it was a local architect, David John Alexander Ross (1898–1975) of the firm of John Ogg Allan (1870–1955) who designed the granite-faced moderne Tullos Primary School, completed in 1939 and notable for its glazed patio doors around the ground floor with a surrounding canopy to keep rain out. The approach may have been inspired by the mid-1930s experimental École en Plein Air at Suresnes near Paris, designed by Eugène Beaudouin (1898–1983) and Marcel Lods (1891–1978), the classrooms of which had pivoted glazed panels to give a semi-outdoor environment.[6] Needless to say, the climate around Paris is considerably warmer and drier than that of Aberdeen.

Back in Edinburgh, the West Pilton Secondary School was another serving a large new housing scheme. The design by James Stewart Johnston (1901–1992) features drum-shaped stair towers with glass brickwork, for which inspiration may have come from Burnet, Tait & Lorne's Burlington School for Girls at Wood Lane in London, opened in 1936 and for which Frederick McManus was the lead architect.[7] Designed in 1937, West Pilton's construction was delayed by the Second World War and it was finally completed a decade late in 1948 and shortly after was renamed as Ainslie Park. Above the entrances, which are at either end of the main frontage, there are bas relief panels, one of a kilted youth holding the torch of Knowledge and the other of a teenage girl holding the mirror of Truth (which is, of course, an Art Deco octagonal one). Johnston's firm went on to design further schools – including Berwickshire High School at Duns and Inchview Primary School at Pilton, neither of which was as visually impressive as Ainslie Park.

Also designed in the late 1930s but finished post-war is Kilsyth Academy, designed by Basil Spence, which

West Pilton Secondary School, Edinburgh
James Stewart Johnston, 1937
Bruce Peter

stands prominently on a lower slope of the Campsie Hills and is arranged asymmetrically as a series of blocks of various sizes emanating from a central six-storey clock tower. The first and second storeys carry a large bas relief panel by Thomas Whalen (1903–1975) entitled 'Knowledge,' depicting a boy being borne aloft in front of a tree. The tower is balanced by a projecting semi-circular glazed stairwell and, as with Spence's earlier Gribloch mansion, the combination of stripped back neoclassicism and picturesque detailing appear Swedish-inspired. Certain elements – for example a partial cladding in stone rubble – are post-war modifications by Spence to his original drawings to incorporate elements of the contemporary style, later brought to prominence by the Festival of Britain (an event in which Spence was to be significantly involved). Kilsyth Academy is therefore a particularly interesting Scottish school, reflecting a pivot point between pre- and post-war design approaches.

The many Carnegie-sponsored libraries built across Scotland in the pre-First World War period meant that few more were needed thereafter. In the densely populated working-class Fountainbridge area of Edinburgh, the existing small library, dating from 1897, was by the 1930s considered inadequate by the city authorities. John Alexander William Grant (1886–1959), an Inverness-born, Glasgow-trained and, from 1922, Edinburgh-based architect, was commissioned to design a replacement.[8] Hitherto, Grant's main specialism had been housing, his designs often being Arts and Crafts-inspired. For the library, by contrast, he evidently sought to express municipal dignity through finely detailed neoclassical frontages in sandstone with Art Deco embellishment. The steel framing enables very large expanses of glazing, the windows being almost floor-to-ceiling with decorative metal interspersing panels concealing the edges of the first floor; these were designed by the sculptor Charles d'Orville Pilkington Jackson (1887–1973) and depict a working man reading while a librarian advises a mother and child, surrounded on either side by stylised papyrus reeds (from which paper, the material of books, was once derived). Above the corner entrance is a carving representing a fountain and bridge.[9] The overall impression is of great precision and coherence – a composition upon which much care was evidently

expended, even if the angular forms are rather staid for their time and also possibly a little too redolent of industrial premises.

Upon entering, the lofty three-storey octagonal vestibule's cantilevered stairway with bronze railings and lotus finials is a striking feature, while the reading rooms are notable for their natural illumination, not only from the sides but from glazed clerestories too. By the time that the library was completed in 1940, unfortunately, wartime black-out conditions were being enforced and so all of the glazing was covered over until after peace returned, when the interior's extensive fenestration and the lightness it enabled could at last be appreciated.[10]

Fountainbridge Library, Edinburgh
John Alexander William Grant, 1940
Bruce Peter

Healthcare

First World War conscription had starkly revealed just how many young men were unfit to fight, suffering from the effects of poor diets and lifestyles. Consequently, in the 1920s the beginnings of a significant expansion of healthcare provision began. Art Deco and moderne were arguably highly appropriate styles for new medical buildings, reflecting as they did positivist images of youthful beauty and vigour.

The first such Scottish facility to incorporate Art Deco elements was a new Royal Dental Hospital in Glasgow, occupying a north-facing site on Renfrew Street in Garnethill, only one block away from Glasgow School of Art. The design was by the partnership of Alexander Wright (1877–1972) and Edward Grigg Wylie (1885–1954) who had until 1909 been employees of Sir John Burnet. Wright was born in Garnethill and Wylie was a former student and close friend of Eugène Bourdon, whose Beaux Arts approach was of great influence. In the 1920s, Wright and Wylie tutored at the Glasgow School of Architecture and in 1925 Wright was appointed as its Course Director. The Dental Hospital's amply fenestrated four-storey facade with a stair tower at each end reflected Bourdon's influence – though it could equally have fronted factory offices or a school. The horizontal accenting of the top floor windows was perhaps even a subtle homage to Mackintosh's nearby School of Art. While design work was underway, in 1928 Wylie and Wright took into partnership Wylie's nephew, Frederick Robert Wylie (1904–1982) and it was under the new joint name of Wylie, Wright & Wylie that the project was completed in 1932.

In that year, an architectural competition was held for a new Infectious Diseases Hospital to occupy a large greenfield site by the White Cart River at Hawkhead near Paisley. The assessor, James Miller, had earlier designed several hospitals, large and small, and so had a thorough knowledge of what was required. The winning submission, by Thomas S Tait, who had recent experience from his Royal Masonic Hospital project in London, was a radical departure from anything previously attempted in Scottish healthcare. Rather than designing a single unit throughout which disease could spread, Tait arranged a series of separate, oblong one- and two-storey pavilions with patio doors and long extruded balconies to bring in plentiful fresh air and sunshine. Curved ends, flat

Royal Dental Hospital, Glasgow
Wylie, Wright & Wylie, 1932
Bruce Peter

roofs with over-sailing canopies, white paintwork and entrances highlighted with bands of coloured glazed brick engendered a moderne sense of dynamism and purpose while plentiful greenery created a soothing atmosphere.[11] In reaching this solution, Tait appears to have drawn upon elements of new healthcare buildings on the continent, notably the Zonnestraal sanatorium in Hilversum in the Netherlands by Jan Duiker (1890–1935), Bernard Bijvoet (1889–1979) and Jan Gerko Wienbenga (1886–1974), built between 1925 and 1931.

Tait's design probably inspired James Miller and his son, George James Miller, to produce a comparable solution for the Canniesburn Hospital near Bearsden, the site for which was secluded and looked out towards the Campsie Hills. The hospital was to provide extra capacity and convalescent care beds for the Royal Infirmary of Glasgow, for which Miller senior had been responsible earlier. Canniesburn Hospital was

Hawkhead Infectious Diseases Hospital, Paisley
Thomas S Tait of Sir John Burnet, Tait & Lorne, 1936
Bruce Peter

completed in 1935, some of the buildings featuring curving glazed stair towers, while others are wholly cubistic in form.[12] The designs of the Hawkhead and Canniesburn hospitals elegantly implied aims towards healthfulness, hygiene and recovery in a way that arguably too few subsequent Scottish healthcare buildings have done.

Francis Lorne and Ludovic Gordon Farquhar of Burnet, Tait & Lorne, meanwhile, had designed an extension for the Glasgow Eye Infirmary, converting a further section of the mid-nineteenth-century terrace it occupied in Sandyford Place, off Sauchiehall Street to the west of Charing Cross. They rearranged the spaces behind the existing sandstone frontage, adding a new attic storey and installing a moderne curved entrance canopy, flagpoles and a sign in gold mosaic, which presumably they chose for the visual pleasure it engendered. Remarkably, these mid-1930s additions all remain in situ today.

Canniesburn Hospital
James Miller & Son, 1935
Bruce Peter

Fitness and sport

Throughout 1930s Europe, the idea of exposing as many as possible to the health-giving benefits of sunshine and fresh air found widespread support across the political spectrum and, in Scotland, despite uncertain weather, the sun-worshipping phenomenon was embraced, with several notable seaside leisure developments being brought to fruition. Municipalities with jurisdiction over seaside resorts realised that investing in new leisure infrastructure might help to attract additional visitors. Modern architecture's taking inspiration one way or another from the layout and symbolism of passenger ships often encouraged light-coloured designs with sweeping lines, redolent of being at sea.

The latter Victorian and Edwardian eras had witnessed the construction of new indoor swimming baths in many British towns and cities. In the interwar period, there followed the British response to a Europe-wide wave of development of outdoor pools, often fashionably referred to as 'lidos', where it was possible both to swim and sunbathe. At the bigger examples there was often also a cafe and sometimes terracing for spectator events, such as professional swimming displays and beauty contests. As the outdoor pools were usually sited on public land along resort promenades, it was typically the local borough engineer's department that designed them, sometimes with an architect also involved to draw up the pool pavilion, in which changing facilities were housed. The styles of these bifurcated between the preferred neoclassical of municipal architecture and engineering departments and more up-to-date but usually blocky Art Deco-derived forms with minimal embellishment. Architectural style was, however, subordinate to engineered necessity, as the written content of a short-lived mid-1930s specialist journal, *Bath and Bath Engineering*, demonstrated. Although its title used a jovial overlapping Art Deco font, the articles it contained were overwhelmingly concerned with analyses of constructional issues and of the best ways of carrying out filtration and of controlling the growth of bacteria and algae in pool water.

Outdoor pools fell into two distinct categories: one comprised the relatively few very costly examples contained within their own walled reinforced concrete basins, entirely separate from the sea and supplied with filtered and aerated water. The other consisted of the many more 'tidal' pools with low surrounds over which

Dunoon Bathing Lido
Thomas Beveridge, 1937

replenishing sea water flowed at each high tide. Which solution was preferable depended on each municipality's willingness to risk investing. Sometimes, pools were gradually upgraded, for example the initial 1880s manifestation of Dunbar's outdoor pool was of the tidal variety but it was extended in the late 1920s with concrete perimeter walls between the rocky outcrops that had originally defined it. On the Firth of Clyde, Troon and Prestwick gained large new outdoor pools in 1931 with rectilinear basins and pavilions of neoclassical colonnaded design. At Saltcoats, a tidal pool dating from 1894 was improved with a new pavilion in 1933 but at Rothesay and Dunoon the idea of building pools was vetoed on account of cost and so bathing stations from which swimmers entered open water gained new, commodious changing facilities in 1934 and 1937 respectively.[13] Gourock Outdoor Swimming Pool, first opened in 1909 and occupying a superb promontory site with a backdrop of mountains across the firth, was rebuilt in the 1935 at a cost of over £14,000 with new Art Deco entrance porticos at street level and renovated changing facilities below.[14]

Scotland's most capacious self-contained outdoor pools were on the bracing but usually less rainy East Coast. The Arbroath Outdoor Pool, which opened in 1934 to a design by the borough engineer, Thomas A Hogg (1895–1944), was ambitious in scale, costing £22,000 and accommodating up to 1,200 bathers plus 4,000 spectators; stylistically it was, however, rather lumpish.[15] Born in Selkirk, Hogg had trained in Edinburgh in the office of Dick Peddie (1853–1921) and Walter Todd (1888–1944).[16] The Gaumont film company recorded the pool's opening for a newsreel, the commentary stating that Arbroath had been the sunniest place in Scotland during the previous four years – albeit with 'invigorating' sea breezes from the North Sea. A fashion show was presented in which 'mannequins show[ed] the ladies what to wear when they take the plunge, are on the beach or maybe go on a cruise'.[17]

Arbroath Outdoor Pool
Thomas A Hogg, 1934

Tarlair Outdoor Pool, Macduff
John C Miller, 1936
HES DP108839

Needless to say, there were rather substantial economic and social gaps between the pool's typical clientele and those whose wealth enabled them to cruise – but by reclining in a deckchair on the poolside terrace, one could always dream. Nearby Stonehaven also gained an open-air pool in the same year, albeit somewhat smaller, stylistically more traditional and costing a mere £9,000. Its pavilion, designed by the Aberdeen architect Robert Robb Gall (1878–1950) of Gregory & Gall, has pilasters flanking the entrance and pitched tiled roofing.[18] The Tarlair Outdoor Pool, located in a picturesque bay near MacDuff and comprising separate ponds for swimming and for boating, designed by the Burgh Surveyor of MacDuff, John C Miller, was constructed slowly between 1931 and 1936 as money was gradually raised.[19] Burntisland's commodious pool was likewise completed in 1936, the Burgh Surveyor James A Waddell providing a high brick perimeter wall for shelter, which gave an appearance comparable to recent municipal pools in and around London. At first floor level, there was a balcony for spectators with a cafe at the landward

end above the changing rooms; it was thus a popular suntrap on summer days – though, as was typical of Scotland's unheated outdoor pools, the water was reliably purgatorial.[20] Away from the seaside, the inhabitants of the Ayrshire mining town of Cumnock decided in 1935 to build an outdoor pool in Woodroad Park where there was a natural hollow; this was further dug out, lined and completed by the summer of 1936 at a cost of £5,500.

The finest and final Scottish outdoor pool was at Portobello, Edinburgh's seaside resort, where the City Engineer's Department, led by William Allan Macartney and assisted by James Sheill and George Geddes, worked with Ion Warner (1897–1987) of the City Architect's Department. Together, they designed a pool of Olympic dimensions with lockers

Portobello Outdoor Pool advertisement
Illustration by Tom Curr, c1938

Portobello Outdoor Pool
Ion Warner and William Allan Macartney, 1936
Bruce Peter collection

for 1,284 bathers and terracing accommodating 6,000 spectators. A most ingenious aspect of the project was the use of cooling water from the town's power station, located adjacent to the pool's site, enabling the unique attraction of swimming outdoors in relative warmth. The west terracing was protected by a cantilevered reinforced concrete shelter, opposite which was a set of concrete diving boards, which were the project's most daring stylistic flourishes. By comparison, the pavilion, containing a cafe, was another tamely rectilinear composition, which by the time of the pool's inauguration in 1936 appeared a little dated.[21]

Several other Scottish seaside municipalities considered investing in new pools, but decided against on account of expense, including at Fraserburgh, Bo'ness and Ayr.[22] In the long run, caution proved wise as the pools also needed ongoing investment to maintain, especially as salty seawater caused the slow decay of the reinforced concrete from which they were built.

In Aberdeen, a magnificent new indoor municipal pool, the Aberdeen Baths, was opened in 1940. A joint effort by the City Architect's and Engineer's Departments, the architectural work was by Alexander McRobie (1913–1992) and Leo Durnin (1902–1988),

who were assistants of the Chief Architect, Robert Mackay (1898–1941). The structure enclosing the pool consists of reinforced concrete arches, a technique earlier used at the New Horticultural Hall in London's Westminster, designed in the mid-1920s by Easton & Robertson. The granite-faced entrance block facing Justice Mill Lane may lack finesse but the circulation spaces within are notable for their inlaid terrazzo flooring and for the crisp detailing of the doorways and the wall finishes. Terraces for spectators line the pool's sides and, altogether, the edifice is notable for its generous scale and good facilities, demonstrating the importance attributed to the aim of better fitness in the 1930s and the prime role of municipalities in achieving this.[23]

Sports pavilions were programmatically very similar to those of outdoor swimming pools, albeit with playing fields adjacent, rather than water. The example at Penilee near Paisley, designed by James Steel Maitland in 1939, features a bow window, originally for a cafe, with an open balcony above. At Mountblow near Dalmuir the sports pavilion is a three-storey design by James George McKenzie (1908–1992), recently appointed as Senior Architect in the office of the Clydebank Burgh Surveyor. It comprises a plinth containing storage, above which rise two storeys accommodating changing rooms with south-facing balconies, linked by a fin-shaped stair tower.

In addition to municipal provision, Glasgow and Aberdeen Universities invested in moderne sports pavilions for their students. In 1936 Glasgow University's favoured architect, T Harold Hughes, designed the Sports Pavilion by the University's playing fields at Garscadden. This was, for Hughes, a rare, wholly moderne offering comprising a glazed semi-circular cafe and a clock tower containing stairs and a water tank with the changing rooms in wings on either side.[24] At Aberdeen University, the King's Pavilion for students of King's College was completed in 1941 to a design by A G R Mackenzie. It contains an indoor swimming pool to the rear of a strikingly clean-lined front block. External stairways link to a slim projecting balcony while a matching roof overhang above provides some shelter.[25]

Mountblow Sports Pavilion, Glasgow
James George McKenzie, 1937
Bruce Peter

King's Pavilion, Aberdeen
A G R Mackenzie of A Marshall Mackenzie & Son, 1941
Bruce Peter

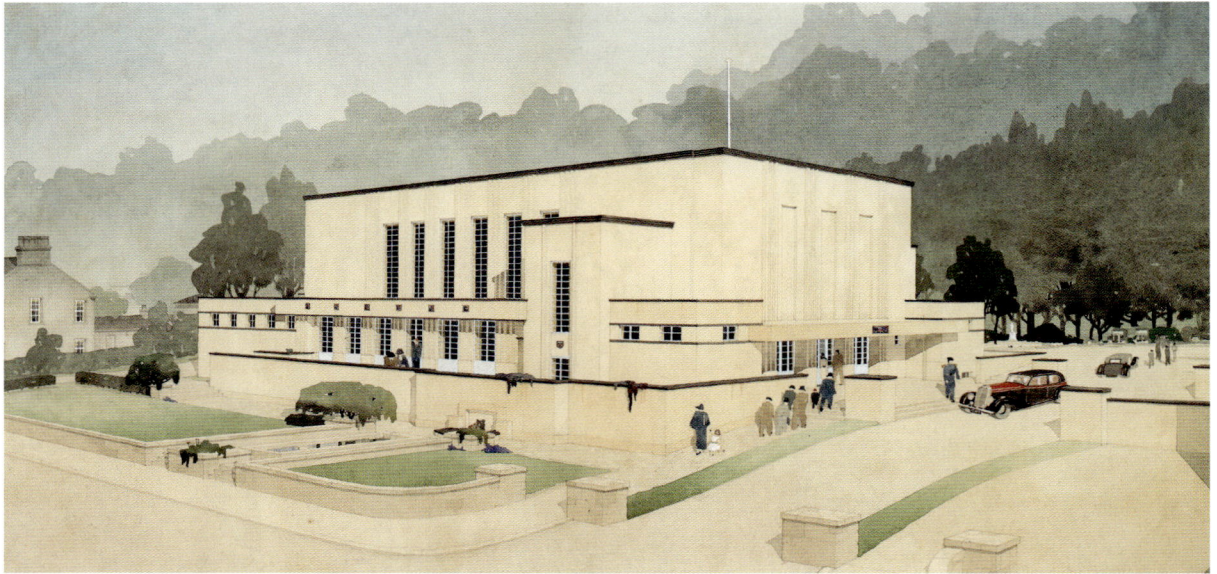

Pavilions

Perhaps more cost-effective alternative investments for seaside municipalities than swimming pools, and more adaptable than sports pavilions, were multi-functional pavilions. These were capable of hosting dancing, variety and entertainment shows, public meetings and displays – and also with cafes as daily attractions where passers-by could shelter from inclement weather to enjoy a cup of tea or a light lunch. On England's south coast, the De La Warr Pavilion at Bexhill, completed in 1935, provided a state-of-the-art model for such venues, even if many locals there found its appearance controversial. Lacking an indoor entertainment venue, Gourock on the Clyde Coast likewise held an architectural competition in 1935 for the Cragburn Pavilion; this was won by a recent Glasgow School of Architecture graduate, James A Carrick (1911–1989), who was the son of an established Ayr architect, James Carrick (1880–1940), both of whom had started out as employees of James Miller. Carrick Junior – who was a fashion-conscious architect favouring moderne whenever a client would accept it – produced an economical rectangular hall with a stage at one end, a cafe and terrace on the ground floor of the long elevation facing the Firth of Clyde and a balcony with six tall windows above.[26] By the time it was in build, Carrick had won a further pavilion competition in 1936 with a more architecturally ambitious solution for Rothesay on the Isle of Bute, which was considered

Cragburn Pavilion, Gourock

James A Carrick of J & J A Carrick, 1935

HES DP039197

to be the most distinguished of the Clyde Coast resorts.[27]

Completed in 1938, the Rothesay Pavilion's rectilinear frontage to the promenade is enlivened by a huge glazed semi-circular projection from the first floor at one end containing a cafe and buffet with an outdoor terrace above, sheltered by a matching canopy; perhaps Carrick had been inspired by the very similar combination of forms used by William Kininmonth for his Edinburgh home and by Thomas S Tait for the Hawkhead Infectious Diseases Hospital. The much-publicised De La Warr Pavilion would have been another obvious source of inspiration for the overall compositional approach, though Carrick chose a weather-resistant tiled facing rather than copying its painted exterior. Not only did his design appear dynamic while offering superb views outward, but also the interior was very generously proportioned with commodious hallways, floored in inlaid terrazzo, wide stairways and cloakrooms in which wet outdoor clothing could be hung to dry. At first floor level, the multi-purpose auditorium was well-equipped and, throughout, cove lighting and bold moderne forms in plasterwork made visiting a chance to experience the latest in interior style.[28]

Rothesay Pavilion
James A Carrick of J & J A Carrick, 1938
Bruce Peter collection, HES SC1389132, HES SC1169522,
HES SC1169523, HES SC636577

Dunfermline Fire Station
James Shearer, 1936
HES SC879285, SC864923

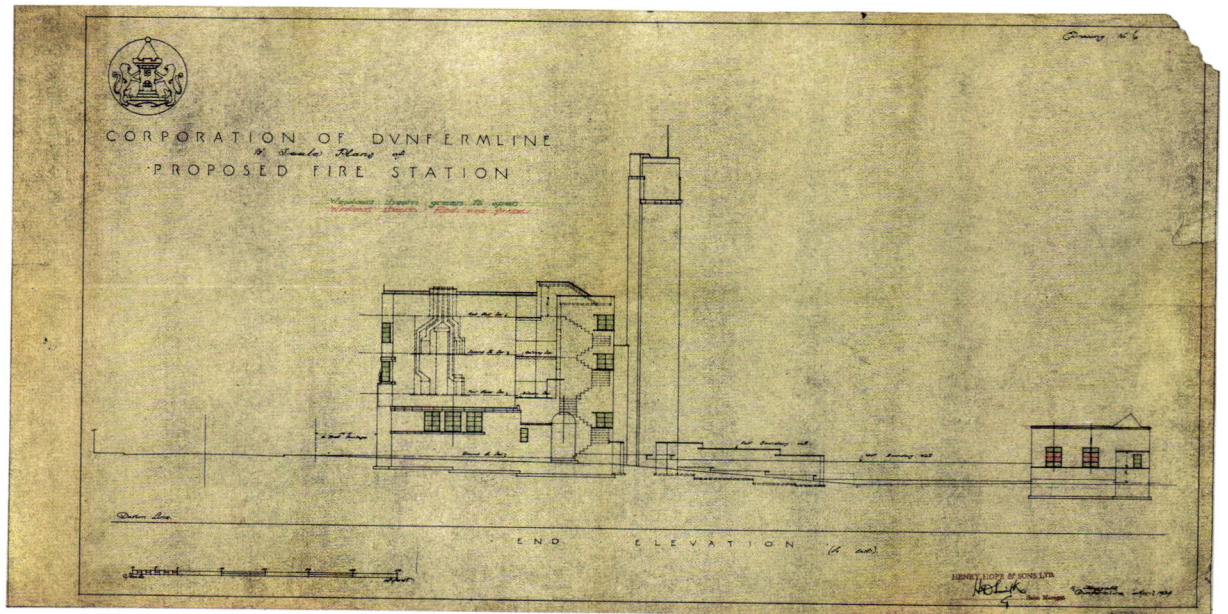

Fire and light

If the Rothesay Pavilion exemplified municipal provision at its most up to date and glamorous, more typical investments by local authorities in new buildings were for comparatively mundane uses but, even so, a high architectural quality was often achieved. In Dunfermline, for example, a new fire station was completed in 1936 to a design by a local architect, James Shearer (1881–1962), who was a graduate of the Glasgow School of Architecture and former employee of Burnet.[29] Although a traditionalist by instinct, in this instance, Shearer produced a rectilinear composition incorporating restrained Art Deco elements, perhaps influenced by the Burnet offices' most recent projects. Dark grey facing brick was chosen for the ground floor to highlight the fire station's standard bright red doors. The correspondent from *The Architect and Building News* claimed to detect the influence of Mackintosh in the massing and colour contrasts, though these are not so different from other comparable buildings of the period.[30] Kirkcaldy's new fire station, drawn up by the town's Burgh Engineer and Surveyor George Duffus (1882–1970) was built almost concurrently and has a similar layout, suggesting that Shearer may

Kirkcaldy Fire Station
George Duffus, 1936
Bruce Peter

have been consulted, although its detailing is not quite as neatly resolved as at Dunfermline.[31] Both are lent distinction by slender towers, the inclusion of which was permissible as their shafts were to be used to hang wet firehoses for drying.

In late-1930s Glasgow, meanwhile, as electrical street lighting gradually superseded gas, a new control station was constructed on Millbrae Road in Battlefield on the city's Southside. Its design was by Sam Bunton (1908–1974), a young, ambitious and versatile Glaswegian architect who mostly produced housing. He devised a striking arrangement of differing volumes of grey brick, apparently inspired by Dudok, with boldly horizontal continuous glazing around much of the ground floor and, at the corner, a vertical accent of internally illuminated glass blockwork.[32] Bunton's solution showed how even a very utilitarian requirement could be lent civic dignity through well-considered composition and attentive detailing.

St Andrew's House

The new home of the Scottish Office in Edinburgh, the eventual St Andrew's House, designed by Thomas S Tait, would be the largest, most prestigious and architecturally impressive public edifice erected in interwar Scotland. That it emerged with these qualities was far from inevitable. Its final form was the outcome of a long, controversial and at times acrimonious gestation process, spanning a quarter of a century. When in 1911–1912, the Liberal government of Herbert Henry Asquith brought forth legislation for a Scottish Board of Agriculture and a Scottish Land Court, a new centralised administrative headquarters for Scotland's growing bureaucracy appeared necessary. The Secretary of State for Scotland, Captain John Sinclair, Lord Pentland, believed that the most obvious location for this would be the site of Calton Prison, which stood on the southern slope of Calton Hill, a rocky outcrop that had earlier been imagined as an equivalent of the Acropolis in Athens. Built in stages between 1791 and 1817, the prison was considered an embarrassment by enlightened denizens of Edinburgh and the fact that it was the first sight rail passengers arriving from the south typically saw only made matters worse. The Office of Works' Principal Architect in Scotland, William Thomas Oldrieve (1853–1922), prepared a national romantic scheme for

St Andrew's House, Edinburgh
Thomas S Tait of Sir John Burnet, Tait & Lorne, 1939
Bruce Peter

government offices to replace the prison. This retained some of its castellated perimeter wall, behind which a picturesque composition of interlinked buildings, which from a distance somewhat resembled Falkland Palace, was proposed. The outbreak of the First World War, however, caused development work to be suspended.[33]

Calton Prison was closed in 1925. Over time, the Scottish Office's administrative brief had been expanded to cover Health, Education, Fisheries and Agriculture, these remits being inefficiently split between 18 different offices in central Edinburgh. At the same time, a new National Library was being planned to occupy the site of the Sheriff Courthouse on George IV Bridge, which would consequently need to be moved elsewhere. (The library was designed by Reginald Fairlie in a monolithic neoclassical idiom and built between 1936 and 1955.) The decision was therefore taken to replace the prison with government offices and a new Sheriff Court, making the proposed complex far bigger and potentially more domineering on the city's skyline.[34]

St Andrew's House, Edinburgh
Thomas S Tait of Sir John Burnet, Tait & Lorne, 1939
Bruce Peter

With regard to the design, it was decided for expediency to have this carried out by the Office of Works with neither external consultation nor competition. By the 1920s, the role of Principal Architect in Scotland had disappeared, the Office of Works' Architecture Department being centralised in London. Inevitably, the Scottish architectural profession were outraged and the Arts and Crafts architect Sir Robert Lorimer, a greatly respected senior figure in the cultural and architectural worlds and since 1928 President of the RIAS, protested loudly and vigorously. The recently created Royal Fine Art Commission for Scotland, established in 1927 and led by the highly cultivated Sir John Stirling-Maxwell with Lorimer its member for architectural matters, weighed in too.[35] In London, the conservative architectural heavyweight Sir Reginald Blomfield (1856–1942) wrote haughtily to *The Times* that 'with all respect to the very capable architects of the Office of Works… it cannot be contended for one moment that the best architectural ability of the country is confined within its walls' and that the lack of open competition was symptomatic

of 'the inordinate appetite of bureaucracies' which, he felt, was 'a standing menace in the modern State which should be closely watched and firmly resisted'.[36]

By the summer of 1929 a design had nonetheless been prepared; this comprised a large six-storey quadrangle of government offices, linked by arches to a five-storey Sheriff Court block, the elevations having continuous pilasters with neither variation nor a central focus.[37] The proposal made no concessions to context and could equally have been designed for the vicinity of Whitehall or, for that matter, Washington DC or Berlin. Those responsible had evidently failed to grasp Calton Hill's historic, symbolic and aesthetic significance. John Summerson, at that time a lecturer at Edinburgh College of Art, was so concerned that he commissioned one of his students, Pat Ronaldson (1912–1943), to draw a perspective from the Office of Works' model and this was published in *The Scotsman* newspaper.[38]

Stirling-Maxwell requested that the design be modified through the introduction of bolder effects of light and shade and that it be better related to the rock foundation on which it would stand. A portico and end pavilions were thus added on the block containing offices, while the Sheriff Court became a much more compact, separate unit, somewhat resembling a mausoleum. Despite these changes, the

St Andrew's House, Edinburgh
Thomas S Tait of Sir John Burnet, Tait & Lorne, 1939
Bruce Peter

scheme still remained in essence a derivative exercise in governmental neoclassicism. Following the death of Sir Robert Lorimer, his successor on the Fine Art Commission, James Miller, argued that the Office of Works' revised design proposal had too vertical an emphasis and that a horizontally stepped composition would respond more pleasingly to the site's topography. The Cockburn Association, led by Lord Elphinstone, had meanwhile formed a Calton Hill Scottish National Committee to coordinate objections; the Duke of Atholl – a much-decorated veteran of the army who was greatly admired in governmental circles and who had sat on an initial project committee back in 1913 – lent it his support, while Patrick Geddes, the polymathic urbanist and cultural thinker, unequivocally stated of the proposed design that 'we really must not allow it'. A very large number of other prominent aristocrats, academics and industrialists expressed their agreement. In response, the Secretary of the Office of Works, Sir Lionel Earle, remained adamant that it alone should produce the plans, or there would be none.[39]

The effects of the Wall Street Crash led the newly elected Labour government of Ramsay MacDonald to suspend the project, but with the return of the Conservatives in August 1931, it was revived, albeit no longer including the Sheriff Court, which instead would be built in the Old Town, between the Royal Mile

and the Bank of Scotland (a building subsequently integrated into the High Court). A speech in the House of Commons in November 1932 by John Buchan, popular novelist and Member of Parliament for the Scottish Universities, argued that Scotland had suffered a progressive loss of identity and that any new buildings constructed on Calton Hill offered a prime opportunity to correct this deficit.[40] The new Secretary of the Office of Works, Major William Ormsby-Gore, took note, but worried that an architectural competition would merely add costs and complexity, risking the scheme being abandoned altogether. Moreover, in the government's experience, limited competitions had a reputation for disputes leading to costly compensation payments. Therefore, as with his predecessor, Earle, Ormsby-Gore favoured a wholly in-house design by his own architectural staff and decided that to avoid the risk of objectors defeating that aim, a step-by-step approach should be used. Under his plan, the general outline, then the layout and, finally, the elevations, would be designed and, at each stage, agreement would be sought among the interested parties.[41] At this point, the

Sculpture over entrance to St Andrew's House
Alexander Carrick and Phyllis Mary Bone, 1939
Bruce Peter

distinguished elderly Edinburgh architect Sir George Washington Browne (1853–1939), who had designed numerous notable buildings in the city – including churches, commercial edifices and the Central Library – and had been a founder of the Fine Art Commission, attempted to break the impasse by proposing a grouped layout in two tiers. In his design, the side of the main block facing over the tracks at Waverley Station was lower than the other three sides and there were separate, smaller blocks located at each end. Although this solution would be costlier to build than a monolith, it responded much more pleasingly to its context than the previous proposals and so it gained the Fine Art Commission's support. The Office of Works then produced its own version with the side blocks altered into extruded wings.[42]

In July 1933, after Their Majesties King George V and Queen Mary had received a briefing paper on the project, the Queen's Assistant Secretary wrote to Ormsby-Gore that she had expressed anxiety about the scheme and hoped that 'something noble and worthy of the site may be built'. Having for so long resisted

the idea of any kind of external architectural input, the Office of Works was at last forced by this Royal intervention to concede that a distinguished architect would now need to be selected. Thomas S Tait of Burnet, Tait & Lorne was chosen; having recently been overlooked for designing new offices in Whitehall, this would be his consolation.[43]

Following more than two decades of gestation, there remained only four months for Tait to produce a design in response to what was a large and complex brief.[44] Prodigiously hard-working and skilful but also unassuming and self-contained, he would have been very aware that this would most likely be the building for which he would be best remembered. His own commentary in a report accompanying his design drawings emphasised the attention he paid to the characteristics of the site and of the existing nearby buildings. He observed that 'not many architects have had the good fortune to be asked to design a building for such an imposing and dramatic situation'. In the elevations, he sought to reflect 'the long low-lying lines of the hillside without interfering with its outline or the monuments crowning its crest', his intention being that the whole composition should appear as 'one fine piece of sculpture work'.[45] So far as aesthetics were concerned, Tait's solution ended up being as modern as he probably felt he dared be, combining elements of the rectilinear neoclassicism of the Daily Telegraph building in London, the Anglo-American headquarters in Johannesburg and an unsuccessful competition entry he submitted for Norwich Town Hall, with the introduction of moderne elements reminiscent of the Royal Masonic Hospital only at the extremities. In carrying out the project, he was assisted by his long-standing Burnet, Tait & Lorne colleague, Andrew Bryce (1890–1943), with whom he had worked closely on many diverse designs from the British Museum onwards and who was equally fastidious.

Darnley stone was chosen for the external walls with grey and black polished granite and faience details, the main roofs being of shallow-pitch, clad in copper. Facing onto Regent Road, the centre block is of seven storeys, the basement opening onto an internal courtyard to the rear. The main entrance sits between semi-circular bastions with thistle-heads and thistle-patterned collars, above which is a bas relief heraldic panel in stone depicting the Royal Arms of the United Kingdom as used in Scotland, created by Alexander Carrick (1882–1966) and Phyllis Mary Bone (1894–1972), who sculpted its lion and unicorn.[46] The outer storm doors were designed by Walter Gilbert and depict in low-relief the Divine Call to St Andrew, who is flanked by St Ninian, St Kentigern and St Magnus against a St Andrew's Cross; these were made in cast bronze by H H Martyn of Cheltenham.[47] Above the long cornice of the blank first storey, which in sunlight is authoritatively underlined by a strong shadow, there soar six square pilasters, capped by allegorical figures modelled by Sir William Reid Dick and sculpted by Carrick. These represent Architecture, Statecraft, Health, Agriculture, Fisheries and Education and are reminiscent of the two pilasters above the Royal Masonic Hospital's entrance. The treatment of the roofline is monumental, with shallow step-backs culminating in a long, rectilinear parapet. At each end, this steps down to flanking stair towers and twice more to long symmetrical four-storey wings, each of 12 bays and with the top storey recessed. The gates to the subsidiary entrances have lions rampant, cast by Thomas Hadden of Edinburgh after Tait's sketches. In the front courtyard, pylons carrying lighting and

Office of the Secretary of State for Scotland, St Andrew's House

Thomas S Tait of Sir John Burnet, Tait & Lorne, 1939
HES SC2660821

flagpoles are the frontal aspect's most obviously moderne elements and are reminiscent of comparable devices forming the frontage of Tait's Coal Pavilion at the Glasgow Empire Exhibition of 1938 (see Chapter 5).[48]

The south elevation is contrastingly deferential to its hilly and craggy context and was very deftly organised by Tait as a series of receding layers and set-backs, stepping down the slope. The underlying concept owed much to Washington Browne's proposal and generations of civil servants working in the offices have had much to thank both him and Tait for as they enjoyed the consequent daylight and vistas. (The Office of Works' own unrealised designs would instead have had offices entirely surrounding a lightwell, which would have been finished in harling, rather than the stone and faience used by Tait.) A roof-garden, planted with bright yellow St John's Wort and other flowers selected by Tait, was intended to give office workers looking out of the rear windows of the Regent Road block a beautiful

Sculptures on main frontage of St Andrew's House

Sir William Reid Dick and Alexander Carrick, 1939

Bruce Peter

foreground to enjoy, but this was never installed.[49] The semi-circular, south-facing end pavilions and glass-enclosed stairways are among the moderne-looking aspects of the main structure, but they also reference the form of the retained circular Governor's House from the old Calton Prison.

Tait's scheme won the approval of the Fine Art Commission and was published in *The Times* in November 1934.[50] Construction began in April 1937, but only once this was in progress did officials realise that more office space would be required than they had allowed for and so Tait was required to provide this as unobtrusively as possible through the enlargement of the south-facing range.

Consequent budgetary constraints forced Tait to carry out some judicious pruning of his designs for the interiors, most of which ended up being merely clean-lined and serviceable. The entrance hall is the only two-storey space and is floored in travertine slabs, rather than the linoleum used everywhere else. Tait purpose-designed clocks, door furniture and stairway balustrading with a repeating thistle motif. For the conference rooms, located on the third storey, and for the Secretary of State's office on the fifth floor, a high standard of finish was required. The former are panelled in grey Indian veneer with moderne banding in laurel while the latter features opulently figured veneer from a walnut tree reputedly planted by Mary, Queen of Scots. The offices originally for the Under Secretary of State and the private secretaries have Nigerian walnut dadoes. The furniture, also of Tait's design, was made by A H McIntosh of Kirkcaldy and was upholstered in fabrics by Donald Bros of Dundee, who also supplied the curtains.[51]

St Andrew's House was completed in 1939 and intended to be formally opened by King George VI and Queen Elizabeth in October of that year, but this was cancelled owing to the outbreak of war, Their Majesties instead making a low-key visit in February 1940.[52] Notwithstanding the building's importance in the Scottish architectural canon, it therefore never achieved the international attention given to the numerous other new governmental buildings constructed in Europe and the Americas in the interwar era. As an architectural achievement, it compares favourably with the best of these and, more than 85 years after completion, continues to provide a spacious, attractive and flexible working environment.[53]

CHAPTER 5
THE EMPIRE EXHIBITION OF 1938

Thomas S Tait's patience and dedication, and the focused work he and his colleagues carried out on the St Andrew's House project won the respect of the upper echelons of the Scottish Office and of the Office of Works. Consequently, when the UK government decided in 1936 to try to boost West Central Scotland's still sluggish industrial economy by holding an Empire Exhibition in Glasgow, he and his colleagues were considered the obvious architects for the task of designing it. If St Andrew's House remains as Scotland's finest Art Deco public building, the Empire Exhibition would emerge as the biggest, most comprehensive and spectacular expression of moderne to be achieved anywhere in 1930s Britain – though, lasting just six months, also the most ephemeral.

In 1931 the Secretary of State for Scotland, William Adamson, established a Scottish National Development Council to commence initiatives likely to stimulate growth and employment.[1] The idea of staging a great exhibition in Glasgow was first mooted by the council in the spring of 1936 and by summer the idea had begun to gain momentum with the strong encouragement of the shipbuilder Sir James Lithgow and other business leaders.[2] At first, it was thought

that the proposal could come to fruition either in the summer of 1938 or 1939, but political and economic imperatives quickly led to selection of the earlier option.[3] A Finance and General Purposes Committee was established to raise the necessary funding, its inaugural meeting taking place in October 1936.[4]

Glasgow had earlier hosted major exhibitions in 1888, 1901 and 1911, each one of which had provided a remarkable snapshot of Scotland's political and aesthetic concerns at these moments. The plan for 1938 was to stage an Empire Exhibition, which would avoid any need to seek the diplomatic approval required for truly international events. The previous British Empire Exhibition, held at Wembley in 1924–25, had, however, achieved disappointing attendance, though as deliberations for the Glasgow exhibition got underway, preparations for an Empire Exhibition in Johannesburg in 1936–1937 were well advanced and certain aspects of its design and layout would influence the subsequent Glasgow event. Of far greater international significance, however, were the Exposition Internationale des Arts et Techniques dans la Vie Moderne in Paris in 1937, and the World's Fair in New York in 1939.

Glasgow's previous exhibitions had all been staged in Kelvingrove Park, but for the Empire Exhibition, it was felt to be too limited in size and without sufficient car parking space and so it was decided instead that the venue should be the much larger Bellahouston Park, covering 169 acres on the city's Southside. Edward James Bruce, The Earl of Elgin and

Illuminated Tower of Empire and North Cascade, Empire Exhibition

Thomas S Tait of Sir John Burnet, Tait & Lorne and Launcelot Ross, 1938

Courtesy of Ian Johnston

Kincardine, was appointed as the Empire Exhibition's President and the event's aims were stated as being:

- To illustrate the progress of the British Empire at home and overseas.
- To show the potentialities of the United Kingdom and the Empire Overseas to the new generations.
- To stimulate Scottish work and production and to direct attention to Scotland's historical and scenic attractions.
- To foster Empire trade and a closer friendship among the peoples of the British Commonwealth of Nations.
- To emphasise to the world the peaceful aspirations of the peoples of the British Empire.[5]

The promotion of Imperial brotherhood was, of course, highly idealistic and masked the real diplomatic and political tensions within the Empire at that time. As India was seeking independence it decided not to participate with a pavilion of its own.[6] Ireland, which already had become a Free State, did exhibit, no doubt because there was a very big community of Irish background in Glasgow. The use of the term 'Commonwealth of Nations' was therefore more appropriate, while the desires for peace and prosperity reflected the contemporary troubled times.

One might have expected that an Empire Exhibition would have been entirely jingoistic, and indeed a predictably positivist spin was applied to most of what was shown. Yet, perhaps wishing to be seen to differentiate Britain from continental Europe's totalitarian regimes, a certain amount of reflective criticism was tolerated. Writing in *SMT Magazine and Scottish Country Life*, T Drummond Shiels, a former Under-Secretary of State at the Colonial Office, noted that:

> The association of Scotsmen with the Empire is a fascinating story … containing chapters bright with the sparkle of high courage and adventure, and others more sombre, telling of the cruelty and folly of governments and landowners, and of the persecution and privation of the common people… Scotland herself has paid a heavy price for serving the Empire in the persistent drain of some of her finest human material.[7]

In the Clachan, which evoked a traditional highland village, the presence of a derelict and abandoned cottage spoke poignantly of the origin of the huge Scottish diaspora. Yet, Shiels ignored the very extensive Scottish involvement in Caribbean slavery, writing that 'there is little trace of Scottish influence in the early history of the West Indies. Michael Scott of Glasgow developed sugar planting in Jamaica.'[8] In the end, the prominence given to Scotland's history, culture, society and industrial and engineering achievements made the Empire Exhibition – just like its Victorian and Edwardian predecessors in Glasgow – primarily a Scottish event. Yet, it also provided a late snapshot of a British Empire glamorously reframed using up-to-date architecture and design as masks to conceal an accelerating decline.

Preparation time was tight and a Scottish architect capable of working on a grand scale and in a suitably dignified but up-to-date style was urgently needed. Thomas S Tait was formally appointed as Architect-in-Chief in October 1936 to plan the exhibition site and to oversee the designing of most of its contents. The civil engineers were John Hogg and Liston Carnie of Crouch & Hogg.[9] A total budget of around £10 million was allocated, a minor part of which was provided by the UK government and by Glasgow Corporation while most came from the administrations of the Empire nations and from commercial sponsors.

As with the St Andrew's House project, in which Tait was involved concurrently, the time allowed for the design work was brief, there being a mere four months until the ground plan, covering 150 acres, was to be presented in February 1937. The first sod was to be cut less than a month thereafter by Lady Elgin.[10] Tait was enthused about the project's potential, later writing for *SMT Magazine and Scottish Country Life* upon its successful realisation that 'it is only once in a lucky lifetime that [an architect] has the chance to plan on a big scale, to plan huge buildings each of which is only a unit in a greater plan, to say "Let there be an avenue here, and here, and here"'.[11]

Tait was assisted not only by ever-dependable Andrew Bryce but also by three recently graduated additions to Burnet, Tait & Lorne's workforce. Margaret Brodie (1907–1997) had trained at the Glasgow School of Architecture and had won a travelling scholarship to Italy, about which she wrote vividly in the RIAS *Quarterly Illustrated*, recording that her adventures there had begun 'under a cloud

Initial design sketch for pavilions on Dominions Avenue, Empire Exhibition
Thomas S Tait of Sir John Burnet, Tait & Lorne, 1937
Bruce Peter collection

Final design for the Canada Pavilion, Empire Exhibition
Thomas S Tait of Sir John Burnet, Tait & Lorne, 1937
Bruce Peter collection

of depression… I was a unique object of curiosity for the natives of Turin… who were unsparing'.[12] A rare woman architect in a male-dominated profession, Brodie applied herself with great determination and was a central figure in Tait's small and focused planning and design group. Working in consort with her were Alexander Esmé Gordon (1910–1993), who was a recent Edinburgh College of Art graduate, and Tait's son, Gordon Tait (1912–1999), whose life had been lived wholly in London, where he attended the Architectural Association and served as Clerk of Works on Burnet, Tait & Lorne's Mount Royal hotel and flats project. Other leading Scottish architects of progressive persuasion – Basil Spence, Thomas Waller Marwick (1903–1971), James Taylor Thomson (1886–1953), Launcelot Hugh Ross (1885–1956) and Jack Antonio Coia (1898–1981) – contributed designs for particular structures or interiors, working in liaison with Tait and his colleagues.[13] Marwick was the third generation of an Edinburgh architecture dynasty, the family firm of T P Marwick & Son having been founded in 1917 by his grandfather. The firm's wider output in the era comprised banks and large shops in Edinburgh, often notable for their imaginative design. Thomson was likewise from Edinburgh but had worked in New York between 1912 and 1920 in the office of Bertram Goodhue, thereafter being employed in Glasgow by Burnet, Son & Dick. He established his own firm in 1937 with the Empire Exhibition as its initial project. Ross was born in Aberdeen, though moved to Glasgow in 1907, working for Burnet there and in London until 1912 when he commenced independent practice, designing mainly retail premises in and around Glasgow. Coia came from Wolverhampton, studied at the Glasgow School of Architecture in the early 1920s and joined the practice of the much older John Gaff Gillespie (1870–1926) and William Kidd (1879–1929) in which he was made a partner in 1927. Under Coia, the design of churches for the Archdiocese of Glasgow became an important activity and the firm's output was notable for its inventiveness. Distinguished architects from elsewhere in the UK also received individual commissions to design certain pavilions or exhibits, while others were devised by commercial exhibitors and their chosen architects, though all proposals were vetted for suitability by Tait.

The Bellahouston Park site was a large, mostly flat, expanse of cut grass with rises to Bellahouston Hill in the centre, on which there were mature trees, the felling of which was embargoed by Glasgow Corporation. Tait's layout therefore was focused on utilising the lower ground on the south, west and north sides of the hill for the main circulation areas and pavilions, devising three grand set-piece compositions, one on each side. The main aim of the layout was to engender a modernist sense of space, light and horizontality, in stark contrast to Glasgow's dense, dark and vertiginous inner-city urbanity. Rectangular ponds with illuminated fountains were to be central features, the extensive use of water being a leitmotif throughout the exhibition and a metaphor for hygiene at a time when too few Glasgow homes as yet possessed private toilets or bathrooms. Bellahouston Hill in the middle, meanwhile, was to feature restaurants and a tall tower, which was to be the Exhibition's centrepiece and symbol. Towers were frequently found in interwar great exhibitions, the Pavillon du Tourisme at the Paris Exposition of 1925, designed by Rob Mallet-Stevens, being an early moderne example with design characteristics similar to those of the far bigger tower Tait would now be designing for Glasgow. Illuminated water cascades with fountains would connect this and the principal circulation areas adjacent to the main entrances. At the north-east corner it was decided to add a Clachan as the one at the 1911 Scottish National Exhibition had been a popular attraction, while in the south-east corner a huge amusement park would be created and operated by the famous British fairground and holiday camp entrepreneur, Billy Butlin. These features were, however, peripheral and did not impinge on Tait's main masterplan.[14]

The size and complexity of the exhibition increased as the planning progressed. An initial idea promoted by Australia was that it, Canada, New Zealand, South Africa and Ireland would jointly contribute one large pavilion.[15] Prevarication by the last four meant that nothing further came of this and, instead, Tait devised a row of separate but outwardly identical pavilions for the masterplan, pending decisions by each dominion regarding what it would actually build. So enthusiastic was the uptake from manufacturers wishing to exhibit in the Palace of Industries that an additional hall needed to be added (they were suffixed 'West' and 'North'). As there was great interest too from commercial, scientific, transport, religious and media organisations, a large number of extra, smaller pavilions were added, filling out the spaces between the bigger ones and often having the most eye-catching designs, contrasting with the larger structures under Tait's control, in which he sought to achieve a high degree of aesthetic coherence.

The cumulative outcome was that the Empire Exhibition as built had considerably more diverse content than had at first been expected and was therefore also much more akin to one of the really big international exhibitions of its era than might have been expected of an event in a Depression-stricken regional city. That it was also architecturally and artistically among the finest was thanks largely to Tait's refined taste, cultivation, sense of drama and feeling for occasion. The overall conception and detailing of the elements reflected the exceptional ability of an architect at the height of their powers, ably assisted by a phalanx of other remarkable talents. Tait carried out the design work in London, sending Brodie and Gordon to Glasgow to survey the Bellahouston site and to supervise the civil engineering works that would provide the basis for the pavilions, circulation and water displays. For the two young architects, the task must have felt in equal measure daunting and invigorating.[16]

With regard to architectural style and the choice of construction materials, Tait explained that 'when an architect has suddenly to switch over from building in a permanent way with stone and steel to temporary structures of light steel, wood and asbestos, he has to reorganise his ideas… Big temporary buildings mean a new technique… easily erected and… easily dismantled.'[17] Lightweight steel framing, such as was also used for light industrial buildings, clad in asbestos cement sheeting, appeared to be the best choice and the construction was a boon for suppliers such as Sir William Arrol & Co and Turner's Asbestos Cement Ltd.

Tait most likely used as an initial design reference the influential De La Warr Pavilion at Bexhill, for which he had been the competition judge in 1933. Its construction of light steel framing with cladding panels and its formal arrangement of cuboid and glazed drum volumes expressed in up-to-date terms the 'dignity and gaiety' he sought to engender.[18] Another probable influence was the Stockholm Exhibition of 1930, Tait's designs for the frontages of the Colonial pavilions in

Layout of the Empire Exhibition

HES SC1063411

Map of the Empire Exhibition

Bruce Peter collection

PLAN OF EXHIBITION

With Reference Numbers of Certain Buildings

3. Physical Fitness Pavilion.
4. Peace Pavilion.
8. Administration Offices.
9. An Clachan (Highland Village).
10. North Bandstand Café.
11. North Bandstand.
12. Church of Scotland.
13. Palace of Art.
14. Royal Reception Rooms and Arts Tea-room.
15. Press Club.
17. Paisley Road Main Entrance.
18. Royal Fountain.
19. North Cascade.
20. Scottish Pavilion— South.
21. Scottish Pavilion— North.
23. B.B.C.
24. The Times
25. Bellahouston Drive Entrance.
26. Concert Hall.
27. United Kingdom Government Pavilion.
28. Telephone Exchange.
29. Technical Offices.
32. City of Glasgow Pavilion.
34. Scottish Milk Marketing Board Model Dairy.
38. Palace of Industries— West.
42. Agriculture, Fisheries and Forestry.
43. Cinema.
44. Mosspark Boulevard Main Entrance.
46. West African Colonies.
47. Southern Rhodesia and East Africa.
48. Empire Tea Pavilion.
49. Malaya, British West Indies, Composite Colonial Exhibits.
51. Lake and Pylons.
52. Union of South Africa.
53. New Zealand.
54. Canada.
55. Ireland.
56. Australia.
57. South Bandstand.
62. British Railways.
67. Palace of Industries— North.
68. Post Office.
70. Burma.
72. Ministry of Labour.
73. Post Office Exhibit.
74. Women of the Empire Pavilion.
75. Atlantic Restaurant.
76. Tower of Empire.
77. Roman Catholic Pavilion.
78. Garden Club.
79. Grand Staircase.
80. South Cascade.
83. Georgic Restaurant.
84. Army and Royal Air Force Pavilion.
85. Christian Science.
86. Episcopal Church of Scotland.
88. Palace of Engineering.
94. Coal Pavilion.
96. Rubber Pavilion.
97. Amusements Park.
98. Amusements Park Restaurant.
99. Dance Hall.
100. Car Park.
102. Information Bureaux.
104. Amusement Park

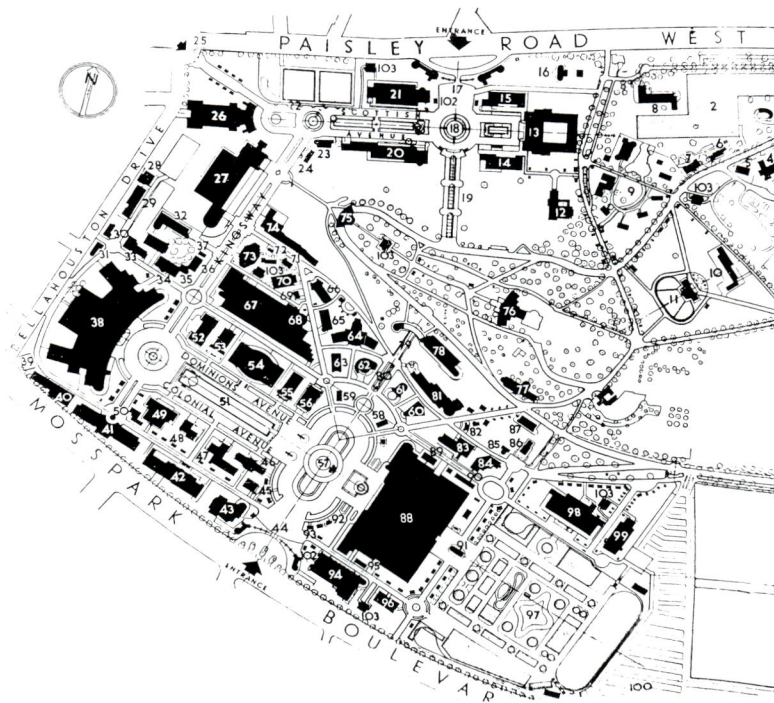

particular being very similar to some of those created for it by Erik Gunnar Asplund, Sven Markelius and their colleagues. Moreover, it too was distinguished by 'scores of banners and murals, bright sunshades and awnings, and hundreds of thousands of flowers' which Tait also specified for Bellahouston. He wanted 'John Citizen' during his visit to 'consider himself on holiday' and to be able 'to escape from everyday things'.[19] This desired atmosphere would be achieved architecturally by 'long, clean lines without any fussiness' and the use of 'a uniform colour scheme' to cover the whole exhibition.[20] Tait justified his aesthetic approach for the pavilions' exterior faces in perfect modernist terms:

> Good building and good architecture are simply the honest use of materials you have to handle… Big temporary buildings mean a new technique. The buildings at Bellahouston are therefore ones which are suited to the function they have to fulfil and the materials from which they are made. They are long and low, because light steelwork lends itself to big spans. They have great sweeping lines…[21]

Perhaps wishing to counter culturally conservative readers' suspicions of 'modernism by the back door', he added that 'some people may call them modernist. That is a word I do not like. In this case it means nothing, for the design has been conditioned by function and materials, and not by time.'[22] This too was a typical modernist justification, but one with which it was hard to argue, not least because 'function' was a rather nebulous concept.

Tait's stylistic approach was reflective of what was being produced by way of new architecture throughout the British Empire in the second half of the 1930s, to which he himself contributed. From India to Canada, and from South Africa to Australia, Art Deco and moderne buildings were being built in substantial numbers, many examples being significantly bigger and fancier than the largest ones in Britain itself – and in some instances their architects were Scots-born and trained. For example, in Vancouver in Canada, George Colvill Nairne (1884–1953) from Inverness co-designed numerous significant Art Deco edifices, including the 17-storey Georgia Medical Dental Building, completed in 1929, and the 23-storey Marine Building, finished

Marine Building, Vancouver
George Colvill Nairne, 1930

in 1930. Nairne's partner was John Young McCarter (1886–1981), a Canadian of Scots descent. In Cape Town in South Africa, meanwhile, William Hood Grant (1879–1957), who was born and educated in Dundee, emigrating in 1901, was responsible for several impressive Art Deco blocks, such as the Commercial Union Insurance Building of 1930 and the Commonwealth Building of 1938. Grant's architectural partner there from 1903 was Donald MacGillivray (1871–1949) from Muir of Ord in Ross-shire, who in 1907 moved to Bulawayo in Rhodesia (now Zimbabwe), designing in the 1930s Art Deco buildings there and in Salisbury (now Harare) in partnership with his son, Ian Donald MacGillivray (1901–1968). In Hong Kong, Richard McNeil Henderson (1886–1972), a civil and mechanical engineer who had

Commercial Union Insurance Building, Cape Town
William Hood Grant, 1930

Jonathan Boonzaier

Commonwealth Building and Colosseum Theatre, Cape Town
William Hood Grant, 1938

Jonathan Boonzaier

Wan Chai Market, Hong Kong
Richard McNeil Henderson, 1937

Bruce Peter

arrived from Glasgow in 1911, was made Director of Public Works in 1932 and was licensed as an Approved Architect under the Hong Kong system, in which role he was involved in the design and construction of numerous buildings, including the streamline moderne Wan Chai and Central Markets, which opened in 1937 and 1938 respectively.[23] In India, the British government's architects George Wittet (1878–1926) of Perthshire and John Begg, who was born in Bo'ness, supported the foundation of The Indian Institute of Architects in Bombay in 1917, which in 1925 gained affiliation with the RIBA. The Institute nurtured a first generation of Indian modern architects, whose striking Art Deco designs transformed the city in the 1930s when a large new district was built on land reclaimed from the Arabian Sea.

Back at Bellahouston, between the springs of 1937 and 1938, a remarkably focused and coordinated civil engineering and construction effort transformed the park into the most complete and spectacular display of the moderne style in interwar Britain. Reviewing the outcome in the *Architectural Review*, the editor and renowned writer on buildings J M Richards was generous in his praise for what was achieved and he attributed the success to Tait's having 'played the role of architect in the widest sense' in realising a high degree of visual and spatial coordination.[24] He observed approvingly that 'the rectangle … of the standard asbestos sheet formed a unit on which all buildings were based as on a grid, in plan and elevation'. Although its use might be criticised for 'making the exhibition appear to be made of cardboard', nonetheless, 'the light and temporary appearance that results … is exactly the quality exhibition architecture should have'.[25]

South Cascade, Tower of Empire and Garden Club, Empire Exhibition

Thomas S Tait of Sir John Burnet, Tait & Lorne and Launcelot Ross, 1938

Courtesy of Ian Johnston

North Entrance turnstiles, Empire Exhibition
Thomas S Tait of Sir John Burnet, Tait & Lorne, 1938
Courtesy of Ian Johnston

Writing in 1988, the design historian Paul Greenhalgh coined the term 'ephemeral vista' to describe in essence the views that visitors to such great exhibitions experienced.[26] The implied paradox of spectacular layout, offset by flimsy, temporary construction was as true of this event as it was of most of the others of its era. Writing for British *Vogue*, Raymond Mortimer captured the effect achieved:

> You go through the turnstile, and at once you are in another civilisation, separated by continents, by centuries, from the sulky, soot-blackened granite [sic] of Victorian Glasgow. Flags and pennons fluttering, fountains soaring like towers, towers throwing like fountains, multi-coloured pavilions like giant models of the diagrams of Euclid, colonnades curving like the fuselage of an air-liner, a restaurant in the shape of a ship, floodlit trees that seem the painted setting for *A Midsummer Night's Dream* – the entire effect is gay, welcoming, and, so to speak, 'future'.[27]

This was possible because 'buildings that are here to-day and gone to-morrow can afford to be blue and duck's-egg green and fanciful… They are scenery, a dress-rehearsal of architecture… At Glasgow, Britannia has thrown the coal-scuttle off her head and tilted a yachting-cap in its place; stripped the encumbering draperies, and emerged, rejuvenated, in very well-cut white drill shorts'.[28]

In *SMT Magazine and Scottish Country Life*, Alastair Borthwick informed would-be visitors that 'Facing you as you enter… are the Cascades – seventeen waterfalls pouring 400 feet down the hillside – and the Grand Staircase, which is a double flight of steps running up either side of the cascades'.[29] Soaring above these at the crest of Bellahouston Hill was the exhibition's 'sensational and symbolic centrepiece' – the 300-feet-high Tower of Empire, which Thomas S Tait designed with assistance from Launcelot Ross

Illuminated Tower of Empire, Empire Exhibition
Thomas S Tait of Sir John Burnet, Tait & Lorne
and Launcelot Ross, 1938
HES SC2535960

and from the structural engineer James Mearns.[30] During construction, the tower's complex steel skeleton gave little hint of the dramatic effect which would be achieved once it was clad in silvery metal-surfaced ribbed asbestos panels, which ordered its form into a succession of overlapping planes soaring upward. In height, it was equivalent to a skyscraper – a building type most Scots would have known only from illustrations in newspapers and magazines – but the effect of slenderness Tait achieved also made it suggestive of some sort of futuristic science fiction fantasy structure that might be used to tether airships, for example. Its design captured the imaginations of all who saw it and it was undoubtedly the exhibition's one truly awe-inspiring building. Borthwick marvelled at Tait's design, which was 'so slender that it is difficult to believe that you may share the top galleries with six hundred people'.[31] At its summit, a vane to counteract

wind torque appeared to pierce the sky. From the galleries, commanding views could be enjoyed to a 'frieze of mountains right on the horizon', including Ben More and even Ben Cruachan, 70 miles away.[32] By night, the whole ensemble was aglow with 'coloured lights, reflected by mirrors; and the colours are constantly changing. Submarine lights below the lake play constantly. Every building is floodlit. Each of the hundreds of trees on the crest of the hill is floodlit in colour. And above them all is the Tower, every inch of it lit, with a beam shooting upwards from its crest which is visible half-way across the country.'[33]

Palace of Engineering, Empire Exhibition
Thomas S Tait of Sir John Burnet, Tait & Lorne and
Launcelot Ross with murals by C L Davidson, 1938

The Dominions and Colonial Avenues vista

The Dominions and Colonial Avenues formed the grandest of the Empire Exhibition's three main axial vistas. The lake in the centre was 'over 400 feet long, and sprayed by a score of fountains. At one end is a fountain which spouts its jet of water, not vertically, but in a long arc which travels a hundred feet… Scores of banners line the avenues and the place is blazing with flowers'.[34] At the eastern end, next to the main entrance from Mosspark Boulevard, the Palace of Engineering, another major contribution by Tait and Launcelot Ross, was the exhibition's largest building, though constructed in just three months.[35] It was entered through six square columns set in a proscenium-like recess in its monumental frontage. The curved lower wings on either side were adorned with strikingly expressionistic Art Deco murals by the illustrator C L Davidson (d 1941); these depicted the liner *Queen Mary* and the battleship HMS *Hood*, surrounded by other products of modern Clydeside engineering.[36] (Otherwise employed by *The Bulletin* newspaper, Davidson had also recently illustrated a

children's adventure story, *Aboard the Bulger*, by the Scottish novelist Anna Scott-Moncrieff.[37]) Projecting outward to the left of the frontage was a restaurant seating 600, the exterior of which featured a rounded glazed drum at one end while the interior had 'Indian red walls, turquoise doors [and] draped curtains'.[38] In the lofty display hall to the rear, the lattice framework of columns and girders provided a suitably engineered setting. Among these, a key exhibit was a 230-ton steel ingot, appearing to enter a fiery furnace. The displays otherwise included a commemoration of the Greenock engineer James Watt, examples of shipbuilding, civil and structural engineering, including the design of bridges, and recent developments in electrical engineering and communications.[39] Reporting in *Vogue*, Raymond Mortimer admired 'propellers that are much more beautiful than most sculpture, and an irresistible collection of model ships from John Brown and other great Scottish shipbuilders'.[40]

Between the Palace of Engineering and the lake, the bandstand, designed by the architect and architectural acoustics pioneer Hope Bagenal (1888–1979), was a single curved wedge, coming straight out of the ground, then curving to form a canopy which reflected the sound towards the seated audience. This was adorned with a whimsical painted composition of musical instruments and notation.

Finishing the Western end of the vista, the Palace of Industries (West), designed by James Taylor Thomson, had a contrastingly horizontal emphasis, its concave curving frontage joining together three separate display halls to the rear, arranged in a splayed E-shaped plan. The cream, pale green and pink colour scheme was devised by John Christie of Guthrie & Wells, who also designed murals, including one depicting the 'Angel of Energy', on the frontage.[41] Within, beneath glazed clerestories, were 'hundreds of stands showing anything from lawnmowers to lipstick'.[42] Their overall effect was much like a conventional trade fair of the kinds frequently held in Glasgow's Kelvin Hall or at Earl's Court and Olympia in London. At one end was a Restaurant and Milk Bar, decorated in pink and turquoise and with seating for 500.[43]

Bandstand, Empire Exhibition
Philip Hope Edward Bagenal, 1938
Courtesy of Ian Johnston

Palace of Industries (West), Empire Exhibition
James Taylor Thomson with murals by John Christie of Guthrie & Wells, 1938
Courtesy of Ian Johnston

Palace of Engineering, Empire Exhibition
Thomas S Tait of Sir John Burnet, Tait & Lorne, 1938
Courtesy of Ian Johnston

Illuminated fountains between the Dominions and Colonial Avenues
Thomas S Tait of Sir John Burnet, Tait & Lorne, 1938
Courtesy of Ian Johnston

Dominions Avenue with the Canada Pavilion and Palace of Industries (West), Empire Exhibition
Thomas S Tait of Sir John Burnet, Tait & Lorne and James Taylor Thomson, 1938
Courtesy of Ian Johnston

Ireland Pavilion, Empire Exhibition
Sir John Burnet, Tait & Lorne, 1938
Courtesy of Ian Johnston

Along the length of Dominions Avenue were national pavilions in a variety of typically moderne shapes devised by Tait and his colleagues after discussions with the commissioning nations, all rendered in pastel shades with darker colour accents. The frontages of Australia's large cream-painted, bunker-like pavilion featured two slanting, internally lit red fins. Inside was a model of Sydney Harbour Bridge, the portals of which Tait had also designed, with ferries passing under and cars and trains moving across. There was also an Australian bush scene with a 'forest filled with native living birds' (which were, of course, in cages).[44] Ireland's more modest pavilion contained a model for a new trans-Atlantic airport at Shannon.[45] The biggest of the group belonged to Canada, for which Tait had produced three different proposals. The one selected was a symmetrical composition with a fin-shaped tower as its centrepiece.[46] The entire structure, apart from the steel framework, was imported, the Canadians being particularly proud of the effect achieved by the asbestos cladding. Unfortunately, during erection in January 1938, it was severely damaged in a storm, necessitating the quick ordering of replacement materials for a rebuild.[47] Upon entering, visitors saw a giant mural depicting idealised images of Canadian life and culture. The National Parks Bureau showed stuffed animals in a diorama and 30 Canadian firms exhibited their wares.[48] The greatest attraction for visitors, however, were four mounted policemen, who perhaps reminded them of the 1936 romantic hit film *Rose Marie* (in which a 'Mountie', played by Nelson Eddy, succeeded in getting his girl, Janette MacDonald). New Zealand's pavilion had stylised versions of Māori *pouwhenua* (land poles) outside while, within, there were prosaic displays of natural resources and food exports.[49] In the *Architectural Review* J M Richards caustically dismissed the displays within the Dominions' pavilions as 'a mixture of conventional… stands and even

New Zealand Pavilion, Empire Exhibition
Sir John Burnet, Tait & Lorne, 1938
Courtesy of Ian Johnston

more pathetically… of national product; the familiar accumulations of pyramids of apples, stuffed fish and coloured photographs of spectacular scenery'.[50]

Negotiations had been required with regard to each pavilion's style, though nearly all exhibitors accepted Tait's overall moderne design concept. South Africa, however, insisted on building a replica of an old Dutch settler's farmhouse, to design which it employed the architect James Miller and his son, George, both of whom could quite easily have instead produced a moderne solution to harmonise with the others. The displays inside included gold and diamonds, grapes, peaches, citrus fruit and wine.[51] There were also 15 busts of 'typical members of native tribes' and examples

Australia Pavilion, Empire Exhibition
Sir John Burnet, Tait & Lorne, 1938
Courtesy of Ian Johnston

of sculpture and painting by modern South African artists.[52] *Scottish Field*'s correspondent, the conservative George Scott-Moncrieff, considered the pavilion to have 'quite the best individual exterior at Bellahouston … Compared with it, any of the others, if isolated from its surroundings, would appear gimcrack and flashy, although together they are admirable'.[53] South Africa's choice of stylistic traditionalism over modernity was more a reflection of the taste of those doing the choosing than of the architectural situation in the nation itself, in whose cities several notable Art Deco and moderne edifices had recently been constructed – but one would not have known this by viewing what was chosen for display in Glasgow.

A short walk away from South Africa, tucked discreetly behind the Palace of Industries (North) was the Burma Pavilion. This was the only other national pavilion to diverge markedly from the exhibition's predominant moderne aesthetic, appearing from the front as a traditional temple building with highly ornate roof eves appended to an otherwise quite mundane rectangular structure with a pitched tiled roof. The location was a political consequence of Burma's wish to be certain that it would not risk being next to an Indian pavilion, were one to have been built.[54]

Opposite the pavilions of the Dominions was Colonial Avenue, where the general style tended more towards stripped back neoclassicism than moderne, there being a dearth of curves but instead plentiful rectangular columns and deep cornices, suggestive of shade in the tropics (but also proving useful in giving shelter from Glaswegian downpours). The Colonial Hall contained exhibits by Malaya (part of current-day Malaysia), the West Indies, Cyprus, Malta, Ceylon (Sri Lanka), North Borneo (Indonesia), the Falkland Islands, Somaliland (part of Somalia), Bechuanaland (part of Cape Province in South Africa), St Helena and Hong Kong. These included a tropical scene with rubber and mango trees, cooking demonstrations and displays of indigenous arts and crafts. The Tea Pavilion of the Empire Tea Marketing Expansion Bureau promoted tea imports from not only India and Ceylon but even the Dutch East Indies, which were interlopers from another empire altogether.

Southern Rhodesia's pavilion contained one main exhibit – a replica of Victoria Falls, 120 feet wide and 14 feet deep, cascading at a rate of one-and-a-half million gallons a day. For added realism, submarine propellers churned up the rapids below the falls and

Burma Pavilion, Empire Exhibition
Sir John Burnet, Tait & Lorne, 1938
Courtesy of Ian Johnston

Rhodesia Pavilion, Empire Exhibition
Sir John Burnet, Tait & Lorne, 1938
Courtesy of Ian Johnston

chemicals produced foam while lights played on steam to make rainbows and the roar was recreated with loudspeakers. The overall effect was 'almost alarmingly realistic'.[55] By comparison, the joint pavilion of the West African Colonies of Gambia, Sierra Leone, Gold Coast and Nigeria was more mundane, though the Nigerian government employed Tait personally to design its display, which emphasised its timber production. The nations of the Empire occupying individual, bespoke pavilions were thus nearly all ones where white populations dominated, implicitly reflecting the racialised structure of British imperialism, which the exhibition's veneer of modernity could only partially conceal.

Colonial Pavilion, Empire Exhibition
Sir John Burnet, Tait & Lorne, 1938
Courtesy of Ian Johnston

Nigeria display, Colonial Pavilion, Empire Exhibition
Thomas S Tait of Sir John Burnet, Tait & Lorne, 1938
Courtesy of Ian Johnston

The Kingsway vista

The Kingsway axis, running north–south, commenced with the Palace of Industries (North), which stretched back in parallel with the rears of the pavilions lining Dominions Avenue. It was a late addition to accommodate an overspill of exhibitors and so Tait delegated its design to Jack Coia of Gillespie, Kidd & Coia, who was already drawing up a Roman Catholic church for elsewhere in the exhibition. Whereas the firm's typical output of churches combined modernised Romanesque details and Dutch-style geometric brickwork – St Peter in Chains at Ardrossan, built concurrently with the exhibition and consecrated in October 1938, being a fine example – for the Palace, Coia produced an appropriately structurally expressive solution.[56] With hindsight, its gently curved aircraft hangar-like roof appears to have been among the exhibition's more prescient structures, moving beyond moderne and perhaps towards the contemporary idiom used widely at the 1951 Festival of Britain. The entrance to the Palace was via a rust-coloured half-drum with glazing at one end. Within, the Scottish

Kingsway with the South Africa Pavilion and Palace of Industries (North), Empire Exhibition
Thomas S Tait of Sir John Burnet, Tait & Lorne, 1938
Courtesy of Ian Johnston

Furniture Manufacturers' Association exhibited changing displays by the leading cabinetmakers in the entrance area, while in the main hall the Scottish Committee of the Council for Art and Industry had a large stand devoted to Scottish domestic wares in general. It also financed the erection of two fully furnished houses; one was a model country house with a spacious entrance hall containing a curved staircase, two reception rooms, three bedrooms, a bathroom, a maid's room, a kitchen, pantry stores and an adjoining garage, while the other was a model working-class house of considerably more modest proportions and fit-out.[57] Although the Committee was apparently satisfied at a job well done, the worldlier *Vogue* critic, Raymond Mortimer, was appalled, warning readers planning to visit these displays that they should:

United Kingdom Government Pavilion, Empire Exhibition
Herbert J Rowse, 1938
Courtesy of Ian Johnston

**United Kingdom Government Pavilion,
Empire Exhibition**
Herbert J Rowse, 1938
Courtesy of Ian Johnston

**Coal Hall in United Kingdom Government Pavilion,
Empire Exhibition**
Misha Black, 1938
Bruce Peter collection

prepare… for a shock. Some people no doubt will appreciate the tartan tea-cosies, Modernistic stair carpets, the trays so ingeniously made of butterfly wings… The foreign visitor to Glasgow cannot fail to be impressed by our skill in the manufacture of pumps and submarines and boilers… Could he not be equally impressed by our chintzes and our rayons, our china, our glass, our carpets, our wallpapers and our clothes?

Viewed across a pond, the United Kingdom Government Pavilion on Kingsway by the prominent Liverpool architect Herbert J Rowse (1887–1963) was in a monumental moderne idiom akin to his Mersey Tunnel portals and Liverpool Concert Hall, completed in 1934 and 1939 respectively – and also rather similar to the new architecture of Mussolini's Italy. The biggest of the national pavilions, it was 450 feet long, equal to the length of St Paul's Cathedral and three times the size of the British Pavilion at the 1937 Paris Exhibition.[58] Accessed by a bridge, the main entrance was flanked by gilded lions of dubious stylistic merit while at the opposite end, above the exit, there was a bas relief of Britannia. Within, the displays were devised by the up-and-coming London-based designer, Misha Black (1910–1977), for whom providing exhibition content and interpretation were particular talents and specialisms. (After the Second World War, Black co-founded Design Research Unit, a leading

General Post Office Pavilion, Empire Exhibition
GPO Architects and HM Office of Works, 1938

Courtesy of Ian Johnston

British design agency, and coordinated a large part of the 1951 Festival of Britain Southbank Exhibition in London.) The pavilion's entrance hallway contained what was believed to be the largest spinning globe ever constructed which revolved 'serenely in its starlight space without visible means of support, showing the countries of the world in their eternal journeying from day into night and night into day. It is one of the most fascinating things at Bellahouston…'[59] Beyond were four exhibition halls, one being a 'Fitter Britain' display featuring an 11-foot-tall mechanical man with a pump for a heart, cameras for eyes and bellows for lungs which 'rival[ed] the metal woman of *Metropolis* … Frankenstein would be a circus midget beside him.'[60] This was made by Richard Huws (1902–1980), a Welsh-born, Liverpool-based shipyard engineer who became a sculptor and was noted for his ingenious kinetic and mechanical designs. In another hall, the Shipping display featured a full-size ship's bridge with captain and first officer on duty, but where visitors could handle the controls, and also a cavitation tunnel to show research into more efficient ship's propellers.[61] There followed scientific exhibits focusing on biology and genetics.[62] With hindsight, the latter would appear to have been morally dubious, but the subject was of great fascination at the time.

On the opposite side of Kingsway was the General Post Office's attention-grabbing pillar-box red and gold pavilion, which was designed in-house by its own architects, who refused to cooperate with Tait. In the *Architectural Review*, J M Richards regretted this decision and castigated its 'aggressive and vulgar' appearance and 'old-fashioned jazz-modern design' which he found to be 'quite out of keeping with the general architectural setting'.[63] What Richards found architecturally reprehensible, other less exacting critics considered appropriately novel. For example, the *Scottish Field* journalist Alexander Reid admired what looked to him to be a 'futuristic facade' behind which was 'displayed an extraordinary variety of the GPO's latest equipment – the teleprinter, a fascinating representation of the TIM clock, among a score of others – and opportunity has been taken to show the extent and reliability of the Air Mail services, now multiplying rapidly'.[64] The GPO Film Unit, led by the innovative Scottish director John Grierson, had recently made *Night Mail* with poetic commentary by W H Auden and a soundtrack by Benjamin Britten; this was among the films shown.[65]

Adjacent was the contrastingly discreet and demure Women of the Empire pavilion in dove grey, its complex multi-level interior layout and lack of gratuitously attention-seeking external gestures being closer to the modernist mainstream than most others.[66] The designer was Margaret Brodie, 'a gifted product of the Glasgow School of Architecture', according to the critic Anne Bruce, who recorded in *SMT Magazine and Scottish Country Life* the pavilion's layout and characteristics:

> Her L-shaped plan embraces … sections for Empire, Commercial, and Domestic exhibits, while adjoining the main building a handsome fashion theatre designed like a Greek arena will be the scene of many wonderful dress shows, displaying the creations of leading British fashion experts. Inside the Pavilion, the three principal sections lead out of each other on different levels, and a turning to the left connects with a wide circular gallery, which holds the fine collection of historical costumes, and overlooks the fashion theatre.[67]

The interior colour scheme of rose, cream and French grey was selected for being 'kindest to feminine complexions'.[68] The idea for the pavilion originated with Katherine Bruce, the Countess of Elgin and Kincardine, who was convenor of the Women's Committee, her vision for it being 'a haven to entertain and enrich the mind'.[69] As well as displays about the 'professions, crafts and trades practised by women all over the Empire' there was also one about 'the new English silkworm industry, started by Lady Hart Dyke, whose silk was used for the Coronation robes'.[70] In the courtyard, a bas relief by Norman John Forrest (1898–1972) depicted the rise of woman, from bondage to freedom, while in the interiors there were decorative panels by the stained glass artist Sadie McLellan (1914–2007).[71] Alastair Borthwick noted that 'men should not despair when their wives move towards [the Fashion] Theatre. The mannequin parades

Women of the Empire Pavilion and Atlantic Restaurant, Empire Exhibition
Margaret Brodie of Sir John Burnet, Tait & Lorne and Thomas W Marwick, 1938
Courtesy of Ian Johnston

show the best of British fashions, and the display of period dress is beautiful and, to the male eye, frequently very funny. The bustles are grand.'[72]

At the junction of Kingsway and the Scottish Avenue were the pavilions of the BBC and of *The Times*, representing emergent and established British media institutions. While the former presented an entirely glazed curving frontage, the latter, which was the work of the traditionalist Clough Williams-Ellis, more resembled part of a First World War cemetery in Flanders and stylistically would have fitted in well at the previous British Empire Exhibition at Wembley in 1924.

The Scottish Avenue vista

Adjacent to the Paisley Road West entrance, the two Scotland Pavilions on the Scottish Avenue, designed by Tait with interiors by Basil Spence, mirrored each other in plan and elevation and were patriotically shaded in pale and dark blue. Each had a slender fin-shaped tower articulating the junction between the entrance block and exhibition hall, their design echoing the forms of the Tower of Empire. Such fins were indeed a repeated leitmotif throughout the exhibition, appearing in various sizes and colours on various other pavilions, at significant junctions and denoting the stairways on the flanks of Bellahouston Hill.

The hallway of the Scotland (South) pavilion contained a statue of the young St Andrew by Archibald Dawson, who died shortly after its completion. On the window behind, the shadow of the old St Andrew was sandblasted, appearing as though watching over his younger self. From there, visitors entered the Hall of History, which was hung with banners and contained displays about Scotland's past since prehistoric times. Period rooms were 'completely furnished as they would have been at different stages in the country's history'.[73] By contrast, the outwardly similar Scotland (North) pavilion was filled with propaganda for public services from birth to old age. In the entrance hall, a large figurative sculpture by Thomas Whalen entitled 'Service' clutched the torch of Knowledge and staff of Health in her hands. In one section of the main display hall, innovations in childcare, the reduction of infant mortality and education were celebrated. There was a sculpture by Andrew Dods (1898–1976) allegorising Youth and also compositions of

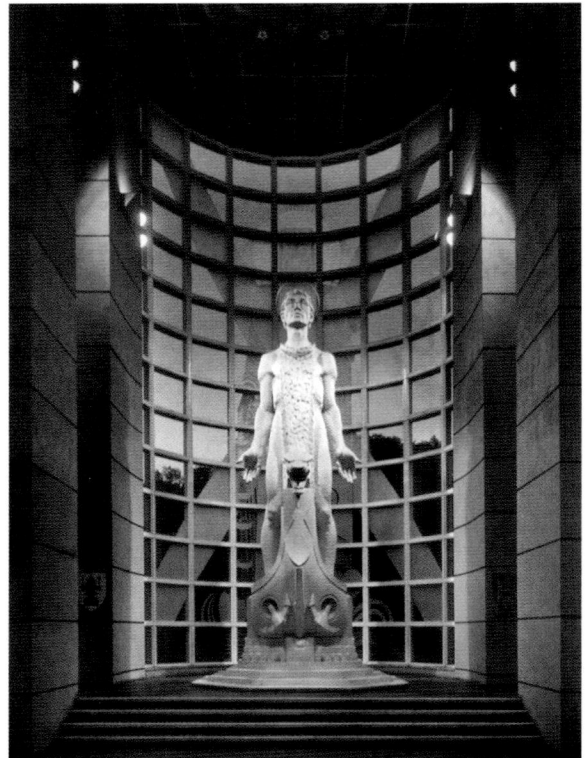

Statue of St Andrew in the Scotland (South) Pavilion, Empire Exhibition
Archibald Dawson, 1938
Courtesy of Ian Johnston

Statue of Youth with photomontage in the Scotland (North) Pavilion, Empire Exhibition
Andrew Dods, 1938
Courtesy of Ian Johnston

Scottish Avenue with Scotland Pavilions and Concert Hall, Empire Exhibition
Thomas S Tait of Sir John Burnet, Tait & Lorne and James Taylor Thomson, 1938
Courtesy of Ian Johnston

Scotland Pavilions viewed from Tower of Empire, Empire Exhibition
Thomas S Tait of Sir John Burnet, Tait & Lorne, 1938
Courtesy of Ian Johnston

Palace of Art, Empire Exhibition
Launcelot Ross, 1938
Courtesy of Ian Johnston

photographs showing the work of Scottish charitable and social organisations.[74] In another section, a relief map of Scotland was sunk beneath floor level with lights, models and neon tubing to show the nation's infrastructures of railways, airways, broadcasting stations and lighthouses.[75]

Facing the ends of the Scotland pavilions was the Palace of Art, which Launcelot Ross designed. Intended as the exhibition's legacy building, its relatively solid construction from blocks of grey reconstructed stone (comprising granite chippings in cement with a polished surface) with shallow-pitched roofs made it somewhat more reminiscent of recent German buildings by the National Socialist neoclassical architect Albert Speer (1905–1981) than the other light and temporary asbestos-faced edifices.[76] Square in plan with long galleries arranged around a central courtyard, it contained what was claimed to be 'the first representative show of Scottish old masters ever gathered under one roof.'[77] Also nearby was the pavilion of the Church of Scotland, which built a replica of a

typical Danish rural church of the fifteenth century – mostly from asbestos, of course. By contrast, the Roman Catholic church by Jack Coia appeared reminiscent of contemporaneous Italian streamlined design. Also typical of recent practice there was the liberal adornment of the exterior with murals of biblical scenes.

Flanking the Palace of Art's main facade were the Press Club and the Royal Reception Rooms, the latter consisting of an entrance hall, lounge, dining room, a boudoir for the Queen and a retiring room for the King. The interiors, designed by Tait, were notable for their fine finishes and detailing.[78] The entrance hall flooring was in narrow strips of contrasting Nigerian veneers ranging from a creamy colour to dark brown. The doorway had sapele pilasters and an obobo cornice. In the lounge, the walls and floor were of opepi, the

Royal Reception Room, Empire Exhibition
Thomas S Tait of Sir John Burnet, Tait & Lorne, 1938
Courtesy of Ian Johnston

panelling interspersed with horizontal fillets in dull gold. Tait designed all of the furniture which Wylie & Lochhead made using opepi, agba, obechi, sida, obobo and pearwood. The curtains were of a Donald Bros Old Glamis design named Foam in turquoise and old gold.[79] They were the exhibition's grandest expressions of moderne interior design and furnishing. The spaces demonstrated Tait's refined taste and attention to detail and also the abilities of leading Scottish craft and industrial makers of interior adornments.

James Taylor Thomson was responsible for the Concert Hall, located at the opposite extremity of the Scottish Avenue. In contrast to the somewhat conservative Palace of Art, it was among the structures tending more towards modernism than moderne, being a rectangular volume in front of which slender pilotis columns held aloft a large box with a gently curving glazed frontage containing a restaurant.[80] Despite its modern comforts, attendances initially were so poor that consideration was given to closing it down, until variety shows were introduced and these proved to be resoundingly popular.[81] The ornamental fountain in front contained a sculpture of dolphins and a dancing nymph by Charles d'Orville Pilkington Jackson.

The southern perimeter and Bellahouston Hill

On the southern edge of the site, behind the pavilions facing Colonial Avenue, and on the flanks of Bellahouston Hill, were a larger number of pavilions of various sizes, promoting particular industries, companies and organisations. Several were located along the southern perimeter wall with their backs to Mosspark Boulevard. Of these, the Coal Pavilion was adjacent to the Palace of Engineering and likewise designed by Tait, using an exposed structure and curving roof similar to Coia's Palace of

Coal Pavilion, Empire Exhibition
Thomas S Tait of Sir John Burnet, Tait & Lorne, 1938
Courtesy of Ian Johnston

Rubber Pavilion, Empire Exhibition
Sir John Burnet, Tait & Lorne, 1938
Courtesy of Ian Johnston

Industries (North). Its frontage was distinguished by three pylons, comparable in form to those in front of St Andrew's House in Edinburgh, out of the tops of which sudden jets of steam and smoke shot upwards. These and the glass-fronted entrance and exit with bold three-dimensional lettering in red perhaps hinted at avant-garde Soviet or Italian Futurist architecture. By comparison, the Rubber pavilion, in the south-eastern corner, was dreary, its blocky form doing nothing to suggest the tactility of the material its displays were meant to interpret. On the opposite side of the exhibition entrance were the Empire Cinema by Alister G MacDonald (1898–1993) and the Wool Pavilion, both with corner towers, the latter's surmounted by a sculpture of a Jacob's Ram. MacDonald was the son of the Labour leader and prime minister, Ramsay MacDonald. A graduate of the Slade School of Art and Bartlett School of Architecture, both parts of the University of London, he was well-connected, widely travelled and cosmopolitan. Designing cinemas was his prime speciality (see Chapter 7).[82]

Shipping and Travel Pavilion, Empire Exhibition
Esmé Gordon of Sir John Burnet, Tait & Lorne, 1939
Courtesy of Ian Johnston

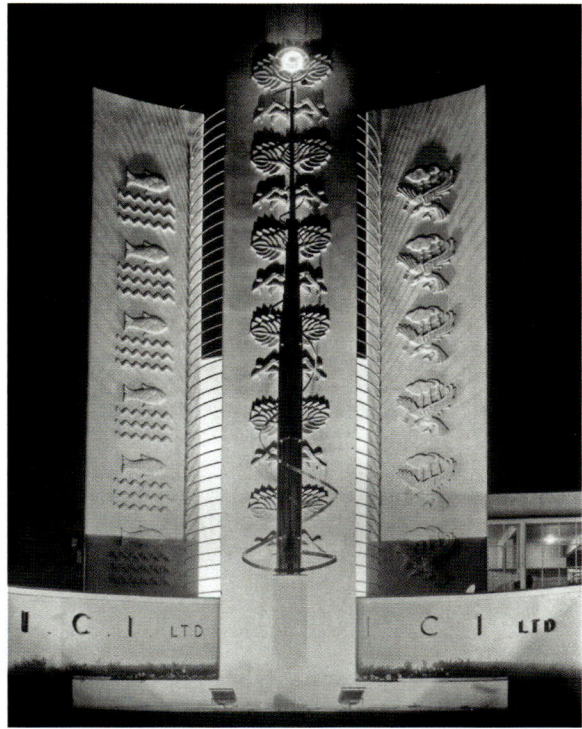

Imperial Chemical Industries Pavilion, Empire Exhibition
Basil Spence, 1938
Courtesy of Ian Johnston

Moving west along the southern perimeter were, in sequence, the Agriculture Pavilion and the Shipping and Travel Pavilion by Esmé Gordon, which had a glazed rotunda and lively facade murals depicting The Spirit of Travel. Although the Exhibition's organisers had hoped that the Aircraft Constructors' Association would co-sponsor a separate pavilion dedicated to air travel, it had refused to cooperate, with the result that aviation was conspicuous for its absence.[83] Finally, the Scottish Co-operative Wholesale Society pavilion – also with a tower – was next to the Palace of Industries (West). Within, the displays tended towards didacticism (in Agriculture, for instance, panels on bacon production in Ulster were unlikely ever to provoke wonderment).

On the sloping southern and western flanks of Bellahouston Hill were yet more, generally smaller pavilions, several of which were of more imaginative

design than the larger structures along the main avenues. To either side of the Southern Cascade and behind the *Glasgow Herald* and *Daily Mail* newspaper pavilions were two minor design triumphs. One of these was the pavilion of Imperial Chemical Industries which Basil Spence devised, showing an early talent for exhibition work that would be applied repeatedly throughout his long and distinguished career.[84] The design featured three pylons, representing air, earth and water. Raymond Mortimer in *Vogue* found it to be 'livelier both inside and out than anything else of its sort'.[85] Directly across the cascade, the 'Big Four' railways (the London, Midland and Scottish; London and North Eastern; Great Western; and Southern), exhibited jointly as 'British Railways', some nine years prior to their nationalisation. Joseph Emberton, a former colleague of Tait, designed their pavilion with a glazed rotunda rising from a single-storey

British Railways Pavilion, Empire Exhibition
Joseph Emberton, 1938
Courtesy of Ian Johnston

lower block, somewhat resembling both Emberton's concurrent designs at Blackpool Pleasure Beach and also recent LMS station architecture. Within was a vast, multi-track model railway, around which Gauge One Bassett-Lowke models clattered at great speed; it was every schoolboy's dream.

Flanking these were the somewhat less demonstrative pavilions erected by Shell-Mex Oil and the Glasgow Corporation Gas Department, while to the rear, slightly higher up the slope, were those of the Distillers Company (designed by Tait and containing a whisky bar), the steelmakers Colvilles and Beardmore, the carpetmaker, James Templeton, the liquor distiller Chivers and the Dunlop Rubber Company. In a happy coincidence, the latter was able to celebrate the jubilee of the invention of the pneumatic tyre by the Scottish veterinary surgeon, John Boyd Dunlop in 1888.[86] While these all provided further variations on the moderne theme, the compact pavilion of the Scottish Motor Traction Company, designed by its own advertising department, hinted at Californian surf culture with its curving, wavy design and a boldly angled roof, on top

of which was mounted a luxury coach with bodywork made by W Alexander & Sons which visitors could inspect by climbing up stairs.[87]

Higher again on the hillside, the exclusive members-only Garden Club, designed by Thomas W Marwick, appeared particularly indebted to the De La Warr Pavilion. At one end of the complex was a shopping rotunda with six small kiosks, linked by a curved canopy to a terraced complex containing a cocktail bar, lounge and restaurant with dancefloor, intended to reproduce 'the surroundings of an elegant country club and … open only to members and their friends'.[88] A spiral staircase led to a roof garden where 'a beautiful background of woodland … with abundance of flowering plants and a fountain [provided] an ideal retreat in the warm days of summer'.[89] The structure was further adorned with sculptures by Hew Lorimer (1907–1993) and Thomas Whalen.

Colvilles and Beardmore Pavilion, Empire Exhibition
Sir John Burnet, Tait & Lorne, 1938
Courtesy of Ian Johnston

Scottish Motor Traction Pavilion, Empire Exhibition
Publicity Department of Scottish Motor Traction, 1938
Courtesy of Ian Johnston

Garden Club, Empire Exhibition
Thomas W Marwick, 1938
Courtesy of Ian Johnston

Atlantic Restaurant, Empire Exhibition
Thomas W Marwick, 1938
Courtesy of Ian Johnston

Jutting out on the western flank of Bellahouston Hill, above the Women of the Empire pavilion, was another exclusive destination, the ship-like Atlantic Restaurant, also designed by Marwick, which was sponsored and operated by the leading Glasgow shipping company Anchor Line.[90] The exterior even had a bow while within were 'pale pink walls with doors of eau-de-nil green. The visitor "going aboard" is immediately transported into the atmosphere of a

luxury liner; meals are served "on deck", where a mast and rigging give colour to the illusion of being at sea, or on the sheltered tea deck above, and the waiters are dressed as stewards. Here one may sit and dream of a

Treetops Restaurant, Empire Exhibition
Thomas S Tait of Sir John Burnet, Tait & Lorne, 1938
Courtesy of Ian Johnston

voyage to the seacoasts of Bohemia in an ideal setting for romantic imaginings.'[91]

Highest of all, at the base of the Tower of Empire, was the Treetops Restaurant, which enclosed mature trees. With regard to its design, Tait recorded that 'for some time we puzzled to know how to plan [it] to avoid the trees which were particularly thick at that point. At one stage we decided to raise the restaurants on stilts which would carry them clear above the trees but later we realised that a much better effect could be obtained if we shortened the stilts and allowed the topmost branches to project upwards through the floor. Now we have the branches growing between the tables.'[92] Tait was evidently proud that no mature trees were felled for the Exhibition and, with hindsight, the approach seems to have been very progressive, aligning with current-day concerns for sustainability. The food critic Mary Fleming, who reviewed the catering provision for *SMT Magazine and Scottish Country Life*, thought that the restaurant gave diners an impression of being 'like Peter Pan and Wendy among the treetops'.[93] Unfortunately, the wet and

stormy weather of 1938 led to gale damage shortly before the Exhibition's closure, when some customers were injured by falling branches crashing through the structure.[94]

Altogether, including kiosks, the Empire Exhibition comprised over 100 different buildings.[95] In addition, lampposts, litter bins, seats and benches were all of bespoke designs, complementing and enhancing the overall aesthetic. The Amusement Park, adjacent, was a separate commercial venture exclusive to Billy Butlin. It occupied a further 16 acres and included the Amusement Park Restaurant, which seated 900 and was decorated in 'coral, sage green, old rose and yellow' to 'make a perpetual summer in its cheerful interior'.[96] Attractions included a Giant Racer capable of 63 mph on a mile-long track, a Rocket Ride, the Wall of Death, the biggest Dodgem track in the world

Speedway ride in the Amusement Park
Billy Butlin, 1938
Courtesy of Ian Johnston

and the Brooklands Racer, which promised the 'thrill of feeling like going at 100 mph in a car you drive yourself'.[97] Many of the rides and sideshows were adorned with ornately painted Art Deco patterns and graphics, updating the baroque of the traditional fairground. Butlin's reflections of Empire were, however, unsophisticated and couched in a manner redolent of the Victorian-era; his 'Savage West Africa' display purporting to present 'Chief Ober Mekewwhe [sic] and his Yoruba Tribe' while the design of the Indian Theatre closely followed the one at the 1901 exhibition. These apparently proved highly popular with a majority of visitors. Nonetheless, it can be imagined that any guests from the West African colonies could have been very offended to discover their culture being represented as savage.

Impact of the Exhibition

Surviving images of the Empire Exhibition suggest in a Glaswegian context an event of unprecedented slickness, colour and cleanliness – but while design aesthetics could be relatively strictly controlled, the prevailing surrounding culture was less amenable to change. Fifty extra police officers were recruited to supervise at the event and this proved a wise precaution as arrests for fighting and drunken and disorderly behaviour did, of course, occur.[98] The Exhibition's organisers had expected 20 million attendees and 15 million were required to break even, but by the time the exhibition was closed, only a figure of 12 million was achieved.[99] This was in large part because it received only perfunctory press attention outwith Scotland. Writing reflectively in *SMT Magazine and Scottish Country Life*, the polymathic journalist, writer and academic Charles Oakley recalled seeing: 'practically no references to the exhibition in the American press. The worst cut was when *Life* published its only photograph … The caption said "an exhibition at Glasgow, England".[100] By comparison, the forthcoming New York World's Fair of 1939 was receiving substantial coverage in the Scottish press while the Empire Exhibition was still in progress.[101] Most visitors who had travelled to Scotland were from elsewhere in Britain, though some came from overseas.

A further unexpected disappointment was the terrible weather throughout the summer of 1938, with torrential rain, gales and unseasonably low temperatures which naturally deterred would-be attendees. Briefly, consideration was given to reopening in 1939, but the worsening international political context with war looming put paid to that idea. A Peace Pavilion, designed by Alister G MacDonald with a Peace Garden among the trees, had reflected the troubled times, but its pacifist message was in the end a forlorn hope. While some wanted the Tower of Empire to be retained, because of its potential as a guide-mark for enemy aircraft, its demolition was ordered in July of that year.

Looking back on what had been achieved, Oakley felt the exhibition to have been 'something brilliantly, stimulatingly modern, suddenly planted in the midst of a nation which had not seen much new happening' and that it had 'given Scotland a new outlook'.[102] Although some of the displays were of variable merit, the best ones, such as those within the United Kingdom Government Pavilion, had impressed with their 'brilliant colours … well-drawn in hard, clear-cut lines'.[103] Oakley, however, concluded that the exhibition's greatest lesson for Scotland was the benefit of cooperation for a country in which industrial relations often were fractious. 'The remarkable achievement of building the exhibition in a few months, and having it ready on time, was made possible by the joint efforts of many thousands of men and women… the greatest instance of unified effort yet seen in Scotland.'[104]

Another commentator, the Liberal satirical writer and broadcaster A G Macdonell, was less optimistic, noting that despite the exhibition, 22,000 more Scots were unemployed in October 1938 than had been in October 1937 and blaming the nation's sluggish performance on 'a mass of inertia and complacency'.[105] Such growth as could be measured in heavy engineering during 1938 was thanks to new warship orders placed under the government's rearmament programme.[106] In conclusion, he asked rhetorically 'Stands Caledonia where she did?' His answer was 'Yes, she does. But the rest of the world has gone on'.[107]

The outbreak of war and the hiatus in non-essential building that it necessitated meant that the Empire Exhibition came to be looked back upon as a period ensemble, rather than the springboard to a new Scotland that those who planned it had hoped for. The international political situation meant that the demolition of the tower was not unexpected, and the imminent war was causing more pressing worries. By the time that economic and political will for radical updating returned in the 1950s, concepts of what was modern in architecture and planning had moved on. Nonetheless, several of those subsequently involved in Scotland's post-war development would have been visitors, retaining memories of spaciousness, cleanliness, coordination and colour.

CALEDONIAN INSURANCE COMPANY HEAD OFFICE

ST ANDREW SQUARE EDINBURGH

LESLIE GRAHAME-THOMSON A·R·S·A F·R·I·B·A
OF LESLIE GRAHAME-THOMSON & CONNELL · ARCHITECTS EDINBURGH

J NETHERBY GRAHAM DELT

CHAPTER 6
COMMERCIAL AND RETAIL

Art Deco and moderne are conventionally framed primarily as commercial styles, used to make the modern appear desirable at the point of consumption. Despite the challenging economic conditions of the 1930s, much construction and renovation occurred along Scotland's urban commercial streets during the decade. New edifices were often distinguished by bright facade finishes to contrast with their soot-stained neighbours while, at street level, the design of shop fascias underwent a radical revolution with regard to form, materials and graphic design.

Office buildings

In the first three decades of the twentieth century, there were significant expansions in the banking, insurance and financial service industries. Insurers did well from the First World War, charging high premiums to protect at-risk assets. In the 1920s, companies in the finance sector invested in impressive new premises, their architectural aim being to signify establishment security and solidity in an uncertain world. In Glasgow, the leading architects of such properties – especially James Miller and his assistant Richard Gunn and Edward Grigg Wylie of Wright and Wylie – took degrees of inspiration from

Caledonian Insurance Company, St Andrew Square, Edinburgh
Leslie Grahame Thomson & Connell, 1938
HES SC465228

American Beaux Arts-style bank buildings. These used steel framing with facades usually composed of rusticated bases from which rose giant fluted pilasters, the windows recessed in the bays between and interspersed by patterned metal infill panels with deep cornicing around the roofline. Entrance halls, lobbies and stairways made copious use of marble and granite – hard, shiny finishes suggestive of resilience and prosperity.

Wright and Wylie's Scottish Legal Life Assurance Society building, completed in 1931 and filling a whole block bounded by Bothwell, Blythswood and West Campbell streets, is a massive Chicago-style edifice exemplifying these characteristics. The project was designed concurrently with the same architects' Glasgow Dental Hospital, enabling an intriguing comparison between the comparatively light treatment of its Beaux Arts exterior and the very much weightier composition of the Scottish Legal Life frontages. On the main facade facing Bothwell Street, Art Deco was introduced in the form of comparatively minor sculptural panels by Archibald Dawson, depicting Industry, Prudence, Thrift and Courage, inserted among the rusticated stone blocks of the first floor.[1] In the hallway, the pilasters have polychromatic Egyptian capitals, details reminiscent of Alexander 'Greek' Thomson designs in an otherwise marble-lined Beaux Arts-style space.

Miller and Gunn's design for the Commercial Bank of Scotland at the junction of West Nile Street and West George Street, also completed in 1931 and faced

Scottish Legal Life Assurance Society, Bothwell Street, Glasgow
Wright & Wylie, 1931
HES SC1388762

Bas relief sculpture of Prudence, Scottish Legal Life Assurance Society, Glasgow
Archibald Dawson, 1931
Bruce Peter

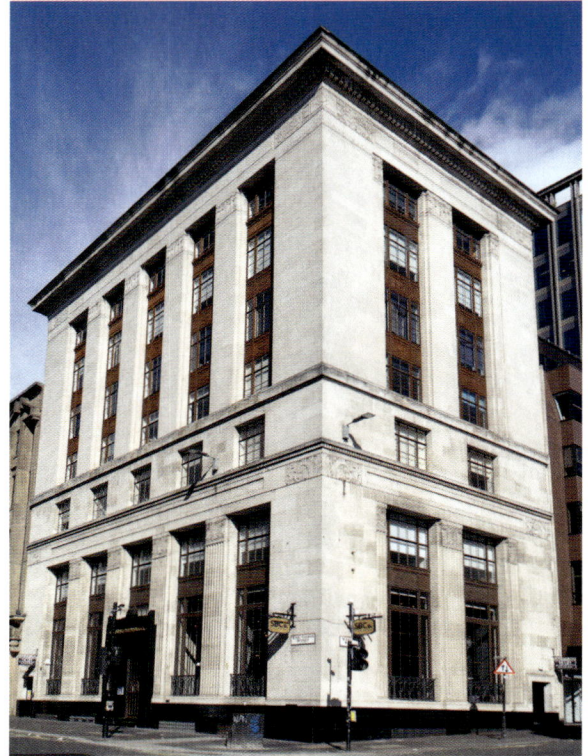

Commercial Bank of Scotland, West George Street and West Nile Street, Glasgow
James Miller and Richard Gunn, 1931
Bruce Peter

in pale creamy-grey Portland stone, likewise retains most of the usual Beaux Arts compositional elements, but replaces neoclassical swags and garlands with Art Deco patterning in low relief. A further Glasgow city-centre property for the same bank and by the same firm of architects at the corner of Bothwell Street and Wellington Street, opened in 1935, is compositionally much more evolved, its frontages, again clad in Portland stone on a granite base, achieving a sense of monumentality by being largely flat.[2] The entrance is accessed between three-storey-high Corinthian columns fronting a deep recess and there are matching fluted pilasters interspersed with fenestration on the return elevation. Above, six Art Deco bas relief panels modelled by Gilbert Bayes and sculpted by Joseph Armitage (1880–1945) depicting 'The Qualities of Man in Society' intersperse windows to form friezes while, above again, a very deep and flat parapet lends a sense of solid mass.[3]

In Edinburgh, the Caledonian Insurance Company's new headquarters by St Andrew's Square, designed by the Edinburgh-trained Leslie Grahame Thomson (1896–1974) and Frank J Connell (1910–1992), was completed in 1938. Its composition has a vertical emphasis, reflecting Thomson's position on modern architecture, as expressed in the RIAS *Quarterly Illustrated* in 1932 in which he argued that 'the mechanistic theory, as propounded by Le Corbusier

Commercial Bank of Scotland, Bothwell Street and Wellington Street, Glasgow
James Miller and Richard Gunn, 1935
Bruce Peter

Commercial Bank of Scotland, West George Street and West Nile Street, Glasgow
James Miller and Richard Gunn, 1931
HES DP061450

Bas relief sculptures on the Commercial Bank of Scotland, Wellington Street, Glasgow
Gilbert Bayes and Joseph Armitage, 1935
Bruce Peter

and others, seems to me fallacious: the whole analogy is false, for a building is a static, and not a dynamic structure'.[4] In 1934, Connell had used money he was awarded as a recipient of the Rutland Prize for architectural draughting to tour the Nordic capitals. Most likely influenced by buildings he encountered in Stockholm and Helsinki, his Caledonian Insurance Company design shows a distinctly Scandinavian national romantic influence. As it was necessary to build within an acceptable timescale and budget, brick construction was selected for the external walls, rather than the stone used for the remainder of the New Town. This was then concealed beneath a hard-looking cladding of granite, the ground floor being faced in black polished blocks while grey slabs cover the five storeys above.[5] The outcome thus appears as though it might have been better suited for an Aberdeen location.

Caledonian Insurance Company, St Andrew Square, Edinburgh
Leslie Grahame Thomson & Connell, 1938
HES SC1208851

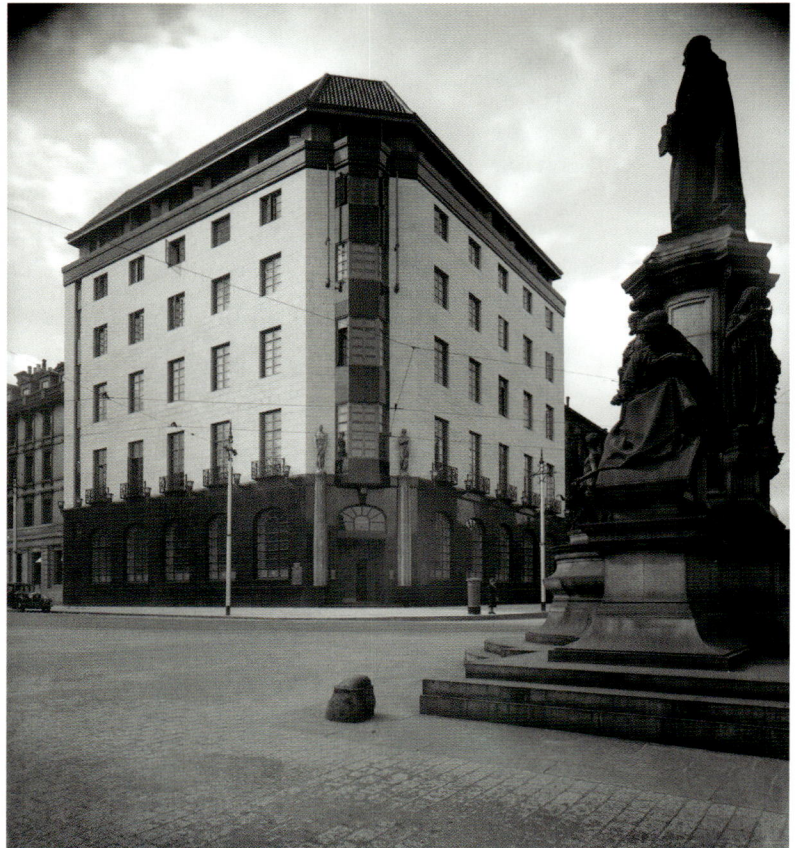

Sculpture on the Caledonian Insurance Company, St Andrew Square, Edinburgh
Alexander Carrick, 1938
Bruce Peter

Detail of carved frieze on doors of the Caledonian Insurance Company, St Andrew Square, Edinburgh
Design possibly by Leslie Grahame Thomson, 1938
Bruce Peter

Nine-foot-tall bronze statues of parent and child figures by Alexander Carrick, which represent Insurance and Security, flank the corner entrance and are mounted on reeded columns. The teak outer doors are carved in Art Deco style with insurance-associated imagery – a building on fire, a motor car, a steam locomotive and an aeroplane.[6]

Arguably the most remarkable banking office to open in 1930s Scotland was the temporary headquarters for the National Bank of Scotland in Edinburgh's George Street, for which the Edinburgh-trained Philip McManus (b 1907) of T P Marwick & Son designed a conversion of an existing building in 1937. The idea was that this would be used until the bank's main premises in St Andrew Square could be renovated. McManus's facade treatment was subtle and sophisticated, its five bays having tall, recessed windows interspersing slender mullions with slightly projecting triangular infill panels between each storey. The upper row of these were adorned with small Art Deco sculptures by Thomas Whalen, above which were vertical slits where the top-floor directors' suite had a narrow balcony. Viewed from a distance, the composition had the appearance of having been folded from card, just like a model kit, but actually the facing comprised slim panels of stone. Inside, the banking hall was moderne with curving corners and horizontal banding in the wall veneer.[7] Despite being planned for a short existence, it actually lasted until the early 1970s, when it was demolished.

In high streets all over Scotland, dozens of regional bank branches were modernised with new Art Deco street frontages and interiors, usually strongly referencing neoclassicism and faced in polished granite, travertine, or reconstructed stone to lend the required sense of sobriety. In addition, a smaller number of new branches were constructed, often using similar finishes. A particularly impressive example is the Commercial Bank of Scotland in Glasgow's Gallowgate, completed in 1937 and the finest of a large number of local premises the bank built in the 1920s and 1930s, nearly all of which were designed by its master of works, James McCallum. Located where the Gallowgate Meat Market had once been, the site's history is commemorated in an Art Deco sculptural

National Bank of Scotland, George Street, Edinburgh
Philip McManus of T P Marwick & Son, 1937
Architectural Press Archive / RIBA Collections

Commercial Bank of Scotland, Gallowgate, Glasgow
James McCallum, 1937
Glasgow City Archive

panel of a bullock's head on the building's corner clock tower. Although in recent decades many such local bank branches have been closed and have since been repurposed, in most instances their frontages survive in good condition on account of their original robust and quite costly design.

As with offices for financial services, the growth of the mass media in the interwar era required an expansion of newspaper offices and printworks. In the period before the First World War, Charles Rennie Mackintosh and his Honeyman and Keppie colleagues had designed new headquarters in Glasgow for the *Daily Record* and *Glasgow Herald* newspapers. By the interwar era the Scottish printed press was, for the most part, solidly established in its existing premises. In the 1930s, Britain's most successful newspaper was the London-based *Daily Express*, owned by the Canadian-born newspaper baron Lord Beaverbrook, which provided news, pithy opinion and illustrated celebrity and fashion features – a combination that millions of readers perceived as modern and in tune with their values and aspirations. In keeping with this up-to-date image, the proprietor commissioned the talented and progressive architect-engineer Sir Owen Williams to design concrete-framed offices for the newspaper's production in London's Fleet Street, in Manchester and in Albion Street in Glasgow, out of which the *Scottish Daily Express* was distributed from 1939 onwards.[8] All of these buildings are distinguished externally by claddings of black Vitrolite glass held in stainless steel strapwork. Initially, the intention was that the Glasgow office would feature an illuminated beacon on its roof, formed of translucent glass blocks, though this was never built. Much later, extra storeys of offices were added, set back from the original street frontage.

Whereas the late-Victorian and Edwardian eras had experienced booms in the speculative construction of office blocks, the comparatively unpropitious economic climate of the 1930s meant that few further examples were then added. A relatively rare exception is Lothian House in Edinburgh, a very large block with shop units along the ground floor and a cinema at one end, occupying the site of an infilled basin at the end of the Union Canal, adjacent to Lothian Road. Its architect was Stewart Kaye (1885–1952) of Stewart Kaye and Walls, who was Dundee-trained and had worked in London and Cardiff before taking over the established Edinburgh practice of Robert Macfarlane Cameron (1866–1920) following the latter's death. Kaye's

Daily Express building, Albion Street, Glasgow
Sir Owen Williams, 1939
Bruce Peter, HES SC2535673

main speciality thereafter was the design of municipal and private housing, most of which was stylistically undistinguished. In contrast, Lothian House, completed in 1939, is an imposing angular Art Deco edifice with boldly detailed stonework surrounding the many window bays, in which the glazing is interspersed by jazzily patterned metal infill. By comparison with the emphatically dignified premises of the financial institutions, its style is rather brash.

In central Glasgow, the area known nowadays as the Merchant City was until the 1970s mostly occupied by warehouses in which commodities were stored and wholesaled. In the mid-1920s and early 1930s a number of reinforced concrete-framed examples in the American Beaux Arts-style were constructed there, a notable group comprising five-to-seven-storey red sandstone-faced blocks along the south side of Wilson Street. Those completed between 1932 and 1937 to designs by James Taylor Thomson and Alexander Hood MacLeod (1889–1941) of Thomson, Sandilands and MacLeod feature Art Deco forms applied to door architraves and to cast infill panels interspersing their metal-famed glazing.

Lothian House, Lothian Road, Edinburgh
Stewart Kaye of Stewart Kaye & Walls, 1939
Bruce Peter

Retail

Very similar compositional approaches were often used for the frontages of the large new retail stores that were built in much greater numbers, reflecting an expanding middle-class consumerism and the greater efficiency of modern factory-based fashion-clothes manufacturing, making mass-produced items relatively cheap and available in quantity. The Art Deco style, as with Art Nouveau before it, was in any case closely associated with fashion retailing, both having originated in Paris and having from the outset been related to French couture imagery. The main entrance to the Paris Exposition across the Pont Alexandre III was lined on both sides with display windows showing the latest couture. Within the site, the Parisian department stores each had their own quite large pavilion in which to present their wares.

In a 1933 article in the RIAS *Quarterly Illustrated* on the design of shop fascias, Robert Rennie (1906–1969) observed that 'Paris, in the shop front at least, has maintained a leadership in smartness and brilliance' and that Parisian retailers uniquely had 'the faculty of being able to play fast and loose with decoration, without making it vulgar'.[9] Yet, already in Scotland, Rennie noted with anxiety, 'many discordant methods have been adopted', which, perhaps predictably, he blamed on designs most often being devised by shopfitters rather than architects. In his opinion, the former were mere 'mass-production experts … who have, except in rare cases, little knowledge of design, but have picked up from the Continent some ideas of what is smart and "catchy"'. Warming to this theme, he condemned their use of 'coloured glass and jazz panels' as representing 'the worst phases of the modernist movement', whereas 'the best modern work on the Continent is plain and severe'.[10] This was a familiar complaint of would-be modernist architects, who sought to present themselves as providing uniquely superior cultural gravitas and aesthetic refinement. Yet, as Rennie also observed, successful retail design needed to address, 'the psychological problem of attracting the public and inducing them to buy what they perhaps did not intend to buy' and so 'a shop must proclaim itself above the din and rush of modern traffic'.[11]

Arcading, whereby access to the shop interior was recessed behind covered entrance passages, was one solution that came to be commonly applied in shops of all sizes. Rennie noted approvingly that 'showcases forming pathways arouse curiosity, and invite one to wander from the crowded pavement into its alleyways and enjoy in peace a review of the wares exhibited'.[12] In wet Scottish weather, moreover, an arcaded entrance provided shelter for passers-by who would then browse the window displays and perhaps make spontaneous purchases. The introduction of three dimensions to fascias and the partial dematerialisation of exterior and interior were also, of course, signifiers of modernity and modernism, as was the application of up-to-date materials:

> The use of steel for window astragals, mullions, transoms, and grilles… which can be dull finished or polished to a degree of brilliance that eclipses the brilliance of polished silver, and which can retain that brilliance in any atmosphere, is now on the market. An extremely novel idea has been introduced which eliminates astragals at the angle of plate glass windows, by merely clipping the two sheets together with small metal clips at intervals… Concealed lighting for show windows and shop interiors is widely used with excellent effect… Neon tubing, which has quite recently come into vogue, is now extensively used for lettering and signs.[13]

Rennie illustrated his article with drawings of shop fronts in Paris, London, New York and Edinburgh, the last being the Lotus & Delta shoe shop on Princes Street, owned by the shoemakers and retailers Earl & Earl Ltd, which had opened in 1928, built to a design by Joseph Emberton. He praised its engraved glass upper windows, with a 'surround [of] beige coloured marble, the metalwork silveroid' as 'exceedingly decorative by day and when lighted at night; a very good example of the right kind of advertising'.[14]

The latest Parisian and London fashions, as featured in British *Vogue*, could be bought at some cost in the established Scottish department stores which mainly dated from the latter nineteenth century, famous examples being Jenners in Edinburgh and Wylie & Lochhead, Pettigrew & Stephens, Copeland & Lye and Trerons in Glasgow. Scottish high-end clothing design and manufacture excelled mostly in producing tweeds for country living, which *Vogue* and other society and lifestyle magazines, ranging from *Scottish Field* to *Tatler*,

Lotus & Delta Shoes, Princes Street, Edinburgh
Joseph Emberton, 1928
RIBA Collections

also promoted. Stylish women in county towns were encouraged to wear tweed skirts cut just above the knee and matching jackets with small and shapely hats pinned on their short, waved hair. Around Glasgow were a cluster of manufacturers of fashion clothes mostly aimed at the mid-market, including corsets and undergarments by R K Smith & Co, hosiery by Arthur & Co, coats and frocks by H J Coutts & Co, skirts and jackets by Wallace & Weir, overcoats by A & J Mandel and Stewart & McDonald and furs by Fred Nettler & Co. In the 1930s, a woman could dress stylishly almost entirely using off-the-peg items made within the city.[15] Many Scottish regional towns had their own smaller versions of the city department stores. Bespoke facsimiles of up-to-date styles could also be made-to-measure by the many dressmakers and tailors, who created and altered garments in close consultation with customers, who made appointments for measuring, fabric selection and fitting.

The late 1920s and early 1930s were a notable period for the development of fashion retail, with inspiration arriving from a new source, supplementing the established fashion leaders in London and Paris. The advent of 'talking' motion pictures in 1929 quickly led to a symbiotic relationship between leading couturiers, Hollywood film studios and the emergent new generation of American-based movie stars. They acted as living mannequins promoting the latest in style to wide international audiences. On screen they were able to present fashion as part of a wider set of consumerist and lifestyle possibilities, also involving hairstyles, jewellery, make-up and holding and smoking cigarettes in particularly memorable ways. Spoken American slang witticisms and terms such as 'guy' and 'doll' entered Scottish dialect through the cinema, the audiences apparently greatly influenced by what they saw on screen. British high street retailers who could supply the means of emulation at reasonable cost were among the greatest beneficiaries.

In the latter 1920s, the R W Forsyth department store sought to cultivate a more up-to-date image than its rivals. To achieve this aim, it commissioned Sir John Burnet's Glasgow office, Burnet, Son & Dick, to renovate its store on Edinburgh's Princes Street, a prominent building opposite Waverley Market and Station which Burnet himself had earlier designed in the Edwardian baroque manner. The new interiors were made and installed by George Parnall & Co, a long-established upmarket shopfitting specialist originating in Bristol but headquartered in London. Completed in 1929, they comprised multicoloured inlaid flooring, Art Deco cabinets and display units, and loose and built-in furniture, all of bespoke design, new pendant lighting with frosted glass diffusers and some charming wall murals that complemented a cheerful colour scheme. The Hairdressing Department, in particular, was state-of-the-art with the latest chairs, octagonal

bevelled mirrors, mood lighting and fancy plate glass vitrines to contain displays of perfumes and beauty products. Whereas the neighbouring Jenner's store was grand and traditional, Forsyth's was henceforth contrastingly youthful and fashionable.[16]

Towards Princes Street's east end, close to R W Forsyth's store, T P Marwick & Son designed new premises for Jay's household furnishers. Above the two-storey showroom were a further three storeys containing hotel bedrooms, which formed an annexe to the adjacent Cranston's Old Waverley Hotel. Completed in 1938, the building's austere stone-faced facade, split into two flat planes derived from the Golden Ratio with a flagpole at their junction and featuring two small bas reliefs by Thomas Whalen, lacked the elegance of the same architects' National Bank of Scotland frontage, located only a short walk away.[17]

Renovated interiors of R W Forsyth, Princes Street, Edinburgh
Burnet, Son & Dick and George Parnall & Co, 1929
Bruce Peter collection

Binns, Princes Street, Edinburgh
Richardson & McKay, 1935
HES SC1119784

While Glasgow and Scotland's other regional towns and cities gained substantial numbers of new retail premises of all sizes and types, Edinburgh received fewer, not least because suitable large sites for redevelopment were harder to find. In the mid-1930s, the fire-damaged former Maule's department store at the West End of Princes Street was purchased by Binns of Newcastle, which carried out a substantial rebuild with a new Art Deco main block designed by the partnership of John Ross McKay (1884–1962) and James Smith Richardson (1883–1970), both of whom were Edinburgh-trained and former employees of Lorimer.[18] Their facade composition's giant fluted pilasters and heavy cornices was similar but not quite identical to the neighbouring Royal Bank of Scotland branch, adjoining the return elevation on Hope Street and later annexed for a store extension. The corner is cut back at a 45-degree angle with scalloped edging to the parapet and, on the ground floor, plate glass windows in bronzed frames, set into polished granite surrounds. The intention for the important corner site was appropriately grandiose, but the elements are perhaps a little too compressed and truncated to properly achieve this impression.

Despite the era's economic difficulties, Glaswegians were enthusiastic purchasers of the latest styles. In the city's Argyle Street, the very large Royal Polytechnic department store opened in 1929 and was soon taken over by the Lewis's chain, headquartered in Liverpool.[19] A mighty but bland neoclassical edifice faced in Portland stone, it was designed by the Leeds architect George Walter Atkinson (1860–1950) and was intended to cater to a growing and aspiring middle market. Serving a similar clientele was the locally owned Watt Brothers store at the junction of Sauchiehall Street and Hope Street, the original 1915 premises of which were expanded in 1929–30 with a new four-storey Art Deco wing in matching red sandstone at the junction of Hope Street and Bath Street, the design of which was by Keppie & Henderson. A rare project in the style by this firm, the distinctive faceted bay windows in slim metal spandrels

C&A, Sauchiehall Street, Glasgow
North, Robin & Wilsdon, 1931
Glasgow City Archives

are a feature also used in the new C&A store built shortly afterwards just two blocks away in Sauchiehall Street, but to more dramatic effect. The Dutch-owned chain, founded in the mid-nineteenth century, had entered the British retail market earlier in the 1920s, benefitting from the great interwar expansion in

Watt Bros, Hope Street and Bath Street, Glasgow
Keppie & Henderson, 1930
HES SC2599991

the ready-to-wear fashion market and the desire for continental glamour. C&A's London architects, North, Robin & Wilsdon, the main partners in which were Sidney Vincent North (1872–1951) and William John Wilsdon (1866–1951), had previously designed stores for F W Woolworth & Co and so understood what was required of modern, mass-market retailing. Having rebuilt existing premises for C&A in Leeds and Liverpool, their first entirely purpose-built store for the company was in Manchester, opening in 1928 and in an angular Art Deco style, clad in faience. The Glasgow branch, completed in 1931 and containing five levels of sales floors, represents a further stylistic development.[20] The vertical accentuation of its glazing, which at the corner extends upward by an extra sixth storey to form a small tower feature, hinted at the forms of new New York skyscrapers and was comparable with recent retail architecture in Berlin. At street level, by contrast, a horizontal emphasis was achieved with wide expanses of plate glass inset within flat fascia panels with chamfered corners, the store name being in bulging, illuminated lettering. C&A also opened a store on Edinburgh's Princes Street, converted from the two lower storeys of existing premises, unsympathetically refaced with horizontal glazing and resulting in a clash with the Louis XV style of those above. Using such brash approaches helped fashion chain stores of this kind quickly to became prominent features of the 1930s retail scene.

At the very busy junction of Buchanan Street and Argyle Street, another rapidly expanding off-the-peg retailer, the menswear chain of Montague Burton, was concurrently constructing its large new store with sales floors spread over four of the five storeys and administration above. Burton, who had been born Meshe David Osinsky in Lithuania, had arrived in Britain in 1900, aged 15, establishing himself as a tailor in Chesterfield just three years thereafter. He believed that smart clothes enhanced a man's self-respect and aimed to offer suits that appeared made-to-measure but were in fact efficiently factory-manufactured and sold at popular prices. The heart of his operation was a vast factory in Leeds; begun in 1922, it was repeatedly extended, employing around 10,000 in the latter 1930s. Burton had a reputation for being a benevolent employer who provided benefits and recreational facilities and who wrote on industrial relations. He was thus admired by aspiring working people.[21] He also understood the benefits of good publicity involving

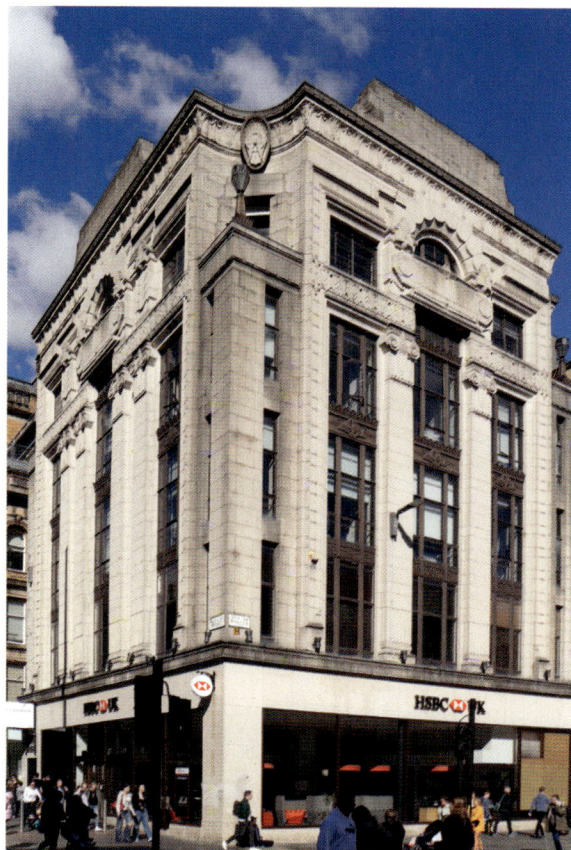

Burton, Buchanan Street and Argyle Street, Glasgow
Harry Wilson, 1931
Bruce Peter

Burton, High Street, Dumbarton
Harry Wilson, 1938
Bruce Peter

Burton, Dumfries
Harry Wilson, 1937
Bruce Peter collection

Burton and The Fifty Shilling Tailor, Kirkcaldy
Harry Wilson, 1937
Bruce Peter collection

the patronage of male celebrities and sportsmen. Many Burton's stores included a billiard room as an added inducement to encourage would-be shoppers to enter their premises. Altogether, Burton was quite visionary in his approaches to running and promoting his business. Intending to cultivate a moderately up-to-date image, his was one of the high street companies, alongside the major cinema chains, that spread Art Deco all over Britain.

Burton's stores were designed under the direction of the company's in-house architect, Harry Wilson (1884–1973) of Leeds, whose assistants in the late 1920s included the Aberdeen-born Henry Erskine Hill (1902–1989) and Arbroath-born, Dundee-trained William Fyfe Henry (1905–1980), though the latter emigrated to Rhodesia. The Glasgow store opened in 1931 and was evidently considered prestigious, having complex Art Deco facade treatments with Egypto-Greek ornamentation, moulded from blocks of grey reconstructed stone.[22] Another large branch was located on Aberdeen's St Nicholas Street, clad in granite and with the company name carved for posterity in a roofline frieze. In Paisley and Kirkcaldy, mid-sized stores of three storeys were built in the 1930s, their facades in Beaux Arts style with Art Deco detailing sweeping round prominent corner sites.[23] The Burton's branches in smaller towns featured a variety of treatments, the one in Dumfries being clad in local pink sandstone, while Dumbarton's was finished in faience, including sunburst window heads; long after

the store's closure, it still retains the original name sign, moulded into the blocks of faience forming the pediment. The most striking of all the smaller branches was in Ayr, the relatively narrow frontage of which was originally finished in polished black granite with golden metallic details. It was the only Scottish example designed in this way, though there were several others in various English towns, the ones in Mexborough and Stratford-on-Avon being almost identical. The inspiration for polished granite facades was probably Ideal House in London by Raymond Hood (1881–1934) and Stanley Gordon Jeeves (1888–1964), which was completed in 1928.[24]

Burton's emphasised that it was 'The Tailor of Quality', which justified its prices not being the cheapest. Other perhaps less reputable menswear entrepreneurs sought to undercut its offerings, an example being in Kirkcaldy where The Fifty Shilling Tailor was located directly opposite Burton's store, its flashy neon-lit Art Deco signage emphasising only the low cost of its wares. Using the fascia to communicate cheapness obviously marked out such tailors as downmarket and aiming at a clientele for whom affordability trumped other niceties.

Design perspective of Marks & Spencer, Argyle Street, Glasgow
J M Monro & Son, 1930
HES SC675537

Marks & Spencer, Murraygate, Dundee
J M Monro & Son and Robert Lutyens, 1936
Bruce Peter

Woolworths, Sauchiehall Street, Glasgow
Bruce Campbell Davidson, 1936
Glasgow City Archives

Marks & Spencer was another expansionist British retailer to decide in the late 1920s to build new premises in Glasgow, replacing an existing, quite small store there. As with Burton, its founder, Michael Marks, was a Jewish immigrant to Leeds who entered the retail trade in the mid-1880s and in consort with an employee, Thomas Spencer, went on to develop a nationwide chain of outlets. For the new Glasgow store, they employed the well-established local firm of J M Monro & Son, founded in 1893 by James Milne Monro (1840–1921) and his son, Charles Ernest Monro (1874–1945). The latter was the senior partner when M&S became a client, assisted by a third generation, Geoffrey James Monro (1907–1985), a Glasgow School of Architecture graduate who had been taught by T Harold Hughes and who joined the firm in 1929. By then, construction of the five-storey edifice on Argyle Street was already under way. Clad in reconstructed stone, moulded in rectilinear forms, it opened in 1930, the store filling the lower floors, while those above were leased out to other businesses. Its success led the company to acquire a second Glasgow site on Sauchiehall Street, opening there in 1935. The symmetrical cream faience exterior of the latter and also

those of subsequent M&S stores were of a more-or-less standard design (which could be adapted for use in any city or town) devised by the interior designer Robert Lutyens (1901–1971), son of the architect Sir Edwin Lutyens, whose firm Lutyens & Simmonds had decorated the homes of M&S directors. In 1934 he was appointed to the company's board, acting as its design adviser to achieve stylistic consistency across its stores, including the composition of facades, though J M Monro & Son were retained to handle the architectural design of what lay behind. Within a year of opening, the Sauchiehall Street store was extended with a slightly taller additional bay at one end containing extra vertical circulation and more sales floor space. The M&S store in Dundee's Murraygate, completed shortly after, is of very similar design.[25] All of the Scottish M&S branches, including smaller stores in Ayr, Kirkcaldy and Paisley, were arranged according to a standard modular layout.

Whereas the Burton's and M&S operations were to an extent American-influenced, another prolifically expanding high street retailer, F W Woolworth & Co, actually was an American-headquartered multinational. Founded by Frank Winfield Woolworth

Falkirk and District United Co-operative Society, Bank Street, Falkirk
James G Callander, 1937
Bruce Peter

Leven Reform Co-operative Society, Durie Street
Andrew D Haxton, 1937
Bruce Peter

in New York in 1879 as a so-called 'five-and-dime' discount store, it expanded rapidly cross North America and opened its first British stores in 1909. In the 1930s, F W Woolworth continued its British expansion with new Art Deco-fronted stores, large and small, being erected throughout the country. Their architect was Bruce Campbell Davidson (1896–1977), who was born in Ireland into a Scottish family. He had first been employed by Woolworth in the early 1920s, working in the Liverpool office of its chief architect, William Priddle (1885–1932), and designing its new shops in Scotland and the north of England. When Priddle died in 1932, Davidson replaced him, superseding the established Beaux Arts neoclassical style with Americanised Art Deco, the stores' frontages often being entirely clad in moulded faience. The biggest Woolworth's for which Davidson was responsible was on the promenade at Blackpool, next to the Tower, and containing a cafe and restaurant as well as extensive sales floors.[26] In Scotland, somewhat smaller versions were opened, the branch on Glasgow's Sauchiehall Street, adjacent to Marks & Spencer, being a re-cladding in faience of an existing building.[27] Other significant Scottish Woolworth stores were in Dundee,

in Dunfermline and in Clydebank.[28] Many more smaller branches, finished in faience, stone or brick, were also built in towns and suburbs that were not large enough to support a Burton's. They were indeed the only Art Deco buildings in high streets such as those in Airdrie, Helensburgh or St Andrews.

In Scottish regional towns, affiliates of the Scottish Co-operative Wholesale Society (SCWS), founded in 1868 and inspired by the English co-ops that had followed the 1840s Rochdale pioneers, built notable Art Deco stores. In Leven, the already quite commodious Edwardian-vintage premises of the Fife Co-operative Wholesale Society was given a substantial extension designed by Andrew D Haxton in his typically angular and symmetrical style. Faced in stone, it has a wide pediment and ornately detailed oxidised copper infill panels depicting beehives, symbolising the 'industry' of its Co-operative owners, as well as intricate Art Deco stained glass fenestration.[29] The Falkirk Co-operative store by James G Callander is particularly impressive, standing on a prominent corner site and composed of stone dressings with scalloped edges and bronze infill panels featuring Mayan-inspired imagery. Both the Leven and Falkirk projects were completed in 1937. Numerous other co-operative stores were designed by the SCWS's in-house architect, Cornelius H Armour (c1881–1955), a notable example being an extension of the Kinning Park Co-operative's drapery store on Glasgow's Bridge Street with a richly ornamented sandstone frontage, likewise Mayan-inspired. Armour designed many more, smaller SCWS stores, often only single-storey with slim Art Deco pediments above the name signage and shop windows.

In complete contrast, a large extension to the St Cuthbert's Co-operative store, tucked away on Edinburgh's Bread Street, was arguably Scotland's most architecturally avant-garde large shop of the 1930s. Completed in 1937 to a design by David Harvey (1908–1975) and Philip McManus in the office of T P Marwick & Son, it was the country's first to have a frontage almost entirely composed of a glass curtain wall – a bold and unusual choice, particularly in the context of Edinburgh. On a shallow canopy, large three-dimensional sans serif chromed lettering spelled out the name.[30] Before the project was completed, McManus emigrated to South Africa, practising thereafter in Durban.

St Cuthbert's Co-operative Association, Bread Street, Edinburgh
David Harvey and Philip McManus of
T P Marwick & Son, 1937
HES SC710123, SC710124, Bruce Peter collection

Glasgow Corporation Gas Department, Sauchiehall Street, Glasgow
Alexander Graham Glen of McInnes Gardner, 1935
Glasgow City Archives

Burgh of Dunfermline Gas Department, Canmore Street, Dunfermline
Robert Henderson Motion, 1939
Bruce Peter

The requirements of retail were not limited to department stores or local shops. Showrooms displaying the latest domestic appliances were needed to communicate their products' technological benefits. Gas cookers and fires promised relative cleanliness and reduced labour in comparison with ones fired by coal or anthracite. Intending to cultivate a desirable image, the Glasgow Corporation Gas Department employed the architectural firm of McInnes Gardiner, best known for its designs for the luxurious interiors of ocean liners, to plan its showroom near to the Charing Cross end of Sauchiehall Street. The design was by the firm's senior partner, Alexander Graham Glen (1891–1976) and featured an unusually large fascia panel, emblazoned with the word 'GAS' in big, three-dimensional moderne letters.[31] Elsewhere in Scotland, a notable free-standing Art Deco gas showroom was built for the Burgh of Alloa Gas Department to a

design by William Kerr (1867–1940) and John Gray (1878–1946) of local architects John Melvin & Son. Completed in 1938, it fills an entire irregularly shaped block also containing offices and a depot.[32] A smaller but equally notable example is the showroom of the Burgh of Dunfermline Gas Department, which Robert Henderson Motion (1886–1967) designed and which opened in 1939. Above the sales floor was a lecture theatre where presentations were given about the fuel's advantages over alternatives for domestic use.[33]

Shop buildings, of course, constituted only a minority of high street retail premises; the vast majority were units occupying the lower floors of mixed-use edifices, typically with office space or housing filling their upper storeys. Nearly all of these structures pre-dated

**Burgh of Alloa Gas Department,
Bank Street, Alloa**
William Kerr, 1938
HES SC681660

the 1930s – but often shop fascias and interiors were modernised during the decade by specialist shopfitters. The leading British companies involved in this type of work were E Pollard & Co and Frederick Sage & Co of London – but there were also several Scottish-based firms. Of the Edinburgh shopfitters, the longest established was Donald Grant & Sons, founded in 1831 (and still extant today as Grant Westfield).[34] Heggie & Aitchison dated from 1887 when Alexander Heggie and John Aitchison took over an existing joinery business in Rose Street. Aitchison died in 1900, Heggie thereafter specialising in shopfitting with a workshop in Grove Street, which he ran until 1932 when his son Maurice took over.[35] Adam Currie founded his joinery and shopfitting business around 1891, in the mid-1930s employing the young architect Stanley White Edgar (1909–1991), previously an assistant of Reginald Fairlie, as in-house shop designer.

In Glasgow, meanwhile, Archibald Hamilton had developed a shopfitting business from one initially founded in the late 1860s as brass engravers and lithographers but which increasingly found engraving and etching shop windows to be a lucrative area of activity.[36] By the 1890s, its workshop in Ann Street in Cowcaddens was producing whole shop fascias and at around the turn of the century, display units for interiors came to be made there too.[37] Showroom premises were then acquired in Glassford Street to display the range of shop fittings it could offer, the emphasis being particularly on items to equip draper's stores, the outfitting and modernisation of which were by then its prime specialities.[38]

Although in the 1930s all of these shopfitters produced fascias and interiors in a range of design styles as required by their clients, those by the Glasgow firm of Archibald McEwan were outstanding for their boldness and modernity. Founded in Ibrox around 1903, McEwan soon moved to larger premises in Woodside, which was more proximal to the city centre where most shop interiors were installed.[39] In the 1930s, the business was run by his son, James F McEwan, and moved its showroom from Ingram Street into new premises of their

Swears & Wells, Sauchiehall Street, Glasgow
E Pollard & Co, 1928
Glasgow City Archives

Style & Mantle, Mitchell Street and Argyle Street, Glasgow
Designer not known, c1930
Glasgow City Archives

own design on Hope Street in 1932, which featured a sleek black polished granite frontage with chromed metal casements around a plate glass window and a circular illuminated name sign with moderne lettering. The younger McEwan was even invited to address the Annual Trade Dinner of the Scottish Federation of Drapers in 1935 on the subject of 'Shop fronts and shop fitting and lighting'. This he illustrated with sales charts demonstrating the benefit to trade of the imaginative modernisation of these elements.[40]

As shopfitting companies such as these could remodel shop units more quickly and much less expensively than complete retail buildings could be designed and constructed, they were more readily able to reflect evolving stylistic trends. In some instances where a shop occupied both the ground and first floors, a new two-storey fascia would be imposed upon whatever existing facade was already there. While such appendages to older frontages reflected a commercial logic, for design reformers they were anathema as they added to what the more idealistic within the architecture and design communities viewed as visual corruption (as opposed to either classical or modernist totality of form).

In Glasgow, an early Art Deco example of this style of modernisation was the Sauchiehall Street boutique of the upmarket London furriers and outfitters Swears & Wells, which opened in 1928. It featured a two-storey portico in the Egyptian style, designed by E Pollard & Co of London and including a clock featuring gold scarab wings above its recessed entranceway. Furriers, though nowadays disparaged, were then considered highly glamorous and aspirational and so they invested in designs for their premises to appeal especially to upwardly mobile women shoppers for whom image was all-important. Indeed, as Art Deco was associated with Parisian haute couture, it quickly came to be favoured for women's fashion boutiques of all kinds. A striking example from around 1930 was Style & Mantle Ltd's premises, filling two storeys at the junction of Mitchell Street and Argyle Street, the top corners of the display windows of which were splayed and set into framing entirely clad in black Vitrolite with shiny angular lettering. Another was the Art Fabrics textile and dressmaking shop at 373–375 Sauchiehall Street, opened in 1935 and featuring a two-storey frontage in polished reconstructed stone with a ground floor arcade, the design of which was commissioned from E Pollard

but executed by McEwan. Probably the shop's owner thought that employing a London firm to carry out the design work, if not the actual installation, would ensure an outcome reflective of the latest in West End chic. By the mid-1930s, the angular style was, however, becoming passé and McEwan's own designs were by then often more advanced.

A subsequent Pollard design carried out by McEwan in around 1937 for the furrier Whitney's in Buchanan Street received a boldly three-dimensional frontal treatment with projecting display windows flanking a deeply arcaded entrance passage with columns along the centre, supporting an island canopy. Above was a wide, flattened arch around which the fascia was clad in cream and black faience with the name in three-dimensional red lettering. Whitney's premises reflected 1930s retail design

Art Fabrics, Sauchiehall Street, Glasgow
E Pollard & Co and Archibald McEwan Ltd, 1935
Chris Doak

Martin's Dyers & Cleaners, Sauchiehall Street, Glasgow
Archibald McEwan Ltd, 1936
Bruce Peter collection

Whitney's, Buchanan Street, Glasgow
E Pollard & Co and Archibald McEwan Ltd, 1937
Glasgow City Archives

at its most confident with all of the typical period characteristics of form, signage and materials used to striking effect.[41]

McEwan designed and outfitted numerous small shops, located all over Glasgow and beyond, their alterations often making mundane activities appear instantly conspicuous and memorable. A notable example was Martin's dry cleaners, located in the small unit to the right of the entrance to the Regal cinema on Sauchiehall Street. Redolent of up-to-date American design practice, its pink, black and cream Vitrolite fascia panelling curved around the window glazing at one end, the highly stylised lettering in red accentuated by repetitive parallel lines, suggestive of speed and efficiency.

Glasgow's Great Western Road, leading from St George's Cross via prosperous Kelvinbridge to Anniesland, was also home to numerous shops that were given Art Deco and moderne re-stylings. Near the St George's Cross end, the glass merchant and glazier James McPhie commissioned Wylie, Shanks and Wylie, formerly Wylie, Wright and Wylie, in which George Ferguson Shanks (1898–1985) had been made a

Design perspective of Cleghorn, Princes Street, Edinburgh
Basil Spence, 1936
HES SC357574

James P McPhie, Great Western Road, Glasgow
Wylie, Shanks and Wylie, 1938
Chris Doak

partner in 1936, to transform its premises. Completed in 1938, the black Vitrolite fascia was adorned with aluminium trim and matching Art Deco lettering.[42] The firm of architects was nothing if not versatile; its output encompassed grand city centre blocks at one extreme but also minor design gems such as this shop at the other.

More sophisticated than any of these, however, was the Edinburgh premises of the leather goods retailer Cleghorn on Princes Street, which Basil Spence designed in 1936. Two-thirds of its double-height plate glass exterior was so deeply recessed as to provide space for what was effectively a sheltered outdoor courtyard in which stood three free-standing display vitrines. The interior featured a series of circular voids between the two sales floors, which were connected by a curving stairway to the rear.[43] The Cleghorn store reflected Scottish 1930s retail architecture at its finest – but, as with pretty much every other example of an Art Deco or moderne-style outlet of shop unit size, it has long-since disappeared. Fortunately, Spence's surviving original rendering of the interior with its boldly drawn curves and subtle colours eloquently records for posterity his original very elegant design intention.

THE GHOST GOES WEST

CINEMA

REGAL CINEMA
SHOTTS

E. WEIR
DELT.

CHAPTER 7
ENTERTAINMENT

If involvement in commercial house-building and the outfitting of retail premises represented two areas of architectural practice which some within the profession considered disreputable, the design of popular entertainment venues was potentially worse still. But in the early 1930s the entertainment business was one of the few other growing sectors in which there were architectural jobs to be found. The interwar era indeed witnessed a great development of new and improved media. The first British radio broadcast happened in 1920 and the British Broadcasting Corporation was founded in 1922. The first mainstream narrative film with a soundtrack, *The Jazz Singer* starring Al Jolson, was released by RKO in 1927 and the Scottish John Logie Baird pioneered television broadcasting in 1929, though it did not become a mainstream medium until the 1950s. Better printing techniques enabled illustrated newspapers and thick, heavily illustrated lifestyle magazines to be produced at lower cost, and so a symbiotic relationship developed between journalism, showbusiness celebrities, fashion and cosmetics houses and retailers. As we have seen in the previous chapter, the public were encouraged to take stylistic inspiration from the stars of the glamorous-looking and alluringly cosmopolitan worlds of film and fashion.

The Regal, Shotts
John Ross McKay of Richardson & McKay;
sketch by Ernest John Weir, 1939
HES DP103635

All of this had architectural and design implications for entertainment venues, with the creation of superficial stylistic commonalities between the spaces apparently inhabited by the wealthy and famous – whether they be Hollywood mansions, film sets or First Class ocean liner saloons – and those appearing in the 1930s to house popular entertainment, such as cinemas and dance halls. Popularised versions of modern architecture and interior décor were considered by growing numbers of architects and entertainment providers to be highly suitable for such venues, engendering fashionable and escapist images and allowing audiences to experience – however briefly – fantasy versions of how the future might look, achieved with cost-effective budgets.

Viewed through the politicised critical filters of the intelligentsia, mass entertainment provoked alarm; cultural conservatives viewed the imagery emanating from the USA as threatening to established British, Scottish and local identities, while left-wingers, viewing through Marxist lenses, merely saw cultural opiates which would distract the urban poor from the true poverty of their lot. The cinema – which enabled higher levels of immersion than the other mass entertainments – was considered most problematic in these regards and such thinking undoubtedly tainted perceptions of the buildings in which films were shown.[1] Yet, the fact that venues for popular entertainment might enable indoctrination could also potentially help to 'sell' the positive virtues of up-to-date design to the public. Entertainment venues were mostly windowless and all-enveloping, meaning that designers could produce sustained stylistic effects that audiences would be able to enjoy (or tolerate) for the relatively brief duration of their attendance. They could therefore experience the latest in fashion in a short snatch during a moment of relaxation, being able thereafter to contrast this with their everyday experiences and living conditions in the 'real world'.

Cinemas

In terms of quantity, cinemas were the most numerous commercial building type to be constructed in Scotland during the interwar period. The same was true throughout much of the world as, following initial experimental showings in the second half of the 1890s by various inventors (such as the Lumière brothers in France, Thomas Edison in the USA and William Friese-Greene in the UK), the medium was appropriated by showmen and impresarios and it spread globally with remarkable rapidity. Many cinemas, particularly those occupying suburban sites, were examples par excellence of a typical approach to commercial design that the American architects and educators Robert Venturi (1925–2018), Denise Scott Brown (b 1931) and Steven Izenour (1940–2001) would much later identify as being a 'decorated shed' – the antithesis of the modernist ideal of a 'total form', designed to be equally significant on all sides.[2] In Scottish cities, suburbs, towns and even villages, cinemas were usually the most prominent and showy examples of Art Deco and moderne with frontages intended to contrast with surrounding buildings, signifying modernity and escapism.

By the time of the release of *The Jazz Singer*, it had been a mere 18 years since the passing of the Cinematograph Act of 1909, which was the first British legislation concerning public safety at film shows.[3] This regulated the design of cinema buildings, ensuring separate, fire-proof projection booths and adequate emergency escape routes, which brought about an initial boom in the construction of purpose-built examples, as opposed to ones temporarily set up in shop units, for instance. Prior to 1914, some purpose-built cinemas were constructed in Scotland, including the Hippodrome in Bo'ness by Matthew Steele in 1912 and the Campbeltown Picture House in 1913 by Albert V Gardner (both architects would later design Art Deco edifices). During the First World War, the building of cinemas was suspended in Britain but not in the USA, where the Hollywood studios and other big businesses invested enthusiastically in increasingly large and lavish examples, the baroque ostentation of many of which outdid the grandest European opera houses. In Scotland, several very large cinemas were built in the second half of the 1920s that sought to copy the typical American approach, the Green's Playhouse in Glasgow and the Playhouse in Edinburgh, both of which were designed by John Fairweather (1867–1942), being notable instances.[4]

Cinema operation benefited from economies of scale and so during the 1920s circuits of venues expanded first locally and then nationwide. These enabled the centralisation of administration, including the booking and distribution of films. Cinemas with seating capacities of over 1,000 were commonplace in urban areas, the biggest examples, fewer in number, having over 3,000 seats. Financiers came to view cinemas as lucrative and relatively secure investments, especially when new projects were backed by established circuits with good records of profitability.

In the 1920s, films may have been black and white and without soundtracks, but the decoration of cinema venues had the potential to generate a sense of escapism. In the USA, exotic thematic treatments came to be favoured. Often inspiration was taken from either the near or Far East, such as at Grauman's Chinese Theater in Hollywood, while the fascination for ancient Egypt that followed the unearthing of the treasures in Tutankhamun's tomb gave rise to the same owner's Egyptian Theater. In Scotland, the considerably more modest Govanhill Picture House on Glasgow's Southside, completed in 1926 to a design by Eric A Sutherland (1870–1940), has an Egyptian-inspired entrance portico in white and grey faience with a scarab and golden domes, while the Regal in Dunfermline by the Edinburgh architect Thomas Bowhill Gibson (1895–1949), who made designing cinemas a speciality, was opened in 1931. In neither case was the Egyptian style perpetuated within the interiors, which were rather plain and reflected Scottish cinema operators' cost-saving preference for continuous performances with the houselights constantly dimmed. An alternative strategy developed in America by the architect John Eberson (1875–1954) was the so-called 'atmospheric' interior, whereby the auditorium was decorated to resemble a romantic outdoor courtyard with exotic buildings in plaster low relief forming the side walls and a smooth, blue-painted ceiling to resemble a sky. This idea originated during the Renaissance with the Teatro Olimpico at Vicenza of 1585, designed by Andrea

**Auditorium of the Moray Playhouse,
High Street, Elgin**
Alister G MacDonald, 1932
Bruce Peter collection

Palladio (1508–1580), which was a notable precedent for Eberson's designs; in turn, they influenced those of the small number of cinemas with atmospheric interiors that were built in Scotland, such as the Orient cinemas in Glasgow and Ayr.[5]

In Germany, an entirely different design approach simultaneously came to be applied which used smooth, elongated forms and concealed effects lighting to create a unique architectural style for what was, after all, an up-to-date and light-based entertainment medium.

Angus Playhouse, John Street, Montrose
Alister G MacDonald, 1933
Bruce Peter collection

The architecture critic Philip Morton Shand was so impressed by this approach that he wrote and had published in 1930 a book entitled *The Architecture of Pleasure 1: Modern Theatres and Cinemas*, largely featuring recent German exemplars, which he hoped might provide design inspiration for British architects to follow suit.[6] While he was writing it, the first similarly styled British cinema, the New Victoria, was already under construction in central London to a design by a young architect there by name of E Wamsley Lewis (1898–1977). Its elevations feature repeated parallel horizontal and vertical ribs lit by strips of neon, while its auditorium walls are adorned with stacks of large shell-like lighting sconces in plaster, which were originally interspersed with cascading illuminated glass lights resembling stalactites. The overall effect was intended to resemble a fantasy futuristic mermaid's cave and even the carpets were woven in wave patterns. Best of all from the perspective of the New Victoria's owner, Gaumont British, its final cost was £189,000, significantly less than the £250,000 budgeted.[7] The New Victoria would go on directly to influence cinema design in Scotland through the work of Alister G MacDonald, who had been invited to the opening ceremony, and who in the second half of the 1920s had been the Clerk of Works of the London-based cinema and theatre architects Frank T Verity (1864–1937) and Samuel Beverley (1896–1959).[8]

Thanks to MacDonald, it was in the North East of Scotland, rather than the Central Belt, that the first cinemas to be comprehensively designed in an Art Deco manner were built. Shortly after the New Victoria opened, MacDonald was commissioned by Caledonian Associated Cinemas (CAC), which was Scotland's largest independent cinema circuit, to design a number of new venues, of which the Moray Playhouse in Elgin, completed in 1932, was the first.[9] CAC had its head office in Inverness and its properties were concentrated in the Highlands and along the North-East coast between Inverness and Aberdeen, with subsidiaries in Fife, East Lothian and the Borders. MacDonald's treatment of the auditorium side walls was very evidently inspired by what he had seen in the New Victoria, albeit on a much smaller scale and realised with an even tighter budget. Whereas the Elgin cinema was entered through an existing shop unit and therefore had no facade of its own, the subsequent Angus Playhouse in Montrose had a long frontage with the auditorium running parallel to the street.[10]

The Playhouse, Murray Street, Perth
Alexander Cattanach and Thomas Bowhill Gibson, 1933
HES SC1029721

MacDonald's treatment of this exterior also showed the New Victoria's influence. His inexpensive but elegant volumetric design seamlessly tied the tapering auditorium into the foyer block with smooth, coloured render and bold horizontal lines. The staircase was emphasised by a tall window, while the auditorium made use of layered plasterboard, the shadows of the edges picked up by concealed lighting. The Playhouse had 1,059 seats, including a fully cantilevered balcony and tea-room, all for only £15,000.[11] In the 1930s, cinemas with capacities of over 1,000 seats were not atypical of such county towns, which served large farming hinterlands.

MacDonald went on to design the Playhouse in Peebles for CAC, followed by the Broadway in Prestwick and the Lyceum in Dumfries, all of which opened between 1933 and 1936, the latter's interior being also very similar to that of the New Victoria.[12] Subsequently in London, MacDonald produced a series of ingenious news theatres, showing newsreels interspersed with cartoons, the finest of which were located on the concourses of the Victoria and Waterloo railway stations.[13]

At the same time, CAC appointed the Kingussie-based Alexander Cattanach to design a further batch of new cinemas, which included its flagship property,

the Playhouse in Perth (1933). He was probably inspired by MacDonald's clean-lined designs, as these were achievable within CAC's intended budgets, and he sought advice about cinema construction from Thomas Bowhill Gibson. The 1,700-seater Playhouse was completed in only nine weeks from laying the first brick – a feat which *The Ideal Kinema and Studio* magazine considered a record.[14] The exterior is symmetrical and, like that of the New Victoria, features horizontal ribs that curve inward to meet a taller block with vertical ribs over the entrance doors.[15] Five years later, Cattanach produced a similar design for the Regal cinema in Rothesay, which eventually joined the CAC circuit too.[16] His further projects for CAC included the Playhouse in Dunbar in 1937, the Regal in Lossiemouth and the Playhouse in Fraserburgh, which both opened in 1939.[17]

Concurrently with the designing of the earlier of the Art Deco cinema projects of MacDonald and Cattanach in the North East of Scotland, another considerably grander scheme was being planned for the

**Facade, doors and foyer of the Capitol,
Union Street, Aberdeen**
David Stokes of A Marshall Mackenzie & Son, 1933
Bruce Peter

centre of Aberdeen. The Capitol, which also opened in 1933, was likewise a flagship venue, it being the pride of the Aberdeen Picture Palaces circuit. However, it emerged as an Art Deco design only as a result of the death of the originally commissioned architect, Clement George (1879–1932), whose practice was absorbed into that of Alexander Marshall Mackenzie, who also died. His son, A G R Mackenzie, based in London, then sent his young assistant, David Stokes, up to Aberdeen to take over the running of the office there and it was he who directed the Capitol's design. George's fairly conventional and undistinguished plans were subjected to a bold reworking which was accepted on the basis that a rival circuit was already building another cinema on a site immediately to the rear and so it was felt important to achieve the best possible outcome. The existing Union Street frontages (which George had intended to keep) were swept away and replaced with a new flat granite facade, the centrepiece of which is three tall windows, rising to a pediment and originally outlined at night with blue neon and floodlighting. The interior style was announced by four sets of entrance doors with modish stainless steel semi-circular windows and hand plates; these form fully circular 'targets' when the doors are closed. The foyers and auditorium were symmetrical and in line.

As in the New Victoria, blue and silver tones were used throughout because Aberdeen was, after all, 'the silver city by the sea'. The balcony staircase was the lobby's central feature with its sweeping chromed tubular steel railings and flanking stairs down to the stalls crush hall. The auditorium, which contained seating for 2,100, made use of concealed effects lighting behind coves to suffuse the space in a cyclorama of colours. As a city-centre cinema on an important thoroughfare, the Capitol had a restaurant, full stage facilities and a cinema organ. The ladies' powder room, accessed off the balcony foyer, was replete with bevelled mirrors, make-up tables with fluted bases in modish black, cream and mint green and a stylish Art Deco carpet.[18] The Capitol was included in the Royal Institute of British Architects' centenary exhibition in London, entitled International Architecture 1924–1934, as an example of good design practice. Although Stokes apparently did not enjoy his sojourn in Aberdeen, he would have been unlikely to have achieved such a large and prestigious completed project at that time had Mackenzie not sent him there.

Elsewhere in Aberdeen, the architect and business entrepreneur Thomas Scott Sutherland later designed the Astoria, Kittybrewster in 1935 and the Majestic on Union Street in 1937, but these ponderous granite-faced edifices lacked the sophistication of the Capitol and neither survives today.[19]

Following the inauguration of the Capitol, the North East of Scotland could boast a fine array of Art Deco cinemas, as yet unequalled in the Central Belt. This situation occurred partly by chance as the architects commissioned to design these projects happened to be of progressive persuasion, but it was also in part because the clients needed solutions that were relatively inexpensive and quick to realise. In Glasgow, by contrast, the city centre was already very well served by cinemas designed in the 1910s and 1920s in ornate historicist styles. It was the British subsidiary of the American Paramount Corporation that decided to build the first outstanding Art Deco example there. The project was part of a wider plan by Paramount to open very large and lavishly appointed cinemas in the centres of various British regional cities. It followed earlier investment in flagship cinemas in London's West End and in Paris, both of which were designed by the London architects Frank T Verity and Samuel Beverley. Paramount's idea was that cinema audiences would experience a curated environment reflecting the lavish and aspirational style of the movie settings.

After Paramounts had opened in Manchester, Newcastle and Leeds, designed by Verity and Beverley in collaboration with Paramount's American interior decorator, Charles M Fox, it was Glasgow's turn to receive a Paramount in 1934. This would occupy an entire block between Renfield Street and West Nile Street. The Art Deco facade to Renfield Street is clad

Ladies' powder room of the Capitol, Union Street, Aberdeen
David Stokes of A Marshall Mackenzie & Son, 1933
Bruce Peter collection

in moulded blocks of reconstructed stone with five tall windows above the corner entrance, separated by fin-shaped mullions. Originally, the entire composition was outlined with the most extensive display of neon lighting yet seen on any building in Scotland, a six-foot-high neon name sign in Paramount's cursive font dominating the skyline.[20] Glasgow had never seen a piece of architecture quite like it. But from any other angle than Renfield Street, the building presented nothing more than unrelieved masses of dark red industrial brick and was arguably a blight on its immediate surroundings to the sides and rear.

Where most of the budget was spent was on decorating the interior. The fully carpeted two-storey-high entrance hall had a grand staircase at the summit of which was the Balcony Café, adjacent to which was the Paramount Restaurant. The latter was also two floors high and positioned over the main entrance behind the five tall windows. Rattan chairs, white linen tablecloths and swathes of curtaining were combined with Art Deco carpets and subdued lighting to engender an atmosphere suggestive of hotelier luxury. The auditorium seated 2,784 and was decorated in shades of copper, green and silver. There was a large stage and several dressing rooms for variety programmes with full orchestral accompaniment, plus a Compton theatre organ with a silver console. A centralised vacuum cleaning installation meant that vacuum cleaner pipes could be connected to nozzles located at

**Exterior, auditorium and restaurant of the
Paramount, Renfield Street, Glasgow**
Frank T Verity and Samuel Beverley, 1934
Bruce Peter collection

intervals around the auditorium so that the carpeting could be kept pristine. The Paramount employed a staff of approximately 200, those facing the public being specially trained in deportment and dressed in suitably stylish uniforms, all to create a very Americanised illusion of high living.[21]

In Dundee, the equivalent of Aberdeen's Capitol and Glasgow's Paramount was Green's Playhouse, which was opened in 1936. The Greens were showmen from Wigan who moved to Scotland in the 1890s and were early to invest in travelling collapsible cinema booths, hauled and powered by steam traction engines. After the Cinematograph Act of 1909, they built permanent venues in Glasgow's inner-city districts, followed in the 1920s by their first huge Green's Playhouse in central Glasgow. The same architect, John Fairweather, was employed to draw up the auditorium block for Dundee, decorating its interior in a similar neoclassical manner as the one in Glasgow, but the facade and foyer were separately designed by Joseph Emberton.[22] By the 1930s, Emberton had come to be employed by Blackpool Pleasure Beach to add new attractions and redesign existing ones. There, his expressionistically moderne approach with whimsical details created an appropriate sense of levity. One of his assistants in this work was Fairweather's nephew, George Fairweather (1906–1985), and it was through this connection that Emberton came to design for the Greens in Dundee.

As the street frontage to Nethergate was narrow, Emberton designed an 85-foot-tall tower, clad in white render and glass with internal illumination in blue using timed flashers to create a waterfall-like effect, while the cinema's name was in neon-outlined lettering. The foyer had a great expanse of cream terrazzo flooring with sycamore panelling and lighting troughs in the ceiling. On Sundays, when cinemas were not allowed to open for film performances, the tables and chairs from the adjacent cinema cafe were moved into the foyer and the carpet in the cafe itself was then rolled up to reveal a maple dance floor so that Green's Playhouse could still make money as a venue for tea dances. A white marble stairway with illuminated balustrades to make a 'fountain of light' effect, rather like the more famous example in the foyer of the Strand Palace Hotel in London, linked to Fairweather's 4,114-seat auditorium with its vast Corinthian columns along either side. There, the only Art Deco features were plaster grilles with fountain-like lighting sconces in front that flanked the proscenium.[23] These were contributed by John

Foyer and cafe of Green's Playhouse, Dundee
Joseph Emberton, 1936
Bruce Peter collection

Foyer of Green's Playhouse Dundee with cafe seating for Sunday opening
Joseph Emberton, 1936
Bruce Peter collection

Auditorium of Green's Playhouse, Dundee
John Fairweather & Son of M Alexander & Son, 1936
Bruce Peter collection

Exterior of Green's Playhouse, Nethergate, Dundee
Joseph Emberton, 1936
Bruce Peter collection

Alexander, a Newcastle-based interior decorator whose company, M Alexander & Sons, had been founded in 1893. During the 1930s Alexander created several lavish cinema interior schemes, mostly for venues in the north east of England.[24]

※

The film release system meant that new films were shown first in city-centre venues that were tied to major studios before being shown weeks later in the inner, then outer suburbs. Many new cinemas were built during the second half of the 1930s in these latter areas in particular. The great boom in cinema construction led certain Scottish architectural practices – often ones with experience dating back to the cinema's early days – to more-or-less specialise in their design. The Glasgow firms of Albert V Gardner (1884–1944), Gavin Lennox (1878–1956) and Daniel MacMath (1880–1956), James McKissack (1875–1940) of John McKissack & Son, and Charles J McNair (1881–1955) and Robert Elder (1899–1963), as well as the Edinburgh architect Thomas Bowhill Gibson, are all synonymous with Scottish Art Deco and moderne cinema architecture. Between them, they were responsible for many of the most prominent and assertive examples of the styles. The building and equipping of cinemas also benefited a number of Scottish contractors and suppliers, mainly located in the Glasgow area. Toffolo Jackson, founded in 1916, was the leading Scottish specialist in the laying of Art Deco and moderne patterned terrazzo flooring in cinema foyers and toilets.[25] Paterson & Co, established three years thereafter, made auditorium seating.[26] Ornamental metal fabricators such as Walter Macfarlane & Co and David King & Sons, both of which originated in the mid-nineteenth century, cast Art Deco and moderne stairway balustrades and parts for entrance canopies.[27] The Glasgow cinema supply cluster was, however, minor in comparison with those in London and the Midlands, which provided stiff competition; often Scottish cinemas were equipped with seating and many other items that were sourced in the south.

In Glasgow's industrial districts there were very large audiences, many of whom did not mind so much if a film wasn't the latest, just so long as the cinema in which it was shown was close at hand and affordable. In such districts, Albert V Gardner produced designs for some high-capacity venues. His family were from

Gloucestershire and they had moved to Glasgow in 1901, after which he began architectural studies at the Glasgow School of Architecture. By 1908, he had his own small practice and he designed his first cinema projects in around 1910–11. In 1931, the 4,002-seat Astoria on Glasgow's Possil Road was completed to his design and was claimed to be the 'world's largest working-class sound kinema'. Externally, it more resembled a factory than a place of entertainment, but the interior was brightly decorated in the jazz moderne style.[28] (The link between mass work in industry and the concomitant industrialisation of leisure was, of course, one frequently cited by cultural critics of the era and since.) Another Gardner creation was the Orient in the city's Gallowgate, opened in 1932, which was a 2,570-seater with an Art Deco ziggurat above the entrance, but, inside, the auditorium was contrastingly in the 'atmospheric' manner.[29] For Ayr, meanwhile, he designed a smaller cinema of the same name, seating 1,648 and again with a striking Art Deco frontage while atmospheric within.

The Orient, Gallowgate, Glasgow
Albert V Gardner, 1932
Bruce Peter collection

Rendered sectional drawing of auditorium of the Granada, Duke Street, Glasgow
John Christie of Guthrie & Wells, 1935
Glasgow City Archives

The 2,300-seat New Bedford in Eglinton Street on the fringe of the Gorbals district was completed in 1932 to a design by the partnership of Gavin Lennox and Daniel MacMath for the Glaswegian entertainment entrepreneur, Bernard Frutin.[30] Lennox was a farmer's son, born near East Kilbride, whose apprenticeship was in Perth and who came to Glasgow in the early 1900s where he became an employee of the firm of Thomson & Sandilands. There, he met the English-born MacMath, entering practice with him in 1906. Until the latter 1920s, Lennox and MacMath designed mainly small churches and halls in Glasgow's hinterlands but thereafter cinemas became their main output. The New Bedford's largely flat, symmetrical frontage has a lunette as its centrepiece while the interiors were designed and decorated by Guthrie & Wells in the jazz moderne manner. A little later, the same design team were responsible for the 2,400-seat Granada at the Parkhead Cross end of Duke Street in the city's East End, which opened in 1935 and was also run by Frutin. Though the name alone might have suggested a Spanish theme, both its relatively small street frontage and its cavernous interiors were again jazz moderne, the latter achieved by making imaginative use of a cheap and simple material – layers of plasterboard cut into patterns by jigsaw to make zig-zag, wave and sunburst forms – all of which were painted in bright, contrasting shades of yellow, red, blue and black.[31] It was as though the contemporaneously fashionable ceramicist Clarice Cliff's patterns had materialised on an architectural scale – a spectacular contrast to the unlovely environment outside the cinema as the neighbourhood was dominated by the black corrugated masses and belching chimneys of Parkhead Forge. Elsewhere, Lennox and MacMath designed the 2,600-seat Tudor cinema in Giffnock for Frutin, opened in 1936 and the name of which was as misleading as that of the Granada, as it was largely a moderne design with a curving corner frontage.[32] Its context was middle-class outer suburbia and so it never reached the success of its equivalents in working-class Parkhead and Gorbals. Smaller and simpler Lennox and MacMath cinema designs included the 1,300-seat Globe in Johnstone, which was of comparable external appearance to the Tudor, and the 730-seat Rex in the South Lanarkshire village of Newmilns, both opened in 1939.[33]

James McKissack – who was himself a keen amateur cinematographer and had designed early Glasgow cinemas after the enactment of the Cinematograph Act – had begun his architectural career in 1899 as an apprentice in his father's practice, John McKissack & Son, which had initially designed mainly churches and industrial buildings. He attended Glasgow School of Art, gained partnership status in 1900 and made a study tour of Italy and France. Following the death of McKissack senior in 1915, cinema design became the main speciality.

James McKissack's main client, Richard Singleton, had been both an early cinema entrepreneur and a founding supporter of the Labour Party. His son,

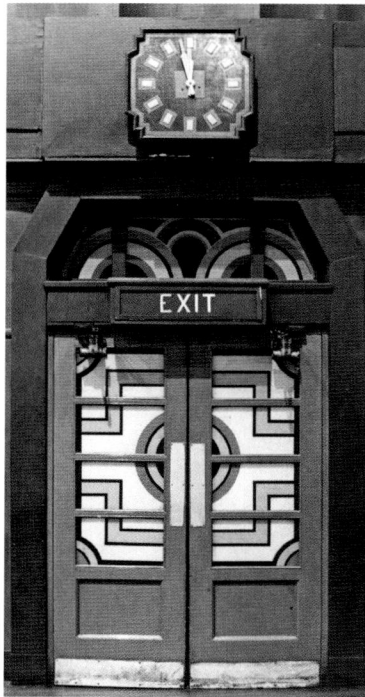

**Auditorium exit doors of the Mecca,
Balmore Road, Glasgow**
James McKissack of John McKissack & Son, 1933
Bruce Peter collection

The Commodore, Dumbarton Road, Glasgow
James McKissack of John McKissack & Son, 1933
Bruce Peter collection

George, perpetuated the business and opened his first purpose-built venue, the Broadway in Shettleston, in 1930. His other major clients, George Smith and James Welsh, were Labour councillors who had first shown films in a rented hall in Denniston in 1910. By the 1930s, Smith had become the city's Housing Convenor and the pair commissioned from McKissack the 1,620-seat Mecca Picture House, which opened in 1933, to serve the new Possilpark corporation housing scheme. For this cinema and others, McKissack clad not only the auditorium roof but also its sides and rear in panels of corrugated asbestos cement – a cheap and quick solution which Albert V Gardner also used for the rear-quarters of some of his designs.[34] At the same time, McKissack designed for Singleton the Commodore at Scotstoun, which was followed in 1936 by the Vogue cinemas in Rutherglen and Strathmartine Road, Dundee – all of which featured faience tiled porticoes in various rectilinear Art Deco polychromatic designs

to denote their entrances.[35] The Vogue name was, of course, highly aspirational, referencing the American-owned glossy fashion magazine. In the same year, the Embassy cinema in Shawlands on the city's Southside was also built to his design. The client on this occasion was the Glasgow Photo Playhouse Company, which before the First World War had employed McKissack to draw up its La Scala cinemas in central Glasgow and in Helensburgh. The exterior of the Embassy featured twin towers embellished with moulded faience.[36] Within, McKissack's cinemas were all very plain, however, the only decoration being of the door architraves, which were more likely to be noticed in the near-dark. In September 1936, Singleton sold his entire circuit to the Birmingham-based Odeon chain, which was anxious to gain a Scottish foothold.[37]

In Edinburgh, McKissack enlarged the five-year-old Caley Cinema on Lothian Road in 1928, approximately doubling its capacity to 1,800 by

The Vogue, Langlands Road, Govan, Glasgow
James McKissack of John McKissack & Son, 1938
Bruce Peter collection

Auditorium exit doors of the Vogue, Govan
James McKissack of John McKissack & Son, 1938
HES SC2542738

building its auditorium upwards. In such a rapidly expanding commercial field of business, projects of this kind were commonplace and, in this instance at least, he did an excellent job, achieving the enlargement by matching the building's existing French Empire-style frontage to a new mansard roof, which few would have guessed had not been part of the original design intention. On the interior, though, the latest jazz moderne style was used for the new plaster mouldings and for panels of stained glass in the foyer.[38] In 1933 he similarly converted the 20-year-old Tivoli cinema on the city's Gorgie Road into the New Tivoli, doubling its capacity to 1,200 and adding a new entrance portico in matching red sandstone with jazz moderne embellishments.[39] Although McKissack again evidently tried his best, the bricked-up original entranceway remained very obvious, even after repurposing as a poster display space. He also designed entirely new cinemas to serve peripheral Edinburgh

housing estates – for example, the Carlton in Piershill, opened in 1935, and the Embassy in Pilton of 1937, both for the local Robert McLaughlin circuit.[40] The following year he planned the Raith in Kirkcaldy for the same owner, with an idiosyncratic cloud-shaped entrance portico, and he gave a similar treatment to the Embassy in Troon, built in 1937 for the Ayrshire-based A S Blair circuit.[41] By this point, McKissack was sharing design work with an assistant, William J Anderson (1883–1950), who was the son of a cabinetmaker and had attended Glasgow School of Art from 1904 to 1908.

Back in Glasgow, George Singleton used finance accrued from his Odeon deal to commission the 2,500-seat Vogue in Govan from McKissack, which was completed 1938 and had a curving cream frontage in fluted tiles carried to full height, each vertical rib having a strip of coloured neon attached.[42] Interviewed by the author in the early 1990s, the elderly Singleton recalled flying from Renfrew to London shortly after it opened and feeling very proud upon seeing the scintillating colours of his cinema far below.[43] Smith & Welsh's Riddrie, with 1,791 seats, was located in the suburban housing scheme of that name and has a streamline moderne frontage of horizontal emphasis building up to its centrally placed name sign.[44] Their 2,500-seat Aldwych in Cardonald was, by contrast, severely rectilinear, finished in render and with a deep cornice; both were also opened in 1938.[45] These three were McKissack's most impressive suburban cinemas.

McKissack's final cinema design was again for Singleton, who had been persuaded by his friend Charles Oakley to build a city-centre venue in Glasgow's Rose Street to show good-quality continental films that on account of their foreign-language soundtracks were unavailable in mainstream Hollywood-dominated venues. The solution was devised by McKissack's assistant William J Anderson, who was significantly influenced by Burnet, Tait & Lorne's Curzon cinema in London's Mayfair. His scheme was similarly faced in Dutch-style brown brick, though Singleton insisted on the base being of faience to enable easy cleaning.[46] Named the Cosmo, short for 'cosmopolitan', the cinema's two-storey foyer featured a globe over the stalls entrance while the auditorium seated a mere 850.[47] Opened in 1939, its motto was 'Entertainment for the Discriminating' and Oakley's cartoon of the bowler-hatted 'Mr Cosmo', modelled on George Singleton, was its trademark.[48]

Glasgow's other prolific cinema specialist, Charles J McNair, had designed his first cinema, Scott's Electric Theatre in the city's Gallowgate, in 1911. This

The Riddrie, Cumbernauld Road, Glasgow
James McKissack of John McKissack & Son, 1938
HES DP337352

Exterior, foyer and proscenium of the Cosmo, Rose Street, Glasgow

William J Anderson of John McKissack & Son, 1939

Bruce Peter collection

cinema was built for a local entertainment impresario and construction entrepreneur, George Urie Scott, who subsequently founded the Cinema Construction Company to build nearly all of the many other cinemas which the McNair practice designed in the 1930s. The son of a butcher from Ayr, in 1898 McNair had joined the local architectural firm of James Morris (1857–1942), moving to Glasgow in 1903 to work with John Nisbet (1868–1951), whose focus was the design of tenement housing, the construction of which ended abruptly as a result of the Finance Act of 1909, which taxed developers for increasing land values. McNair thereafter took over the practice and shifted specialism to cinemas. From 1927 onwards, his junior partner was Robert Elder, who had studied at the Glasgow School of Architecture, joining McNair shortly after graduation.[49]

The Regal, Maxwell Place, Stirling
Charles J McNair and Robert Elder, 1932
Bruce Peter collection

Working with them in the latter 1930s was a young assistant, Robert Forsyth (1913–1998), who in the mid-1990s recalled to the author that:

> McNair was a genial wee man – very good with clients. Scott would come into the office with large-scale maps of districts around Glasgow. He'd have selected suitable sites for building cinemas and drawn concentric rings around them to find out how many people were living within a one-, two-, three-mile radius and he'd know how many tram routes there were passing by and what the frequency of service was. Elder, who became a partner in the early 1930s, did most of the designing. He was a bachelor who was pretty much married to his drawing board. A man of few words, he sat quietly chain-smoking as he drew up the projects, which he then handed to me or one of the other assistants to detail.[50]

The Regal, Princes Street, Falkirk
Charles J McNair and Robert Elder, 1934
Bruce Peter collection

Auditorium of the Regal, Ellis Street, Coatbridge
Charles J McNair and Robert Elder, 1934
Kevin Gooding collection

As a developer, builder and operator of cinemas, Scott was unusual, but his approach to analysing local commercial potential before committing to sites probably was fairly typical practice in the industry as a whole. McNair & Elder designed cinemas for Scott's own companies, for the prominent A B King circuit and, most importantly, for the powerful and expansive Associated British Cinemas (ABC) circuit, which had been founded by a Glasgow solicitor, John Maxwell, and which in the 1930s was running cinemas the length and breadth of Britain. In 1929 McNair converted a ballroom into the flagship ABC cinema in Glasgow, the Regal on Sauchiehall Street. He added a new entrance portico, detailed to reflect the design of the adjacent Grecian Chambers building by Alexander 'Greek' Thomson, and through which was accessed an opulent neoclassical interior.[51] The Rex in Riddrie and the Regal in Hamilton, both of which opened in 1931, were similarly decorated, but the Regal in Stirling, completed in 1932, and the Regals in Paisley and Falkirk, both opened in 1934 with the latter a conversion from an older theatre, had jazz moderne décor.[52] The Regal, Coatbridge, the Plaza, Govan and the Princes, Springburn were

Auditorium of the Regal, Maxwell Place, Stirling
Charles J McNair and Robert Elder, 1932
Kevin Gooding collection

completed in 1936, all with impressive streamlined interiors, which McNair & Elder became particularly adept at designing, though their external aspects were comparatively unsophisticated.[53] Whereas McKissack usually preferred shiny faience for frontages, McNair & Elder tended to use render, giving most of their designs a much more austere appearance. Typical seating capacities were between 2,000 and 2,400. Usually, there was an oval void formed by the balcony front and the tapering side walls flanking the proscenium, the latter being punctured by horizontal slits containing decorative grillwork, focusing attention on the screen. Above, deep cornices concealed colour-change lighting, which suffused the walls and ceiling in slowly changing colours. According to Robert Forsyth, construction followed a well-organised process:

> Having erected the steel frames, the roof would be fitted, then teams of Irish brickies would come on site to build the outside walls. While this was happening, the balcony cantilevers would be assembled. Its main girder was always the heaviest piece of structure and one of the first items to arrive on site right at the beginning of construction. Next, while the floors were being laid, wooden batons would be attached to the

steelwork onto which expanded metal sheeting was fixed. Specialist plasterers sprayed this with layer upon layer of plaster to make the domed ceiling, which was the best shape for acoustic reasons. The rest of the auditorium would then be lined in plasterboard, which was also sprayed with a skin of coarse plaster to lessen the reverberation. Pegboard tiles were fitted to the rear walls further to dampen this.[54]

Later McNair & Elder projects for George Urie Scott himself and for A B King had much more inspired exteriors as well. Their 1,600-seat State cinema which opened in King's Park in 1937, stood at the crest of a hill. It was particularly impressive, with the receding volumes of the foyer spaces expressed in white render and the structure of the auditorium exposed in darker horizontal bands and held within a low white rendered wall with vertical fins. It was one of two cinemas built for Scott's Cathcart Picture Playhouse Company – the other was the 2,009-seat State, Shettleston.[55]

The State, Castlemilk Road, King's Park
Charles J McNair and Robert Elder, 1937
Glasgow City Archives

Exterior and foyer of the Lyceum, Govan Road, Glasgow
Charles J McNair and Robert Elder, 1937
Glasgow City Archives and Bruce Peter collection

McNair & Elder's two best designs, however, were both for cinemas controlled by A B King, whose role in the development of the cinema industry in Scotland was seminal, not only as a major exhibitor but also as an organiser, lobbyist and diplomat. Between the wars, he was responsible for booking films for many of Scotland's independent cinemas. He was a member of the General Council of the Cinema Exhibitors' Association, chairing their Entertainments Tax Committee. In the 1935 Budget, this Committee was instrumental in securing a remission in Entertainment Tax for cinema seats costing up to 6d, a great relief to the small independent exhibitors whom King supported so enthusiastically.[56] The first of these notable projects came after the Lyceum in Govan, a former theatre, burned down, and King commissioned McNair & Elder to design a suitable replacement. The old theatre had followed the line of the neighbouring tenements but, as there was insufficient space for the planned 2,600-seater successor, this was located at right-angles further behind. The new building is

The Ascot, Great Western Road, Glasgow
Charles J McNair and Robert Elder, 1939
Glasgow City Archives

Drawing of facade of the Ascot, Glasgow
Robert Elder of McNair & Elder, 1939
GSA Archives

therefore distinguished by a three-storey-high curtain wall frontage which sweeps around the street corner in a graceful curve, but has open space directly behind it. Above the doorways and canopy are what appear to be five tall, recessed windows, formed of panels of reeded glass and interspersed with blue tiled mullions. The remainder is clad in tiles and facing brick and the flowing lines are emphasised by a narrow cornice. There are prominent display panels, carefully placed to be in line with the top deck windows of passing tramcars. The foyer is circular, floored in shiny terrazzo and with an 'island' ticket booth in the centre.[57] A greater contrast with the sooty ashlar tenements next door would have been difficult to imagine.

McNair & Elder's final cinema project, the 1,963-seat Ascot at Anniesland, completed in 1939, obviously used design inspiration from the Empire Exhibition, being very similar in appearance to the Palace of Engineering. Built for Great Western Cinemas, a company in which A B King was involved, its name was allegedly chosen as a result of its being partly financed by a winning bet by another of the directors.[58] Five tall windows with slim fins between were recessed in the cream-tiled frontage with flanking drum-shaped volumes containing the stairs to the balcony. The war, and materials rationing, started during construction and so permission was needed to complete it.[59]

Edinburgh offered fewer development opportunities for cinema entrepreneurs than Scotland's other cities. Glasgow had 139 cinemas in operation at the outbreak of the Second World War – more cinema seats per head of population than any other city in the country – whereas Edinburgh had only 65. Its Old Town was already densely built upon and the dignified Craigleith stone edifices in the New Town did not lend themselves to augmentation with what some residents would have considered Americanised brashness. Outwith the centre, however, Thomas Bowhill Gibson designed the elegant Dominion in Morningside, which opened in 1938 and has been enduringly successful.[60] His subsequent County in Portobello, completed in 1939, is notable for its symmetrical facade with flanking drum towers, between which there originally rose a tall fin with glass blocks illuminated from within by colour-change lighting.[61] The interiors of both are notable for their striking moderne plasterwork.

More productive in the churning out of designs for cinemas than either McKissack or McNair & Elder was the Glaswegian-born and educated, though London-based, William R Glen (1885–1950). Formerly the architectural partner of Albert V Gardner, Glen was appointed by ABC cinemas in 1929 as its in-house architect, running a drawing office within its London headquarters at Golden Square in Soho and designing more than 70 of its new cinemas in England. Photographs of Glen at the height of his powers in the 1930s show a stylish man who was reputedly a snappy dresser, wearing sharply cut double-breasted suits and white spats over his shoes. His daughter, Gari Todd, recalled that he was 'very proper, very gentlemanly, liked us to speak, dress and behave nicely… and, so far as we could judge, was very formal in dealings with others'.[62] Glen was fortunate that ABC always sought a strong presence in the high street, rarely accepting sites that allowed only narrow entrances and usually buying sufficient ground to set the auditorium block some way back. He became particularly adept at handling foyer spaces, usually making them airy double-height volumes, lit by chrome pendant light fittings, while the walls were often adorned with medallions and friezes in low relief. Grand staircases on either side met an open landing bridge in the middle, with a decorative metal balustrade. Auditoria were tall with conspicuous decorative grillwork and boldly modelled ceilings with dramatically sculpted ribs, illuminated troughs and scalloped edges picked out in gold, stepping down

The Dominion, Newbattle Terrace, Edinburgh
Thomas Bowhill Gibson, 1938
Bruce Peter collection

Auditorium of the Dominion, Edinburgh
Thomas Bowhill Gibson, 1938
Bruce Peter collection

Facade and sectional drawings of the County, Bath Street, Portobello
Thomas Bowhill Gibson, 1938–1939
HES DP228692

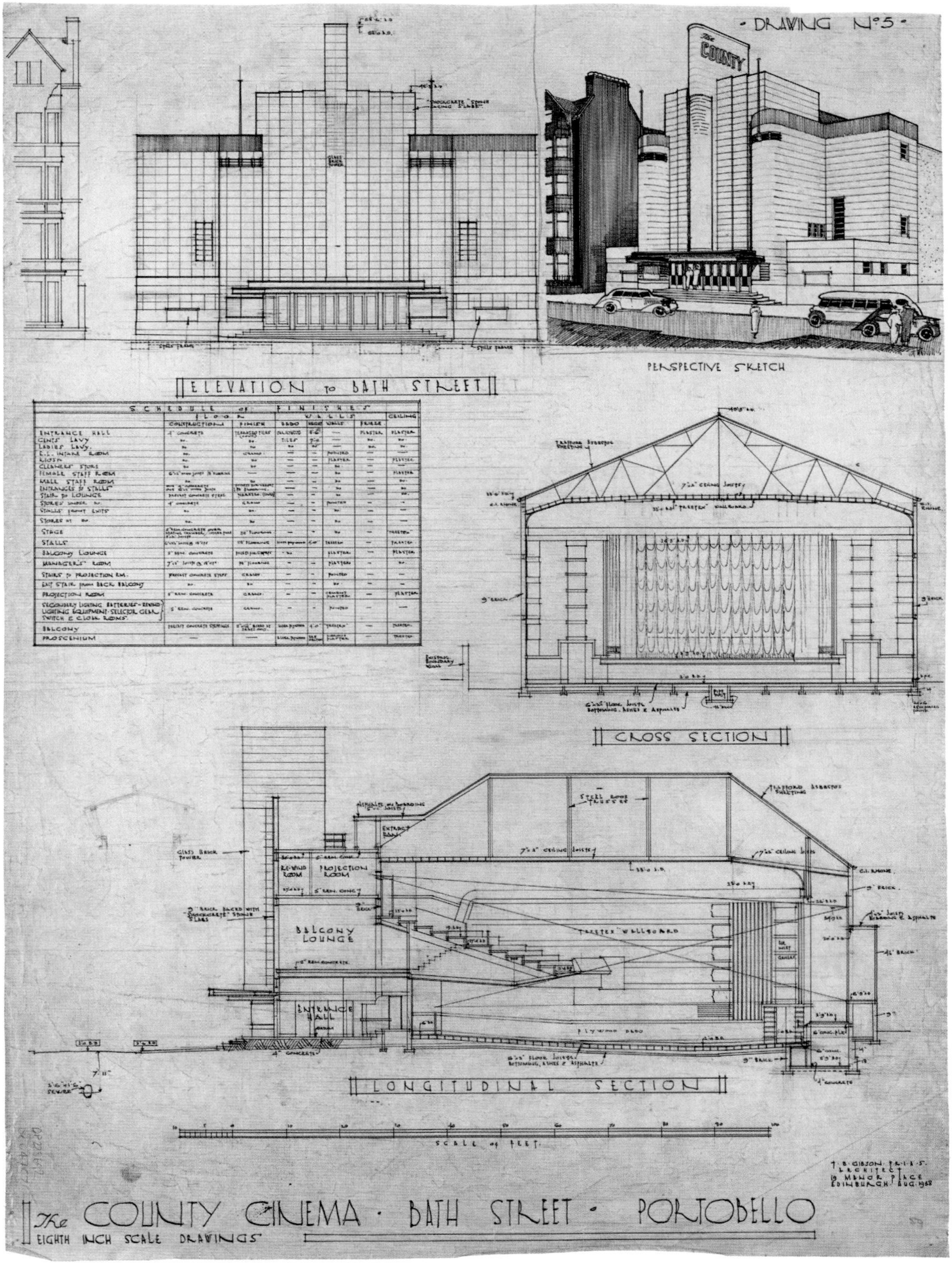

THE COUNTY

PERSPECTIVE SKETCH

[ELEVATION TO BATH STREET]

SCHEDULE OF FINISHES

CROSS SECTION

BALCONY LOUNGE

PROJECTION ROOM

RE-WIND ROOM

ENTRANCE HALL

LONGITUDINAL SECTION

SCALE OF FEET

The COUNTY CINEMA · BATH STREET · PORTOBELLO
EIGHTH INCH SCALE DRAWINGS

Auditorium of the Regal, Lothian Road, Edinburgh
William R Glen, 1939
Kevin Gooding collection

towards the screen opening. The front emergency exits from the circle faced backwards with short slips and the auditorium would therefore narrow in front of the circle and taper further inwards towards the screen. Though no two cinemas from Glen's office were the same, they had in common ingenious planning and the skilful manipulation of space.[63]

In Scotland, Glen was responsible for only two projects for ABC, the remainder being by McNair & Elder. The Regal in Edinburgh, which opened in 1939, was incorporated into the Lothian House office and retail development on Lothian Road by the architectural practice Stuart Kaye and Walls. Only the canopy and entrance doors distinguished it externally but the interior represented Glen's work at its best, the auditorium being adorned with ornate ventilation grilles to either side of the screen opening and also illuminated painted panels. For an ABC cinema, it was large with 2,769 seats and a cafe.[64] The 1,488-seat Palace in Arbroath, completed in 1940, replaced an older cinema of the same name and was evidently built

to a much tighter budget, though it too had a double-height foyer while the auditorium walls around the screen were embellished with Glen's typically complex Art Deco plasterwork.[65]

In England in the second half of the 1930s, it was the Odeon circuit, founded by a Birmingham entrepreneur, Oscar Deutsch, which asserted the most dynamically up-to-date architectural identity and boldly brought an expressionistic moderne aesthetic to many otherwise architecturally traditional regional towns. In Scotland, Odeon expanded mostly through buying up existing cinemas, such as those bought from Singleton in 1936. In 1938 three new Scottish Odeons were built in Ayr, Hamilton and Motherwell to designs by Thomas Braddock (1887–1976), who was an assistant of the company's London architect, Andrew Mather (1891–1938).[66] The Ayr Odeon, which seated 1,700, was the most impressive-looking of the three, being located on a prominent site facing onto Burns Statue Square and next to the railway station – and it is the only survivor today.[67] Deutsch next proposed a number of much larger Odeons to be developed, mainly around Glasgow. Another Mather assistant,

**Drawing of proposed Odeon cinema,
Partick, Glasgow**
Keith P Roberts of Andrew Mather, 1939
Bruce Peter collection

Keith P Roberts (1910–1994), drew up schemes for
Odeons at Bridgeton, Partick, Townhead, Dumbarton
and Falkirk.[68] None were built owing to financial
difficulties and materials shortages caused by the
worsening political situation in Europe, but Roberts'
scheme for Partick would have been a particularly
impressive building.[69]

The Scottish cinema that came closest to emulating
the distinctive style of the best of the English Odeons
was the independently owned, 2,648-seat La Scala
in Clydebank. It was also completed in 1938 for a
company controlled by A B King to a design by Lennox
D Paterson (1902–1984), who had inherited the firm
of Gavin Paterson (1866–1934) of Hamilton. Just like
many Odeons, La Scala's corner-entrance was denoted
by a tower feature clad in brick and tilework. The
recent completion of the giant ocean liner *Queen Mary*
by the nearby John Brown shipyard and the ordering

La Scala, Graham Avenue, Clydebank
Lennox D Paterson of Gavin Paterson & Son, 1938
Bruce Peter collection

of the *Queen Elizabeth* inspired a nautically themed treatment of the interior, the screen curtains having appliqué depictions of the soaring bows of the two Cunard 'Queens' pointing in from each side.[70]

Cinemas were not restricted to the cities and larger industrial towns. Rural market towns also were lucrative places as they were route centres and could therefore easily be accessed by thinly spread populations. For many farm workers, going to 'the pictures' was a treat on market day. To enable development, local businessmen – such as shop owners, solicitors and even haulage contractors – would collaborate, usually with A B King, to source the necessary operational expertise and also a reliable supply of films. Typically, such projects would be financed by a combination of these entrepreneurs' own investment, a share issue and, if necessary, a bank loan. Such locally owned cinemas offered many patrons the unaccustomed luxuries of fitted carpets, concealed colour-change interior lighting and several sets of appliqué and festooned curtains over the screen. The romance of the movies affected every aspect of their design and operation. The Regal in Lanark, a large and well-appointed 1,316-seater with a cafe, designed by Lennox D Paterson and opened in 1936, was owned and financed in this way.[71]

Andrew D Haxton of Leven made designing cinemas for smaller towns a significant aspect of his practice in the second half of the 1930s. As with his other commercial buildings, such as the Leven Co-operative store extension, cited previously, these had symmetrical frontages with pediments, while their entrance doorways and interiors were notable for their vigorously coloured and patterned Art Deco detailing. The prototype for this type of cinema was the Troxy in Leven, which opened in 1935, and was followed by the Regal in Broxburn, West Lothian, in 1936.[72] A local cinema circuit, Lothians Star Theatres, owned by Messrs Millar and Walker of Bathgate, then commissioned two further cinemas from Haxton – the Regal in Armadale, which opened in 1937 and the Regal in Bathgate, which opened the following year.[73] The latter's interior was the fanciest of all, featuring remarkably camp bas relief panels on either side of the screen depicting nude muscular Roman charioteers with firm buttocks, designed and made by John Alexander of Newcastle.[74] (Identical panels were installed in the Forum cinema in Hexham in Northumberland). The same owner's Regals in

The Regal, Bannatyne Street, Lanark
Lennox D Paterson of Gavin Paterson & Son, 1936
Bruce Peter collection

Facade drawing of the Regal, Broxburn
Andrew D Haxton, 1936
HES DP029774

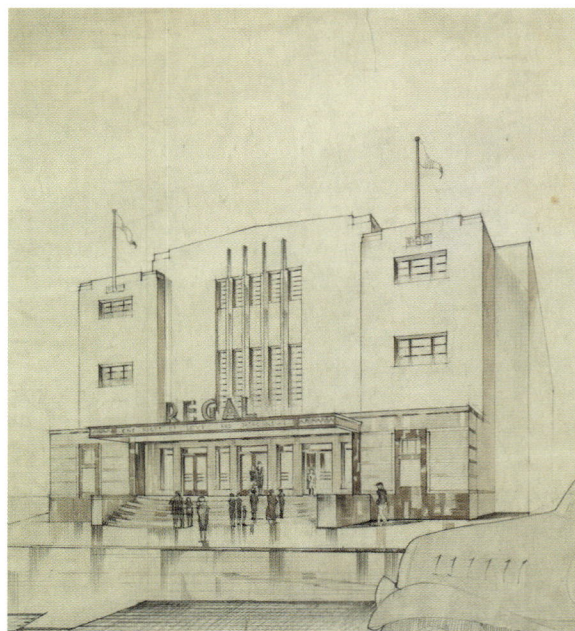

The Regal, Bridge Street, Bathgate
Andrew D Haxton, 1938
Bruce Peter

Plaster grille by the screen in the Regal, Bathgate
John Alexander of M Alexander & Son, 1938
Bruce Peter, HES SC800184

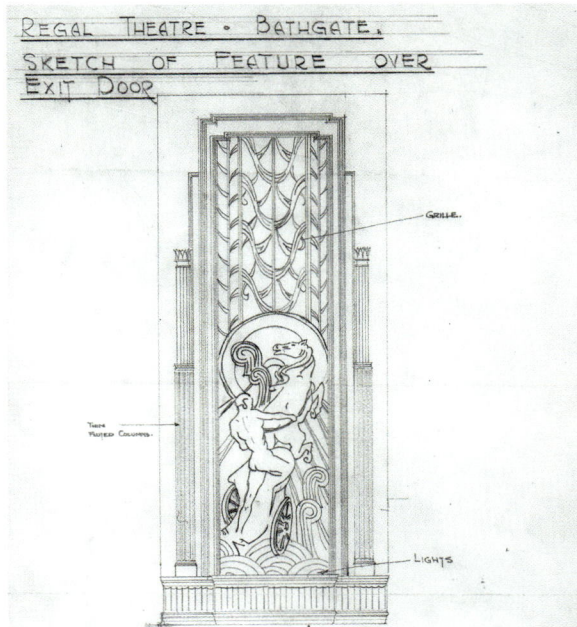

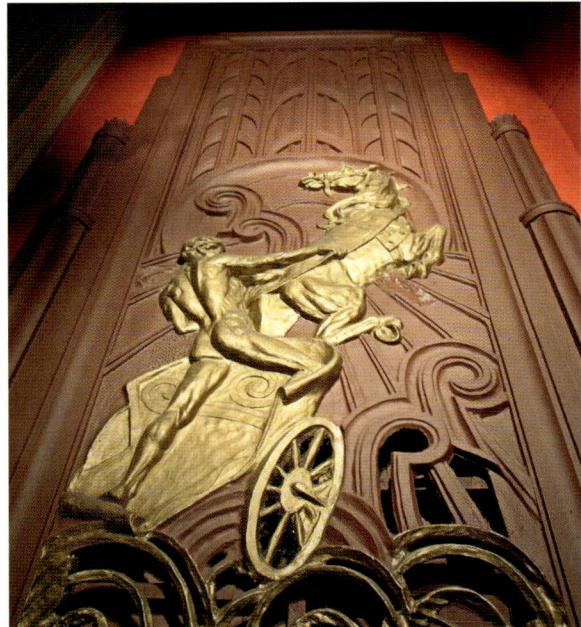

The Regal, Station Road, Shotts
John Ross McKay of Richardson & McKay, 1939
Bruce Peter collection

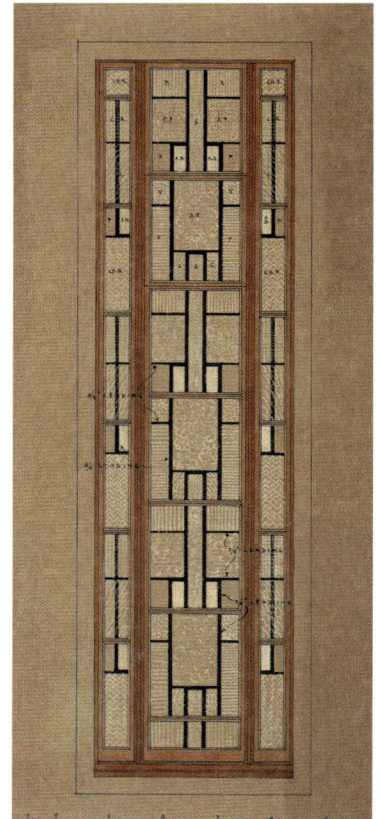

Detail drawing of glazing of the Regal, Shotts
John Ross McKay of Richardson & McKay, 1939
HES SC1381441

West Calder and Shotts opened in 1938 and 1939 respectively, and were the work of John Ross McKay of Edinburgh, their facades having a tower feature at one end in the moderne 'Odeon' manner.[75] These all had capacities in the 800 to 1,000-seat range.

In Ayrshire, the vividly imaginative Glasgow School of Architecture-trained, Kilbirnie-based architect James Houston (1893–1966) produced two of Scotland's most outlandish but memorable cinema designs. From an artistic family, he excelled in his studies, winning medals for his draughting and, following naval service in the First World War, he became a lecturer at the Royal Technical College in Glasgow. His wider output consisted mostly of bungalows and villas of unexceptional design, plus some shops, agricultural and industrial buildings.

The cinema designs – plus a cafe and restaurant complex in Largs – were his most notable projects, demonstrating a playful imagination. The 1,200-seat Radio in Kilbirnie was completed in 1938 and, as with the famous Radio City Music Hall in New York City, took the 'miracle' of the transmission of radio waves as its theme. It has a low, curvaceous frontage with chrome eagles' heads with wings at each corner and a fake radio beacon soaring above the entrance with a flashing light and purple neon zig-zags to broadcast its presence to the neighbourhood.[76] Bearing in mind that the Radio stands at a crossroads in an otherwise quite staid little Ayrshire village of sandstone terraces and villas, this design was more than a little audacious. Houston's subsequent Viking at Largs, which opened in 1939 and had a similar

The Radio, Bridgend, Kilbirnie
James Houston, 1938
HES

Auditorium of the Radio, Kilbirnie
James Houston, 1938
HES

capacity to the Radio, took its inspiration from the Battle of Largs of 1263. A fantasy fortress in red, white and blue, it stood in landscaped gardens with a replica of a Viking longboat projecting from the entrance. Patrons entered between buttressed walls beneath battlements. A portcullis, which advertised the cinema's programme, was shut over the doors for security at night.[77] The interiors of both the Radio and the Viking were designed by Guthrie & Wells and perpetuated the themes of the buildings' exteriors. Their design for the Viking was particularly vigorous, featuring Art Deco mural panels of imagined scenes from the Battle of Largs on the splay walls flanking the proscenium and a mix of ancient Norse and jazz moderne patterns on the side walls.[78] The Viking's colourful thematic design would have delighted visiting holidaymakers. It was indeed one of several fun-looking buildings constructed in the 1930s along the town's waterfront, another being the Mooring's Café, for which Houston also was responsible (described in the following chapter).

The Viking, Irvine Road, Largs
James Houston, 1939
HES SC910631

Facade drawing of the Viking, Largs
James Houston, 1938–1939
HES SC879095

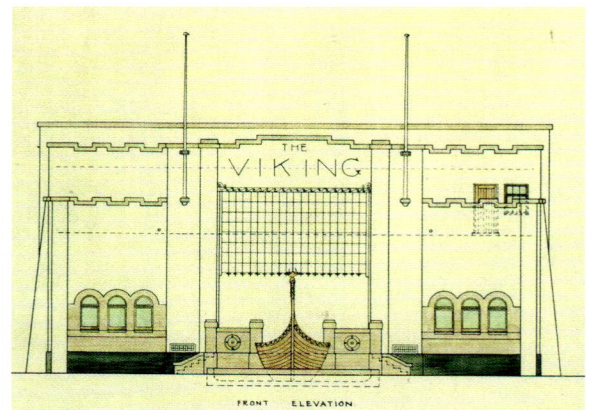

**Rendered sectional drawing of auditorium of the
Viking, Largs**
John Christie of Guthrie & Wells, 1938–1939
Glasgow City Archives

**Design for one of two decorative panels flanking
the screen in the Viking, Largs**
John Christie of Guthrie & Wells, 1938–1939
Glasgow City Archives

In smaller and more remote communities, new cinemas needed to be built as economically as possible and so a Glasgow steel fabricator, F D Cowieson & Co Ltd, owned by the architect-engineer Frederick D Cowieson (1877–1945), spotted an opportunity to design and build these. Its range of products otherwise included kits for 'churches, chapels, halls, pavilions, hospitals, bungalows, sanatoria, schools, also church furniture, etc', and even bus bodywork.[79] Among its 1930s cinema output were the 1,114-seat Playhouse in Oban opened in 1933, the 950-seat Playhouse in Stornoway and the 800-seat Regal in Anstruther, both of which were completed in 1934.[80] Another Glasgow company offering a similar 'design and build' offer was Stellmacs Ltd, the proprietors of which were Frank F Maxwell (1897–1996), Archibald M H Stewart (b 1887) and William J Maxwell (b 1890), who sought to entice cost-conscious clients by providing outline designs and estimates free-of-charge. Between 1931 and 1939 Stellmacs Ltd was responsible for building 20 cinemas, most of which were in Ayrshire and Lanarkshire towns and villages.[81] Typical examples were the 565-seat Palace in Castle Douglas and the Regal in Dalry, both inaugurated in 1934. The windows in the latter's facade were located to resemble eyes and a nose (with the doors below being the mouth).[82] The 665-seat County Cinema

The Playhouse, Beach Street, Stornoway
Frederick D Cowieson & Co, 1934
Bruce Peter collection

in Kinross and the 1,500-seat Regal in Peterhead were built by them in 1938 and 1939 respectively for the Dundee-headquartered J B Milne circuit. Even if their angular jazz moderne styling was by then a little dated, the frontal treatment of the County was at least carried out with brio.[83]

A third Glaswegian design-and-build contractor producing complete cinemas was Spiers Ltd, the office of which was in Blythswood Square. Founded in the late nineteenth century by the entrepreneur John Spiers

The County, Station Road, Kinross
Stellmacs Ltd, 1938
Bruce Peter collection

Cinema De Luxe, Glasgow Road, Denny
J Abercromby of John Spiers Ltd, 1939
Bruce Peter collection

as a manufacturer of power looms for the textile industry, it diversified from the 1880s onwards into the fabrication of iron-framed churches, schools and village halls, iron fencing and railway equipment. A London office was opened in 1902, when hospitals and bungalow housing were added to its range. Among the cinemas for which it was responsible was the 850-seat Cinema De Luxe in Denny, which was designed by its engineer, J Abercromby and opened in 1939.[84] Its cream-painted facade was distinguished by a stepped pediment and three vertical triangular projecting windows, the two flanking the entrance illuminating the balcony stairways. It stood out boldly in a town otherwise dominated by dark sandstone frontages.

But even these companies' efforts did not quite represent Art Deco in Scottish cinemas at the most basic. To find this, one needed to visit the back streets of Dundee's working-class districts where the J B Milne circuit operated some very primitive halls of older vintage, featuring bench seating and exposed ceiling trusses. To these, Milne appended Art Deco canopies, pediments and name-signs above the usually narrow entrance doorways while, inside, screen curtains with Art Deco patterning were hung. Names such as the Rex and Broadway may have been suggestive of stately or Americanised glamour, but the

The Broadway, Arthurstone Terrace, Dundee
Allan & Frisken, 1931
Bruce Peter collection

name of the Dundee Rex instead was reputedly inspired by the owner's dog.[85] In such locations, the experience of Art Deco was about as far from the glamour of the Paris Exposition as could be imagined.

The Rex, Alexander Street, Dundee
Architect for modernisation not known,
originally built 1913
Bruce Peter collection

Ballrooms and ice rinks

Similar lightweight steel framing systems and corrugated asbestos cladding panels as were employed to build cinemas and the pavilions of the Empire Exhibition were also used to enclose other types of leisure and entertainment facilities. In the Edwardian era, the waltzes of Strauss had formed a soundtrack to the greater toleration of unmarried mingling and embracing in public ballrooms, albeit within a formalised structure, policed by stewards to ensure propriety. Dance hall operators were very keen to present respectable, romantic images and feared the revoking of their licences if standards of decorum were not maintained.

Prior to the First World War there were also passing crazes for ice skating and roller skating, for which arguably the first large but utilitarian 'leisure sheds' with show facades were erected. Whereas the roller rinks came and went, ballroom dancing became increasingly popular in urban Scotland, especially following the advent of American-influenced popular music in the 1920s and its associated fashion imagery as viewed on-screen in cinemas. In local ballrooms, there were indeed many who hoped briefly to feel themselves to be like Fred Astaire and Ginger Rogers. The décor of the ballroom environment provided a glamorous context for dressing up, seeing and being seen, socialising and perhaps eventually finding a partner for life. Even the title of 'Palais de Danse', commonly used by British commercial dance hall operators, was intended to connote continental elegance and romance.[86]

As with cinemas, many Scottish ballrooms predated the era of the Art Deco and moderne styles and therefore needed updating. Since the design of ballrooms involved many of the same structural, aesthetic and regulatory requirements as cinemas, unsurprisingly cinema architects were often responsible for their design. One Glasgow ballroom was the F&F Palais at Partick, owned by the local entertainment entrepreneurs Fyfe & Fyfe Ltd, which occupied a hall that had previously been an early cinema and, before that, workshop premises. In the latter 1930s, Guthrie & Wells carried out a thorough redecoration, involving the superimposition of jazz moderne plasterwork and a typically vivid paint scheme, while a new moderne frontage was erected on Dumbarton Road.[87] Of venues that were from the outset in the moderne idiom, Glasgow's Barrowland Ballroom was a well-known example. Occupying the upper floor of a very

Advertisement for the Plaza Ballroom, Eglinton Toll, Glasgow
Edward Patrick Kinsella, c1920
Courtesy of Lesley Wood and Ken MacGregor

austere factory-like moderne block, the lower level contained a market hall, which housed part of the Barras street market. Opened in 1933 its design was by Joseph Boyd (b 1873), who in the 1930s was the only surviving partner of the Glasgow firm of Bryden, Robertson & Boyd, and who otherwise mainly carried out modernisations of cinemas.[88] A more stylish-looking ballroom elsewhere in city's East End was the Dennistoun Palais, designed by McNair & Elder and opened in 1938, which externally was a roughcast brick box, the entrance being via a faience-clad corner, cut back at a 45-degree angle and illuminated by neon; this looked most appealing at night.[89]

The Art Deco elements of other Scottish ballrooms were mostly signage and paintwork as this genre of leisure building did not receive as much investment input as cinemas. Perhaps one reason why fewer

Dennistoun Palais, Duke Street, Glasgow
Charles J McNair and Robert Elder, 1938
Newsquest

Kirkcaldy Ice Rink, Rosslyn Street, Kirkcaldy
Williamson & Hubbard, 1938
Bruce Peter

Detail of facade of Kirkcaldy Ice Rink
Williamson & Hubbard, 1938
Bruce Peter

ballrooms were built was that there already existed large numbers of municipal halls that were suitable for dancing. A rare, purpose-built example of a municipally owned dance venue was the Beach Ballroom in Aberdeen, designed by Thomas Roberts (1875–1955) and William Hume (1878–1941) and opened in 1929. Its faience facades used a material later closely associated with Art Deco but the design, outside and in, was entirely neoclassical; had it been built only a few years later, its detailing almost certainly would have been different.[90]

Ice rinks, although contained in similarly constructed enclosures to ballrooms, tended to be bigger and with raked perimeter seating for spectatorship at sports events, as well as a refrigeration plant to freeze the main arena. Viewed through a moderne sensibility, the speed and potential grace of ice skating, at least if professionally done, had obvious popular aesthetic appeal. Although the interiors of rinks were very utilitarian, their facade treatments and foyers, to greater or lesser degrees, had commonalities with those of cinemas and swimming pools. Typically, ice rinks were commercial speculations with set days for competitive ice hockey as well as professional ice-skating shows on others and also public skating or ballroom dancing (on an un-iced floor). Cafes and bandstands were thus often included to provide musical accompaniment and refreshments.

With regard to architectural treatment, there were two approaches. One option was for an Art Deco or moderne entrance portico appended to an otherwise largely featureless shed, exemplified at Dundee Ice Rink by local architect William Mollison Wilson (1901–1990) and at Kirkcaldy Ice Rink by Williamson & Hubbard; both opened in 1938.[91] An alternative option was to give some usually quite sparse architectural

Neon design for facade of Ayr Ice Rink
James Carrick of J & J A Carrick, 1938–1939
HES DP043403

Arena in Ayr Ice Rink, Station Road, Ayr
James Carrick of J & J A Carrick, 1939
HES DP036994

modelling to the entire front elevation with horizontal bands of Crittall windows, portholes, flagpoles, signage and neon. Examples were Falkirk Ice Rink by the local partnership of Robert Wilson (1886–1963) and Henry Wilson (1880–1961), which opened in 1938, and Ayr Ice Rink by James Carrick, completed early in 1939.[92] Murrayfield Ice Rink in Edinburgh by Herbert G Dunn (1906–1995) was another and it too should have opened in 1939 but, owing to the outbreak of war, it was instead requisitioned for use as a storage depot. Released in 1948, ice skating was finally able to commence almost a decade later than had been intended.[93] By then, a moderne symmetrical frontal block containing a cafe had been appended to the original design. Lanarkshire Ice Rink in Motherwell, which Jack Coia and T Warnett Kennedy (1911–2000) of Gillespie, Kidd & Coia designed, was never constructed – a pity as Coia's Palace of Industries (North) at the Empire Exhibition was highly accomplished and perhaps showed the approach to form and detailing he may have had in mind.

**Perspective of initial design for Murrayfield Ice
Rink, Edinburgh**
Herbert G Dunn of J B Dunn & Martin, 1938

Murrayfield Ice Rink, Edinburgh
Herbert G Dunn of J B Dunn & Martin, 1939–1948

Greyhound racing stadia

While operators of cinemas and ballrooms worked
hard to create respectable images in the face of moral
suspicion about the possible degenerative effects of
watching popular films and of unmarried couples
dancing, the proprietors of greyhound racing venues
– another highly popular commercial entertainment
in the 1930s – faced even greater challenges. The fact
that working-class men were the prime clientele and
that betting was involved led many critical observers to
believe that those who attended were 'going to the dogs'
in every sense. Greyhound racing had evolved from the
cruel rural sport of hare-coursing but the commercial
'electric' stadia that first appeared in the 1920s used a
motor to propel a dummy hare, which the racing dogs
instinctively chased. Particularly in southern England,
lower-division football clubs introduced racing as
an extra money-spinning attraction. The National
Greyhound Racing Society was founded in 1928 to

Entrance to Shawfield Stadium, Rutherglen Road, Glasgow
John Easton, 1937
Glasgow City Archives

represent the owners of the larger and more overtly commercial venues, which thereafter dominated. In popular culture, as the 1930s progressed, greyhounds came to embody the aesthetically desirable moderne traits of sleekness and speed.[94]

In the second half of the decade many stadia were upgraded with additional trackside facilities in the form of bars and restaurants, while their entrances and Totalisator (or Tote) boards often were re-clad with Art Deco and moderne forms and graphics. In Glasgow, there were eight greyhound racing venues by 1935, all fairly insalubrious relative to their better-funded counterparts around London. The Shawfield Stadium in Glasgow's East End, which was home to Clyde Football Club and had first hosted greyhound racing in 1932, was sold three years thereafter to the Shawfield Greyhound Racing Company, co-owned by John Bilsland, a Glaswegian who already ran the Stanley greyhound stadium in Liverpool. He commissioned the architect John Easton (1898–1977), who in the 1920s had assisted in the practices of the cinema designers

William Beresford Inglis and Albert V Gardner, to design a modernisation. Since 1932, Easton had attempted to establish himself in independent practice, which proved difficult on account of the prevailing Depression conditions and, having carried out only minor projects and produced a design for a cinema in Ibrox that had failed to come to fruition, the Shawfield rebuild was his first significant success. He devised a showy new entrance comprising brightly painted steel Art Deco entrance gates set in a brick portico with stepped sides, tiled pilasters and lanterns.[95] Within, a new grandstand was constructed and so the venue was transformed into a comparatively stylish one where even young couples were attracted to attend alongside the existing male clientele.

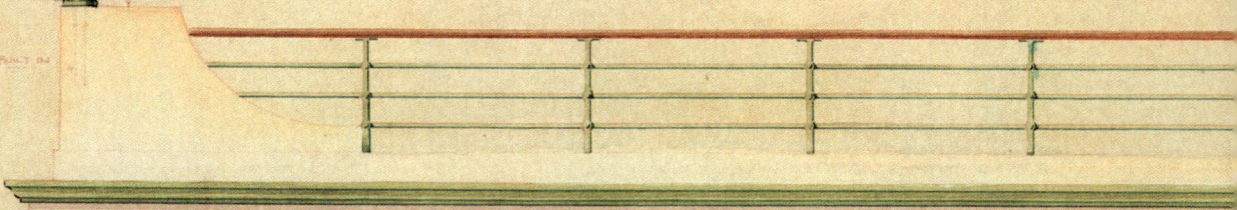

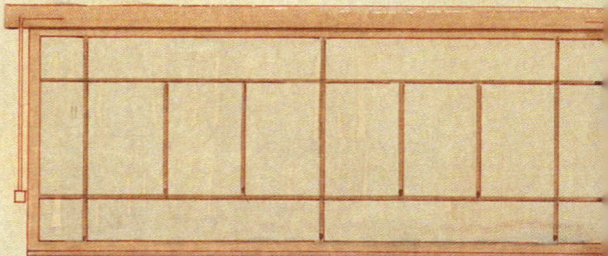

THE MOORINGS

ELEVATION

CHAPTER 8
HOSPITALITY AND CATERING

Eating, drinking and overnighting in glamorous, up-to-date environments were activities frequently represented in popular 1930s films and novels as being romantic and desirable. A greater awareness of continental and American methods of provision and presentation, disseminated through a lively professional journal, *The Caterer and Hotel-Keeper*, encouraged British hotel, restaurant, cafe and bar owners to emulate the latest overseas trends. Scotland's tourism grew during the 1930s and so expanded and modernised hotel and catering infrastructures were required to accommodate and feed travellers on the move.

Hotels and roadhouses

Growing car ownership and the construction of trunk roads resulted in an expanded hotel geography in the 1920s and 1930s. The existing larger properties had been built to serve the railways but now additional examples were needed in different locations for drivers and their passengers – including seaside holidaymakers and guests visiting Glasgow for the Empire Exhibition. In some ways, the new 'roadhouses' represented an update of the concept of the roadside inns of the pre-railway age.

Viewed from the outside, hotels may have had superficial similarities to other types of commercial building of their era – but beyond their facades, in terms

The Moorings, Largs
James Houston, 1936
HES SC879099

of structure, they were more complicated. Unusually among types of commercial premises, they required comparatively large spans on the lower floors for the public rooms with shorter spans for the bedroom storeys above, which also needed to be no deeper than two rooms with a corridor between so that all would have windows. This meant that a relatively long length of external wall was necessary, sometimes in large properties with an internal light-well in the centre of a block. The requirement for many bathrooms and toilets, kitchens and laundries all added to hotels' complexity and so, given the Depression conditions of the early 1930s, it is unsurprising that finance to build new ones was hard to come by. It was only in the decade's second half that construction recommenced.[1]

In London's West End, the fashionable and exclusive hotels used by high society as venues for the 'London Season', such as Claridge's and the Savoy, were among the first buildings in Britain of any kind to have Art Deco interiors and their stellar reputations in the hospitality and catering industry perhaps inspired operators and entrepreneurs elsewhere to emulate their style as best they could. Another significant and influential example was the London, Midland and Scottish Railway's Midland Hotel in Morecambe, completed in 1933 to a design by Oliver Hill. Built as an experimental attempt to attract middle-class visitors to what was otherwise a largely working-class resort, the Midland was widely published in architecture, catering and hospitality journals, which meant that its moderne styling became widely known and discussed.[2]

Perhaps owing to the combined effects of British insularity, the First World War and building regulations requiring window ventilation for every bathroom, hoteliers in Britain were slow to adopt the American all en suite model, in which the bathrooms were located adjacent to the corridors and mechanically ventilated. Even the LMS's luxury golfing hotel at Gleneagles, which was opened in 1924 (albeit to a pre-war design by James Miller), initially had just a quarter of en suite rooms. The remainder were retrofitted in a 1935 refurbishment, at which point the cocktail lounge and restaurant were transformed with new moderne interiors, designed by his son George James Miller. His interventions mostly involved installing suspended ceilings, formed of expanded metal and sprayed with plaster, to give a fashionably smooth, streamlined effect. The existing, now unwanted, neoclassical decorative enrichments were thereby entirely hidden from view. At the request of the British Government, the design of the hotel's new Restaurant du Soleil was precisely replicated for a restaurant at the Empire Exhibition in Johannesburg in 1936–1937.[3]

Simultaneously with the Gleneagles renovation, in Glasgow the first new Scottish hotel in the moderne manner throughout was under construction. Far from being a resort for prosperous tourists, it was instead a working men's hostel in the heavily industrialised East End. The Bellgrove Hotel on Gallowgate was designed by the cinema architects McNair & Elder, who faced it in alternative bands of harling and brick with repetitive horizontal lintels with the result that it closely resembled some of the era's new industrial architecture. Its tiled ground floor in bands of cream and black faience obviously related to their cinema output. Within were small rooms and communal showers and toilets.[4] (The building still stands and has latterly provided accommodation for those who would otherwise be homeless.)

Elsewhere, new hotels that were more upmarket were built for leisure and business travellers. As the moderne style lent itself to seaside locations, the task of designing a substantial four-storey extension to the Marine Hotel in Oban gave the Glasgow architect-entrepreneur James Taylor, who otherwise worked for the house builders Mactaggart & Mickel, a superb opportunity. The large new wing, overlooking Oban Bay, was built adjacent to an existing 1890-vintage building. Completed in 1936, its curvaceous projecting ground floor with extensive metal-framed glazing overlooks a sun terrace. This and the facade's stucco finish combined to give the impression that it might equally have materialised in a resort on the English Riviera.[5]

The Empire Exhibition brought about an increased need for hotel accommodation in the vicinity of Glasgow. Siting a new hotel on the Clyde Coast at Gourock was an ingenious solution as there was a busy steamer pier from which there were regular sailings to popular resorts such as Rothesay and Dunoon and an

Bellgrove Hotel, Gallowgate, Glasgow
Charles J McNair and Robert Elder, 1936
Bruce Peter

Marine Hotel, Corran Esplanade, Oban
James Taylor, 1936
Bruce Peter collection

Bay Hotel, Station Road, Gourock
James William Laird of Laird & Napier, 1938
Bruce Peter collection

adjacent railway station from which regular trains ran to Glasgow – many stopping *en route* at Cardonald, close to the Empire Exhibition's site. Opened in May 1938, the Bay Hotel was a four-storey edifice with a curved frontage, featuring a glazed stair tower near the centre. Its design was by James William Laird (1880–1939) of the Glasgow firm of Laird & Napier, which had been founded in the mid-1920s. Both partners were Glasgow trained, Laird hitherto having been in practice with his brother John (1868–1937), while James Napier (1889–1946) was employed by Burnet and by John Fairweather. Apart from the reception areas, the hotel's ground floor was given over to shop units, its public rooms being located on the level above and distinguished externally from the two bedroom storeys by a band of brickwork. A roof terrace provided spectacular panoramic views across the Firth of Clyde. As Gourock was a transfer point for large numbers of Scottish holidaymakers bound for the island of Bute and the Cowal peninsula, it was hoped that, after the Exhibition's closure, the hotel (and the nearby outdoor swimming pool and Cragburn Pavilion) would encourage more visitors to stay in the town, using the steamer routes for day trips to other places.[6]

Back in Glasgow, the Empire Exhibition's organisers had hoped to persuade the London-based Scottish hotelier Thomas Crawford Gordon, proprietor of London's Mount Royal hotel and apartments in Oxford Street, to develop a new property in Glasgow.[7] As he was on the verge of bankruptcy, it was instead the local architect-entrepreneur William Beresford Inglis, whose practice of Weddell & Inglis designed restaurants, bars and cinemas, who stepped in to build and operate the eight-storey, 198-bedroom Beresford Hotel on Sauchiehall Street.[8] To finance the £200,000 cost of the project, Inglis sold the cinemas he operated and borrowed additional funds. The site works alone, involving considerable excavation of the steeply sloping plot to give an unbroken flat expanse at street level and the construction of a retaining wall, cost £10,000. When inaugurated, the *Caterer and Hotel Keeper* described the Beresford as 'Glasgow's first skyscraper hotel' – though this was a considerable exaggeration as the building was no taller than many another in the city at that time. Nonetheless, it occupied:

> A commanding position… and its striking yellow, green and scarlet front has been attracting attention for months. Mr W Beresford Inglis, the managing director told a *Caterer and Hotel Keeper* representative, 'Having specialised in cinema design, I decided to introduce the lines and colour of the cinema in the Beresford. The result is certainly surprising, but has gained universal approval'[9]

Advertisement for the Beresford Hotel, Sauchiehall Street, Glasgow
William Beresford Inglis of Weddell & Inglis, 1938
Glasgow City Archives

Glasgow's Welcome to the World

The Beresford Hotel

The hotel's exterior was entirely clad in faience tiles and was a sharp contrast to the grimy, smoke-blackened sandstone of typical Glasgow buildings. What would otherwise have been a pure cuboid, fitting the city's grid-plan, was enlivened by two drum-shaped projections rising from the first floor to above roof height. These broke the frontage into three sections. In between, a series of fin-shaped verticals was outlined at night in neon.

With regard to the interiors, according to the *Caterer and Hotel Keeper*, the entrance foyer had a terrazzo floor, patterned with waves and the main feature was an illuminated archway, through which the stairwell was accessed:

> Straight through from the entrance is the restaurant which seats 250. The architectural treatment here is bold and massive. The dado is in straight-grained mahogany, and the walls are treated with honey-coloured Opaltex [a multicoloured spray paint finish popular for cinema auditorium walls]. Woven into the texture is a faint suggestion of well-known Scottish landmarks, such as Edinburgh Castle and Ben Lomond… Almost the entire front of the hotel is given over to a writing room and lounge for residents only. The furniture is bleached oak and the walls are fawn coloured with motifs indicating the purpose of the room. The first floor is entirely devoted to public rooms. The hotel lounge, although very large, has been so broken up architecturally that it has a distinctly intimate atmosphere. The woodwork is of walnut and the furnishings are crushed strawberry with blue spots. The walls are in soft shades of orange, and the columns are copper spattered with red. Parts of the ceiling are done in apple green.[10]

Contrasting with all this colour and comfort was 'the smoke room, for men only' which was 'severely plain in dark, reddish oak panelling with hide-covered chairs. The walls are in tones of sepia with motifs of a sporting character'.[11] Its inclusion perhaps suggested a perceived need to cater to the Scottish male psyche by providing a strongly masculine haven in which to bond over cigarettes and whisky.

Lounge, foyer and restaurant, Beresford Hotel, Glasgow
William Beresford Inglis of Weddell & Inglis, 1938
Bruce Peter collection

Lounge, foyer and restaurant, Beresford Hotel, Glasgow
William Beresford Inglis of Weddell & Inglis, 1938
Bruce Peter collection

The bedrooms filled the floors above, which surrounded a central lightwell. The *Caterer and Hotel Keeper* reported that:

> In each of these, the carpet is blue with a wavy black line… the walls are papered horizontally with a rough speckled shade of orange. The ceiling is a sunshine yellow… Curtains are a rich cream with a design in blue, black and orange. The bedspread matches the curtains and the quilt is of powdered blue… There is a wash-hand basin and a telephone in every room.[12]

The hotel reportedly had 'many novel features' including an all-night restaurant to enable fast service to hungry guests arriving back late from the Exhibition, a 'telewriter' to duplicate food orders in the kitchen and for the cashier, loudspeakers in all the public rooms for announcements and music, a telephone exchange with 275 lines and two fast passenger lifts.[13] Yet, bathrooms were only provided for every four bedrooms which by 1938 was a poor show and would ultimately become the hotel's major shortcoming. Another strange omission was of a cocktail bar as by the latter 1930s these had become very popular, not least elsewhere in Glasgow – but perhaps Inglis' novice status as a hotelier was to blame. This lack was, however, rectified in October, by which time the hotel had successfully accommodated around 50,000 guests. Also designed by Inglis and located near the entrance in what had previously been part of the (presumably under-utilised) sitting lounge, the new cocktail bar was 'very colourful' and featured 'a tangerine carpet with black and faun lines [and] a dado of gamboge with a green horizontal motif'. The upper parts of its walls were 'sprayed in yellow, black, red and gold'.[14]

Whereas the Bay and Beresford hotels primarily served rail travellers, the two-storey Newhouse Hotel, opened in May 1938, was located adjacent to the main Edinburgh–Glasgow road in Lanarkshire and was initially intended to accommodate those visiting the

Former Beresford Hotel, Sauchiehall Street, Glasgow
William Beresford Inglis of Weddell & Inglis, 1938
Bruce Peter

Internal doorway showing furniture and lighting, Beresford Hotel, Glasgow
William Beresford Inglis of Weddell & Inglis, 1938
Bruce Peter collection

Empire Exhibition by car.[15] Designed by Alexander Davidson (1879–1976), inheritor of the versatile and prolific Coatbridge-based practice established by his father, James Davidson (1848–1923) in the latter nineteenth century, it was the only example of moderne it ever produced. The flat roof had a terrace, from which the passing traffic could be watched while refreshments were supplied by means of an electric service hoist. Unlike at the Beresford Hotel, each of the ten bedrooms had its own private bathroom, lined in slabs of shiny Vitrolite glass; this suggests that car owners were a pickier clientele, prepared to pay a premium for this additional comfort.[16] Adjacent was a smaller, separate building for the use of lorry drivers, containing four bedrooms, each with four bunks, and a kitchen where they could cook. As the hotel's proprietor, Angus McNab Chassels, bred spaniels, he ensured that spacious kennels were provided so that dog lovers would be attracted to stay.[17] The hotel's lounge featured a bandstand and dance floor and the *Caterer and Hotel Keeper* reported that the dining room was 'large and well-lit with windows on two sides… The chef, Mr John Girdwood, was previously at the Imperial Hotel, Edinburgh and at the Waldorf-Astoria, New York… The kitchen can cater for 300 people.'[18] The appointment of a more experienced and well-travelled chef than might have been expected at a small hotel on the fringes of an industrial conurbation suggests that it was also intended to attract motorists from a wide catchment area to enjoy a stylish evening with dining and dancing before driving home in, hopefully, not too inebriated a state.

Increasing car ownership in the latter 1930s encouraged the development of new hotels in locations far off the beaten track, which were intended as latter-day equivalents of the late-Victorian and Edwardian hydropathics. The remotely sited five-storey Keil Hotel at the south end of the rugged but picturesque Kintyre Peninsula was a rare Scottish example. Designed by the established Glaswegian architect James Austen Laird (1878–1950), its proprietor was a local farmer, Captain James Taylor, who apparently thought that there would be a market for such a coastal retreat. The hotel's moderne aesthetic was rather superficial, however, its having deep roof parapets but traditionally vertical fenestration with sash windows perhaps reflecting its architect's formative knowledge dating from the

Drumossie Hotel, Bogbain near Inverness
Roy Caruthers-Ballantyne of Caruthers-Ballantyne & Cox, 1940
Bruce Peter

Victorian and Edwardian eras. Almost immediately after opening in 1939, the property was requisitioned by the Admiralty for wartime use as a hospital.[19]

In the Scottish Highlands, new hotels appealing to motorists were developed along the northern stretch of the A9 trunk road to Inverness. The Drumossie Hotel at Bogbain just outside the city was developed by Loch Ness Hotels, which in late 1937 purchased the picturesque site. Designed by

Keil Hotel, Southend, Kintyre
James Austen Laird, 1939
Bruce Peter collection

Roy Caruthers-Ballantyne, it is a long and curving three-storey edifice with a projecting semi-circular centrepiece, its overall form being somewhat akin to that of the Midland Hotel in Morecambe. The project took three years to complete, however, one initial major problem being a scarcity of steel brought about by the government's national rearmament programme.[20] This necessitated a redesign to reduce the amount required for framing, with brick supporting walls and shorter concrete beams introduced as substitutes. Consequently, the building's public spaces possibly ended up having less open planning than had been the original intention. Economic instability before the outbreak of the Second World War and a consequent lack of capital then caused further delays. Owing to Caruthers-Ballantyne's suspicion of flat roofs in the wet and snowy Highland climate, those of the bedroom wings are pitched, with lantern windows in Arts and Crafts style. Upon completion, rather than welcoming the first paying guests, the hotel was immediately taken over by the British Government's Air Ministry to accommodate officials and senior military personnel involved in the war effort.[21]

Grampian Hotel, Station Road, Dalwhinnie
Thomas Beveridge, 1941

Bruce Peter collection

The two-storey Grampian Hotel at Dalwhinnie some way to the south on the A9 was commissioned by a locally based entrepreneur, James Wilson Poe, who had moved there from Cambuslang near Glasgow and whose wife's family already ran a hotel in Newtonmore. Poe chose as architect a family acquaintance, Thomas Beveridge (1888–1964), who was Edinburgh-trained and had earlier been employed there by the cabinetmakers Scott Morton and by Sir Robert Lorimer, indicating an Arts and Crafts orientation.[22] In the mid-1920s, he had established practice in Glasgow, where his clients were mainly owners of country houses requiring extension and redecoration.

For the Grampian Hotel, Beveridge was perhaps inspired by new roadhouses elsewhere in Scotland to attempt a moderne design. On the ground floor, the lounge and dining room were to the rear, facing the Cairngorm mountain range. Bedrooms were above with a roof terrace on top, all accessed through a chunkily angular stair tower at one end. Attached to the opposing side elevation was a contrastingly curvaceous concrete external fire exit stairway, which appeared considerably more architecturally adventurous than the remainder. The Second World War began while construction was underway, the project's completion being delayed until July 1941.[23]

Unlike Drumossie, there was no military requisition as it was necessary to maintain provision of hotel rooms

Northern Hotel, Great Northern Road, Kittybrewster, Aberdeen

A G R Mackenzie of A Marshall Mackenzie & Son,
1939–1947

Bruce Peter

at intervals around the countryside for 'bona fide travellers' (those whose occupations required them to travel – for example, salesmen). Owing to the wartime situation, the opening was low-key and was not even mentioned in the local press. [24] It was nonetheless timely as a couple of months before the *Inverness and Northern Counties People's Journal* had predicted heavy demand for tourist accommodation in the Highlands during the summer months. Britons would be heading north for their holidays, hoping temporarily to escape the ever-present threat of being bombed by the Luftwaffe. [25] An advertisement for the hotel in *The Scotsman* emphasised that Dalwhinnie was in a 'Safe Area'. [26] Unfortunately, it proved challenging to keep the Grampian Hotel wind and watertight and it was demolished in the early 2000s. By contrast, Drumossie continues to prosper, doubtless thanks to its design being better adapted to Highland conditions.

The need for the Northern Hotel in the Kittybrewster district of Aberdeen arose owing to the burning down of the existing Palace Hotel there. Thus, notwithstanding the Second World War beginning

while construction was still at an early stage, permission for completion was granted to enable necessary accommodation to be provided locally. Fitted into a Y-fork between roads, the design by A G R Mackenzie was consequently wedge-shaped in plan with a curved corner facing in the direction of the city centre. The fenestration has a strong horizontal emphasis, accentuated by strips of light and dark grey granite, the overall effect being rather severe. Within, the hotel originally contained 32 bedrooms, a restaurant, a cocktail bar with a circular counter and a ballroom, which in plan has the shape of a violin and, as with all of the hotel's interiors, is notable for its starkly minimalistic moderne styling. The unusual shape was, however, practical as it enabled distinct areas for

Ballroom of the Northern Hotel, Kittybrewster, Aberdeen

A G R Mackenzie of A Marshall Mackenzie & Son, 1939–1947

HES SC2520258, Bruce Peter Collection

socialising and for dancing when the space was hired out for wedding receptions and corporate functions.[27]

On the urban fringes, roadhouses without overnight accommodation were built in substantial numbers during the 1930s. Their great attraction was that they avoided city licensing strictures banning the serving of alcoholic drinks on Sundays; such venues could be licensed on the basis that they might serve 'bona fide travellers'. In reality, it was more often the case that city-dwellers would drive out to the roadhouses to eat, drink and perhaps even to dance. For the growing car-owning sector of the middle-class, doing so provided a new and up-to-date kind of experience, allowing car owners to see and be seen amid stylish and hotel-like surroundings.

Edinburgh's fringe suburbs were fertile territory for roadhouse developments, its expanding suburban populous being enthusiastic motorists who could quickly drive out of the city, easily reaching attractive countryside (Glasgow, by contrast, was considerably bigger and more sprawling). The most impressive Art Deco example, the Maybury at Corstorphine, designed by the entrepreneurial architect-developers

Maybury, South Maybury, Edinburgh
William Patterson and James Broom, 1935
Bruce Peter

White House, Niddrie Mains Road, Craigmillar
William Innes Thomson, 1936
Bruce Peter

Delmore, Beauly Road near Inverness
Architect not known, c1936
Bruce Peter collection

William Patterson and James Broom and completed in 1935, appeared as though directly transposed to the 'bungalow-land' there from Miami Beach. Its location was carefully chosen, being at the junction of the A8 and A9 trunk roads to attract motorists and near the tram terminus, meaning that city dwellers who aspired to be drivers could also visit.[28] Unusually in 1930s Scotland, it was of reinforced concrete made in situ, rather than the more typical brick with harling method. The curved entrance block with slim, tall windows was intended to resemble a modern car's streamlined radiator grille cover. Within is a two-storey hallway, panelled in walnut and with a grand Y-shaped staircase with moderne balustrading, resembling the kind found in Hollywood musicals and replicated in cinemas and hotels of the period. There were bars and a restaurant in one wing while the other contained a double-height space with a balcony that was convertible from a daytime configuration with tables and chairs for evening use as a ballroom.

Shortly thereafter, William Innes Thomson (1910–1990), Edinburgh-trained and son of the architect William Nicholas Thomson (1857–1951), designed the smaller and less showy White House in Craigmillar, completed in 1936.[29] McKean records that its flat roof was the choice of the proprietor's daughter, who subsequently had regrets as it enabled easier access for burglars than a pitched design would

have done.[30] Overlooking the Pentland Hills at Fairmilehead was the Hilburn, designed by Thomas Bowill Gibson and, in terms of style, owing much to his concurrent cinema design output. Its roof was fringed in green-glazed pantiles and, within, alongside the usual bars and restaurant, there was a bowling alley, accessed via a curved moderne stairway.[31] In central Scotland, the Silverlinks Roadhouse near the Kincardine Bridge and the Newhouse Roadhouse at Whitburn were comparably hybridised designs with moderne curved corners and pitched tiled roofing. The Delmore Roadhouse on Beauly Road near Inverness was perhaps a little reminiscent of roadside buildings in the American Mid-West on account of its clapboard construction, within which typically moderne elements such as horizontally banded wall panelling and jazzy carpeting were installed. It represented the more ephemeral extreme of 1930s Scottish hospitality architecture – a precursor of the many prefabricated and temporary-looking outlets that would proliferate in the post-war era as car ownership became increasingly widespread and the initial upmarket images of venues serving motorists gave way to mass catering.

Painted panel, 'Diana and her Nymphs' (renamed *The Hunt*)
Robert Burns, c1923
National Galleries of Scotland

Tearooms and cafes

Since the late-Victorian and Edwardian eras, tea and luncheon rooms had been established as important sites of fashionable modernity in Scottish urban life. The highly aesthetic interiors devised by Charles Rennie and Margaret Macdonald Mackintosh for Catherine Cranston's venues in Glasgow set the tone for further developments in the interwar period. Tearooms, which were unlicensed, were the feminine and respectable alternative to the pub and their décor was intended to connote high style, allied with comfort and good hygiene.

In 1923 the Edinburgh bakers D S Crawford gained permission to extend their premises at 70 Princes Street, opposite the Royal Scottish Academy.[32] The intention was to provide an artistically decorated equivalent of Cranston's Willow Tearoom in Glasgow in the heart of the capital. Within a structure planned by the Edinburgh architect Alexander Allan Foote (1886–1969), the Arts and Crafts artist and decorator Robert Burns (1869–1941) was commissioned to paint panels to adorn a new first-floor dining room, his theme being 'the worship of women'. At the top

of the stairway was a large panel entitled 'Diana and her Nymphs', depicting the goddess and acolytes surrounded by leopards in a vibrantly coloured jungle setting featuring copious gold leaf. The dining room itself contained four smaller panels showing Athena, Aphrodite, Hera and Artemis.[33] Burns was President of the Scottish Artists' Society and a member of the Contemporary Artists' Society and, at around the same time as the Crawford's project, he painted decorative panels to adorn the Forestry Hall at the 1924 British Empire Exhibition in Wembley.[34] In 1927, another Crawford's Tea Room opened in Hanover Street, immediately adjacent. Burns panelled its interior with Japanese-style painted screens but, rather than depicting imagined scenes from the East, these showed the wrecking of the Spanish Armada off the Scottish coast following defeat at the Battle of Gravelines in 1588. Chinese-style furniture by Whytock & Reid and fabrics from Jenners department store augmented the Oriental aesthetic.[35] The two venues were subsequently conjoined, the mullions and cornice surrounding their large first floor windows being re-faced in grey granite with Art Deco pediments.

Ca'd'Oro Buffet, Gordon Street, Glasgow
John Christie of Guthrie & Wells and Jack Coia of Gillespie,
Kidd & Coia, 1926
Bruce Peter collection

**James Campbell and Walter Hubbard bakery and
tearoom, Great Western Road, Glasgow**
James Lindsay, 1930
Glasgow City Archives

City Bakeries, St George's Road, Glasgow
William John Brockie Wright, 1939
Glasgow City Archives

In Glasgow, meanwhile, a complex of tearooms and restaurants, known as the Ca'd'Oro, had been opened in 1926. This was located within a mansard roof extension added to an 1870s Venetian-style commercial block by John Honeyman (1831–1914) at the junction of Gordon Street and Union Street. The design of the extra structure was prepared by a youthful Jack Coia of Gillespie, Kidd & Coia, showing his versatility when confronted with a challenging brief. The interior, by contrast, was the work of John Christie of Guthrie & Wells, who melded rectilinear elements reminiscent of late Mackintosh with jazz moderne and oriental details. In the buffet, decorative panels of cavorting ladies in Japanese and Ancient Egyptian-inspired garb were highly reminiscent of the contemporaneous output of the French couturier Paul Poiret. The surrounding wall panelling was finished in silver leaf, giving a shimmery effect, comparable with recent Parisian Art Deco interiors and also those produced subsequently in London by Basil Ionides, among others.[36]

For the more keenly priced catering outlets, commercial success was achieved in large part through economies of scale. The premises for R A Peacock in Glasgow's Union Street, designed by Whyte and Galloway and opened in 1930, had four floors of dining space with administrative offices above, behind a symmetrical Art Deco frontage with extensive glazing to enable daylight to flood in. The interiors featured direct and indirect artificial lighting, and had jazz moderne wall decorations. At Kelvinbridge in Glasgow's West End, meanwhile, James Campbell and Walter Hubbard operated a tearoom, bakery and restaurant within the same faience-clad two-storey Art Deco block, which opened for business in 1930.[37] Its architect, James Lindsay (b 1892), otherwise mainly produced bungalow housing, this being his only significant contribution in the style. Four bay windows fronting the first-floor dining space have complex jazz moderne-patterned leaded glass. Campbell also ran luncheon and tearooms in Glassford Street with similarly vigorous jazzy window top-lighting; both sets of premises were decorated by the shopfitters Archibald Hamilton Ltd.

There were also chains of tearooms, such as the City Bakeries which expanded around Glasgow's districts and satellites as the 1930s progressed. Its regular architect, William John Brockie Wright (1883–1976), had studied at the Glasgow School of Architecture in the 1900s, then worked for James Miller among others before commencing independent practice in the 1920s. Wright's most striking moderne design for the chain was at 276–280 St George's Road, opened in 1939 and comprising shops with a cafe above.[38] Its two-storey tiled fascia, inserted into an existing frontage with a projecting glazed semi-circular illuminated beacon above the entrance, was a superb example of its genre, but was sadly swept away in the 1960s when the side of the street in which it stood was demolished for the M8 motorway.

As well as tearooms, milk bars were a 1930s fashion, through which the dairy industry promoted the health virtues of drinking its products, either as straight from the cow, or more likely sweetened and flavoured as milkshakes, or as cream squirted into buns. The whiteness of the milk was reflected in their clean-lined designs, with light colours, wipe-clean surfaces and modern graphics. Around the West of Scotland, Ross's Dairies opened a chain of milk bars, its flagship outlet being a two-storey example opened in 1930 at the junction of Glasgow's Bath Street and Renfield Street. The existing corner building was remodelled with a

deep parapet to at least gave an impression of there being a flat roof while providing ample space for company branding, outlined in neon and framed by portholes.[39] Such was the company's rate of expansion that later in the decade a new pasteurisation plant was constructed on Crow Road, the centrally located office of which featured very large glazed panels set within symmetrical concrete framework and topped by a clock tower. The impact of moderne in the dairy industry spanned from city streets to the countryside. In the latter 1930s Fenton Barns farm in East Lothian, which had an established reputation for experimentation and innovation, commissioned the Edinburgh partnership of Alexander Arnott (1871–1950) and James Inch Morrison (1878–1944) to design a new building for milking cows on an industrial scale. It even features a

Ross's Dairies, Renfield Street, Glasgow
Possibly Frank C Petrie, c1930
Glasgow City Archives

Broadway Café, Shettleston Road, Glasgow
Architect not known, c1938
Glasgow City Archives

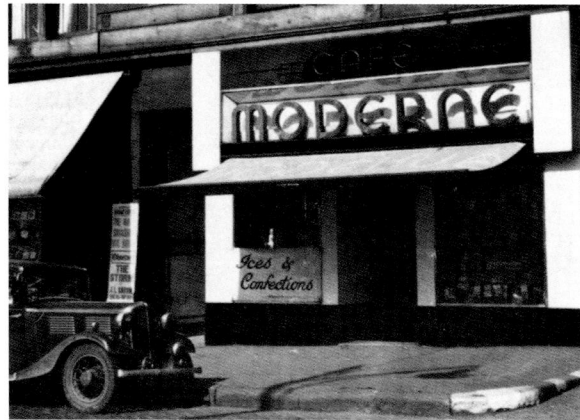

Café Moderne, Pollokshaws Road, Glasgow
Architect not known, c1939
Glasgow City Archives

moderne semi-circular stairway projecting towards the country road in front – an image of stylish modernity at the point of production that was comparable with those of the high street milk bars in which some of its health-giving output was consumed [40].

Glasgow's tearooms and milk bars were, however, outnumbered by its numerous high street cafes, most of which had been established by migrant Italian families who had arrived in the city in the latter nineteenth century. Many came with the intention of going on to the USA but, finding booming trade, instead set up catering businesses, which they passed from generation to generation and modernised along the way to incorporate the latest style trends. Cafes tended to serve fried food and ice cream and usually had wipe-clean table tops with built-in seating, whereas tearooms specialised more in sandwiches and cakes, as well as cooked meals, and usually had individual chairs and tablecloths to promote a more elegant impression. In the 1930s, names such as Café D'Oré, Café del Rio and Café Moderne were suggestive of continental sophistication, an impression also conveyed by striking fascia designs, often using coloured Vitrolite, stained leaded or acid-etched glass and three-dimensional lettering in stylised moderne-style fonts. On the interior, terrazzo flooring reflected Italian tradition while booth seating was robust but also provided relatively intimate spaces for conversation and romance in what were otherwise often densely populated

communities. Polished wood veneer, Bakelite surfaces and mirrored Vitroflex wrapped around columns made fashionable backdrops for the enjoyment of fry-ups or ice cream sundaes.

Two of Scotland's largest Art Deco cafes were located at opposite ends of the beach promenade in Largs on the Clyde coast. Both were purpose-built and free-standing, giving greater opportunity for architectural whimsy. The Nardini cafe, completed in 1935, was the work of Paisley architects Charles James Davidson (1872–1920) and his brother George Veitch Davidson (1879–1964), and is notable for its rectilinear silhouette in stucco with neon-lit moderne signage. Next to the town's pier, meanwhile, the Castelvecchi family, who traded as Castlesons Ltd, opened their three-storey Moorings cafe and restaurant in 1936. Although Castlesons initially considered employing an Italian architectural firm, in the end they opted for James Houston of Kilbirnie. His design was intended to resemble a passenger ship, complete with curving corner cut-backs in the shape of bows, a promenade surrounded by deck railings and a forecastle with mooring eyes. In addition, the Moorings contained an ice cream factory, a bakery and a ballroom. [41] The complex opened for business just as the new Cunard-White Star flagship *Queen Mary* was delivered from the John Brown shipyard in Clydebank, at which point the idea of being aboard a liner was in the forefront of the Clydeside public's imagination. Both the Nardini

and Moorings cafes were extensively glazed to give panoramic views over the firth towards the pretty isle of Cumbrae. Within, gold-sprayed rattan chairs and potted palms engendered an atmosphere perhaps suggestive of the winter gardens of tropical cruise liners or luxury hotels on the Riviera, albeit for a clientele who were unlikely ever to experience what such environments were really like.

Nardini, Greenock Road, Largs
Charles James Davidson and George Veitch Davidson, 1935
Bruce Peter collection

The Moorings, Fort Street, Largs
James Houston, 1936
HES SC2534436

Ballroom in The Moorings, Largs
James Houston, 1936
HES SC2534458

Restaurant in The Moorings, Largs
James Houston, 1936
HES SC2534434

Carron Tea Room, Cameron Street, Stonehaven
Henry Tawse and George J Allan, c1936
Bruce Peter

Interior of the Carron Tea Room, Stonehaven
Henry Tawse and George J Allan, c1936
HES DP097367

A third outstanding example was in Stonehaven, the Carron Tea Room forming part of a new town centre block commissioned in the mid-1930s by the Northern Co-operative Company from the Aberdeen architects Henry Tawse (1890–1959) and George J Allan (b c1891), who had earlier designed the Co-operative's shop in Aberdeen's King Street. While it was rather bland, their Stonehaven design is notable for its exuberant composition, which was perhaps encouraged by the pleasurable seaside location.[42] The complex comprised a Co-operative shop with Art Deco window details facing Evan Street, with the tearoom accessed from Cameron Street, running in parallel to the south. The design for the latter's frontage is sophisticatedly three-dimensional, comprising very large metal-framed windows overlooking a raised sun terrace. This is sheltered by a bow-shaped loggia in brick with render, the open bays of which contain Art Deco metal balustrading, the whole being set behind a front garden through which customers enter, ascending curved steps to gain access. The lofty interior has a vaulted ceiling and built-in lighting strips that continue down the walls, which are wood-panelled with metal details, etched glass and also a clock.

Pubs and bars

Alongside tearooms, cafes and milk bars, pubs maintained their popularity. In Glasgow in particular, the 1930s saw a great modernisation of the traditional Scottish pub, more to reflect the style of the American cocktail bar, or at least the images of these contrived in Hollywood movies. High, ornate ceilings were hidden behind lowered, false ones with built-in concealed lighting; iron columns and tiled bar fronts were re-clad in banded veneer, walls were re-finished with moderne relief plaster and etched peach glass, and inlaid vulcanised rubber flooring superseded encaustic tiles. Whereas hitherto many publicans had blended their own whiskies, requiring a rack of casks behind the serving counter, now shelves for bottled drinks and cocktail ingredients were added in its place – and, in such modernised pubs, sawdust was no longer spread on the floor to soak up spills. Competition between publicans and with other attractions such as super-cinemas and dance halls to attract younger, more upwardly mobile drinkers who sought greater comfort and elegance spurred these developments. While many pub modernisations were superficial with their old atmosphere merely augmented, the most thorough transformations into moderne cocktail bars were very complete, even down to smart uniforms of white mess jackets with brass buttons, stiff collars and bow ties for the servers.

Such swish design and service were to be found in Lang's Bar on Queen Street following renovation in 1937 by its new licensee, Thomas A Mackie, for whom a frontage of black, cream and brown faience was constructed. The Bay Horse on Pollokshaws Road on the Southside was refaced in slabs of granite upon which large sans serif letters in stainless steel with neon inlays were fitted while the windows were used for displays of bottled drinks, which were considered a sign of sophistication.[43] Along Dumbarton Road to the west, The Thornwood was entirely re-faced in yellow Vitrolite with chrome trim and The Neuk was given a rather avant-garde re-design by Sam Bunton using glass bricks, lit from behind, with the name spelled out in a striking font on individual enamelled panels, standing proud of the frontage on a horizontal ledge.[44] Inside, the bar servery too was built up from glass bricks and likewise illuminated.

In a dark, dirty and decayed part of Glasgow's inner city, the short frontage of the Variety Bar

Lang's Bar, Queen Street, Glasgow
Architect not known, 1937
Chris Doak

Bay Horse, Pollokshaws Road, Glasgow
Architect not known, 1936
Glasgow City Archives

The Thornwood, Dumbarton Road, Glasgow
Architect not known, 1938
Glasgow City Archives

The Neuk, Dumbarton Road, Glasgow
Samuel Bunton, 1938
Glasgow City Archives

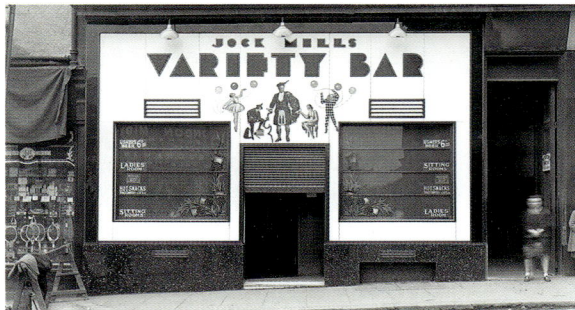

Variety Bar, Cowcaddens Street, Glasgow
Architect not known, 1938
Glasgow City Archives

Portland Bar, Shettleston Road, Glasgow
Alexander Hood MacLeod of Thomson, Sandilands and
MacLeod, 1937
Bruce Peter

on Cowcaddens Street shone out in red and cream Vitrolite after a 1938 renovation. The bar's proprietor was a retired music hall comedian of the Edwardian era, John Mullen, whose stage name was Jock Mills. Painted below the Art Deco name sign was an image of the Scottish entertainer Sir Harry Lauder, flanked by dancers and acrobats.[45] More performers with whom Mullen had been associated were documented in photographs within the cosy interior.

Whereas most Glasgow pubs were likewise built into the ground floors of tenement blocks, a very few examples occupied their own buildings, as was more typical in English cities and towns. Of these, the Portland Arms on Shettleston Road in the East End, a handsome brick-fronted Art Deco pub completed in 1937 to a design by Alexander Hood MacLeod of Thomson, Sandilands & MacLeod for the publican Jonathan Tindal, remarkably survives almost completely intact. The centrepiece of the interior is the large island counter, clad in strips of walnut and zebra wood with chrome edging and glass bottle shelves in the middle. Around the perimeter are groups of booth seating, while the doorways contain acid-etched glass and the illumination is from a mix of cove and pendant lighting.

Although a majority of Glasgow bars were, like the Variety Bar and Portland Arms, aimed at working men, an increasing number sought to appeal also to middle-class male and female drinkers. The Rogano oyster bar and restaurant in Royal Exchange Place was a unique luxury venue, attracting Glasgow's business community, their spouses and guests. It was the vision of a prominent publican and restauranteur, Donald Grant, proprietor of the neo-Tudor-style Grant Arms bar and restaurant in Argyle Street. In 1935 he took over the long-established Spanish-themed Rogano bodega and employed the firm of the Glasgow architect, cinema and hotel entrepreneur, William Beresford Inglis, to transform it, the project being carried out by Inglis's assistant, John David More Thomson (1906–1964). A new fascia in yellow and black Vitrolite with bold, Broadway-style three-dimensional lettering and a painting of an oyster was installed. On the ground floor, champagne, cocktails and plates of oysters were served over a long bar faced in burled walnut, behind which was a whimsical bas relief panel of crustaceans and underwater life by Charles Cameron Baillie (1901–1960), who also made decorations for the prestigious Cunard-White

Rogano, Royal Exchange Place, Glasgow
William Beresford Inglis and John David More Thomson
of Weddell & Inglis, 1935
Glasgow City Archives

Interior of Rogano, Glasgow
Bas relief panel by Charles Cameron Baillie, 1935
Bruce Peter

Steps Bar, Glassford Street, Glasgow

Architect not known, 1949

Bruce Peter

Star liner *Queen Mary*. Baillie's initial training had been as a scientific instrument maker but between 1918 and 1925 he had taken evening classes in painting at Glasgow School of Art, thereafter establishing himself as a portraitist and creator of interior decorations in the Art Deco manner. Adjacent, a small Spanish-style sherry bar remained from the premises' previous incarnation. In the basement, there was a brasserie restaurant, the walls of which featured etched peach glass mirrors of underwater creatures, also by Baillie, while the carpet had a wavy design, giving diners a slight impression of themselves being luxuriously submerged. Following the renovation, Rogano established itself as Glasgow's most stylish eatery; its first restaurant manager was Swiss-trained and his successor was attracted from the Savoy in London.[46]

Art Deco styling continued to be used in hospitality interiors installed after the Second World War, a surviving example being the well-preserved Steps Bar in Glasgow's Glassford Street, which was refitted in 1949 at the behest of a new owner, Thomas Taylor. The fascia features black Vitrolite with floral acid etched windows, while the bar counter has curved ends and concealed lighting. The most charming feature, however, is the snug, in which an illuminated stained-glass panel depicts the *Queen Mary* with a Spitfire flying above, Mr Taylor having flown with Coastal Command during the war.[47]

Illuminated stained-glass panel in Steps Bar snug

Designer not known

Bruce Peter

CHAPTER 9
INDUSTRY AND ENERGY

Art Deco manifested frequently at points of production as well as of consumption. Idealised imagery of heroic workers appeared across 1930s Europe, Soviet Russia and the Americas. In Scotland, similar motifs were included in the Empire Exhibition and in the advertising and promotion of industrial outputs. The more abstract notion of energy – particularly electricity, which was mostly invisible – was given tangible form in Art Deco patterns and forms suggestive of sparks and flashes, while streamline moderne as a whole was an aesthetic concerned with the capturing of rapid movement.

During the Great Depression, the stagnation of Scotland's established heavy industrial economy caused grave concern, but hope for renewed industrial expansion and fresh employment opportunities was found in the expansion of light industries, often powered by electricity. These required new types of industrial building, optimised for efficiency and with up-to-date external styling suggestive of the cleanliness and order of the manufacturing processes enacted within. In the USA, advanced architecture and industrial capitalism were viewed as having a symbiotic relationship. Modern factories enabled a virtuous cycle of greater efficiency, increased profits and, potentially, better pay and conditions for employees. Reinforced

concrete construction enabled great structural strength while light steel framing for roofing allowed wider spans, making buildings better suited to the achievement of these aims.

An early and outstanding Art Deco example in Scotland of the Americanised approach to factory design is the premises of the London-headquartered India Rubber Company, a maker of pneumatic tyres, at Inchinnan near Renfrew, completed in 1930 to a design by Wallis, Gilbert and Partners. It was built using the 'Kahncrete' reinforced concrete construction system, invented in Detroit in 1903 by the entrepreneurial engineer and industrialist Julius Kahn and used in commercial and industrial buildings designed by his brother, the architect Albert Kahn (1869–1942). Julius Kahn formed the Trussed Concrete Steel Company (Truscon) to manufacture 'Kahncrete' beams, after which a third brother, Moritz Kahn, set up a Truscon subsidiary in London in 1913 to apply the technology to the construction of new factories in Britain, often for subsidiaries of American corporations.[1] The Kahns' Truscon system was not new to Scotland, however, as in around 1912 Albert Kahn had used it when designing a factory for the Albion Motor Company in Scotstoun, though its office block was by the Glaswegian Alexander Nisbet Paterson (1862–1947) and of unexceptional appearance.

In London, Truscon's offices in Tothill Street were adjacent to those of the architect Thomas Wallis (1873–1953), who subsequently formed Wallis,

India of Inchinnan, Inchinnan near Renfrew
Thomas Wallis of Wallis, Gilbert and Partners, 1930
Bruce Peter

India of Inchinnan, Inchinnan near Renfrew
Thomas Wallis of Wallis, Gilbert and Partners, 1930
HES SC1256955, Bruce Peter

Gilbert and Partners. Young and ambitious, Wallis was a bricklayer's son and had served his architectural apprenticeship in the office of Sidney R J Smith (1858–1913), including assisting in drawing up plans for the Tate Gallery, before commencing independent practice in 1900 while also working part time as a draughtsman for the government's Office of Works. Julius Kahn evidently recognised a kindred spirit in the hard-working Wallis, and so in 1916 he recruited him as Truscon's architect for new factory buildings in the UK. 'Gilbert', however, is an enigma; whoever he was, he was not a British-registered architect, though he may possibly have been an American business colleague of Kahn, or an office manager dealing with administration and finance. Or perhaps he never existed at all and the name was merely an invention of Wallis to make his firm sound bigger and more impressive; such a move would have been in character as he had a reputation for being an imaginative salesman.[2]

Having designed and built around a dozen major concrete-framed factories in and around London and in the home counties, in the latter 1920s, Wallis and Truscon had successfully established themselves as Britain's leading designers of the most modern and showy Art Deco examples. Among these the Firestone tyre factory at Brentford, completed in 1927, was the newest and most spectacular. The Egyptian-inspired frontage of the administrative block presented a wide expanse of octagonal pilasters with polychromatic tiled bases and capitals, interspersed by bays containing big windows. Unfortunately for Wallis, envious fellow architects were disparaging of its bright colouration for being way too vulgar and 'American' in the worst sense, though, in actuality, its forms were not so far removed from those of Burnet's Adelaide House, for example.[3] (As the latter was faced in natural stone, it seemed demure by comparison – though in the ancient world, many buildings actually were painted in polychromatic designs not dissimilar to those produced by Wallis.)

When the India Rubber Company, which was a rival of Firestone, wanted to build a new factory at Inchinnan, Wallis and Truscon were hired, apparently with the instruction to produce something similar. On the project, Wallis was assisted by John Wishart Macgregor (1901–1988), whose parents were Scottish-born and who had joined his practice in 1928. The outcome was and remains spectacular. The snowy whiteness of the painted walls was the antithesis of typical Scottish factories, while the repetitive rhythm of rectilinear pilasters and bays and brightly coloured Egyptian-inspired ornamentation made its facade an attention-grabbing spectacle for passers-by.[4]

In the 1930s, there was a growing momentum encouraging progressive employment approaches with regard to workers' quality of life. Charles Oakley, who lectured in Industrial Psychology at the University of Glasgow, argued in favour of treating employees well to foster good labour relations, higher levels of commitment, improved efficiency and enhanced quality of outputs.[5] One Glaswegian company with a solid track-record of benevolence was the carpet-maker James Templeton & Co. Whereas most other manufacturers struggled through the Depression years, it found that the emergent culture of home ownership and aspiration towards Americanised luxury, as depicted in the movies, was creating a rapidly growing

James Templeton & Co, Glasgow
Ninian Johnston and George A Boswell, 1935
Bruce Peter

James Templeton & Co, Glasgow
Ninian Johnston and George A Boswell, 1938
Bruce Peter

Nairn & Co, Kirkcaldy
George James Miller of James Miller & Son, 1938
Bruce Peter

demand. Even environments where hitherto having fitted carpets would not have been considered, such as the saloons of trans-Atlantic liners, in which spillages and seasickness were frequent hazards, now needed swathing in plushest Axminster.

Templeton's carpets therefore required additional production space and so, to expand the Victorian Venetian gothic extravaganza William Leiper had earlier designed for them by Glasgow Green, they employed George A Boswell (1879–1952), who was a former assistant of James Miller. Earlier, as an independent practitioner in Edwardian Glasgow, he had specialised in designing cinemas and went on to develop a successful general commercial practice. In the early 1930s he employed the talented Ninian Johnston, recently graduated from the Glasgow School of Architecture. It was Johnston who was the principal designer of the additions to Templeton's premises, the first new wing being completed in 1935.[6] Its granite base with ribbed bands of faience and edge-to-edge fenestration might have won the approval of Walter Gropius – but when another wing was needed, adjacent

to Leiper's polychromatic original, Johnston felt obliged to pay homage with a matching frieze around the roofline in glazed brick.[7] Although the existing building and its new neighbour, completed in 1938, would prove to be effective foils for each other, the *Architects' Journal* was unenamoured, commenting cruelly and in line with the national stereotype that those responsible may have been inebriated when devising that particular solution.[8]

In Kirkcaldy, meanwhile, Nairn & Co, whose linoleum flooring business was likewise flourishing, commissioned a new factory and office block from James Miller's firm, the project being the work of his son, George James Miller. The offices are arranged around a quadrangle, their symmetrical main facades in stone with restrained neo-Georgian details, deep parapets and pitched tiled roofing being very much in the manner of Miller junior's earlier employer, Herbert Baker. Architectural sculpture is by the London-based Joseph Armitage (1880–1945), whom Baker had frequently commissioned. Completed in 1938, the modernised traditionalism of the main frontages

Weir Pumps Ltd, Cathcart, Glasgow
Wylie, Shanks and Wylie, 1937
Bruce Peter

is perhaps a reflection of Nairn's desire to transcend passing fashions; the inlaid linoleum flooring in the hallway was the most obvious Art Deco element – but also the most easily replaced.[9]

Another similarly progressive company, albeit in the traditional engineering sector, was Weir Pumps Ltd of Cathcart in Glasgow, which commissioned Wylie, Shanks and Wylie to design for its premises a new Welfare Building, completed in 1937. The street frontage proclaims forward-looking thinking with a moderne clock tower and glazed curving staircase, while within were a canteen, rest lounge, library, cinema and gymnasium.[10]

An even more attention-grabbing industrial edifice was meanwhile being planned for a site at Shieldhall near Renfrew. Its development was a result of frustration by the Scottish Co-operative Wholesale Society at an international cartel fixing the wholesale pricing of lightbulbs. This led it to join forces with the Co-operative Wholesale Society in England and to solicit the assistance of the Swedish Co-operative Union

Luma factory, Shieldhall, Glasgow
Cornelius H Armour, 1939
Bruce Peter

to begin their own production of lamps and bulbs to be sold in Co-operative stores in Britain and Sweden. The Swedish Co-operative Union was a useful partner as it already had expertise in lightbulb manufacture. In Stockholm, it had opened the Luma bulb and lamp factory at Hammarby in 1930 and this complex of buildings had won praise for its functionalist appearance. Its design was by the organisation's own architecture department, known in Swedish as 'Kooperativa Förbundets Arkitekt- och Ingenjörsbyrå' (or KFAI), the architects responsible being Artur von Schmalensee (1900–1972) and Eskil Sundahl (1890–1974).[11] The Scottish Co-operative Wholesale Society's architect, Cornelius H Armour, took inspiration from their work when planning the Scottish Luma factory, which was completed in 1939.[12] Its most immediate and striking similarity is a moderne two-storey-high glazed beacon with semi-circular ends projecting above the roofline in which new lamps and bulbs were tested, illuminating the factory's surroundings and showing what Luma's products could achieve. The factory is otherwise of very plain appearance, reflecting Armour's Swedish functionalist inspiration and probably also the challenging economic climate in which it was built.[13]

Representing the height of late-1930s modernity in factory office design was a new concrete-framed four-storey administrative block constructed in 1939 at the Zenith metal foundry of Henry Wiggin & Co

Henry Wiggin & Co Zenith Works, Thornliebank, Glasgow
Johnson's Reinforced Concrete Engineering Co, 1939
Glasgow City Archives

in Thornliebank on Glasgow's Southside. This was an outpost of what was a large multinational company ultimately headquartered Canada. The block was designed and built by Johnson's Reinforced Concrete Engineering Co of London and Manchester with an exterior that was almost entirely glass-clad. Window strips on the first and second floor interspersed shiny black Vitrolite panels, while the ground floor, where there were communal showers and locker rooms, and the stair tower were enclosed with glass blockwork.[14] The top floor contained a canteen, in which all employees ate together – a most forward-looking concept at that time. The architect responsible for this striking building has proven elusive to trace, but an original plan names a Mr Beckett, who presumably was employed directly by Johnson's.[15]

Hillington Industrial Estate
In terms of concept and scale, Scotland's first modern industrial estate at Hillington was a unique project in the second half of the 1930s. The idea of building an industrial estate in the Glasgow area was first envisaged in 1934, though the scheme took four years to come to fruition. Clydeside's heavy engineering-based economy had failed to show signs of recovery from the Great Depression, resulting in the Scottish Office declaring it a 'Scottish Special Area' where targeted measures would be taken to encourage the development of new industries to diversify the economy and thereby hopefully encourage fresh employment opportunities.[16] The chosen site was farmland at Hillington between Glasgow and Paisley, adjacent to the railway to Gourock, Ayr and Stranraer, the port facilities on the Clyde and Renfrew Aerodrome.[17] The developer was the specially created Scottish Industrial Estates Ltd, chaired by Sir Stephen Bilsland, philanthropic owner of a successful Glasgow bakery business, which would build and rent out factory units, thereby recouping the government's investment over time. The Glasgow architectural practice Wylie, Shanks & Partners was commissioned to design these, working quickly and within a tight budget.[18] To help design the estate, two recent graduates of the Glasgow School of Architecture, Margaret Jean Sutherland Love (1912–1979) and James Robin (1913–1980), were employed as assistants.

The project was developed concurrently with the Empire Exhibition in Bellahouston Park and there were greater similarities between the two than might be

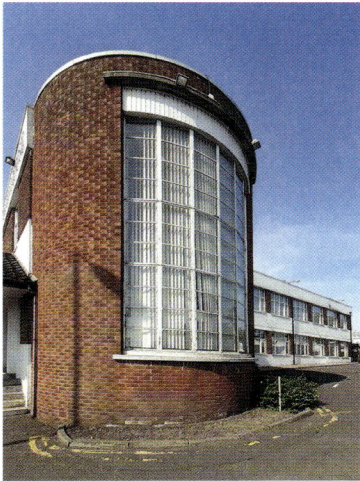

Industrial units, Hillington Industrial Estate near Renfrew
Wylie, Shanks & Partners, 1938–1939
Bruce Peter

imagined. Both used spacious planning with extensive planting and their buildings were built of light steel framing, enclosed with asbestos cement roofing and with horizontally emphasised moderne frontal compositions. The main differences were that, at Hillington, these were built of brick with render and their detailing was considerably less showy, lacking much of the exhibition's joyful accenting, but nonetheless still including the occasional glazed semi-circular stairway with flagpole.

Writing about the industrial estate in *SMT Magazine and Scottish Country Life* in 1938, Mary Fleming emphasised the comparison, writing that the estate was 'within sight of the Tower of Empire, that symbol of the vigour of modern Scotland' and that its site had been transformed within just 12 months into 'a garden suburb of 120 factories' which was 'rapidly spreading over the ground.'[19] She noted with approval that these had 'not wounded or marred the countryside as the "dark Satanic mills" of the industrial revolution' and that there were 'no gaunt chimney-stacks to break the serene skyline and no smoke to defile the hill air'. Instead, she found at Hillington 'a pleasant settlement of cream-coloured buildings bordered with gay flower-beds, and set about with grass verges… Here prosperity will be recaptured for Scotland, not at the price of human well-being but under a regime which makes full provision for the happiness of the worker.'[20] Fleming commented

favourably on the units' appearance, which she found to be 'very light and pleasing, the cream roughcast making an effective contrast with the tawny colour of the facing bricks between the windows, while the window-frames are painted an attractive mid-blue'.[21]

Fleming recorded that the estate's standard units were each '5,000 square feet in area … in blocks of three or four units' with yard spaces and service roads to the rear. Renting one of these cost £208 per annum, including grounds maintenance and fire and insurance costs.[22] There were also 'Nest' factories for what we would nowadays call start-up businesses, each of 1,200 square feet and costing £1 per week in rent with the option of moving into bigger premises at any time.[23] Designs could be modified to suit the needs of occupiers, while established manufacturers wishing to site themselves on the estate could acquire ground and erect their own premises.[24] Inside the units, 'considerable thought has been given to the planning of working space in order to eliminate pillars and other obstructions… In a three-unit block with a floor area of 15,000 square feet there are only four internal columns in the working space… Good lighting is aided by the use of sky lights as well as windows… and ventilation is of the most up-to-date description.'[25] All of the units were centrally heated by underground pipes emanating from a central boiler house, running on smokeless fuel.[26]

The estate's centrepiece was a communal social facility for workers, the Seaforth Canteen, which had a balcony and also a roof terrace, both accessed via an extruded stairway. Within were two dining spaces (in which a three-course lunch could be purchased for 10d), a smoking room and a small swimming pool. Nearby were tennis courts, a playing field for football and bowling greens.

With regard to what the estate produced, Fleming observed that 'a city could… find there a large proportion of the things required to supply its needs'.[27] Among the outputs of the new factories were furniture, shop fittings, neon signs, shirts, knitted jumpers, dresses, bicycles, ice-cream, biscuits, cake-fillings and sweets, bottled fruit juice, preserved meats, chutney and pickles, parts for machinery, tools, bottled oxygen, concrete slabs, pipework, synthetic stone, asbestos cement slates, office stationery, shoe polish and golf clubs. Altogether, the occupants were 'a most intriguing mixture of businesses large and small' making 'furniture, fruit juice and peppermint balls … within a few hundred yards of each other'.[28]

Small industrial unit, Hillington Industrial Estate
Wylie, Shanks & Partners, 1938
Bruce Peter

Hillington Industrial Estate under construction
Wylie, Shanks & Partners, 1938
HES SC1258254

Energy production

The electrical age had brought about a growing need for power generation. This was mostly enabled by coal-fired power stations, but Scotland's hilly topography with fast-flowing rivers also enabled hydro-electric power. In the early 1930s Sir Alexander Gibb and his Chief Engineer James Williamson (1881–1953) were commissioned to design a series of hydro-electric power stations in Galloway and Kirkcudbrightshire in south-west Scotland, with turbine halls featuring restrained Art Deco embellishment, comparable to their recent Kincardine Bridge.[29]

The potential of hydro power for industrial use had already been proven in a scheme developed at the start of the twentieth century by Loch Leven near Fort William to generate electricity for aluminium smelting. This provided inspiration for another at the Falls of Clyde by New Lanark, an eighteenth-century model industrial town in the Central Belt, making use of the river's natural flow to turn turbines. As the location was one of scenic beauty, Sir Robert Lorimer was retained as an adviser to ensure that the designs of the installations would not spoil their surroundings. The scheme was completed in 1927, the turbines being contained in a reinforced concrete hall, detailed in a stripped-back neoclassical idiom typical of its time by James

Tongland Power Station, near Kirkcudbright
Sir Alexander Gibb & Partners and James Williamson, 1935–1936
HES DP104713, SC2503615

Glenlee Power Station, near Dalry
Sir Alexander Gibb & Partners and James Williamson,
1935–1936
Bruce Peter

Taylor Thomson after sketches by Lorimer. A classical temple in the landscape was, of course, an established picturesque ideal.[30]

The electrical engineer behind the New Lanark scheme, Edward MacColl (1882–1951), who had earlier worked on the powering of Glasgow Corporation's tramway system, next turned his attention to long-distance electricity transmission and the development of a national grid under the aegis of the Central Electricity Board, which would enable electricity generated at future more remote hydro-electric schemes to be transferred to where it was needed for general use. Following the inauguration of the grid in 1933, a highly ambitious new scheme for hydro-electric generation, spanning Ayrshire, Galloway and Kirkcudbrightshire, was devised to feed into it.[31] The extent of the development was considerable, covering 38 miles from Loch Doon to Tongland on the Kirkcudbrightshire coast and involving the construction of nine separate reinforced concrete dams. The Parliamentary Assent included a clause requiring reasonable regard to be paid to the preservation of the beauty of the scenery of the districts in which the new structures were to be located. Williamson rose to the challenge of designing dams and infrastructure that would appear handsome as well as effective and an austerely monumental aesthetic in bare concrete was applied. As with Kincardine Bridge,

rectilinear, stepped Art Deco forms were sparingly used to add smaller-scale detail. The five power stations – Glenlee, Tongland, Carsfad, Earlstoun and Kendoon, all of which were completed in 1935 and 1936 – were conceived in a similar idiom with giant outline pilasters interspersed by tall rectangular fenestration, creating a rhythmic effect, suggestive of the dynamism of modern technology while also referencing the neoclassical in their proportions and mass.[32]

A similar approach was later on applied at the Tummel Valley hydro-electric scheme near Pitlochry, which was developed by the North of Scotland Hydro Electric Board (NoSHEB), formed in 1943, and built between 1947 and 1951 to designs by the same engineers.[33] The veteran Edinburgh architect and Royal Fine Art Commissioner Harold Ogle Tarbolton (1869–1947) acted as adviser to NoSHEB, but died before completion. Subsequent post-war schemes in the Highlands have buildings designed in consultation with the Dunfermline-based architect James Shearer, which although of similar form and proportion to Williamson's

Pitlochry Dam and Power Station, Pitlochry
James Williamson & Partners and Harold Ogle Tarbolton, 1950
Bruce Peter Collection, HES SC914038, HES SC914023

designs, tend to be clad in stone and ornamented with decorative panels depicting Pictish motifs, commissioned from sculptors such as Thomas Whalen, whose approach remained redolent of his 1930s work, as seen at the Empire Exhibition.[34] Whether pre- or post-war, the Scottish hydro electric power stations mostly have a familial appearance, representing Art Deco at its most austerely monumental. Viewed from our current perspectives on the environment, these projects appear all the more visionary on account of their successful generation of 'green' energy, achieved with due attention paid to visual amenity.

While hydro-electric power appeared to represent one possible future approach to the supply of energy, Scotland remained very much a coal-based economy. Its extensive mining areas stretched from Ayrshire and Dumfriesshire through central Scotland to Fife and East Lothian and whole communities existed for coal extraction. Urban tenement housing sprouted vast numbers of smoky chimneypots; industry and rail transport belched coal smoke and even new suburban housing estates were built with coal fires in every living room.

After the First World War, a Royal Commission had been convened to consider the partial or complete nationalisation of British coal mines and also ways in which the terrible working and living conditions of coal miners could be improved. Although the Liberal Prime Minister, David Lloyd George, rejected any suggestion of nationalising the coal industry, one of the commission's recommendations that was enacted was to create a Miners' Welfare Fund, administrated by a Miners' Welfare Committee. This was established in 1921 and it raised funds through a levy on all coal extracted to pay for improvements in education, social provision and public health in mining communities.

One pressing concern was that hitherto few coalmines had baths where miners could wash at the end of their shifts. The exhausted men had to return home dirty and often soaking wet from mine water, risking pneumonia and bringing the filth of the coal seams into each home, where their wives were expected to help them bathe and get changed as best possible, probably in a tin bath placed in front of the fire. Therefore, among the Committee's initiatives was to finance the building of dedicated pithead baths at every coalmine in Britain. This would be a massive and costly undertaking, but one that would gradually change miners' working conditions for the better. Over the ensuing 30 years, over 400 pithead baths were built across all of Britain's mining areas, designed by architects appointed by the Miners'

Welfare Committee's Chief Architect, the Liverpool-educated John Henry Forshaw (1895–1973). The drawing office in London was split into regional departments, the North–Eastern and Scotland division being led from 1928 onwards by John Austin Dempster (1892–1956), who was a graduate of the Glasgow School of Architecture and who between war service and his appointment to the Welfare Fund had been a borough architect in Bethnal Green in London's East End. During the ensuing years, he was responsible for the design of over 50 pithead baths in Scotland and northern England, every one of which was of a bespoke design, though all were distinguished by their strikingly modern appearance.[35] Dempster was assisted by Hugh Smith (1899–1967), who had likewise studied at the Glasgow School of Architecture, from which he graduated in 1925, thereafter being employed in HM Office of Works. A brace of draughtsmen worked under their direction.

Dempster wrote in detail in the RIAS *Quarterly Illustrated* about the importance of colliery baths having a high architectural quality to lend much-needed dignity to mine environments and to transform miners' working conditions. He cited continental exemplars from which he took inspiration, finding the layout and equipment of German pithead baths to be particularly satisfactory.[36] Emulating German practice, each baths building he and his colleagues designed contained a sequence of spaces, comprising a 'dirty room' in which miners dressed or removed mine-soiled workwear, a communal showering space and a clean room in which to change into and out of everyday clothes. Some examples even included a canteen and creche and social facilities for miners' families. As the water tank feeding the showers needed a high position to ensure pressure and a boiler flue was also required,

Castlehill Colliery Baths, near Wishaw
James Austen Dempster and Hugh Smith, 1935
HES SC1074158

Fleets Colliery Baths, near Tranent
James Austen Dempster and Hugh Smith, 1936
HES SC1074158

Cardowan Colliery Baths, Stepps, Glasgow
James Austen Dempster and Hugh Smith, 1935
HES SC1073896

Dempster and his colleagues made virtue of necessity by incorporating these into tower features, forming the centrepieces of a variety of otherwise diverse volumetric compositions. The designs built in the second half of the 1930s bifurcated into two distinct approaches, one being geometric compositions clad in facing brick in the manner of contemporary Dutch architect Willem

Marinus Dudok, with the other using painted render finishes upon compositions featuring curved elements, reminiscent of the style of Rob Mallet-Stevens.

The Dudokian baths included those at Bowhill and Aitken collieries in Fife, Manor Powis and Wester Auchengeich in Lanarkshire and Cardowan near Glasgow, the last four evidently inspired in varying degrees by the massing of Hilversum Town Hall in the Netherlands.[37] Newcraighall in West Lothian and Mauchline in Ayrshire were, by contrast, long, low compositions, while Arniston, also in West

Arniston Colliery Baths, near Gorebridge
James Austen Dempster and Hugh Smith, 1936

Lothian, was a striking circular design with a tower in the centre, its form possibly inspired by Southgate London Underground station by Charles Holden.[38] Those with painted rendered exteriors may have been intended to give the false impression that coal was clean and non-polluting, but they did not stand up nearly so well to the Scottish climate as those finished in brick. Nonetheless, when new, they briefly dazzled. The more basic examples of the genre were at Whitehill, Prestonlinks and Hopetoun collieries in Lothian, Castlehill in Fife, Polmaise near Stirling and Auchincruve and Kames in Ayrshire.[39] Bigger and more sophisticated-looking were those at Polkemmet Colliery in West Lothian and Michael Colliery in Fife, both of which were symmetrical compositions with a tall tower in the centre featuring a bow window.[40] Fleets Colliery in East Lothian and Pennyvenie Colliery in Ayrshire were contrastingly asymmetrical with a tower at one end and extensive glazing along the flank, indicating the placement of their social facilities.

The pithead baths were Scotland's biggest and most visually striking single group of moderne buildings, located in working-class communities dedicated to coal extraction. They were also among the shortest lived and all were demolished between the 1960s and the 1980s when the collieries were closed. As they were built for one very specific purpose – washing dirty miners – they would in any case have been very difficult to convert for other purposes.

Polkemmet Colliery Baths
James Austen Dempster and Hugh Smith, 1937

CHAPTER 10
OCEAN LINERS

Among the most magnificent Art Deco environments to emerge from Scotland – or anywhere in the world, for that matter – were the interiors of the large passenger liners constructed in Clyde shipyards for trans-Atlantic, trans-Pacific and colonial routes as well as for leisure cruising. In the first half of the twentieth century, the Clyde was the world's pre-eminent shipbuilding river with over 30 significant yards in operation. Clyde shipbuilding had reached its all-time peak in terms of tonnage output in the Edwardian era and by the period after the 1925 Paris Exposition it was arguably already in the first phase of a long decline (though it is only with hindsight that this came to be realised). In the 1920s, the restricted economic situation in the wake of the Treaty of Versailles led to lower numbers of orders being placed, while the after-effects of the Russian Revolution encouraged unprecedented industrial disputes, resulting in severe delays in completing such vessels as were under construction. Newly industrialised nations, such as Italy, where Mussolini's Fascist government heavily subsidised shipbuilding, provided stiff competition for foreign orders. In the first half of the 1930s, the effects of the Wall Street Crash and the Great Depression meant near-empty order books. Considerable hardship was caused in the

First Class Lounge, *Strathallan*
James Patrick MacBride and Alexander Graham Glen
of McInnes Gardner, 1938
McInnes Gardner

many thousands of households who depended upon the industry for their livelihoods.

It was back in the 1890s that liner companies involved in the trans-Atlantic passenger trade had first begun to conceive of their vessels' First Class accommodations as versions of floating hotels, offering a similar style and level of service as the hotelier César Ritz sought to provide ashore. The leading shipping lines then began to employ architects to design their vessels' First Class interiors in the Ritz style of light and florid Frenchified neoclassicism, which continued to be leading British shipowners' preferred choice prior to the Art Deco era. Until the latter 1920s, trans-Atlantic liners were otherwise mostly designed for the carriage of westbound migrants in Third Class, but sharply declining American quotas and a rapidly growing tourist trade encouraged a more comfortable all-cabin Tourist Class to fill bigger proportions of shipboard space; this in any case enabled a more balanced trade with equalised passenger volumes in both directions and so was more profitable for shipping lines.

From the 1900s, the increasing aesthetic complexity of First Class liner interiors and the desire of shipowners to have greater control over their specification and execution, coupled with the fact that shipyards' prime competencies were in steelwork and heavy engineering, rather than decorative work, led to the interiors being subcontracted to specialist suppliers. The leading Scottish company involved in their making was the Glaswegian cabinetmaker Wylie & Lochhead, though its contribution was slight relative to that of Waring & Gillow, Britain's pre-eminent specialist whose showrooms were in London and Paris but whose workshops were in Lancaster. Towards the end of the 1920s, it added Modern Art Departments to the ranges of interior design services it offered and even had some success in selling Art Deco back to the French.[1]

Among the various other makers of ship interiors, H H Martyn & Co of Cheltenham was also notable for its work in the Art Deco idiom. It operated a vast complex of workshops making finely crafted architectural elements in stone, wood, metal, glass and plaster and first became involved with ship interiors following the commissioning of James Miller by the Cunard Line to design the First Class saloons of its flagship liner *Lusitania*, completed by John Brown & Co of Clydebank in 1907. Miller was already using the company to make interiors of buildings ashore, such as the Anchor Line headquarters in Glasgow's St Vincent Street. After the *Lusitania* was delivered, one of Miller's assistants on the project, David Longden (1886–1970), was recruited by H H Martin to develop its ship interiors business. Another of H H Martin's managers in the interwar period was the noted designer of decorative metalwork, Walter Gilbert.[2]

Art Deco first went to sea two years after the Paris Exposition when, in 1927, the French state-controlled trans-Atlantic liner operator Compagnie Générale Transatlantique took delivery of the *Île de France*, the interiors of which were designed by the same architects and decorators as had been responsible for the main French-sponsored exhibition pavilions. On both sides of the Atlantic – but particularly in New York – the new liner caused a sensation. American enthusiasm for the relentless glamour and modernity of its public rooms and suites was no doubt heightened by prohibition being in force on all US-flagged ships, whereas on this French one, there were numerous very chic saloons in which to down cocktails until the small hours of the morning. The New York smart set were very smitten and soon the liner's interior style came to be emulated there in new office, apartment, hospitality and entertainment venues. It was even name-checked in such popular songs as 'These Foolish Things' and 'A Fine Romance'.[3] In 1928, the German shipping company Norddeutscher Lloyd introduced its streamlined, high-speed, Blue Riband-winning *Bremen* with moderne interiors by Fritz August Breuhaus (1883–1960), while the Swedish American Line took delivery of the German-built *Kungsholm*, decorated in an opulent and elegant Scandinavian national romantic

version of Art Deco by Carl Bergsten (1979–1935), who had designed the Swedish Pavilion at the Paris Exposition.[4]

One might have expected that the relatively conservative culture of British shipowners would have caused there to be a hiatus between the commissioning of such stylistically advanced continental liners and equivalents flying the British Merchant Navy flag, the Red Ensign. However, in actuality, when the *Île de France* entered service, the first Clyde-built examples to display elements of the new approaches were already under construction. International competition and varying marketing strategies targeting diverse clienteles ensured that there was room for the modern alongside the existing historicist grand styles of décor favoured in the British merchant navy.

<hr />

Canadian Pacific was early to sense an opportunity to re-think shipboard provision in both the trans-Atlantic and trans-Pacific trades with a view to encouraging tourist and leisure travel. Perhaps Canada's large French population gave cause to embrace the latest look from Paris. In the 1920s, Canadian Pacific promoted itself as 'the world's most complete transportation system'; its track mileage spanned Canada from coast to coast, while its shipping services encompassed Europe in one direction and the Far East and Australasia in the other. With North America the prime global centre of economic growth in the 1920s, Canadian Pacific was in a good position to capitalise – and the fact that its trans-Atlantic route from Montreal and Quebec to Glasgow and Liverpool had a shorter duration than the lines from New York also gave economic and time-saving advantages, it being possible to complete journeys to other cities in the USA and Canada by rail.

In the second half of the 1920s, the company ordered four moderately sized trans-Atlantic liners, each of around 20,000 gross tons – the *Duchess of Bedford*, *Duchess of Richmond* and the *Duchess of York*, all of which were built by John Brown & Co and delivered between 1928 and 1929, plus the *Duchess of Atholl*, which William Beardmore & Co completed in 1928. The interiors of these Clyde-built ships were the work of the London-based illustrator and interior decorator Percy Angelo Staynes (1876–1953) and the architect Albert Henry Jones (1887–1960). Staynes was born in

First Class stairway, *Empress of Japan*
Percy Angelo Staynes, Albert Henry Jones and
H H Martyn & Co, 1929
Bruce Peter collection

First Class Dining Saloon, *Empress of Japan*
Percy Angelo Staynes, Albert Henry Jones and
H H Martyn & Co, 1929
Bruce Peter collection

Nottingham and had studied at Manchester School of Art, the Royal College of Art and the Académie Julian in Paris. In Bloomsbury at around the turn of the century, he had gone into partnership with the interior decorator Arthur Theobald Wolfe (1870–1944), who came to prominence in Edwardian London for his Art Nouveau wallpaper designs. They operated from premises in Hart Street, right next door to Wylie & Lochhead's London showroom. Jones was primarily a specialist in the design of cinema buildings, the interiors of some of which had decorative similarities to his concurrent work for Canadian Pacific's new liners. Ashore, he also drew up the company's Belfast office and travel bureau in 1929.

The liners' First Class dining saloons, made by H H Martyn & Co of Cheltenham, had octagonal ceilings with brightly painted zig-zag designs. The walls had light veneers, the furniture was unfussy and

the flooring had simple rectilinear inlays. In addition, some of the lighting was indirect, cast upwards on the ceilings from wall sconces. The journal *Shipbuilding and Shipping Record* commented that 'a distinctly new note has been struck... besides possessing an air of novelty, very pleasing to those who have become accustomed to the usual type of decoration on board ship, it has the additional advantage that the basic idea has been to avoid the heavy expense of upkeep'.[5] The modernity of these elements was rather tentative, however, superimposed over compositions that were otherwise essentially neo-Georgian in character.

For the trans-Pacific service, Canadian Pacific next commissioned the *Empress of Japan* from the Fairfield Shipbuilding & Engineering Co in Govan. It entered service in 1929 and was intended to present a cruise-style image through a white-painted hull and fashionable interiors. As Hawaii was becoming a highly desirable tourist destination, Canadian Pacific planned to introduce calls there *en route*. The First Class public rooms, which Staynes and Jones again designed and H H Martyn made, formed a suite of inter-linked spaces on the promenade deck. A notable feature was a high-ceilinged, rectangular grand lobby surrounding the main stairs with wings extending forward and aft on either beam. With its glossy hardwood veneer wall linings, columns with Egyptian-style capitals and concealed ceiling lighting, it closely echoed the style of the lobbies in recent large and upmarket city hotels (of which Canadian Pacific also operated a notable chain). The most ornate elements were the wave-like staircase balustrades, to the rear of which was a large painting by Staynes depicting a Japanese garden scene.[6] Forward, there was a spacious observation lounge and cocktail bar with illuminated Art Deco mirrors.

Most splendid of all was the two-deck-high First Class dining saloon, which was mostly lined with slabs of white-veined black marble, offset by areas of dark polished hardwood, etched mirrors, ornate balustrades and – clearly showing *Île de France* and *Bremen* influences – bands of concealed ceiling lighting. No previous British-flagged liner had ever boasted a space designed in such a thrillingly up-to-date manner – indeed, in the late 1920s the approach still was rare enough ashore in the UK.[7] The *Empress of Japan* also contained an indoor swimming pool and a gymnasium – features that further reinforced the cruise-style image of healthful and leisured travel.[8]

In 1928 Canadian Pacific ordered from John Brown & Co an even bigger liner for its trans-Atlantic Montreal–Quebec–Glasgow–Liverpool route to be named the *Empress of Britain*.[9] Whereas the *Empress of Japan*'s interiors had been fairly stylistically homogeneous, for the new vessel, it was felt that to appeal to the conservative end of the British and North American taste spectrum, it would be necessary to include a far broader range of decorative styles. Staynes and Jones were again retained as coordinating designers for the entire interiors, with the Glaswegian architect Alexander McInnes Gardner (1878–1934) also heavily involved. A graduate of Glasgow School of Art, earlier in his career he had been James Miller's assistant in drawing up the First Class interiors of Cunard's *Lusitania* of 1907. Upon the completion of this work, Gardner commenced independent practice and from the early 1920s onwards made the design of ship interiors his main speciality. When his initial partner,

the London-born and traditionalist George A Crawley (1864–1926) died, a Glasgow-trained assistant of more progressive persuasion, Alexander Graham Glen, was promoted to take the design lead.

The *Empress of Britain*'s high-ceilinged First Class Mall – a multi-functional grand lobby, lounge and shopping arcade on the Promenade Deck – was decorated by Staynes and Jones in a light, silvery palette with ceiling lighting troughs featuring scalloped edges, illuminated frosted glass ziggurats above the shop display windows and a mural in the stairwell by Maurice Greiffenhagen (1862–1931). The décor of the other spaces accessed from the Mall was by a wide variety of artists and decorators and was highly diverse in detailing and atmosphere. The Cathay Lounge, by the French-born but London-based illustrator Edmund Dulac (1882–1953), had a Cantonese-inspired theme in red, black and gold, the aim being to remind trans-Atlantic passengers that Canadian Pacific's liner operations across the Pacific also called at Hong Kong. The Knickerbocker Bar, a relatively small moderne cocktail lounge on the port side, was decorated with a whimsical mural telling the history of the cocktail by the cartoonist W Heath Robinson (1872–1944).[10] By contrast, traditionalists would have gravitated either towards the French Renaissance-style Mayfair Lounge by the upmarket London interior decorator Sir Charles Allom (1865–1947) of White Allom or to the Empress Room ballroom, which was neo-Georgian and had a coral blue and silver colour scheme selected by the artist Sir John Lavery (1856–1941).

Four decks below, Frank Brangwyn contributed decorations to the spectacular Art Deco Salle Jacques Cartier First Class dining saloon, which otherwise was mostly designed by Staynes, Jones and Gardner. Measuring 120 feet in length and with a height of 19 feet, it was the largest passenger space yet attempted at sea without structural pillars. At each end and along both sides of its upper level, Brangwyn painted a series of murals depicting the French explorer's discovery of the St Lawrence River, featuring lush foliage against a silver ground. These were set behind rectilinear polished oak balustrading reminiscent of detailing favoured by Frank Lloyd Wright and Charles Rennie Mackintosh and matching the forms of the chairs and tables. The concealed illumination not only crossed the ceiling from side to side but also continued down the walls. In the centre was a Lalique glass fountain of light, rising from the buffet counter.

Empress of Britain
John Brown & Co and Canadian Pacific, 1931
Bruce Peter collection

First Class Mall, *Empress of Britain*
Percy Angelo Staynes, Albert Henry Jones and Maurice
Grieffenhagen, 1931
Bruce Peter collection

Cathay Lounge, _Empress of Britain_
Edmund Dulac, 1931
Bruce Peter collection

First Class Dining Saloon, _Empress of Britain_
Percy Angelo Staynes, Albert Henry Jones, Alexander
McInnes Gardner and Frank Brangwyn, 1931
Bruce Peter collection

In addition to the main direct and indirect ceiling and wall illumination, there were shaded lamps in the centres of all the tables. The inlaid vulcanised rubber flooring featured a cubist design by Brangwyn, which contrasted with his naturalistic treatment of the murals.[11] The room was for its time a tour de force of high-end fashionable décor, superbly conceived and immaculately executed.

Extensive leisure and fitness facilities were provided, there being an indoor swimming pool, Turkish spa, gymnasium and games courts, as well as facilities for playing on deck. The pool and spa were to have been decorated using tilework designs devised by the celebrity Parisian couturier Paul Poiret, who was renowned for his Art Deco designs but, as his opulent proposal would have needed twice the available budget to realise, these spaces were instead reallocated to Staynes and Jones. The _Empress of Britain_ entered service in 1931, its all-white livery with three buff funnels lending a cruise-style impression to the regular trans-Atlantic liner service. This leisure-orientated

Dining Saloon, *Monarch of Bermuda*
Alexander McInnes Gardner, Alexander Graham Glen and
Wylie & Lochhead 1931
Bruce Peter collection

approach to image and shipboard provision greatly influenced the development of subsequent new liners for other operators.

While the *Empress of Britain* was at an early stage of construction, McInnes Gardner received a very significant commission from the Furness Bermuda Line, which operated a cruise-style, all-First Class, liner service between New York and Bermuda, which was very popular with wealthy Americans wishing to vacation there in style. The order for the line's forthcoming *Monarch of Bermuda* was, however, placed with the North of England shipbuilding and industrial group Vickers-Armstrong and was allocated to its Walker-on-Tyne shipyard. For the Glaswegian architects to imagine what would be required of this vessel must have needed some creativity and considerable research, probably using the *Empress of Britain* as the initial point of reference. Although considerably smaller than it, the *Monarch of Bermuda* contained a remarkable array of facilities. Again, most of the main public rooms other than the dining

saloon occupied the promenade deck with clerestories punching through to the boat deck above. Towards the stern, the ballroom opened directly onto the outdoor swimming pool, creating a close relationship between these two diverse leisure activities and enabling nightlife to occur around the pool terrace. The ballroom, smoking saloon, lounge and dining saloon (the latter aft of amidships within the hull) were all double-height spaces, giving a sense of grandeur reminiscent of much larger vessels while also encouraging coolness in the muggy summer heat.[12]

Gardner and Glen's decoration of most of the interiors was robust in form and vibrant in detail, though strongly rooted in Beaux Arts neo-classicism. Their compositions used polished hardwoods with

Lounge, *Monarch of Bermuda*
Alexander McInnes Gardner,
Alexander Graham Glen and
Hampton & Sons, 1931
Bruce Peter collection

**Tourist Class Dining Saloon,
*Strathallan***
James Patrick MacBride and Alexander
Graham Glen of McInnes Gardner,
1938
Bruce Peter collection

decorative metal inlays and mirrors, stylised bas reliefs and other whimsical elements superimposed. The lighting was notable for its sophistication, coming from multiple sources. Gardner and Glen purpose-designed almost every item of furniture, including the baby grand pianos, to ensure that all would harmonise with the overall design concept.

The entrance hallway, which was made by H H Martyn & Co, set the tone with its zig-zag marquetry inlays, concealed lighting and octagonal void to the deck above, surrounded by ornate metal railings with fountain motifs.[13] The flashily decorated main lounge, made by the London cabinetmakers and decorators Hampton & Sons, had a coffered ceiling with concealed perimeter lighting, moderne fluted pilasters and balconies with sinuous fronts, clad in bird's eye maple. At one end was a stage with a proscenium while at the other there was a bas relief panel with a conch shell in front, from which emanated a sunburst of fountain-shaped peach glass mirrors.[14] Immediately astern, the Veranda Café, also made by Hampton & Sons, was particularly jazz-inflected with a bright inlaid floor forming an abstract sunburst around a central dais from which a combined buffet table, urn and lamp emerged, which appeared to reference the Egyptian revival.

The dining saloon, made in Glasgow by Wylie & Lochhead, was most striking of all, having balcony railings and a concealed lighting scheme both strongly emphasising the horizontal. The walls were panelled in two tones, which further reinforced this effect. Above the central void, the ceiling was illuminated from four lighting panels and the inlaid flooring reflected the rectilinear overall form of the space and the other elements of its outfitting. The ladderback chairs were perhaps a little old-fashioned by comparison but were probably preferred for their comfort and ability to ventilate diners' backs.[15] Only the Smoking Saloon and Library, also by Hampton & Sons, diverged entirely from the predominant Art Deco approach, being decorated in the manner of an English gentlemen's club with oak panelling and large armchairs, the Saloon having lunettes in the clerestory, suggestive of spaces that Gardner might have conceived a quarter of a century before when working for James Miller.

The *Monarch of Bermuda*'s cabins were not only all en suite, but each was equipped with a full-sized bath, making the vessel outstanding in terms of comfort and well up to the standards expected by a clientele otherwise used to splendid hotels such as New York's

brand-new Waldorf Astoria, which opened almost concurrently with the liner's entry into service in 1931. With facilities such as these, notwithstanding the unpropitious economic circumstances in the aftermath of the Wall Street Crash, Furness Bermuda Line found themselves with a winning formula – so much so that a sister vessel was quickly ordered. The *Queen of Bermuda* was also built by Vickers-Armstrong, but at its Barrow-in-Furness shipyard. It entered service in 1933.[16]

When Alexander McInnes Gardner died in 1934, Alexander Graham Glen took over the firm, which continued without a change of name, employing a talented shipyard draughtsman of Scots-Irish descent, James Patrick MacBride (1895–1982), to carry out much of the design work. Born in Edinburgh, he had spent his career to date in the drawing office of the Clyde shipbuilder Alexander Stephen & Sons.[17] Under this new arrangement, McInnes Gardner's next notable client was the Peninsular & Oriental Steam Navigation Company – Britain's biggest and most important liner company – which had recently commenced a bold programme of new-building to transform its services between the UK, India, Australia and the Far East. In each of these destinations, a great many Art Deco buildings were constructed – Australia, in particular, was perceived in Britain as being a young dependency for which modern ideas, including in design, were appropriate.

In planning its new vessels, P&O's directors may well have taken inspiration from Canadian Pacific's *Empress of Britain* because the company's existing black and ochre exterior livery was abandoned in favour of an all-white scheme with three buff funnels. The accommodation MacBride designed for P&O's *Strathmore*, delivered in 1935 from Vickers-Armstrong's Barrow-in-Furness shipyard, was characterised by smooth surfaces with curved corners in polished hardwood veneers and inlaid flooring, all illuminated by concealed ceiling lighting. It was followed by two near-sisters – the *Stratheden* of 1937 and the *Strathallan* of 1938.[18] These liners were also among the earliest to have comprehensive fire-fighting sprinkler systems. In the early 1930s a number of serious shipboard fires on foreign-flagged passenger ships led the British safety authorities to consider mandating the installation of these on new vessels to fight fires automatically as soon as they ignited. In those days, most people smoked and sometimes they even smoked in bed – a particularly dangerous activity onboard ships.[19]

Concurrently with the building of the *Strathmore*, P&O's rival on the London–Sydney route, the Orient Line, was having Vickers-Armstrong build its own new liner, the *Orion*, with moderne interiors by the New Zealand-born émigré architect and designer Brian O'Rorke (1901–1974). Knowledge of this may have been what persuaded P&O's Chairman, Sir William Crawford, to commission similarly up-to-date shipboard accommodation from McInnes Gardner.

The *Queen Mary*

A new flagship ordered in 1930 from John Brown & Co of Clydebank for the Cunard Line's prime trans-Atlantic route between Southampton and New York would, after a protracted design and construction process, emerge as not just the greatest manifestation of Art Deco ever realised in Scotland – but one of the style's most famous and enduring monuments in a global context. Yet, when first conceived, there was no notion that it would contain any elements of the style whatsoever.

In the latter 1920s, Cunard's service was still operated by three liners of Edwardian vintage – the *Mauretania*, the *Aquitania* and the *Berengaria*, which was a war reparation from Germany, replacing the torpedoed *Lusitania*. Cunard's main British-flag rivals, White Star Line and Canadian Pacific, and even lesser British liner companies with which it cooperated, such as the Glasgow-headquartered Anchor and Donaldson Lines, all used newer tonnage. In the latter 1920s, Cunard carried out development work for its new flagship, using the highly successful *Aquitania* as the initial reference for layout, but doubling its size to give much more room for a far higher quality of travel experience, particularly in the two lower classes. Following technical development work, at the end of December 1930 the keel was laid for what was to be a thousand-foot-long giant, then known merely as Yard Number 534.

A month after this event, in the French shipyard of Chantiers de Penhoët at St Nazaire, construction began on a rival project for Compagnie Générale Transatlantique – the eventual *Normandie*, which would be launched in 1932. Outfitted at lavish expense as a glittering showcase of modern French *grand luxe*, it would contain spectacular internal grand vistas, lined with the costliest and most elaborate of finishes. Indeed, the installation of its interiors would last for nearly three years. The placing of these orders in the

shadow of the Wall Street Crash amounted to bold gestures of faith in economic recovery and a better future. As the *Normandie* was being built, British design critics began to fret that Cunard's flagship would emerge with a far less progressive layout and appearance than this and other recent European ships.

When Cunard announced the project in 1930, the after-effects of the Wall Street Crash were being increasingly painfully felt across British industry and, consequently, many potential contributors sought commissions. A very wide variety of styles were speculatively submitted, ranging from a Byzantine swimming pool by Waring & Gillow to a Charles V-style saloon by White Allom. The artist Norman Wilkinson sent an unsolicited suggestion that the First Class smoking saloon should be in a medieval style and that he would produce the necessary painted panels.[20] Cunard's Chairman, Sir Percy Bates, meanwhile decided that it would be necessary instead to appoint an architect of distinction or at least an architectural adviser to design the interiors. Possible contenders were Sir Giles Gilbert Scott (1880–1960), the architect of Liverpool Cathedral and Battersea Power Station, and Charles H Reilly (1874–1948), the Head of the Liverpool University School of Architecture.[21] Sir Percy and the managing director of Cunard's New York office, Ashley Sparks, both thought that as the majority clientele would be American, it would be sensible to employ an American architectural adviser to ensure that any designs would meet their expectations. Conscious that the involvement of any non-British consultant would be controversial, Bates was discreet in selecting and appointing Benjamin Wistar Morris (1870–1944), the architect of Cunard's imposing New York headquarters on Broadway.[22]

Cunard also received unsolicited letters from architects and non-architects who had no direct interest but nonetheless felt an urge to persuade the company away from what they believed would be misguided attempts at evoking the past through the interiors. E Wamsley Lewis, architect of the recently completed New Victoria cinema in London, wrote to recommend a modernist approach. A minor Cunard shareholder, J H Earley, expressed similar sentiments and included with his letter a Design and Industries Association pamphlet entitled 'Shipshape Design' about the benefits of modern architecture and design for ship interiors.[23] Perhaps the most persuasive correspondence came from Christian Barman (1898–1980), editor of the *Architects'*

Queen Mary under construction, Clydebank
John Brown & Co, 1935
HES SC1257773

Journal, a contributor to the *Architectural Review* and subsequently the London Passenger Transport Board's Publicity Officer, who was responsible for the implementation of its modern design identity. At this point, Cunard noted that McInnes Gardner were producing modern interiors for the Furness Bermuda Line and so they might be suitable candidates.[24] Even Cunard's newly appointed architectural adviser, Benjamin Morris, who was known for being an architectural traditionalist who favoured the Beaux Arts idiom, argued in favour of modernity following his own encounter with the recently introduced German liner *Europa*. Feedback from a trip to Canada made by two of his assistants to inspect the new Art Deco Eaton's Department Store in Montreal and the Canadian Pacific liner *Empress of Britain* in Quebec

further encouraged him in a moderately progressive direction. Morris found an ally in Sir Percy Bates' brother, Frederick, also a Cunard director, to whom he wrote in July 1931 that 'The *Empress* seemed to them to provide the stiffest competition in spite of some of her vagaries… I feel that a straight out and out period ship would be a disappointment, no matter how cleverly the unavoidable warfare between structural conditions and traditional proportions were waged.'[25] To reinforce the point, he too referred to the Design and Industries Association's 'Shipshape Design' publication.

In August 1931, Morris wrote to Sir Percy Bates to suggest two potential courses of action. One, known as Scheme A, was for the Morris and O'Connor office in New York to produce outline plans which would be worked up in detail by the design departments of decorative contractors such as Waring & Gillow. The other, known as Scheme B, was to appoint an 'English architect of deservedly high reputation, such as Mr Arthur Davis, London, whose engagement I believe would assure a scholarly performance and generally high standard of taste and scale.' Morris concluded that 'I believe Scheme B would be the better for the company'.[26] Morris also enclosed some initial outline plans. Cunard, however, decided to defer a decision on whether these should be adopted, but it did follow Morris's suggestion of employing Arthur J Davis (1878–1951). Davis had designed the Ritz Hotel in London, which was completed in 1906, with Cunard thereafter hiring him to draw up the highly regarded interiors of its *Aquitania* of 1914, and later to design its headquarters building in Liverpool.

In the late summer of 1931, the worsening economic Depression led Sir Percy Bates to warn about the effects of the difficult trading conditions on Cunard's finances, and in December John Brown & Co offered to slow down construction work, delaying delivery until the spring of 1934, rather than late 1933 as previously intended. Instead, work was halted at Cunard's behest. For over two years, the partially completed liner lay mothballed – a potent symbol of economic failure. Design work continued, however, and in February 1933, Benjamin Morris visited Cunard in Liverpool, using the opportunity to stress the 'trend towards simplification… both on grounds of appearance and economy'.[27]

In 1934, Cunard and its rival, the White Star Line, were forced to merge by the British government, which would subsequently provide loans to complete the vessel. The resumption of the project in May was a great boon for the Scottish economy and for British suppliers more generally. Cunard, meanwhile received permission from Buckingham Palace to use the name *Queen Mary*. (The Clyde excursion operator Williamson Buchanan consequently needed to adjust the name of its *Queen Mary* by adding a suffix 'II'.) The lead British architect Arthur J Davis, however, began to experience ill health and so it was his assistant, J C Whipp, who played the prime role in producing detailed designs for the interiors, derived from outline plans by Morris's architectural partner Robert O'Connor (1895–1993) and his assistants Fecke and Borer. Whipp appears initially to have interpreted the need for aesthetic modernity in a distinctly streamlined and moderne style and when Benjamin Morris saw his proposal for the First Class dining saloon, he was unimpressed. He wrote to Cunard to implore Whipp to adhere more closely to his original drawings in the matter of plain surfaces which were 'preferable to horizontal lines and bands which are indicated on the details'. Morris

continued 'A recent visit to the Italian ship, the *Conte di Savoia*, disclosed very large areas executed in woodwork or composition materials on both walls and ceilings. If however this should not be practicable under the local conditions under which the ship is built, large panels with inconspicuous joints or sinkages would answer the purpose in a reasonably satisfactory manner'.[28] In response, Arthur J Davis agreed that the First Class dining saloon 'should be treated very simply', but he added that 'certain features should be highly decorative' as this was, after all, First Class.[29] By coincidence, in October 1934, Cunard-White Star was contacted by the *Conte di Savoia*'s Italian interior architect, Gustavo Pulitzer Finali (1887–1967), seeking the task of designing all or part of the First Class accommodation. Cunard demurred, explaining that the work was already allocated.[30]

In December 1934 the first tranche of contracts to make and supply the interiors were awarded. Although the wall finishes in the public rooms and much of their furnishing would be created by leading English-based craft makers, so vast was the task that Scottish producers of furniture, fabrics, rugs and carpeting also became involved. Thus, Wylie & Lochhead, McNeil Bros, A H McIntosh, Scott Morton, Donald Bros and James Templeton & Co, among others, received commissions to make and supply furniture, textiles and carpets.

As with Cunard's existing large liners, the *Queen Mary*'s three classes were vertically divided, with First Class (or 'Cabin Class') staterooms and cabins amidships, Tourist Class cabins astern and Third Class cabins towards the bow, where sea motion was usually more pronounced. The First Class restaurant and Tourist Class dining saloon were in the lower hull while the First Class public rooms were in the upper superstructure on Promenade Deck with the Tourist and Third Class saloons respectively aft and forward.

The First Class hallway and shop spaces as well as the Writing Room and Library, which were on the port-side of the Promenade Deck, were all to be made by Waring & Gillow.[31] The Hallway was between the front and middle funnels and its T-shaped circulation area was surrounded by shops with bulging and curving glazed and veneered fascias to promote and sell desirable British merchandise. Above the windows of retailers W H Smith in the centre was a plaster frieze by Maurice Lambert (1901–1964) depicting Sport and Speed.[32]

The Drawing Room to starboard was outfitted by Hampton & Sons and was oval-shaped with walls

First Class Hallway, *Queen Mary*
Benjamin Morris, Robert O'Connor, J C Whipp of Arthur J
Davis and Waring & Gillow, 1936
Bruce Peter collection

First Class Observation Lounge, *Queen Mary*
Benjamin Morris, Robert O'Connor, J C Whipp of Arthur J
Davis and Waring & Gillow, 1936
Bruce Peter collection Image credit

painted in cream and a carpet in four shades of blue
flecked in canary yellow. At one end was a series of
four folding panels featuring a painting in sections by
Kenneth Shoesmith (1890–1939) depicting a highly
idealised flower market in an eastern Mediterranean
harbour with parasols, picturesque locals and, behind,
the masts and sails of fishing craft. To the rear of
this was a religious altar, which could be revealed
when services were held. A Lecture Room located
to port between the Hallway's forward end and the
Observation Lounge was also by Hampton & Sons
while the corresponding space to starboard was
occupied by a playroom designed and decorated by the
illustrator George Ramon (1910–1984) and containing
a Mickey Mouse cinema, a chute and a camel with a
cave-like space beneath its legs.[33]

Accessed from the Hallway's forward end was a
striking semi-circular Observation Lounge, the main
feature of which was a 30-foot-long American-style
cocktail bar, which faced raised terraced seating
overlooking the bow. Also made by Waring & Gillow,
the balustrades and the bar itself were liberally
embellished with polished chrome set against black and
with bright red details.[34] It was certainly the flashiest
space in First Class and was to prove among the most
popular owing to its relative intimacy and the superb

views it afforded through an expanse of relatively large windows. Filling the upper wall above the bar was a festive mural featuring caricatures of Londoners celebrating 'Jubilee Night', painted by A R Thomson (1894–1979).

Aft of the Hallway amidships was a complex of First Class saloons. The largest was the two-and-a-half-deck-high First Class Lounge, made by Bath Cabinetmakers Ltd, which had been founded in 1892 by the social progressive Charles A Richter (1876–1945). Richter, in contrast to William Morris and his acolytes, strongly believed in using machines to spare workers from arduous tasks. The firm's output was usually in the fashionable styles of each era; having initially been associated with Arts and Crafts and Art Nouveau designs, by the 1930s it had embraced Art Deco and moderne. The Lounge measured 96 feet in length by 70 feet across and was decorated in gold, grey and green tones. At one end was a curtained stage for live entertainment and there was also a projection booth, enabling films to be occasionally presented. At the other was a fireplace around which was a large decorative panel by Alfred Oakley (1878–1959) and Gilbert Bayes.[35] Above the doors were bas reliefs by Maurice Lambert. Some of the ambient illumination came from ceiling fittings while other lighting came from large urns made of special glass fused with gold which were located at intervals between the seating groups in the lofty centre section.

Aft of the Lounge was the Ballroom, the silver and gold-shaded panelling and furnishings for which were supplied by Hampton & Sons and which were augmented with large painted panels depicting the Four Seasons by a fashionable and talented painter and illustrator of Scottish origin, Anna Zinkeisen (1901–1976).[36] Double doors at either end led through to parallel gallery lounges inboard of the promenades, which acted as annexe spaces, both being the work of Trollope & Colls, another leading London decorators.[37] The Starboard Gallery was panelled in laurel with carved and gilded bas relief panels of forest animals by John Skeaping (1901–1980) while the Long Gallery, which extended further aft on the port-side adjacent to the First Class smoking room, featured two large oil-painted pastoral panels – 'Evening on the Avon' by Algernon Newton (1880–1968) at one end and 'A Sussex Landscape' by Bertram Nicholls (1883–1974) at the other. The carpet had a pattern devised by the multi-disciplinary

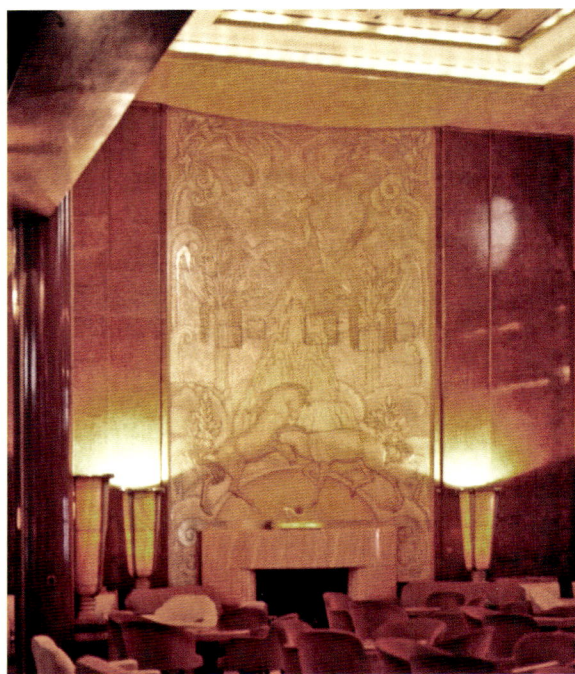

First Class Lounge, *Queen Mary*
Benjamin Morris, Robert O'Connor, J C Whipp of Arthur J Davis, Alfred Oakley, Gilbert Bayes and Bath Cabinetmakers Ltd, 1936
Bruce Peter collection

designer Agnes Pinder Davis (1895–1973) in shades of oatmeal and brown. This and the carpeting in the lounge, drawing room and library were made by James Templeton & Co, which proudly boasted that they were the heaviest and deepest pile carpets it had ever produced and that they gave a 'soft cushioned tread… surpassing anything hitherto known in express trans-Atlantic travel'.[38] Further astern, the First Class Smoking Saloon was made by Trollope & Colls. It contained carved limewood screen depicting swimmers and mermaids by James Woodford (1893–1976) and two large surrealist paintings by Edward Wadsworth (1889–1949) featuring objects connected with the sea and shipping (including the *Queen Mary* itself, approaching from the horizon); these were arguably the most modern of the artworks onboard.

On the Sun Deck, above, was the exclusive extra-tariff Verandah Grill, which overlooked the ship's

First Class Smoking Saloon, *Queen Mary*
Benjamin Morris, Robert O'Connor, J C Whipp of Arthur J
Davis, Edward Wadsworth and Trollope & Colls, 1936
Bruce Peter collection

wake. Made by White Allom, its centrepiece was a
dance floor, around which there were streamlined
balustrades with the tables and chairs arranged on
a slightly terraced floor layout, the varying heights
allowing equally good views towards the dancers and
outward to sea. The background colour was ivory
and the large windows were covered in theatrical dark
red velvet curtains embroidered with silver twinkling
stars, while the lighting was mostly indirect. Doris
Zinkeisen, Anna Zinkeisen's sister, who in the 1930s
was highly sought after among London society and
the theatrical scene, painted long mural panels which
wrapped around the forward bulkhead to the rear
of the bandstand. These depicted a jovial history of
entertainment, comprising cavorting performers from
the circus, the stage and film. In terms of all-round
fabulousness, the Verandah Grill appeared to have it
all – the best ocean views at sunset, live music and
dancing, a captivating artwork, haute cuisine and a
clientele which at times included British royals and
Hollywood celebrities.

First Class Verandah Grill, *Queen Mary*
Benjamin Morris, Robert O'Connor, J C Whipp of Arthur J
Davis, Doris Zinkeisen and White Allom Ltd, 1936
Bruce Peter collection

H H Martyn & Co made the First Class main staircase and its associated hallways and vestibules, and also various special stateroom interiors. Others were by Trollope & Colls, and others still were made by Bath Cabinetmakers (in addition to cabins and associated corridors and connective spaces, plus much of the loose furniture). The First Class cabins and staterooms were amidships within the hull.[39] Every stateroom had unique décor – one might have found in a particular example:

> Walls of ivory-white sycamore… (Your neighbour's may be of bird's-eye maple, African cherry, pearwood, Pacific myrtle or English yew). All your furniture of the same, or blending woods, is built-in; nests of drawers… open silkily, and close with a hand-craftsman's 'click'. Tall mirrors in triplicate move to your every angle. Deep, long-glass wardrobes light up by themselves as you open their doors; the doors do not swing inwards or outwards if you leave them open, but stay put, in whatever mood the ship may be… Your colour-matching telephone stands at your bedside. Your bed lamp is cunningly placed to throw light on the book and nowhere else. Your writing table is cleverly furnished and softly lit… Your carpet, curtains and chair coverings are of fascinating fabrics, infinitely varied, cabin by cabin. Nothing obtrudes harshly upon sense or movement…[40]

Shipbuilding and Shipping Record records statistics illustrating the magnitude of the task of outfitting the *Queen Mary*'s cabins:

> An approximate total of 100,000 fittings have been designed in conjunction with the owners and builders. The installation includes door furniture, finger plates, hat and coat hooks, bath grips, drawer handles, curtain rods, towel rails, thermos jug holders, lamp shades, ash trays, lamp standards… The colour of fittings in the various classes has been selected to harmonise with the paint or woodwork. In Cabin (First) Class and Tourist rooms, mottled onyx has been chosen, in Third Class accommodation mottled auburn. Cabin (First) Class and Tourist Class swimming pool fittings are of a mottled primrose shade while ivory and black fittings are supplied for the public rooms.[41]

Furthermore, in First Class alone, there were 'six miles of carpet and rugs... The pile is an inch thick'.[42] Smaller wall-mounted cabin fittings in all classes were moulded in Roanoid – a hard-wearing, heat-resistant industrial plastic made by Rowan & Boden Ltd of Glasgow. This had been 'subject of tests extending over a period of many years and in view of its decorative qualities, strength and the permanence of colour and polish is ideal for ship use'. Bathrooms were lined throughout with panels of Formica 'beautiful and durable, light in weight, fire-resisting and guaranteed not to blister, crack, craze or lose its lustre'. Flooring was of cork-rubber tiles supplied by Korkoid Decorative Flooring of Glasgow.[43] In addition to the elements supplied by external contractors, John Brown & Co retained responsibility for making and installing large expanses of interior, including the standard cabins in all classes and the great lengths of corridor and other connective spaces.

With regard to the Tourist Class accommodation, the journalist E P Leigh-Bennett characterised it as creating 'an entirely new era in unostentatious luxury for the "next best" aspirants'.[44] The Tourist Class smoking room, by Hampton & Sons, was at the aft end of the Promenade Deck. A large panel in oils by Charles Pears (1873–1958) depicted the old liner *Mauretania* on its scrap delivery voyage in the River Forth. In composition, it had more than a hint of travel poster art, but rendered poignant by the realism of rust and belching smoke from worn-out boilers.[45] For Cunard-White Star, it presumably symbolised progress. The Tourist Class Main Lounge by Trollope & Colls was directly below on the Main Deck, and featured coloured hide wall panels in silver, apple green and red between which were paintings of heavily stylised Japanese ladies by Margot Gilbert (b 1905) depicting 'Dancing through the Ages'.[46] The Cocktail Bar by White Allom was perhaps the trendiest interior in terms of décor, it being entirely lined in red and brown Formica, a material which otherwise was only used elsewhere for cabin bathrooms. The walls had curved corners and repeat horizontal stripes while an abstractly patterned inlaid floor emulated the latest American streamlined style. (Leigh-Bennett described it as 'an insidious place of Chinese red lacquer and biscuit brown glazing'[47]) Trollope & Colls also made the Tourist Class Children's Playroom which featured a naïve painting of Noah's Ark by the illustrator Herry Perry (1893–1962).[48]

Tourist Class Cocktail Bar, *Queen Mary*
Benjamin Morris, Robert O'Connor, J C Whipp of Arthur J Davis and White Allom Ltd, 1936
Bruce Peter collection

The Third Class Garden Lounge was forward on Main Deck with the Smoking Room below on A-Deck and the Lounge below again on B-Deck. All were the work of H H Martyn & Co and were similar in style to First Class spaces on recent Channel and Irish Sea steamers, being solid yet comfortable in their appointments and – in view of their locations in the forward hull where pitching motion was most severe – also easily cleaned.[49]

The dining rooms for the three classes of traveller and the galley were all on C-Deck. The First Class Restaurant, located amidships and supplied by Waring & Gillow, was the largest room ever built on a ship, filling the whole width of the hull, measuring 160 feet in length and with a height of nearly 30 feet.[50] It was entered through decorative bronze doors by Walter and Donald Gilbert (1900–1961), which were surrounded by a vast soaring painted panel by Philip Connard (1875–1958). Entitled 'Merrie England', it depicted a series of highly romanticised vignettes of English life. Across the upper transverse wall at the opposite end was a contrastingly moderne artwork by MacDonald Gill (1884–1947) in the form of a map in painted metal with burnished highlights depicting the *Queen Mary*'s trans-Atlantic route with a glass illuminated model of the liner that moved along in time with its

progress. In between, the great expanses of lustrous veneer panelling were adorned on the upper walls by 14 carved pine panels by Edward Bainbridge Copnall (1903–1973) depicting the history of shipping and sea trade since Ancient Egypt. The lower walls in the side wings featured decorative Japanese-style panels of British and American birds on silver backgrounds by A Duncan Carse (1913–2004). The Tourist Class Dining Saloon, located aft, was also by Waring & Gillow and was only one deck high, its walls containing moulded glass panels by Jacob Drew (b 1909) depicting 'Jason and the Golden Fleece'.[51] The Third Class Dining Saloon, forward, was simpler still and its interior was made by John Brown & Co's own joiners, who were also responsible for the Tourist and Third Class cabins and for the crew's accommodation.

In a context of growing antisemitism in Europe and with German liners especially inhospitable for Jewish people, Cunard-White Star went out of its way to attract their custom. The *Queen Mary* had a

Decorative panel in the First Class Restaurant, Queen Mary
MacDonald Gill, 1936
Bruce Peter collection

separate kosher galley and forward on B-deck there
was a synagogue. This was designed by the Edinburgh-
born but London-based architect Cecil Jacob Eprile
(1897–1982) of Burnett & Eprile, whose work ashore
in the 1930s consisted mainly of Art Deco commercial
buildings, but who also designed an enlargement for
Hackney Synagogue in 1935.

The only communal passenger spaces lower down
in the ship than the dining saloons were the swimming
pools, of which there were two, one for First Class by
Trollope & Colls, which had a Turkish Baths adjacent
with six massage and treatment rooms, and the other
for Tourist Class.[52] The First Class pool was two decks
high, the pool basin itself being 60 feet long by 42 feet
wide. The walls were tiled in buff faience with green
and red inlays and the ceiling soffit was curved and
clad in mother-of-pearl mosaic with indirect lighting
reflecting off it. Its Tourist Class equivalent was only
one deck high and featured pale brown tiled walls with
silver-bronze strips of metal and blue pilasters, between
which were illuminated panels of bubbling fish by
Charles Cameron Baillie.

Making the many highly crafted elements of the
Queen Mary's interiors proved to be a time-consuming
process. By October 1935, John Brown & Co was
becoming increasingly worried by the slow rate of
progress by the decorative contractors.[53] The latter
stages of the outfitting were rather chaotic as large
quantities of interior arrived and required installation,
necessitating the decorative contractors working
overtime at additional expense to ensure that the
delivery schedule would be maintained. The financial
consequences of this effort would be the subject of a
disagreement between Cunard-White Star and John
Brown & Co, extending over a year and a half after
the liner's delivery. Cunard-White Star argued that the
delays were John Brown & Co's fault while the builder
countered that it was delays in the placing of decorative
contracts caused by Cunard-White Star's prevarication
that caused the problems.[54] Cunard-White Star refused
to pay the overtime bills totalling £12,000 which the
decorative contractors had submitted to John Brown

Queen Mary on the delivery voyage, off Greenock
John Brown & Co, 1936
A Ernest Glen

& Co and a firmly toned correspondence then ensued. It took until the spring of 1938 for Cunard-White Star grudgingly to settle the last of the decorative contractors' claims.[55]

When in the spring of 1936 the *Queen Mary* was finally completed after an unprecedented national design, craft making and engineering effort, its interiors divided opinion.[56] The *Architect and Building News*'s reviewer wrote positively of the romance of the ship lying in 'the contrast between the frightening inhumanity of the steel hull cutting its way through inhospitable seas and the cosy intimate interior warmth, within which all facets of everyday human life are lived to the strains of the ship's orchestra and against the background of animated colour and cocktail-hour conversation'. While the craftsmanship and finish, the soft lighting and luxuriant furnishings were praised, he concluded, nonetheless, that the great variety of decoration and artwork created an overall effect of 'mild and expensive vulgarity'.[57]

For its review of the *Queen Mary*'s interiors, *Shipbuilding and Shipping Record* made the inspired choice of commissioning the interior designer Oliver P Bernard to write about them. Bernard was a cultivated observer of recent trends in hospitality design and was best known for having devised striking and showy Art Deco interiors in London's large but fashionable

Strand Palace, Regent Palace and Cumberland Hotels, enabling him to write from a position of considerable practical expertise. He observed that 'Going aboard a liner one fifth of a mile long… is embarking on an adventure of ideas of superhuman scale'. The *Queen Mary* was, he felt, 'a giant experiment' and therefore likely to provoke 'the yapping of mongrel criticism, the scorn of pretentious dilettanti'.[58] Contrary to such critics, he praised 'the extent of craftsmanship contained in public saloons and cabins' which he found 'staggering in terms of quantity alone. An almost uninterrupted uniformity of character is sustained throughout all passenger quarters by continuity of materials employed'.[59]

Measuring 80,774 gross tons and accommodating 2,140 passengers, the *Queen Mary* was by a small margin the biggest ship ever built. It was also the fastest, winning the Blue Riband on its maiden westbound voyage to New York for the fastest trans-Atlantic crossing. Having eclipsed the *Normandie*, which had entered service in 1935, it was fêted with a great welcoming parade of ships. The global reputation

First Class Cocktail Bar, *Circassia*
Waring & Gillow, 1937
Ian Johnston collection

First Class Lounge, *Circassia*
Waring & Gillow, 1937
Bruce Peter collection

of Clyde shipbuilding was at an all-time-high. With hindsight, the *Queen Mary*, perhaps more than any other liner, established an 'ocean liner style' of Art Deco and moderne as the mainstream way of outfitting passenger ships; thereafter it was applied within vessels of practically all sizes and types – and it was also very widely emulated in interiors ashore. In building and outfitting the *Queen Mary*, John Brown & Co and Cunard-White Star had learned a great deal and that knowledge would very shortly be put to good use in the construction of another, even bigger liner, the *Queen Elizabeth*.

Between Cunard-White Star's taking delivery of the *Queen Mary* and the building of the *Queen Elizabeth*, elements of the style of the *Queen Mary*'s interiors were replicated on a much smaller scale on the new Fairfield-built Anchor Line UK–India route motor ship *Circassia*. This entered service in 1937, offering a cruise-style alternative to P&O's provision between Britain and the Subcontinent. The Glasgow-headquartered Anchor Line had suffered badly during the Depression and had gone bankrupt in 1935. It was rescued by the shipping magnate and politician Lord Walter Runciman, who focused investment on upgrading the India service, rather than the loss-making trans-Atlantic one, on which the dominance

of the combined Cunard-White Star could never be overcome.[60]

The *Circassia*'s interiors were designed and supplied by Waring & Gillow. A very comfortable First Class accommodated 321 passengers, though there were in addition 80 berths in Third Class. *The Motor Ship* noted that 'the employment of light panelling in many of the rooms is a satisfactory feature, more particularly for a ship which… spends the greater part of its life under warm and sunny conditions.'[61] Most of the First Class public rooms, apart from the Dining Saloon, were on Promenade Deck. Just like on the *Queen Mary*, a Cocktail Bar overlooked the bow, aft of which was the main Hallway. The Lounge had a two-deck-high central area, the upper part of which was clad in quilted maple. *The Motor Ship*'s correspondent noted 'a large bookcase at the aft end… well filled with quite modern novels'. Modernity thus extended beyond the décor to include cocktail culture, fashionable literature for passengers to read, and dancing, there being an area of parquet floor.[62] A sister ship named the *Cilicia* was completed shortly after and was of very similar internal design.

During 1936 Cunard-White Star placed orders for two additional large trans-Atlantic liners. One of these was with John Brown & Co for an operating partner for the *Queen Mary*; until launching it was known as 'Yard No. 552' but thereafter named the *Queen Elizabeth*. The other was with Cammell Laird & Co of Birkenhead for the somewhat smaller *Mauretania*, completed in 1938. Cunard-White Star commissioned McInnes Gardner to design all of the latter's interiors, their biggest project to date. The resultant spaces were less apparently neoclassical in overall form than those of the *Queen Mary*, there being curved junctions between the columns and beams as well as where the veneered upper walls of the double-height central portions of the saloons met the ceilings of the lower wing spaces. The overall effect was slicker and more obviously moderne than Art Deco. Most impressive were the First Class Dining Saloon and the First Class Lounge, which was known as the Grand Hall.[63]

For the future *Queen Elizabeth*, John Brown & Co were most keen avoid a repeat of the problems experienced in completing the *Queen Mary*'s interiors. Thus, one of the earliest correspondences sent by the yard to Cunard-White Star in October 1936 was a timetable showing exactly when each stage of the interior design, manufacture and installation process would be required to occur.[64] Conceptually and in external appearance, the *Queen Elizabeth* would emerge as a considerably more modern ship than the *Queen Mary*, which from a technical viewpoint was in essence a heavily delayed example of 1920s naval architectural thinking. With only two funnels, which were without guy-wires, the *Queen Elizabeth* had a less cluttered external appearance.

Sir Percy Bates' instinct was again to involve Benjamin Morris in the design of the interiors, but the granting of a government subvention to help pay for the liner's construction made it politic instead to use a prominent British architect. A fellow Liverpool ship owner and confidant of Bates, Alfred Booth of the Booth Line, wrote to recommend George Grey Wornum (1888–1957) on account of his competition-winning design for the Royal Incorporation of British Architects' headquarters in London's Portland Place.[65] Bates also received a letter from Professor Charles Reilly, head of Liverpool University's School of Architecture, recommending Wornum.[66] In September 1936, Benjamin Morris came to London to assist Cunard-White Star in choosing an architect. Of the many firms who offered their services, Morris too selected Wornum. After internal deliberations involving Cunard-White Star's Shipbuilding Committee, it was decided that Morris should be retained as a consultant to ensure

First Class Restaurant, *Mauretania*
James Patrick MacBride and Alexander Graham Glen of McInnes Gardner and W Turner Lord & Co, 1938
Bruce Peter collection

First Class Lounge (Grand Hall), *Mauretania*
James Patrick MacBride and Alexander Graham Glen of McInnes Gardner and W Turner Lord & Co, 1938
Bruce Peter collection

that Wornum's designs would have American appeal. Wornum established a drawing office within the Cunard Building in Liverpool, enabling direct liaison with Cunard-White Star's naval architects, technical staff and Furnishing Department.[67] His wife, the American-born interior and textile designer Miriam Wornum (1898–1989), was also involved in carrying out design work for the project, particularly with regard to the selection of colour schemes and textiles.[68] The overall impression of the Wornums' schemes was that they were rather plainer and more architectonic

First Class Lounge, *Queen Elizabeth*
George Grey Wornum, Miriam Wornum and Trollope &
Colls, 1939–1946
Bruce Peter collection

First Class Restaurant, *Queen Elizabeth*
George Grey Wornum, Miriam Wornum and Maples & Co,
1939–1946
Bruce Peter collection

than those of the *Queen Mary* – indeed, they closely
resemble the spaces within the RIBA building.[69] Their
avoidance of frivolity and whimsicality would, however,
mean that the *Queen Elizabeth* would never quite
achieve the older liner's special élan in the minds of
passengers.

To make and install the *Queen Elizabeth*'s interiors,
Cunard-White Star directed John Brown & Co to
employ a mix of established ship decorating firms and
others that were barely known at all to the shipyard.
This situation reflected the more buoyant passenger
shipbuilding situation in the latter 1930s when the
main suppliers were much in demand. Besides, to outfit
a liner of so great a size required more input than they
could provide alone. The newcomers included the long-
established Edinburgh cabinetmakers Morison & Co,
founded in 1808 in Ayr, who were to be responsible
for the Tourist Class drawing room and library on
Promenade Deck.[70]

The interior fit-out was well underway when the
Second World War was declared in September 1939.
This brought the risk of John Brown & Co being
bombed by the Luftwaffe. Cunard-White Star let it
be known that upon completion in February 1940
the liner would sail for Southampton for drydocking.
Meanwhile, in great secrecy, alternative plans were made
for it to 'vanish' unnoticed from Europe by sailing at
speed directly to the safety of New York, where the
Queen Mary had been berthed since the war had broken
out. Instead of being painted in Cunard's livery, it was
finished in dark grey camouflage and on 27 February
was handed over to Cunard-White Star. It then left the
Clyde without so much as sea trials and headed across
the Atlantic, the speed of the new machinery being
gradually worked up to give over 25 knots. This voyage
passed into Clyde shipbuilding legend as a symbol of the
engineering excellence achievable there. In New York,
the *Queen Mary* and the *Queen Elizabeth* underwent
the first stages of conversion into troop transporters. It
would be at least six years before either liner would be
put to civilian use and, instead, during the war, the two
proved invaluable in carrying whole divisions of soldiers
at a time. Following the cessation of hostilities, the
Queen Elizabeth returned to the Firth of Clyde in March
1946 where, at anchor, John Brown & Co outfitted it
for civilian service. It was thus only in the post-war era
that Cunard-White Star's long-anticipated two-ship
express service commenced to great acclaim and with
considerable economic success.

First Class Lounge, *Queen Elizabeth*
George Grey Wornum, Miriam Wornum and Trollope &
Colls, 1939–1946
Bruce Peter collection

First Class Restaurant, *Queen Elizabeth*
George Grey Wornum, Miriam Wornum and Maples & Co,
1939–1946
Bruce Peter collection

than those of the *Queen Mary* – indeed, they closely
resembled the spaces within the RIBA building.[69] Their
avoidance of frivolity and whimsicality would, however,
mean that the *Queen Elizabeth* would never quite
achieve the older liner's special élan in the minds of
passengers.

To make and install the *Queen Elizabeth*'s interiors,
Cunard-White Star directed John Brown & Co to
employ a mix of established ship decorating firms and
others that were barely known at all to the shipyard.
This situation reflected the more buoyant passenger
shipbuilding situation in the latter 1930s when the
main suppliers were much in demand. Besides, to outfit
a liner of so great a size required more input than they
could provide alone. The newcomers included the long-
established Edinburgh cabinetmakers Morison & Co,
founded in 1808 in Ayr, who were to be responsible
for the Tourist Class drawing room and library on
Promenade Deck.[70]

The interior fit-out was well underway when the
Second World War was declared in September 1939.
This brought the risk of John Brown & Co being
bombed by the Luftwaffe. Cunard-White Star let it
be known that upon completion in February 1940
the liner would sail for Southampton for drydocking.
Meanwhile, in great secrecy, alternative plans were made
for it to 'vanish' unnoticed from Europe by sailing at
speed directly to the safety of New York, where the
Queen Mary had been berthed since the war had broken
out. Instead of being painted in Cunard's livery, it was
finished in dark grey camouflage and on 27 February
was handed over to Cunard-White Star. It then left the
Clyde without so much as sea trials and headed across
the Atlantic, the speed of the new machinery being
gradually worked up to give over 25 knots. This voyage
passed into Clyde shipbuilding legend as a symbol of the
engineering excellence achievable there. In New York,
the *Queen Mary* and the *Queen Elizabeth* underwent
the first stages of conversion into troop transporters. It
would be at least six years before either liner would be
put to civilian use and, instead, during the war, the two
proved invaluable in carrying whole divisions of soldiers
at a time. Following the cessation of hostilities, the
Queen Elizabeth returned to the Firth of Clyde in March
1946 where, at anchor, John Brown & Co outfitted it
for civilian service. It was thus only in the post-war era
that Cunard-White Star's long-anticipated two-ship
express service commenced to great acclaim and with
considerable economic success.

First Class Lounge, *Queen Elizabeth*
George Grey Wornum, Miriam Wornum and Trollope &
Colls, 1939–1946
Bruce Peter collection

First Class Restaurant, *Queen Elizabeth*
George Grey Wornum, Miriam Wornum and Maples & Co,
1939–1946
Bruce Peter collection

than those of the *Queen Mary* – indeed, they closely resembled the spaces within the RIBA building.[69] Their avoidance of frivolity and whimsicality would, however, mean that the *Queen Elizabeth* would never quite achieve the older liner's special élan in the minds of passengers.

To make and install the *Queen Elizabeth*'s interiors, Cunard-White Star directed John Brown & Co to employ a mix of established ship decorating firms and others that were barely known at all to the shipyard. This situation reflected the more buoyant passenger shipbuilding situation in the latter 1930s when the main suppliers were much in demand. Besides, to outfit a liner of so great a size required more input than they could provide alone. The newcomers included the long-established Edinburgh cabinetmakers Morison & Co, founded in 1808 in Ayr, who were to be responsible for the Tourist Class drawing room and library on Promenade Deck.[70]

The interior fit-out was well underway when the Second World War was declared in September 1939. This brought the risk of John Brown & Co being bombed by the Luftwaffe. Cunard-White Star let it be known that upon completion in February 1940 the liner would sail for Southampton for drydocking. Meanwhile, in great secrecy, alternative plans were made for it to 'vanish' unnoticed from Europe by sailing at speed directly to the safety of New York, where the *Queen Mary* had been berthed since the war had broken out. Instead of being painted in Cunard's livery, it was finished in dark grey camouflage and on 27 February was handed over to Cunard-White Star. It then left the Clyde without so much as sea trials and headed across the Atlantic, the speed of the new machinery being gradually worked up to give over 25 knots. This voyage passed into Clyde shipbuilding legend as a symbol of the engineering excellence achievable there. In New York, the *Queen Mary* and the *Queen Elizabeth* underwent the first stages of conversion into troop transporters. It would be at least six years before either liner would be put to civilian use and, instead, during the war, the two proved invaluable in carrying whole divisions of soldiers at a time. Following the cessation of hostilities, the *Queen Elizabeth* returned to the Firth of Clyde in March 1946 where, at anchor, John Brown & Co outfitted it for civilian service. It was thus only in the post-war era that Cunard-White Star's long-anticipated two-ship express service commenced to great acclaim and with considerable economic success.

EPILOGUE
THE ART DECO LEGACY

The Art Deco and moderne styles in Scotland may have reached their apotheosis in the latter 1930s, but they have since had lengthy and intriguing after-lives.

The outbreak of the Second World War in September 1939 began a hiatus which lasted around a decade, during which rationing was enforced and little was built for civilian use. For the war's duration, Scotland's most eminent proponent of the Art Deco and moderne styles, Thomas S Tait, dedicated himself to anonymous governmental work, his public career effectively truncated after the design triumph of the Empire Exhibition. In the post-war era, his talented assistant, Margaret Brodie, became an architectural educator at the Glasgow School of Architecture, building little herself but inspiring many students of the post-war generation. Had the war not occurred, their career trajectories – and those of many other architects – would most likely have developed differently.

When peace returned, building restrictions continued to prevent the construction of many of the types of commercial building featured in the preceding chapters. The government's aim was to get Britain back on its feet again and this meant prioritising construction resources to focus on housing and industry. It was only in 1954 that restrictions ended. Versions of the Art Deco and moderne styles continued to be applied, albeit in stripped-back form to spare expense.

Queen Mary, Long Beach, California
John Brown & Co and Cunard-White Star, 1936
Bruce Peter

The Festival of Britain in 1951 made a new, spindly and picturesque aesthetic, influenced by developments in Scandinavia and the USA and known as 'Contemporary', briefly fashionable. At the main South Bank Exhibition in London, Basil Spence, whose pre-war Imperial Chemical Industries pavilion at the Empire Exhibition had been much admired, came into his element, designing the Sea and Shipping Pavilion with customary brio. But although there was a Scottish sub-exhibition in Glasgow's Kelvin Hall, the Contemporary style was slow to catch on in Scotland with moderne often being perpetuated instead. A couple of new cinemas completed during 1951, the Plaza in Port Glasgow designed by Lennox and MacMath and the George in Bellshill designed by Lennox D Paterson, appeared entirely moderne and as though built in the mid-1930s. Construction of both had already begun in 1939 and permission to complete the George was given following lobbying by the local branch of the powerful National Union of Mineworkers, whose members claimed that it was needed as a recreational amenity.[1] In the same year, a new railway station at Girvan opened, necessitated by the burning down of the previous building in 1946. The design, by British Railways' architects, was in the moderne manner of pre-war English stations for the old LMS.[2] It is, however, the only example of its style ever built on the railways in Scotland.

Other late examples of moderne continued to appear over the course of the ensuing decade. On Glasgow's Alexandra Parade, a mighty red brick cigarette and tobacco factory for W D & H O Wills

Girvan Station, Girvan
British Railways' Architects Department, 1951
HES DP061126

was built between 1949 and 1953 to a design by Imperial Tobacco's Chief Structural Engineer, Cecil Hockin, who earlier had been responsible for a more elaborately Art Deco example in Newcastle. On the Clyde Coast, a new club house at Cardross Golf Club was opened in 1956 as a belated successor to an earlier property destroyed by Luftwaffe bombing in 1941. The curvaceous moderne design was possibly drawn up in the mid-1940s by an assistant of the Dumbarton County Architect, Joseph Weekes (1880–1949), who at that time also produced a replacement for the nearby bomb-damaged farmhouse at Mollandhu. In Edinburgh, meanwhile, a new primary school for the south-western suburb of Longstone was under construction to a design by Reid and Forbes. Opened in 1957, its layout and massing are similar to their 1930s school projects.[3] Nearby, Edinburgh Corporation Transport's Longstone Bus Depot has a moderne-style office block by Thomas Bowhill Gibson.

Back in Glasgow, an eight-storey telephone administration building, Montrose House, was completed in 1957 at the junction of George Street and Montrose Street. Its design was by the Ministry of Works architect Stuart Sim (1898–1988), whose initial plans had been produced in 1939. It features a typical moderne curved corner with recessed glazing interspersed by tall mullions and a deep parapet with flagpoles. Concurrently, at the junction of Queen Street and Ingram Street, a six-storey office block with shops, Royal Exchange House, was under construction to a design by the firm of Frank Burnet & Boston as a replacement for war-damaged premises. Planned

from scratch in the mid-1950s, its curving corner and repetitive fins interspersing window bays likewise appear indebted to typical mid-1930s approaches. On Argyle Street, a large store for Arnott Simpson, planned by the London firm of Stanley Gordon Jeeves, has an overall form replicating that of an unrealised 1939 design for the site for which there already was planning approval. Opened in 1961, it was indeed a very late example of moderne massing, though containing sales floors reflecting the very latest in retailing trends. All of these examples feature simpler, chunkier exterior elements than their 1930s equivalents and were shorn of decorative flourishes. They thus reflect the era's need for economy and also a slowly evolving stylistic taste among the architects responsible. A comparable situation pertained in the passenger accommodation installed in Clyde-built passenger ships of the 1950s. McInnes Gardner, which by then had become well-established as the leading designers of interiors for many of the major British shipping lines' post-war vessels, continued to produce variations of their Art Deco and moderne 1930s work.

Such apparent stasis with regard to architectural approach masked grand plans for a fundamental redevelopment of Scotland, based upon ideas earlier hinted at in the displays within the Scotland pavilions at the Empire Exhibition and, even more presciently in Le Corbusier's Pavillon de L'Esprit Nouveau at the Exposition Internationale des Arts Décoratifs in 1925. The Bruce Report for the total reconstruction of Glasgow, developed by Glasgow Corporation's Engineer, Robert Bruce and published in 1945, embraced the Corbusian 'tabula rasa' approach to urban redevelopment, involving the obliteration of all existing buildings.[4] It took until the early 1960s for such ambitious and costly visions to begin to be enacted. Thereafter, the cityscape was greatly altered by comprehensive demolition and reconstruction – to its detriment, many felt. Edinburgh had sought to apply similar solutions, its Civic Survey and Plan of 1949 by the planners Patrick Abercrombie and Derek Plumstead having proposed the complete clearance of the Leith, Gorgie and Dalry districts for rebuilding, as well as the total reconstruction of Princes Street. Fortunately, it was eventually stymied after effective protesting by amenity groups.[5] By the latter 1950s, any aesthetic other than modernist was dismissed as irrelevant by those with positional power to make planning and architectural decisions.

W D & H O Wills Tobacco Factory, Alexandra Parade, Glasgow
Cecil Hockin, 1953
HES SC1076468

Culture and society also changed rapidly in the post-war period. The coming of age of the Baby Boom generation meant a critical mass of youth with unprecedented spending power, who created and consumed new fashions, music styles and social activities. Technological progress rendered obsolete several of the most prominent genres of Art Deco building and experience. In the 1950s people began watching television rather than going to the cinema and later on began to drive to supermarkets rather than patronising local high street shops. They also began holidaying abroad instead of in Scottish seaside resorts, while for long-haul travel airliners overtook ocean liners in terms of speed and glamour. Very quickly, the built and designed legacies of the 1930s – which had been intended to reflect the fashions and mores of their own era – came to feel as though trapped in a vanished past. Just as the progression of the cycle of taste in the interwar era had caused buildings and artefacts from the Victorian and Edwardian periods to be neglected and disparaged, so interwar examples also came to be discounted. Commercial expediency led several to be

Cardross Golf Club, Main Road, Cardross
Design possibly by Joseph Weekes, 1956
Bruce Peter

cheaply modernised with their most distinctly Art Deco and moderne decorative features removed or covered over. A further factor affecting some 1930s commercial buildings was that they were from the outset intended for finite existences, their quality of building and the materials employed being cheaper than would have been ideal for longevity. Many occupied large sites which in the 1960s became prime development land. In the suburbs, supermarkets often replaced cinemas – instances of a fashionable building genre from one period being superseded by another.

When the architectural conservation movement gained momentum in the 1960s, its initial priorities were buildings of the Georgian and Victorian eras, those from the 1930s being considered too new yet to be thought of as 'heritage'. It was art students and other would-be anti-establishment bohemian types who first re-embraced the decorative modern styles of the twentieth century's first half with the specific intention of challenging and irritating their modernism-obsessed elders. Against this backdrop of renewed stylistic debate, Bevis Hillier's *Art Deco of the 20s and 30s* was published in 1968 and the beginnings of a revival commenced.

Victoria Cafe, Cathcart Road, Glasgow
Designer not known, c1935
Chris Doak

In the mid-1970s, a time when the first reassessment of Art Deco was still in its infancy, students and some staff at Glasgow School of Art's Mackintosh School of Architecture, began to pay positive attention to what remained of the style around the city. The Head of School since 1973, Andrew MacMillan (1928–2014), formerly of Gillespie, Kidd & Coia, had happy childhood memories of visiting the Empire Exhibition and, although of the generation who strongly preferred Corbusian modernism for his own output of designs, he nonetheless encouraged students' interests in alternatives, including Art Deco and moderne. In 1977, a group of GSA architecture students carried out a remarkable act of architectural salvage, rescuing almost the entire interior fittings and the Vitrolite fascia of the Victoria Cafe on Glasgow's Cathcart Road, upon which a demolition order had been served. The cafe was re-installed in the GSA campus as a student venue known as The Vic. At around the same time, individual architecture students Joy Hunter (b 1956) and Chris Doak (b 1956), the latter of whom had been involved in the cafe rescue, wrote dissertations on aspects of Art Deco architecture in the Glasgow area.[6] They were thus at the forefront of the positive reassessment of the style in a Scottish context.

In August 1980, the demolition of the Firestone factory, a prominent West London Art Deco building designed by Wallis, Gilbert and Partners, on the eve of its being listed, caused a furore. The consequent media attention, however, bolstered the recently formed Thirties Society in its campaigns to have other examples protected. The destruction was only the latest of many that had over the preceding two decades obliterated numerous outstanding 1930s buildings from the British urban scene.[7] To an extent, professional architecture historians, such as the highly influential but ideologically prejudiced Nikolaus Pevsner, bore blame for having earlier been very dismissive of Art Deco's significance.

There were wider parallels between the interwar era and the 1970s and 1980s and so it was perhaps unsurprising that a revival of Art Deco then occurred. Half-a-century after the Wall Street Crash, Western nations' economies were again in the doldrums, on this occasion owing to the inflationary after-effects of the 1973 and 1979 oil crises. In Scotland, deindustrialisation was accelerated and unemployment rose. In the years that followed, economic deregulation encouraged the growth of the service sector and, in parallel, a wave of middle-class expansion occurred. Many tenants of council housing became owner-occupiers under the government's Right to Buy scheme and a retail boom then followed. For the style-conscious, Art Deco appeared to form an appropriately chic and showy backdrop for this new consumerism. The emboldened service sector desired new corporate headquarters on which motifs redolent of Art Deco were frequently applied. Office blocks designed in the early 1980s by the American architect Michael Graves (1924–2015), featuring up-scaled and greatly simplified Art Deco-derived forms, provided models for British postmodern architects such as Terry Farrell (b 1938) and Piers Gough (b 1946) and their developer clients to emulate.

In 1980s Glasgow, the design-aware hospitality entrepreneur Ken McCulloch formed a partnership with the Alloa Brewery to buy and sympathetically renovate the Rogano restaurant to attract a new, affluent clientele. He employed the architect John Thomson (1940–2017) of Weddell & Thomson, which was the continuation of its original designers, Weddell & Inglis, to carry out the project. A new cocktail bar in a pleasing 1980s pastiche of Art Deco was installed, carpeting of a design originally used on the *Queen Mary* was fitted and new plasterwork and panelling were added, subtly augmenting genuine 1930s elements.[8] The 1984 outcome appeared even more characteristically Art Deco than the original had done – but hindsight, of course, enables a greater understanding of the prime features of particular design styles to be identified and reprised. McCulloch evidently recognised in Art Deco a style whose moment was returning and the renovated Rogano became one of Glasgow's most chic venues from the second half of the 1980s onwards.

Interior of Rogano, Royal Exchange Place, Glasgow
John Thomson of Weddell & Thomson, 1984
Bruce Peter

Rogano, Royal Exchange Place, Glasgow
John Thomson of Weddell & Thomson, 1984
Bruce Peter

Elsewhere in the city centre, at the junction of Sauchiehall Street and Elmbank Street, an existing pub was renovated as a new Variety Bar, the name and font recalling the earlier Jock Mills' Variety Bar in Cowcaddens, which had been demolished along with the tenement in which it was located only a decade previously. Although the new Variety Bar was of a completely different shape from the original, the design was carried out so convincingly that, after a few years' of use to enable patina to develop, most would have assumed that it was authentic.

In an early 1980s attempt to mitigate the effects of industrial decline, the Conservative Secretary of State for the Environment, Michael Heseltine, advocated the organisation of Garden Festivals to occupy temporarily

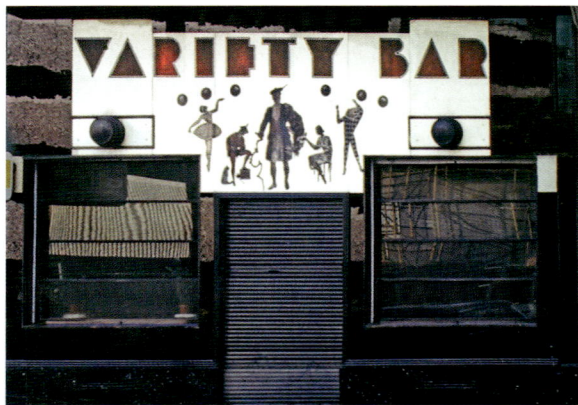

Original Variety Bar, Cowcaddens Street, Glasgow
Designer not known, 1938
Chris Doak

Second Variety Bar, Sauchiehall Street and Elmbank Street, Glasgow
Designer not known, c1987
Bruce Peter

vacant post-industrial dockside land, encouraging subsequent commercial redevelopment. Liverpool hosted the first of these in 1984, followed by Glasgow in 1988. The Glasgow Garden Festival was the city's first and only great exhibition since the Empire Exhibition of 1938, an event still well within living memory at that time. Near the centre of the Garden Festival's site on the Clyde's south bank, the house builder Mactaggart & Mickel collaborated with the Scottish Milk Marketing Board to construct a slightly modified version of a 1930s villa which James Taylor had designed for the Broom Estate in Newton Mearns. Back then, the proposal had failed to find a client and so remained unrealised for over 50 years. Taylor's heyday as an architect had been in the 1930s and thereafter his career had plummeted; shortly after the Second World War he was jailed for tax evasion and his personal reputation never recovered – though, as the Broom Milk Bar posthumously showed, he had been a designer of talent. At the inauguration, Mactaggart & Mickel's Development Manager, Iain Drysdale, stated that the intention of the festival and the Milk Bar was that they were to be a tonic for the Glaswegian and Scottish public, observing that 'we're looking at where Glasgow is today, and where Glasgow was in the thirties with the Empire Exhibition'.[9] From the exterior, the design appeared utterly authentic, the prime difference being internal where, instead of individual rooms, there was a single open-plan cafe space. With its many large windows and open seating terraces, the Broom Milk Bar was among the Glasgow Garden Festival's highlights but at the end of the summer-long event, it was demolished. (Much more recently, Mactaggart & Mickel have built additional houses in the Broom Estate itself, the designs of which reference their 1930s equivalents.)

The 1980s saw momentum build in favour of listing Scottish 1930s buildings, meaning for those selected that a consultation process would be required before significant alterations could be made. Although listing has not in every case provided complete protection, this was nonetheless a great positive change from the situation pertaining only a decade before, when many fine examples were destroyed owing to a lack of safeguard. During the 1990s, even commercial properties such as the former Paramount (latterly Odeon) cinema and the C&A store in Glasgow, the exteriors of which had been updated in the 1970s with over-claddings of corrugated

Broom Milk Bar, Glasgow Garden Festival
James Taylor of Mactaggart & Mickel, 1988
HES SC433103, Bruce Peter

metal and coloured glass panels, were restored to approximations of their original appearances.

While several significant Scottish Art Deco and moderne buildings have been sensitively converted into new uses with period features sympathetically restored, others, fortunately fewer, have sadly been mutilated by uncomprehending owners or lost to redevelopment. Art Deco and moderne housing has survived with mixed success. In some instances, properties have been completely ruined or merely made banal by the replacement of original facings and fenestration with modern, generic materials. In a majority of examples, such houses' special characteristics have been understood, if only for their marketability when selling. Art Deco-fronted shop units have suffered to an even greater extent with entrepreneurial occupiers wishing to impose their desired business identities on properties, irrespective of any Art Deco legacies from previous

King's Cafe, Elmbank Street, Glasgow
Designer not known, c1937
Bruce Peter

B A Kerrigan Tobacconist, South Methven Street, Perth
Designer not known, c1946
Bruce Peter

occupation. Thus, the Vitrolite fascia of the King's Cafe on Glasgow's Elmbank Street, next to the Variety Bar, has recently been covered by an internally lit plastic replacement while, in Rothesay on the Isle of Bute, the striking chrome lettering of Mackinnon's gift shop has been removed – a pity after having remained in situ for almost 90 years. There are now sadly few complete frontages remaining, the B A Kerrigan newsagent and tobacconist in Perth's South Methven Street being a very rare fully intact survivor with angled windows, etched glass and signage all still retained. Within, it

Mackinnon, Victoria Street, Rothesay
Designer not known, c1938
Bruce Peter

is full of typical interwar shopfitting elements. On other high streets, many more partial fragments of what were once Art Deco and moderne shops can still be discerned.

Being large and occupying prime commercial sites, cinemas have proven particularly vulnerable. Between the 1960s and the 1990s, conversion into bingo clubs enabled many former cinema buildings to continue operating commercially with most of their important decorative features intact. One prime example of a super cinema that had survived completely unaltered into the 1990s was the Capitol in Aberdeen, which even at that time retained original 1930s carpeting and upholstery designs, a streamline moderne confectionary stall in the foyer, a gorgeously fancy ladies' powder room and a working cinema organ. Notwithstanding its listed status and successful use as a theatre and concert venue, permission was then granted for a destructive conversion into two separate nightclubs, which badly damaged its interiors, after which the auditorium was demolished for an office development with only the street frontage and part of the foyer retained. This was an exemplar of how not to treat such a rare, preciously complete survivor. Similar 'facade retention' schemes have, however, been less disastrously applied to the reuse of other 1930s buildings of various types, the demolished rear-quarters of which were usually of far lower historic interest than those of the Capitol. Fortunately, elsewhere in Scotland, 1930s cinema buildings have been retained in their entirety and either partially or wholly restored for community use – notable examples being the Radio in Kilbirnie, the Regal in Bathgate and the Birks in Aberfeldy.

With regard to the re-use of other notable Art Deco and moderne buildings, in 2003, the lost Firestone factory's Scottish equivalent, the former premises of India of Inchinnan, was the beneficiary of a sensitive yet imaginative restoration and conversion scheme devised by Gordon Gibb (b 1959). The India building's office block may have been listed, but it was sadly vacant and vandalised when Gibb revived it on behalf of new owners whose business was digital game development, adding new facilities to the rear in a complementarily up-to-date aesthetic using glass and oxidised copper facings.

After the National Health Service moved out in the early 2000s, the former Paisley Infectious Diseases Hospital and the Canniesburn Hospital were eventually converted for residential use. The developers who carried out these schemes evidently recognised in the buildings and their environs qualities of elegance and space that would attract upwardly mobile residents. More recently, the former Kelso High School has been similarly transformed into flats. One may observe that such former hospitals and schools, with their large windows, handsome detailing and expansive lawns, are architecturally so much more appealing than many of their current-day equivalents, which all too often

Renovation of The Birks Cinema, Aberfeldy
Robin Baker Architects, 2013
Bruce Peter

Conversion of India of Inchinnan, Inchinnan near Renfrew
Gordon Gibb, 2003
Bruce Peter

appear as though having been designed primarily to appease particularly mercenary accountants and lawyers.

Whereas factory office blocks, schools and healthcare buildings can relatively easily be repurposed, outdoor swimming pools by the seaside have proved much more challenging to maintain, their great size and exposed locations with salty air causing gradual decay. When, in the 1970s, the availability of affordable package holidays attracted many Scots to Spain's Costa del Sol rather than the bracing conditions of Portobello, Burntisland or Arbroath, the pools fell on hard times and budget cuts forced upon local authorities in the 1980s led most to be closed and thereafter demolished in favour of new fully enclosed leisure centres. These, unlike the outdoor pools, are heated to tropical temperatures, reflecting the desire of the vast majority nowadays to have comfortable leisure. Gourock and Stonehaven retained their lidos and, following a revival of interest in outdoor bathing, many are glad that they did so. The surviving though long-derelict pool at Tarlair is currently scheduled for restoration.

The greatest extant artefact of Art Deco and moderne produced in Scotland in the 1930s, the trans-Atlantic liner *Queen Mary*, has not been seen in the country since it left the Clyde on its delivery voyage in 1936. After a distinguished 31-year operational career through war and peace, it was bought by the City of Long Beach in California to act as a hotel and attraction, which it has since done successfully for many more years than it ever traversed the Atlantic Ocean. Unfortunately, in the decades since arriving there, its various lessees profited but failed to invest to enable sufficient maintenance to be carried out. When the Covid-19 pandemic struck, its operator went bankrupt, leaving Long Beach municipality with a costly dilemma. By then, the *Queen Mary* had become such a symbol of the city that, rather than scrap the old liner where it lay, as some had suggested, it was decided instead to carry out a long-overdue thorough renovation to revive it, keeping the remaining magnificent Art Deco interiors intact.[10]

So powerfully had the *Queen Mary*'s decorative style impacted upon the popular imagination in the interim that when in the early 2000s, Cunard decided to build a new trans-Atlantic liner and cruise ship, the *Queen Mary 2*, the Swedish-owned Tillberg Design and its subsidiary SMC Design in London used the forms, colouration and lighting of its interiors as the main

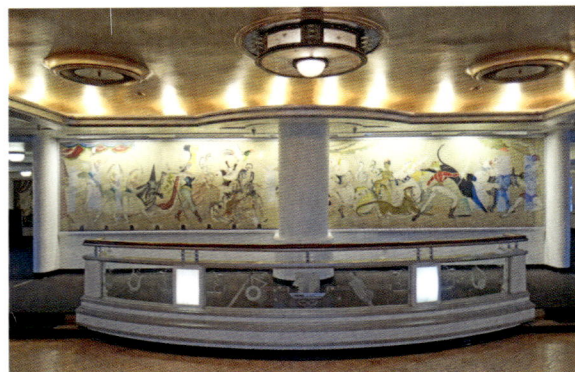

Interiors of the *Queen Mary*, Long Beach, California
Benjamin Morris, Robert O'Connor, J C Whipp of
Arthur J Davis, 1936
Bruce Peter

inspirations.[11] Similar pastiche approaches were then repeated on the subsequent Cunard cruise ships *Queen Victoria* and *Queen Elizabeth*.[12]

Back in Scotland, meanwhile, a New York property developer, Mark Parsinen, commissioned a new links golf course at Castle Stuart between Inverness and Nairn but was initially unsure of how the clubhouse

Castle Stuart Golf Club, near Inverness
Roy Malcolm of G1 Architects, 2011
Courtesy of Roy Malcolm

should be designed. He happened to watch on television a dramatization of Agatha Christie's *Poirot*, set in the famous Art Deco Burgh Island Hotel in Devon, and this inspired him to commission a comparable design for Castle Stuart, which Roy Malcolm (b 1966) of G1 Architects in Strathblane produced.[13] On the undulating coastal site, the building, which was completed in 2011, contributes to a scene somewhat reminiscent of a 1930s railway poster. For Cunard and for Parsinen, as for many others, Art Deco and moderne continue to signify positive associations of pleasure and high-living.

There are, alas, several significant original Scottish Art Deco and moderne buildings currently in states of disrepair and facing precarious futures; in Glasgow, the one-time SMT Leyland garage and the former Lyceum cinema in Govan are two examples. Around Edinburgh, the Hilburn Roadhouse and County cinema in Portobello are similarly in limbo, yet imaginative re-use could make all of these significant and useful landmarks once more. The case of the

Rothesay Pavilion, the moderne multi-functional entertainment and event venue designed in the mid-1930s by James Carrick, gives cause for hope as this outstanding building approaches the end of a lengthy refurbishment and restoration process in which Historic Environment Scotland, among others, has assisted through funding. Its proprietor, Argyle & Bute Council, believes that the venue has the potential to drive regeneration and that, upon re-opening, it will provide a powerful new incentive for visitors to be attracted to the town.

Although many of Scotland's Art Deco and moderne buildings have been lost, hopefully a greater appreciation of their qualities may encourage further similar initiatives to restore and repurpose sympathetically more of those that remain.

Conclusions

In Scotland, imagery which later would come to be categorised as Art Deco first appeared relatively early on, both before and shortly after the 1925 Paris Exposition. The Great Depression caused a hiatus in investment, but during the mid-to-late 1930s, Scotland gained a remarkably large number of highly varied architectural examples of Art Deco and moderne, spread across a wide geographical area. Scottish architects of all kinds quickly became proficient in the Art Deco and moderne styles, whether the profession's prominent names or little-known local practitioners, commercial firms or employees of municipalities.

Sources of inspiration from continental Europe underpinned Art Deco's initial impacts in Britain and Scotland but over the course of the 1930s American influences – which also had European points of origin – gradually came to dominate. This was a reflection of the USA's increasing economic and cultural power, with which many Scots came to feel an affinity. Viewed as a whole and with the benefit of hindsight, much of the Art Deco and moderne created in Scotland was, as one would expect, provincial in scale and character. Perhaps inevitably, there was little to withstand comparison with the styles' greatest exemplars in America – but what was remarkable was their ubiquity as they percolated in modified forms even to very small and remote places. This notwithstanding and

Nardini, Greenock Road, Largs
Charles James Davidson and George Veitch Davidson, 1935, renovated 2008
Bruce Peter

despite protestations to the contrary, relatively few of the architectural manifestations of Art Deco and moderne in Scotland clearly reflected distinctly Scottish characteristics. Perhaps the chunky harled exterior of Basil Spence's Gribloch country house and the massive stone expanse of Thomas S Tait's St Andrew's House government offices in their own ways came closest to achieving a Scottish modern aesthetic. Other municipal and governmental buildings – which represented the serious end of the Art Deco architectural spectrum – were occasionally adorned with sculpture and ornamentation referencing Scottish history and mythology. For every example displaying these traits, there were many more domestic and commercial edifices that could equally have been located almost anywhere in the British Isles, or overseas. Certainly, there was no discernible national modern architectural approach comparable with the well-defined aesthetics that emerged in each of the Nordic nations in the interwar era, for example. Especially in commercial contexts, a reason for using the Art Deco and moderne styles was to provoke a sense of escapism and to persuade users to imagine themselves as being in places other than Scotland. The aims appear to have been to connect with locations such as the Continent, the USA, aboard an ocean liner or even the leafier parts of the English Home Counties or South Coast resorts. A consequence was that maintaining some Art Deco and moderne buildings could be challenging when their designs made few concessions to the realities of Scottish climatic conditions.

The stylistic diversity of Scottish interwar architecture reflected the fact that cultural and economic authority over what appeared in the built environment was very widely distributed. Furthermore, Britain's dominant liberal, commercial beliefs encouraged stylistic differentiation, even if, for opposing reasons, pro-modernist and national romantic commentators would both have preferred greater uniformity. Yet, the prevalence of the Art Deco and moderne styles in Scotland is indicative of an outward-looking aesthetic culture, keen to reflect emergent trends in architecture and design in the wider world.

Scottish design outputs in the interwar period were, if anything, even more variable than architecture and ranged from high-quality textiles to furniture and commercial vehicle bodywork, which attracted criticism on account of their less resolved appearance. Whereas design theorists of the mid-twentieth century favoured visual coherence and simplicity, Scottish-based makers fluctuated between believing that fancy-

looking solutions would attract positive attention in the marketplace and thinking that the avoidance of fashionable traits would offer better long-term value. Consequently, Scottish design outputs tended to be criticised for being either too flamboyant or, conversely, too mundane. Nonetheless, for broad ranges of Scottish practitioners of architecture and design in the 1930s, the styles we recognise with hindsight as Art Deco and moderne, represented what being modern meant to them.

The Art Deco and moderne styles provided – and, for some, evidently still provide – effective means of enabling objects of many kinds and scales to be appealingly and strikingly aestheticised and thereby lent distinction. They manifested in Scotland across a wide geographical locus and found favour at many levels of the social hierarchy. After the Second World War, however, much of Scottish modern architecture took a distinctly utilitarian turn and thus too often failed to achieve a comparable popularity. The long-term successes of Art Deco and moderne also reflect their abilities to accommodate expressions of modernity, of tradition, of the foreign and 'exotic', and, very occasionally, of local vernaculars. Century-long existences mean that the styles have accumulated rich lexicons of symbolism and associations and it is through knowledge of these that we now look at, interpret and appreciate Art Deco and moderne buildings, objects and images.

NOTES

INTRODUCTION

1   Bevis Hillier, *Art Deco of the 20s and 30s*, London: Studio Vista, 1968.

2   Le Corbusier, 'L'art décoratif d'aujourd'hui', *L'Esprit Nouveau*, 1925 (English translation 1987).

3   Bridget Elliot, 'Modern, Moderne, and Modernistic: Le Corbusier, Thomas Wallis and the Problem of Art Deco' in Pamela L Caughie (ed) *Disciplining Modernism*, Basingstoke: Palgrave Macmillan, 2009, 128–46.

4   Musée des Arts Décoratifs, *Les Années '25' Art Déco/Bauhaus/Stijl/Esprit Nouveau*, Paris: Musée des Arts Décoratifs, 1966.

5   'Sir Henry Cole: An Organiser of Exhibitions', *Times*, 1 October 1932.

6   'Paris Exhibition: The British Section', *Glasgow Herald*, 18 May 1925, 20.

7   Gladys H Gow (b 1903 Greenock) – framed sampler; Catherine K Liston (b 1904 Kilbride) – framed sampler; R S Blair – framed sampler; Mary Cullen (b 1903) framed sampler; Janet C Kant (b 1884; possibly GSA staff) – silver brooch; Isobel T Smith – enamel buckles (champlevé); Mary Henderson – copper and enamel triptych; Robert Henderson – copper candle sconce; Mary H Maxwell – brass decorative plaque.

8   Tag Gronberg, *Designs on Modernity: Exhibiting the City in 1920s Paris*, Manchester: Manchester University Press, 1998.

9   Charlotte Benton, Tim Benton and Ghislaine Wood, *Art Deco 1910–1939*, London: V&A Publications, 2003.

10 Susan Sontag, 'On Style' and 'Notes on Camp', *Against Interpretation*, London: Penguin, 2009, 15–38 and 275–92.

11 Clement Greenberg, 'The Avant Garde and Kitsch', *Partisan Review*, autumn 1939, 34–39. Clement Greenberg, 'Towards a Newer Laocoon, *Partisan Review*, July–August 1940, 296–310.

12 Henry Russell Hitchcock and Philip Johnson, *The International Style*, New York: Museum of Modern Art, 1933.

13 Owen Jones, *The Grammar of Ornament*, London: Day & Son, 1856.

14 Hugh Ferguson, *Glasgow School of Art: The History*, Glasgow: Glasgow School of Art, 1995. Christopher Frayling, *The Royal College of Art: One Hundred and Fifty Years of Art and Design*, London: Hutchinson, 1987, 11–64. Deborah Jewison, Policy and Practice: Design Education in England from 1837–1992, with particular reference to furniture courses at Birmingham, Leicester and the Royal College of Art, PhD thesis, Leicester: De Montfort University, 2015, 36–105, De Montfort University Library.

15 Max Donnelly, *Christopher Dresser: Design Pioneer*, London: Thames & Hudson, 2021.

16 Ann Wyllie, Guthrie & Wells: Interior Decorators 1920–1930, MA Decorative Arts dissertation, Glasgow: University of Glasgow, T0010, 1988.

17 Guthrie & Wells Collection, Glasgow City Archives, Mitchell Library, Glasgow, TD655/9/10.

18 Gavin Stamp, *Alexander 'Greek' Thomson*, London: Laurence King, 1999. Anna Ferrari (ed), *Visions of Ancient Egypt*, Norwich: Sainsbury Centre of the Arts, 2022.

19 Frances Fowle, Alex Reid in Context: collecting and dealing in Scotland in the late-19th and early-20th centuries, PhD thesis, Edinburgh: University of Edinburgh, 1994, University of Edinburgh Library.

20 John Duncan Fergusson: *La Terrasse, Café d'Harcourt*, c1908–1909, National Galleries Scotland, www.nationalgalleries.org/art-and-artists/59266.

21 Perilla Kinchin and Juliet Kinchin, *Tea and Taste: Glasgow Tearooms 1875–1975*, White Cockade Publishing, 1991, 81–124.

22 Roger Billcliffe, *Charles Rennie Mackintosh: The Complete Furniture, Furniture Drawings and Interior Designs*, London: Taplinger, 1979.

23 University of Glasgow Collections Hunterian Archive GLAHA:41137, GLAHA:41477, GLAHA:41478, GLAHA:41486, GLAHA:41492, GLAHA:41987, GLAHA:41503, GLAHA:53097 and GLAHA:53095.

24 Wolf-Dieter Dube, *German Expressionism: Art and Society 1909–1923*, London, Thames & Hudson, 1997. Christophe Rauhut, *Fragments of Metropolis in Berlin: Berlin's Expressionist Legacy*, Berlin: Hirmer, 2016.

25 Robert Proctor, 'Evolution and Tradition: The Glasgow School of Architecture under Eugène Bourdon', in Alison Brown, Ray McKenzie and Robert Proctor (eds), *The Flower and the Green Leaf: Glasgow School of Art in the Time of Charles Rennie Mackintosh*, Edinburgh: Luath Press, 2009, 80–94. Gavin Stamp, 'An architect of the Entente Cordiale: Eugène Bourdon (1870–1916) – Glasgow and Versailles', *Architectural Heritage*, vol 15, no. 1, November 2004, 80–116.

26 Anthony Jackson, *The Politics of Architecture*, London: Architectural Press, 1970.

27 Eric Nash, *Manhattan Skyscrapers*, New York: Princeton Architectural Press, 2005, 47.

28 Patrick Elliott and Sacha Llewellyn, *True to Life: British Realist Painting in the 1920s and 1930s*, Edinburgh: National Galleries of Scotland, 2017.

29 The author's grandfather, A Ernest Glen, who was a teenager at the time of the Scottish Exhibition of National History, Art and Industry, recalled with fondness 'Alexander's Ragtime Band' being frequently played and requested at the event.

30 Howard Rye, 'The Southern Syncopated Orchestra 1919–1922', *Black Musical Research Journal*, vol 29, no. 2, fall 2009, 153–228. Howard Rye, 'Chronology of the Southern Syncopated Orchestra: 1919–1922' *Black Music Research Journal*, vol 30, no. 1, spring 2010, 5+.

31 David Boulton, *Jazz in Britain*, London: W H Allen, 1958, 61–3.

32 Cyril Stapleton, 'Satchmo's Column', *Scottish Daily Express*, 16 May 1956, 10.

33 Regina Stephan, Charlotte Benton and Ita Heinze-Greenberg, *Erich Mendelsohn: Architect 1887–1953*, New York: The Monacelli Press, 1999.

34 Michael White, *De Stijl and Dutch Modernism*, Manchester: Manchester University Press, 2003.

35 Herman van Bergeijk, *W M Dudok*, Rotterdam: Nai010, 2001.

36 Philip E J McManus, Jnr, 'The Town Hall, Hilversum, Holland', *Quarterly Illustrated of the Royal Incorporation of Architects in Scotland*, no. 45, 1933, 35–40. Hamish P Hastie, 'Modern Methods in Dutch Architecture', *Quarterly Illustrated of the Royal Incorporation of Architects in Scotland*, no. 53, 1935, 22–6. Francis R Yerbury, 'Hilversum Town Hall, Architect: W M Dudok', *The Architect and Building News*, 26 May 1933, 225–8.

37 Eva Rudberg, *The Stockholm Exhibition 1930: Modernism's Breakthrough in Swedish Architecture*, Stockholm: Stockholmia, 1999.

38 Elena Ovsyannikova and Nikolai Vissiliev, *Boris Velikovsky: Architect of the Russian Avant-Garde*, Stuttgart: Arnoldsche, 2017. William Craft Brumfield, *The Origins of Modernism in Russian Architecture*, Berkeley: University of California Press, 1991. Anatole Kopp, *Constructivist Architecture in the USSR*, London: St Martin's Press 1986.

39 Rob Shields, *Places on the Margin: Alternative Geographies of Modernity*, Abingdon: Routledge, 1991, 3.

40 RIAS, 'About RIAS', www.rias.org.uk/about, accessed 31 January 2024.

41 In the mid-1980s, the architectural historian Charles McKean sought to identify a Scottish 'moderne' with these characteristics. Charles McKean, *The Scottish Thirties: An Architectural Introduction*, Edinburgh: Scottish Academic Press, 1987.

42 Stephen Constantine, *Social Conditions in Britain 1918–1939*, Abingdon: Routledge, 2006.

43 Ken Walpole, *Here Comes the Sun: Architecture and Public Space in Twentieth Century European Culture*, London: Reaktion, 2000.

44 Clough Williams-Ellis, *England and the Octopus*, London: Geoffrey Bles, 1929.

45 Catriona MacDonald, *Scotland and the Great War*, Edinburgh: John Donald Publishing, 2014.

46 Gordon Barclay, 'Duties in aid of the civil power: The deployment of the Army to Glasgow, 31 January to 17 February 1919', *Journal of Scottish Historical Studies*, vol 38, no. 2, 261–92.

47 William Kenefick, *Red Scotland! The Rise and Fall of the Radical Left, c1872 to 1932*, Edinburgh: Edinburgh University Press, 2007. Robert Keith Middlemas, *The Clydesiders: A Left-Wing Struggle for Parliamentary Power*, London: Hutchinson & Co, 1965.

48 Christopher Reichow, *US Intentions with the Dawes-Plan toward Germany*, Munich: GRIN Verlag, 2011.

49 Neil K Buxton and Derek H Aldcroft, *British Industry between the Wars: Instability and Industrial Development 1919–1939*, London: Scholar Press, 1979. Harry W Richardson, 'The Economic Significance of the Depression in Britain', *Journal of Contemporary History*, vol 4, no. 4, 1970, 3–19.

50 Stewart H M Begg, 'The Nationalist Movement in Scotland', *Journal of Contemporary History*, vol 6, no. 1, 1971, 135–52.

51 Charles McKean, *The Scottish Thirties: An Architectural Introduction*, Edinburgh: Scottish Academic Press, 1987, 34.

CHAPTER 1

1 Charles McKean, *The Scottish Thirties: An Architectural Introduction*, Edinburgh: Scottish Academic Press, 1987.

2 Earle Schultz, 'The Quest of Maximum Efficiency', *Quarterly Illustrated of the Royal Incorporation of Architects in Scotland*, no. 19, autumn 1926, 88.

3 Francis Orr Templeton, 'Notes on the Work of Contemporary French Architects', *Quarterly Illustrated of the Royal Incorporation of Architects in Scotland*, no. 30, summer 1929, 37–8.

4 Francis Orr Templeton, 'Notes on the Work of Contemporary French Architects', *Quarterly Illustrated of the Royal Incorporation of Architects in Scotland*, no. 32, winter 1930, 106. Francis Orr Templeton, 'Notes on the Work of Contemporary French Architects', *Quarterly Illustrated of the Royal Incorporation of Architects in Scotland*, no. 33, spring 1930, 8.

5 Francis Orr Templeton, 'Notes on the Work of Contemporary French Architects', *Quarterly Illustrated of the Royal Incorporation of Architects in Scotland*, no. 33, spring 1930, 10.

6 Michel Roux-Spitz, *Batiments et Jardins*, Paris: Éditions Albert Lévy, 1928.

7 Guthrie & Wells, *Craftsmanship*, author's collection, also Guthrie & Wells collection, Glasgow City Archives, Mitchell Library, Glasgow, TD655/9/10.

8 As note 7.

9 V Blake, 'Adelaide House, London', *Architectural Review*, February 1925, 61–73. 'Trade and craft: Adelaide House, London Bridge' *Architectural Review*, June 1925, lb, liib, livb.

10 Sir John Burnet, Thomas Tait and David Raeside, *The Architectural Work of Sir John Burnet and Partners with a Preface by A Trystan Edwards*, Geneva: Masters of Architecture, 1930, 48–50.

11 'New Offices for the *Daily Telegraph*', *Architects' Journal*, February 1929, 239–42. 'New Offices for the *Daily Telegraph*: Details of the Main Front', *Architects' Journal*, February 1929, 243–5.

12 Sir John Burnet, Thomas Tait and David Raeside, *The Architectural Work of Sir John Burnet and Partners with a Preface by A Trystan Edwards*, Geneva: Masters of Architecture, 1930, 16–22. Sir John Burnet, 'The New Entrance Loggia at Selfridge's: Graham, Anderson, Probst and White', *Architects' Journal*, May 1929, 751–8.

13 Francis Henry Crittall, *Fifty Years of Work and Play*, London: Constable, 1934.

14 Robin Carpenter, *Mr Pink: The Architectural Legacy of Walter Francis Crittall (1887–1956)*, Chelmsford: Essex County Council and Braintree District Council, 2007.

15 Sir John Burnet, Thomas Tait and David Raeside, *The Architectural Work of Sir John Burnet and Partners with a Preface by A Trystan Edwards*, Geneva: Masters of Architecture, 1930, 86–105.

16 'The Late Henry Pynor', *Architecture*, January–March 1947, 279.

17 E Maxwell Fry, 'At the Royal Academy: The Architecture Reviewed', *Architects' Journal*, May 1931, 644–50. 'Royal

Masonic Hospital', *Academy Architecture and Architectural Review*, January 1931, 10–13. 'New Freemasons' Hospital', *Times*, 20 May 1932, 11. 'Freemasons' Hospital and Nursing Home, Ravenscourt Park, W', *Builder*, 18 August 1933, 254, 255, 260 and 262–72. Susan Gold, 'The Royal Masonic Hospital', *Thirties Society Journal*, no. 2, 1982, 29–34. 'The Royal Masonic Hospital, London, England, Sir John Burnet, Tait and Lorne, Architects', *American Architect*, January 1935, 58–64.

18 Sir John Burnet, Thomas Tait and David Raeside, *The Architectural Work of Sir John Burnet and Partners with a Preface by A Trystan Edwards*, Geneva: Masters of Architecture, 1930, 86.

19 '£1,000,000 "Flatels" Scheme: Mount Royal nearly ready', *Caterer and Hotel Keeper*, 17 August 1934, 331. 'Perspective view of new shops and flats, Oxford Street, W', *Builder*, 20 June 1933, 1044. 'Mount Royal, Oxford Street, W', *Builder*, 2 November 1934, 764–5.

20 Sir John Burnet, Thomas Tait and David Raeside, *The Architectural Work of Sir John Burnet and Partners with a Preface by A Trystan Edwards*, Geneva: Masters of Architecture, 1930, 86.

21 Sir John Burnet, Tait & Lorne, *The Information Book of Sir John Burnet, Tait & Lorne*, London: Architectural Press, 1938.

22 'The New Russell Institute at Paisley opened by Princess Mary', *Illustrated London News*, 26 March 1927, 15, 'Paisley's New Institute', *Scotsman*, 17 March 1927, 12, 'The New Architecture of the Twentieth Century: Facade of the Russell Institute, Paisley', *Sphere*, 31 March 1928, 32.

23 Basil Ionides, *Colour and Interior Decoration*, London: Country Life, 1926.

24 Christopher Hussey, 'The New Savoy Theatre', *Country Life*, 16 November 1930, 18.

25 Charles McKean, *The Scottish Thirties: An Architectural Introduction*, Edinburgh: Scottish Academic Press, 1987, 197.

26 'Church Extension Plans at Aberdeen', *Aberdeen Press and Journal*, 26 June 1935, 9.

27 Philip Long and Jane Thomas (eds), *Basil Spence Architect*, Edinburgh: National Galleries of Scotland, 2008, 35–6.

28 As note 27, 35.

29 Interview with Sir William Kininmonth by Charles McKean, cited in Charles McKean, *The Scottish Thirties: An Architectural Introduction*, Edinburgh: Scottish Academic Press, 1987, 36.

30 Ninian Johnston, 'Members' Column: The Brink – A Reply to Mr John N Graham', *Quarterly Illustrated of the Royal Incorporation of Architects in Scotland*, no. 47, 1934, 52.

31 As note 30.

32 See Canmore, 'Student material. Esquisse for "an entrance to a variety theatre". Perspective' (DP009624), canmore.org.uk/collection/1024750; 'Student material. Esquisse for "a cinema to seat 1,100". Sketch perspective' (DP011933), canmore.org.uk/collection/1030527; 'Drawing entitled "Esquisse Colour for a Bar", depicting a design for a bar by Jean Payton Reid' (DP 266265), canmore.org.uk/collection/1590266; 'Modern Fenestration – "Hague Volharding"' (DP200484), canmore.org.uk/collection/1455188; 'Ladies Fashions' (DP203038), canmore.org.uk/collection/1459303; 'Design of a Shopfront, Street Elevation and Isometric Section' (DP203045), canmore.org.uk/collection/1459310, accessed 14 August 2024.

33 Duncan Glen, *William Williamson: Kirkcaldy Architect*, Kirkcaldy, Akros Publications, 2008.

34 'Falkirk Architect: Sudden death at Edinburgh of James G Callander', *Falkirk Herald*, 7 March 1942, 5. Born in Shotts, Callander died while undergoing surgery.

35 Charles McKean, *The Scottish Thirties: An Architectural Introduction*, Edinburgh: Scottish Academic Press, 1987, 24.

36 Thomas Scott Sutherland, *Life on One Leg*, London: Christopher Johnson, 1957.

37 Charles McKean, *The Scottish Thirties: An Architectural Introduction*, Edinburgh: Scottish Academic Press, 1987, 54–5.

38 Raymond Plumber, *Nothing Need Be Ugly: The First 70 Years of the Design and Industries Association*, London: Design and Industries Association, 1985. Peyton Skipworth, 'Rebels Against Commercial Ugliness', *Apollo*, January 2008, 42–7.

CHAPTER 2

1 Ian G Lindsay, 'Editorial – The Death of Mansfield D Forbes', *Quarterly Illustrated of the Royal Incorporation of Architects in Scotland*, no. 52, 1936, 5. Mansfield D Forbes, 'Attention to Tradition', *Quarterly Illustrated of the Royal Incorporation of Architects in Scotland*, no. 52, 1936, 34–5.

2 Raymond McGrath, 'A Symphony in Glass: Decorations at "Finella"', *Architects' Journal*, December 1929, 974

3 Elizabeth Darling, 'Finella, Mansfield Forbes, Raymond McGrath, and Modernist Architecture in Britain', *Journal of British Studies* 50, January 2011, 125–55.

4 Philip Long and Jane Thomas (eds), *Basil Spence Architect*, Edinburgh: National Galleries of Scotland, 2008, 36.

5 'House in Edinburgh: Basil Spence and William Kininmonth, Architects', *The Architect and Building News*, 23 August 1935, 226–7.

6 Interview with Sir William Kininmonth by Charles McKean, cited in Charles McKean, *The Scottish Thirties: An Architectural Introduction*, Edinburgh: Scottish Academic Press, 1987, 36.

7 'House for Miss Reid at Murrayfield, Edinburgh', *The Architect and Building News*, 9 August 1935, 179. Philip Long and Jane Thomas (eds), *Basil Spence Architect*, Edinburgh: National Galleries of Scotland, 2008, 38–9.

8 'A House in Edinburgh, Architects: Kininmonth and Spence, ARIBA, *The Architect and Building News*, 11 October 1935, 40–1.

9 William Kininmonth, 'Architecture Which Mirrors Today's Thought', *SMT Magazine and Scottish Country Life*, October 1937, 45.

10 As note 9, 44–7.

11 Philip Long and Jane Thomas (eds), *Basil Spence Architect*, Edinburgh: National Galleries of Scotland, 2008, 24.

12 John R H McDonald, *Modern Housing: A Review of Present Housing Requirements in Gt. Britain, a Resume of Post-War Housing at Home and Abroad, and Some Practical Suggestions for Future Housing*, London: John Tiranti & Co, 1931.

13 As note 12.

14 As note 12, 26–8.

15 'A Modern House in Scotland', *Country Life*, 8 June 1935, 604–5. 'A House in Scotland, Architect John R H McDonald, BSc.', *The Architect and Building News*, 21 June 1935, 344–5.

16 'Plaster Spongy', *Daily Record*, 30 May 1939, 13.

17 Dictionary of Scottish Architects, 'John R H McDonald', www.scottisharchitects.org.uk, accessed 31 January 2024.

18 Information from James Munro, occupant of a house designed by Donald Fowler on Culduthel Road, Inverness, visited by the author on 3 June 2023.

19 Duncan Glen, *William Williamson: Kirkcaldy Architect*, Kirkcaldy, Akros Publications, 2008, 71.

20 Miles Glendinning and Diane Watters (eds), *Home Builders Mactaggart & Mickel and the Scottish Housebuilding Industry: 1925–2015 Celebrating 90 Years*, Edinburgh: Royal Commission on the Ancient and Historic Monuments of Scotland, 2015, 45–102.

21 'Colour Home Showhouse in Central Station', *Bulletin*, 13 September 1934, 2.

22 Mactaggart & Mickel advertisement for the Broom Estate, *Glasgow Herald*, 4 May 1935.

23 'Ravelston Garden, one of several blocks of flats at Craigleith, Edinburgh, by Neil and Hurd', *Architects' Journal*, 22 July 1937, 137. 'Ravelston Garden, Edinburgh, by Neil and Hurd, Architects', *Architectural Design and Construction*, October 1938, 381–2.

24 Kelvin Court, Great Western Road, Dean of Guild plans, Glasgow City Archives, Mitchell Library, Glasgow, B4/12/1938/335. 'Newcastle Flat Designer's Death', *Newcastle Evening Chronicle*, 26 August 1940, 3. 'Flats Designer', *Sunderland Daily Echo and Shipping Gazette*, 26 August 1940, 3.

25 Basil Spence Papers, Historic Environment Scotland Archives.

26 Sketch designs by Basil Spence and John Colville, Gribloch collection, Historic Environment Scotland Archives, MS/614/2.

27 As note 26.

28 As note 26.

29 Letter from Perry M Duncan to John Colville, 14 April 1938, Gribloch collection, Historic Environment Scotland Archives, MS/614/11/1.

30 Arthur Oswald, 'Gribloch, Kippen, Stirlingshire I: The home of Mr and Mrs J M Colville', *Country Life*, 12 January 1951, 110–114.

31 Letter from Gordon Russell Ltd to John Colville signed by Nikolaus Pevsner, 2 January 1939, Gribloch collection, Historic Environment Scotland Archives, MS/614/14.

32 Letter from Green & Abbott Ltd to John Colville signed by John Hill, 18 July 1939, Gribloch collection, Historic Environment Scotland Archives, MS/614/18/1.

33 Arthur Oswald, 'Gribloch, Kippen, Stirlingshire II: The home of Mr and Mrs J M Colville', *Country Life*, 19 January 1951, 182–6.

34 Letters from Raymond Subes to John Colville, 16 June, 13 July and 2 August 1938, Gribloch collection, Historic Environment Scotland Archives, MS/614/12/1–4.

35 Osbert Lancaster, *Homes Sweet Homes*, London: John Murray, 1939, 64.

36 *Report on (1) The Incorporation of Architectural Quality and Amenity in the Lay-out, Planning and External Treatment of Houses for the Working Classes; and (2) The Erection of High Tenements*, London: His Majesty's Stationery Office, 1935.

37 Charles McKean, *The Scottish Thirties: An Architectural Introduction*, Edinburgh: Scottish Academic Press, 1987, 147.

38 Roger Emmerson and Mary Tilmouth, *Matthew Steele Architect: A Biography*, Edinburgh: RIAS Publishing, 2010.

39 Elizabeth Denby, *Europe Re-housed*, London: Allen & Unwin, 1944.

40 John Wilson, 'Continental Housing', *Quarterly Illustrated of the Royal Incorporation of Architects in Scotland*, no. 51, 1935, 18–24.

41 'Notes from the Chapters: Edinburgh', *Quarterly Illustrated of the Royal Incorporation of Architects in Scotland*, no. 51, 1935, 38.

42 'Home of Scottish Craftsmanship; Beith and Lochwinnoch manufacturers who have made Scottish traditions', *The Cabinet Maker and Complete House Furnisher*, 24 April 1937, 129.

43 Elizabeth Cumming, *Hand, Heart and Soul: The Arts and Crafts Movement in Scotland*, Edinburgh: Birlinn, 2006, 23, 68, 90, 94, 101, 111,114, 120, 123, 124, 128, 136, 140, 145, 165, 215 and 222.

44 'The Scottish Furniture Industry', *The Cabinet Maker and Complete House Furnisher*, 27 April 1935, 117–18.

45 'News of Scottish Retail Trade: The compromise between quality and quantity – fashion follows the south', *The Cabinet Maker and Complete House Furnisher*, 27 April 1935, 119.

46 'The Scottish Furniture Industry: Its virtues, its achievements, the business outlook', *The Cabinet Maker and Complete House Furnisher*, 27 April 1935, 118.

47 'Glasgow Exhibition – Good display by Wylie & Lochhead', *The Cabinet Maker and Complete House Furnisher*, 18 May 1935, 271.

48 'Three Views of the Modern Style – from Paris, London and Glasgow', *The Cabinet Maker and Complete House Furnisher*, 26 October 1935, 106.

49 'All-Scottish House – plans for Glasgow exhibition', *The Cabinet Maker and Complete House Furnisher*, 5 October 1935, 14.

50 'Success of the Scottish House', *The Cabinet Maker and Complete House Furnisher*, 12 October 1935, 44.

51 'Scottish Manufacturers Exhibition – prominent northern manufacturers well represented in Glasgow', *The Cabinet Maker and Complete House Furnisher*, 12 October 1935, 47.

52 'Scottish Strike Continues', *The Cabinet Maker and Complete House Furnisher*, 6 June 1936, 395.

53 'Scottish Trade's Recovery – prolonged strike of 1936 has not checked expanding markets', *The Cabinet Maker and Complete House Furnisher*, 24 April 1937, 125.

54 'Furnishing Fabrics from Scotland – A comprehensive survey', *The Cabinet Maker and Complete House Furnisher*, 24 April 1937, 134.

55 D D Sneddon, 'What Glasgow Buys: Outlook of the Scottish public', *The Cabinet Maker and Complete House Furnisher*, 4 May 1935, 184.

56 Frank J Donald, 'Article for Svenska Hem', July 1938, 2, Donald Bros Old Glamis Fabrics collection, Heriot-Watt University Textile Archive, Galashiels, DB 10/8/3.

57 Heriot-Watt University Textile Archive, Galashiels.

58 Donald Bros Old Glamis Fabrics collection, Heriot-Watt University Textile Archive, Galashiels, DB 10/8/3, Frank J Donald, 'Old Glamis Fabrics', 1938, 4.

59 Counter books and pattern books, Donald Bros Old Glamis Fabrics collection, Heriot-Watt University Textile Archive, Galashiels, DB 7/6/1/1, DB 7/6/1/2, DB 6/1/3/5 28–29 and DB 6/1/3/9 33–38.

60 Frank J Donald, 'The Bauhaus in Germany and the New Bauhaus in Chicago' (Paper read before the Dundee Art Society, 11 February 1938), Donald Bros Old Glamis Fabrics collection, Heriot-Watt University Textile Archive, Galashiels, DB 10/8/3.

61 As note 60.

62 Philip Morton Shand, *The New Architecture and the Bauhaus*, London: Faber & Faber, 1935.

63 Letter from Philip Morton Shand to Frank J Donald, 12 January 1938, Donald Bros Old Glamis Fabrics collection, Heriot-Watt University Textile Archive, Galashiels, DB 10/8/3.

64 Letter from Philip Morton Shand to Frank J Donald, 12 January 1938, Donald Bros Old Glamis Fabrics collection,

Heriot-Watt University Textile Archive, Galashiels, DB 10/8/3.

65 Lesley Jackson, *Alastair Morton and Edinburgh Weavers Ltd: Visionary Textiles and Modern Art*, London: V&A Publications, 2012, 9 and 19–31.

66 'Furnishing Fabrics from Scotland – A comprehensive survey', *The Cabinet Maker and Complete House Furnisher*, 24 April 1937, 134.

67 Lesley Jackson, *Alastair Morton and Edinburgh Weavers Ltd: Visionary Textiles and Modern Art*, London: V&A Publications, 2012, 29.

68 As note 67, 38–43.

69 'West of Scotland Carpet Industry – 100,000 employed by continuous demand for Home and Empire markets', *The Cabinet Maker and Complete House Furnisher*, 24 April 1937, 128.

70 Fred H Young, *A Century of Carpet-Making 1839–1939*, Glasgow: Collins, 1943, 41.

71 Fred H Young, *A Century of Carpet-Making 1839–1939*, Glasgow: Collins, 1943. R Logan, *The James Templeton Story*, Glasgow: James Templeton & Co, 1960.

72 Frank J Donald, 'The Bauhaus in Germany and the New Bauhaus in Chicago' (Paper read before the Dundee Art Society, 11 February 1938), 3, Donald Bros Old Glamis Fabrics collection, Heriot-Watt University Textile Archive, Galashiels, DB 10/8/3.

73 Glasgow School of Art Stoddart-Templeton Collection GB 248 STOD/201/1/9/1 'Report on the Library' cited in Jonathan Cleaver, The interrelationship of carpet weaving technologies and design in the work of James Templeton and Company, Glasgow, carpet manufacturer, 1890–1939, PhD thesis, University of Glasgow, 2021, 173.

74 'Where Carpets are Made: James Templeton & Company', *National Floorcoverings Review*, April 1932. Fred H Young, *A Century of Carpet-Making 1839–1939*, Glasgow: Collins, 1943, 41. The Stoddard-Templeton Archive at The Glasgow School of Art contains the books that were in James Templeton & Co's design library.

75 'Retirals: James Kincaid', *Templetonian*, December 1939, 3. 'Obituary: James Kincaid', *Templetonian*, spring 1965, 19.

76 'West of Scotland Carpet Industry – 100,000 employed by continuous demand for Home and Empire markets', *The Cabinet Maker and Complete House Furnisher*, 24 April 1937, 128.

77 As note 76, 128.

78 Augustus Muir, *Nairns of Kirkcaldy: A Short History 1847–1956*, Cambridge: W Heffer & Sons, 1956.

79 'Scottish Trade's Recovery – prolonged strike of 1936 has not checked expanding markets', *The Cabinet Maker and Complete House Furnisher*, 24 April 1937, 125.

80 'Glasgow Furnishing: Corporation's 1s-a-week scheme starts next week', *The Cabinet Maker and Complete House Furnisher*, 31 August 1935, 279.

CHAPTER 3

1 'Empire Exhibition, Scotland – 1938, Administrative Committee minute of thirtieth meeting, 21 July 1937', University of Glasgow Archives and Special Collections, ACC2207/22/7.

2 'Rail Transport Past, Present and Future Commemoration – 1930', jstor.org/stable/community.26330280, accessed 31 January 2024. Malcolm Thwaite, 'The George Bennie Railplane and Hugh Fraser Air-rail Systems of Transport', *Transactions of the Newcomen Society*, vol 75 (1), 2005, 37–84. Lawrence D Taylor, 'The monorail "revolution" of the 1950s and 1960s and its legacy', November 2016, 236–257. 'A New Type of Railway', *Architects' Journal*, 2 January 1936, 32.

3 'The LNER Coronation Express', *Railway Magazine*, August 1937, 79–81. 'The New Flying Scotsman: London–Edinburgh in Six Hours', *Architects' Journal*, 8 July 1937, 45.

4 'The Coronation Scot, LMSR', *Railway Magazine*, July 1937, 39–42. 'The New LMS and LNER Speed Records', *Railway Magazine*, August 1937, 111–16.

5 O S Nock, *British Locomotives of the Twentieth Century Volume 2: 1930–1960*, London: Guild Publishing, 1984, 76.

6 'Surbiton Southern Railway Station', *Architectural Design and Construction*, April 1938, 137.

7 'Richmond Southern Railway Station', *Architectural Design and Construction*, April 1938, 138. 'Railway Stations: Modernisation on the Southern Railway', *Architectural Design and Construction*, December 1938, 463.

8 Maxwell Fry, *Autobiographical Sketches*, London: Elkon Books, 1975, 125.

9 Beverly Cole and Richard Durack, *Railway Posters 1923–1947 from the Collection of the National Railway Museum, York*, London: Laurence King, 1992.

10 'Mr Norman Wilkinson', *Times*, 1 June 1971, 12.

11 Beverly Cole and Richard Durack, *Railway Posters 1923–1947 from the Collection of the National Railway Museum, York*, London: Laurence King, 1992, 98.

12 As note 11, 15.

13 As note 11, 117.

14 As note 11, 145.

15 Ronald W Ferrier, *The History of the British Petroleum Company Volume 1: The Developing Years 1901–1932*, Cambridge: Cambridge University Press, 1982.

16 '42 Years of Service to Scotland', *Commercial Motor*, 11 February 1949.

17 Sam McKinstry, *Sure as the Sunrise: A History of Albion Motors*, Edinburgh: John Donald, 1997, 100–122.

18 '42 Years of Service to Scotland', *Commercial Motor*, 11 February 1949.

19 Bruce Peter, *Scottish Buses: A Global Success Story*, Ramsey: Lily Publications, 2021, 21.

20 As note 19, 26.

21 'Expedited daily SMT Scotland–London Services', *Commercial Motor*, 28 April 1931, 63.

22 Bruce Peter, *Scottish Buses: A Global Success Story*, Ramsey: Lily Publications, 2021, 28.

23 'Modern Bodywork Features as revealed at the Scottish Show', *Commercial Motor*, 23 November 1934, 40.

24 Gavin Booth, *Alexander Coachbuilders*, Glossop: The Transport Publishing Company, 1980, 35–6.

25 As note 24, 35–44.

26 As note 24, 45–6.

27 Ian Stewart, *The Glasgow Tramcar*, Newton Mearns: Scottish Tramway Museum Society, 1983, 108–16.

28 'Transport – Exhibition Preparations – New Tramcars to be built at Copelawhill', *Glasgow Herald*, 4 February 1937.

29 Ian Stewart, *The Glasgow Tramcar*, Newton Mearns: Scottish Tramway Museum Society, 1983, 118–128.

30 As note 29, 148–156.

31 Lindsay Farquharson, *General Wade's Legacy: The Eighteenth Century Military Road System in Perthshire*, Perth: Perth & Kinross Heritage Trust, 2011. Julian Glover, *Thomas Telford: Man of Iron and the Building of Britain*, London: Bloomsbury, 2018.

32 Christopher Hussey, 'New Bridges and Concrete Structure', *Country Life*, 28 April 1928, 594.

33 As note 32, 596.

34 As note 32, 597.

35 Robert Bruce, 'The Great North Road over the Grampians', *Proceedings of the Institution of Civil Engineers*, January 1931, 121–2.

36 Christopher Hussey, 'New Bridges and Concrete Structure', *Country Life*, 28 April 1928, 597.

37 J Guthrie Brown, 'Kincardine-on-Forth Bridge', *Proceedings of the Institution of Civil Engineers*, April 1937, 750.

38 As note 37, 687–759.

39 As note 37, 746.

40 As note 37, 746.

41 As note 37, 747.

42 As note 37, 748–9.

43 'New Garage in Aberdeen', *Aberdeen Press and Journal*, 3 July 1937, 8.

44 'Latest in Garages is like Wells' Dream Come True', *Aberdeen Press and Journal*, 2 July 1937, 11.

45 As note 44.

46 *Kilmarnock and District Directory 1936–39*, 284, R941-42KK, Burns Monument Centre, Kilmarnock. As plans are not archived, there is no description in local newspapers and the building was never published in any architecture or construction journal, it has proven impossible to ascertain who its architect was.

47 Jack Hunter, *A Flight Too Far: The Story of Lady Mackay of Glenapp*, Stranraer: Stranraer & District Local History Trust, 2008.

48 Stuart McKay, *Cabin Moths*, Tonbridge: Air-Britain, 2024, 72–76.

49 National Museums Scotland Blog, 'Winnie Drinkwater: The Pioneering Scottish Woman Aviator' (11 April 2023), blog.nms.ac.uk/2023/04/11/winnie-drinkwater-the-pioneering-scottish-woman-aviator, accessed 31 January 2024.

50 Stuart McKay, *Cabin Moths*, Tonbridge: Air-Britain, 2024, 77–78.

51 R Mervyn Noad, 'New Club-House at Renfrew Aerodrome', *Architects' Journal*, September 1935, 369–71. 'Renfrew Aerodrome', *Builder*, 31 June 1935, 1152–3, 1158 and 1162.

52 'Death of a well-known architect, the late Mr Alex Mair', *Kilmarnock Standard*, 1 January 1944, 5. 'The Late Mr Alex Mair: Pulpit Tribute', *Ayr Advertiser*, 6 January 1944, 6.

53 'Prestwick Aerodrome', *Kilmarnock Herald and North Ayrshire Gazette*, 4 October 1935, 1.

54 'Opening of Central Scotland Airport at Grangemouth', *Falkirk Herald*, 8 July 1939, 4. 'Central Scotland Airport: Official Opening Next Month', *Scotsman*, 6 June 1939, 16. 'Scotland's New Airport', *Scotsman*, 30 June 1939, 14.

55 John Clifford, *De Havilland and Hatfield 1910–1935*, Stroud: Fonthill Media, 2015, 110, 120, 135–8, 162, 167–8, 185.

56 'The direct-drive turbine steamer *Queen Mary*', *Shipbuilding and Shipping Record*, 1 June 1933, 538.

57 'Clyde Paddle Steamer', *Shipbuilding and Shipping Record*, 8 February 1934, 150. 'The New Clyde Paddle Steamers *Mercury* and *Caledonia*', *Shipbuilding and Shipping Record*, 10 May 1934, 495.

CHAPTER 4

1 'Kirkcaldy's Municipal Buildings', *Fife Free Press and Kirkcaldy Guardian*, 10 September 1949, 3. 'Kirkcaldy's Municipal Buildings', *Fife Free Press and Kirkcaldy Guardian*, 17 September 1949, 3. 'Kirkcaldy's Municipal Buildings', *Fife Free Press and Kirkcaldy Guardian*, 29 April 1950, 3.

2 'New County Offices', *Scotsman*, 6 May 1937, 16.

3 'Inverness High School', *The Architect and Building News*, 23 February 1934, 268. 'Inverness School Rearrangements', *Scotsman*, 10 December 1936, 7.

4 'Edinburgh: Niddrie Marischal School', *The Architect and Building News*, 27 September 1935, 374. 'A Work of Peace: Opening of Niddrie Marischal School Hoping for the Best', *Edinburgh Evening News*, 6 October 1938, 9. 'Opening of New Edinburgh School – Space, Sunshine and Comfort, chances that were denied parents', *Scotsman*, 7 October 1938, 7.

5 'Kelso High School', *Builder*, 11 August 1933, 245. 'Kelso High School', *Southern Reporter*, 25 June 1936, 6. 'Education News: Kelso High School 4 new buildings scheme approved', *Scotsman*, 25 September 1936, 10. 'Kelso High School Ceremony', *Hawick Express*, 21 June 1939, 2.

6 'Suresnes, France by Beaudoin and Lods', *Architects' Journal*, 28 May 1936, 820–2.

7 'Burlington School for Girls, Hammersmith Designed by Sir John Burnet, Tait and Lorne', *Architects' Journal*, 21 January 1937, 137–43.

8 'A Change of Name', *Edinburgh Evening News*, 26 July 1938, 6.

9 Ray McKenzie, *Public Sculpture in Edinburgh Volume 1*, Liverpool: Liverpool University Press, 2018, 112–14.

10 'New Edinburgh Public Library', *Scotsman*, 12 March 1940, 10.

11 'Infectious Diseases Hospital, Paisley: Sir John Burnet, Tait and Lorne, Architects', *Architectural Review*, September 1936, 104–108. 'Infectious Diseases Hospital, Hawkhead Road, Paisley,' *Builder*, 14 January 1938, 79–84. 'Hospital at Paisley by Sir John Burnet, Tait and Lorne', *Architects' Journal*, 3 September 1936, 295–8. 'Paisley Infectious Diseases Hospital – Sir John Burnet, Tait and Lorne', *Architects' Journal*, 24 June 1937, 1128–9.

12 'Glasgow Royal Infirmary Auxiliary Hospital and Convalescent Home, Canniesburn', *Builder*, 20 May 1938, 980.

13 Eric Simpson, *Wish You Were Still Here: The Scottish Seaside Holiday*, Stroud: Amberley, 2013, 71.

14 'Gourock', *Bath and Bath Engineering*, January 1935, 21.

15 'Arbroath', *Bath and Bath Engineering*, August 1934, 134.

16 'Death of Thomas A Hogg', *Arbroath Guide*, 8 July 1944, 5.

17 National Library for Scotland Moving Image Archive, 'Arbroath's New Swimming Pool' – Gaumont British, 7 July 1934 (Ref. 2372), movingimage.nls.uk/film/2372, accessed 31 January 2024.

18 'Stonehaven', *Bath and Bath Engineering*, June 1934, 92.

19 Eric Simpson, *Wish You Were Still Here: The Scottish Seaside Holiday*, Stroud: Amberley, 2013, 71.

20 'Burntisland', *Baths and Bath Engineering*, October 1934, 179.

21 'Portobello Swimming Pool, Edinburgh, W A McCartney, AM

Inst CE, City Engineer', *The Architect and Building News*, 1 January 1937, 13–15. 'Diving Stage at Edinburgh', *Architects' Journal*, 12 March 1936, 398.

22 'Developments in the Baths World: Notes and News from All Quarters', *Baths and Bath Engineering*, January 1934–December 1935.

23 'Aberdeen Baths Near Completion', *Aberdeen Press and Journal*, 2 April 1940, 5. 'New Aberdeen Baths Opened', *Dundee Evening Telegraph*, 31 August 1940, 4.

24 'Glasgow University Sports Pavilion, Architect: T Harold Hughes FRIBA', *The Architect and Building News*, 29 January 1937, 158–9.

25 'The swimming pool in the new pavilion at King's College, Old Aberdeen, which will be opened shortly', *Aberdeen Press and Journal*, 18 February 1941, 2. 'College Sports Pavilion', *Aberdeen Press and Journal*, 2 April 1941, 2.

26 'Cragburn Pavilion', *The Architect and Building News*, 15 February 1935, 237. 'Gourock – The Glad Eye of the Clyde', *Daily Record*, 14 May 1936, 22.

27 'Rothesay Pavilion Competition', *The Architect and Building News*, 21 February 1936, 259.

28 'Rothesay Pavilion Site', *Scotsman*, 24 April 1935, 9. 'Rothesay Pavilion: Ayr Architect's Success in Plans Competition', *Edinburgh Evening News*, 5 February 1936, 10. 'Grand Opening Ball, New Super Dance Pavilion Rothesay 1 July 1938', *Sunday Mail*, 19 June 1938, 29.

29 'New Buildings in Scotland: Dunfermline Fire Station', *Builder*, 4 August 1933, 206.

30 'Dunfermline Corporation Fire Station, Architect: James Shearer', *The Architect and Building News*, 1 May 1936, 123–5. 'Dunfermline Fire Station Plans', *Dundee Courier*, 31 March 1934, 8. 'Dunfermline Town Council yesterday inspected the new Dunfermline Fire Station', *Dundee Courier*, 31 August 1935, 6. 'Dunfermline Fire Station', *Dundee Courier*, 14 April 1936, 8. 'New Dunfermline Fire Station', *Fife Free Press and Kirkcaldy Guardian*, 18 April 1936, 2.

31 'Kirkcaldy's New Fire Station', *Dundee Evening Telegraph*, 9 September 1935, 3. 'Kirkcaldy Fire Station', *Leven Advertiser & Wemyss Gazette*, 7 April 1936, 6.

32 Control station for the Glasgow Corporation Lighting Department, Millbrae Road, 1940, Glasgow City Archives, Mitchell Library, Glasgow, D-CA8/2063.

33 David M Walker, *St Andrew's House: An Edinburgh Controversy 1912–1939*, Edinburgh: Historic Scotland, 1989, 5–7.

34 As note 33, 8–12.

35 As note 33, 13–16.

36 'Official and Private Architecture', letter to the Editor, *Times*, 9 July 1929, 12.

37 HH45/51, St Andrew's House, Edinburgh, Accommodation of government departments in Edinburgh on the central site. Notes for the guidance of the architect. Schedule of accommodation to be provided. Plans of the building. Newspaper cuttings. Notes. Correspondence etc., 1925–29, National Records of Scotland.

38 'Calton Hill Buildings', *Scotsman*, 11 December 1929, 9.

39 HH45/47, St Andrew's House, Edinburgh, Collection of newspaper cuttings regarding the erection of the building. Representations. Plans of the building. Correspondence etc., 1929–33, National Records of Scotland.

40 'Parliamentary Report: Scottish Home Rule Debate in the Commons, Scheme for a Centralised Government Building in Edinburgh, Transfer of Government Officials from Whitehall', *Scotsman*, 23 November 1932, 10.

41 HH45/47, St Andrew's House, Edinburgh, Collection of newspaper cuttings regarding the erection of the building. Representations. Plans of the building. Correspondence etc., 1929–33, National Records of Scotland. David M Walker, *St Andrew's House: An Edinburgh Controversy 1912–1939*, Edinburgh: Historic Scotland, 1989, 16–22.

42 As note 41, 22–6.

43 HH45/46, St Andrew's House, Edinburgh, Selection of Mr Thomas Smith Tait, FRIBA to be the architect of the new building. Newspaper cuttings. Correspondence etc., 1933–54, National Records of Scotland.

44 HH45/46, St Andrew's House, Edinburgh, Selection of Mr Thomas Smith Tait, FRIBA to be the architect of the new building. Newspaper cuttings. Correspondence etc., 1933–54, National Records of Scotland. David M Walker, *St Andrew's House: An Edinburgh Controversy 1912–1939*, Edinburgh: Historic Scotland, 1989, 27–8.

45 As note 44.

46 MW5/135, St Andrew's House, Edinburgh, Preparing models and executing stone carving of panel over main entrance and two side panels (2nd floor level), 1936–9, National Records of Scotland.

47 HH45/52, St Andrew's House, Edinburgh, Luncheon Club facilities. Furniture and internal fittings. Themes incorporated in the bronze doors to the main entrance of St Andrew's House. Correspondence etc., 1929–42, National Records of Scotland.

48 HH45/47, St Andrew's House, Edinburgh, Collection of newspaper cuttings regarding the erection of the building. Representations. Plans of the building. Correspondence etc., 1929–33, National Records of Scotland. MW5/102, St Andrew's House, Edinburgh, Erection of new office building, 1935–40, National Records of Scotland.

49 MW5/106, St Andrew's House, Edinburgh, Layout of trees, shrubs etc., 1939, National Records of Scotland.

50 'Government Buildings in Edinburgh: Plans approved by Fine Art Commission', *Times*, 30 July 1934, 14. 'Design for new Government Buildings in Edinburgh', *Times*, 2 November 1934, 18. 'New Edinburgh Buildings: Calton Hill Site: Harmony with the surroundings', *Times*, 2 November 1934, 19. 'New Government Building, Edinburgh', *Builder*, 8 May 1935, 920.

51 MW5/102, St Andrew's House, Edinburgh, Erection of new office building, 1935–40, National Records of Scotland. HH45/52, St Andrew's House, Edinburgh, Luncheon Club facilities. Furniture and internal fittings. Themes incorporated in the bronze doors to the main entrance of St Andrew's House. Correspondence etc., 1929–42, National Records of Scotland.

52 MW5/180, St Andrew's House, Arrangements for opening ceremony – cancelled due to war, 1938–41, National Records of Scotland.

53 'New Government Offices, Edinburgh, Architect: T S Tait, FRIBA of Sir John Burnet, Tait & Lorne', *The Architect and Building News*, 20 October 1939, 58–60.

CHAPTER 5

1   Angus Mackenzie, 'Self-Help and Propaganda: Scottish National Development Council 1931–1939', *Scottish Journal of Historical Studies*, vol 30, no. 2, Edinburgh: Edinburgh University Press, 2010, 123–54.

2   'Plans for Empire Exhibition', *Glasgow Herald*, 31 July 1936, 9.

3   'Exhibition may be held in 1938 or 39', *Glasgow Herald*, 1 July 1936, 10.

4   'Exhibition to be held in Glasgow', *Glasgow Herald*, 6 October 1936, 11.

5   *Empire Exhibition 1938 Official Guide*.

6   'Empire Exhibition, Scotland – 1938 Administrative Committee', 18 October 1937, University of Glasgow Archives and Special Collections, ACCN2270/22/9. 'Empire Exhibition, Scotland – 1938 Administrative Committee', 1 November 1937, University of Glasgow Archives and Special Collections, ACCN2270/22/9.

7   T Drummond Shiels, 'How Scotland has Helped the Empire', *SMT Magazine and Scottish Country Life*, May 1938, 84.

8   As note 7, 87.

9   Captain S J Graham, *Empire Exhibition, Scotland – 1938, Bellahouston Park, Glasgow, 3rd May to 29th October 1938: Report to the Administrative Committee by the General Manager, 11 January 1939*, University of Glasgow Archives and Special Collections, ACC 2270/24/1, 39.

10 'Cutting of first sod – Countess of Elgin cuts first sod', *Glasgow Herald*, 20 March 1937, 11.

11 Thomas S Tait, 'Planning an Empire Exhibition' *SMT Magazine and Scottish Country Life*, May 1938, 88.

12 Margaret Brodie, 'Omnibus', *Quarterly Illustrated of the Royal Incorporation of Architects in Scotland*, No. 41, 1932, 20–3.

13 Captain S J Graham, *Empire Exhibition, Scotland – 1938, Bellahouston Park, Glasgow, 3rd May to 29th October 1938: Report to the Administrative Committee by the General Manager, 11 January 1939*, University of Glasgow Archives and Special Collections, ACC 2270/24/1, 38.

14 As note 13, 90–2.

15 Letter from S M Bruce of Australia House, London, to Sir Alan Anderson, 12 June 1937, University of Glasgow Archives and Special Collections, ACC2270/23/5.

16 I am grateful to Clio and Norman Barr, retired architects and former students of Margaret Brodie in the 1960s at The Glasgow School of Architecture, who maintained a friendship with her and took notes on her life and work, for providing information about her contributions to the Empire Exhibition.

17 Thomas S Tait, 'Planning an Empire Exhibition' *SMT Magazine and Scottish Country Life*, May 1938, 89.

18 As note 17, 88.

19 As note 17, 88.

20 As note 17, 88–9.

21 As note 17, 89.

22 As note 17, 89.

23 Tony Lam Chung Wai, 'From British Colonization to Japanese Invasion: 100 Years of Architects in Hong Kong 1841–1941', *HKIA Journal*, no. 45, 2006, 51.

24 J M Richards, 'Glasgow 1938: A Critical Survey', *Architectural Review*, July 1938, 3.

25 As note 24, 4–5.

26 Paul Greenhalgh, *Ephemeral Vistas: The Expositions Universelles, Great Exhibitions and World's Fairs, 1851–1939*, Manchester: Manchester University Press, 1988.

27 Raymond Mortimer, 'If you go to Glasgow', *Vogue*, 8 June 1938, 57.

28 As note 27.

29 Alastair Borthwick, 'Introduction to Bellahouston', *SMT Magazine and Scottish Country Life*, May 1938, 35.

30 'Symbol of Unity of the People', *Scottish Field*, May 1938, 6. Captain S J Graham, *Empire Exhibition, Scotland – 1938, Bellahouston Park, Glasgow, 3rd May to 29th October 1938: Report to the Administrative Committee by the General Manager, 11 January 1939*, University of Glasgow Archives and Special Collections, ACC 2270/24/1, 38.

31 Alastair Borthwick, 'Introduction to Bellahouston', *SMT Magazine and Scottish Country Life*, May 1938, 39.

32 As note 31.

33 As note 31.

34 As note 31, 38.

35 'Modern Industry', *Scottish Field*, April 1938, 7. Captain S J Graham, *Empire Exhibition, Scotland – 1938, Bellahouston Park, Glasgow, 3rd May to 29th October 1938: Report to the Administrative Committee by the General Manager, 11 January 1939*, University of Glasgow Archives and Special Collections, ACC 2270/24/1, 38.

36 Captain S J Graham, *Empire Exhibition, Scotland – 1938, Bellahouston Park, Glasgow, 3rd May to 29th October 1938: Report to the Administrative Committee by the General Manager, 11 January 1939*, University of Glasgow Archives and Special Collections, ACC 2270/24/1, 60–1.

37 Anna Scott-Moncrieff and C L Davidson, *Aboard the Bulger*, London: Methuen, 1935.

38 Mary Fleming, 'Where Shall We Eat?', *SMT Magazine and Scottish Country Life*, May 1938, 108.

39 Charles Oakley, 'Scotland's Prowess in Engineering', *SMT Magazine and Scottish Country Life*, May 1938, 79–82.

40 Raymond Mortimer, 'If you go to Glasgow', *Vogue*, 8 June 1938, 98.

41 As note 40.

42 Alastair Borthwick, 'Introduction to Bellahouston', *SMT Magazine and Scottish Country Life*, May 1938, 38.

43 Mary Fleming, 'Where Shall We Eat?', *SMT Magazine and Scottish Country Life*, May 1938, 108.

44 Alastair Borthwick, 'Introduction to Bellahouston', *SMT Magazine and Scottish Country Life*, May 1938, 38.

45 As note 44.

46 'Empire Exhibition, Scotland – 1938, Administrative Committee Minute of twenty-sixth meeting of committee, 21 June 1937', University of Glasgow Archives and Special Collections, ACC2270/22/7.

47 'Canadian Pavilion almost wrecked by storm', *Glasgow Herald*, 31 January 1938, 11.

48 'Canada's Striking Exhibit in Glasgow', *The Imperial Review*, 1938, 157, University of Glasgow Archives and Special Collections, ACCN2270/8/4/3.

49 T Drummond Shiels, 'How Scotland has Helped the Empire', *SMT Magazine and Scottish Country Life*, May 1938, 86.

50 J M Richards, 'Glasgow 1938: A Critical Survey', *Architectural Review*, July 1938, 6.

51 T Drummond Shiels, 'How Scotland has Helped the Empire', *SMT Magazine and Scottish Country Life*, May 1938, 86.

52 Alastair Borthwick, 'Introduction to Bellahouston', *SMT Magazine and Scottish Country Life*, May 1938, 38.

53 George Scott-Moncrieff, 'The Month in Scotland', *Scottish*

Field, June 1938, 13.

54 'Empire Exhibition, Scotland – 1938 Administrative Committee', 21 July 1937, University of Glasgow Archives and Special Collections, ACCN2270/22/7.

55 Alastair Borthwick, 'Introduction to Bellahouston', *SMT Magazine and Scottish Country Life*, May 1938, 38.

56 St Peter in Chains was most likely the work of Jack Coia's assistant, Thomas Warnett Kennedy (1911–2000). Johnny Rodger (ed), *Gillespie, Kidd & Coia: Architecture 1956–1987*, Glasgow: The Lighthouse, 2007, 13.

57 'The Empire Exhibition: Scotland's elaborate plans for biggest exhibition since Wembley', *The Cabinet Maker and Complete House Furnisher*, 30 April 1938, 135–6.

58 Alexander Reid, 'Our Property among the state exhibits', *SMT Magazine and Scottish Country Life*, May 1938, 96.

59 As note 58.

60 As note 58.

61 As note 58.

62 As note 58, 97.

63 J M Richards, 'Glasgow 1938: A Critical Survey', *Architectural Review*, July 1938, 9.

64 'The GPO at Work', *Scottish Field*, September 1938, 52.

65 Harry Watt and Basil Wright (directors), *Night Mail*, GPO Film Unit, 1936.

66 Captain S J Graham, *Empire Exhibition, Scotland – 1938, Bellahouston Park, Glasgow, 3rd May to 29th October 1938: Report to the Administrative Committee by the General Manager, 11 January 1939*, University of Glasgow Archives and Special Collections, ACC 2270/24/1, 71–75.

67 Ann Bruce, 'Women's Work at Bellahouston: The contributions from women of the Empire', *SMT Magazine and Scottish Country Life*, May 1938, 117.

68 'Building an Exhibition', *Scottish Field*, March 1938, 41.

69 Empire Exhibition folder 0109, University of Glasgow Archives and Special Collections, ACC 2270/24/2.

70 Amelia Defries, 'These Exhibitions', *Vogue*, 13 April 1938, 114.

71 Ann Bruce, 'Women's Work at Bellahouston: The contributions from women of the Empire', *SMT Magazine and Scottish Country Life*, May 1938, 118.

72 Alastair Borthwick, 'Introduction to Bellahouston', *SMT Magazine and Scottish Country Life*, May 1938, 38.

73 As note 72, 36.

74 *Scottish Pavilions Official Guide*, University of Glasgow Archives and Special Collections, ACC2270/23/1.

75 Alastair Borthwick, 'Introduction to Bellahouston', *SMT Magazine and Scottish Country Life*, May 1938, 36.

76 Captain S J Graham, *Empire Exhibition, Scotland – 1938, Bellahouston Park, Glasgow, 3rd May to 29th October 1938: Report to the Administrative Committee by the General Manager, 11 January 1939*, University of Glasgow Archives and Special Collections, ACC 2270/24/1, 65–70.

77 Alastair Borthwick, 'Introduction to Bellahouston', *SMT Magazine and Scottish Country Life*, May 1938, 36.

78 Captain S J Graham, *Empire Exhibition, Scotland – 1938, Bellahouston Park, Glasgow, 3rd May to 29th October 1938: Report to the Administrative Committee by the General Manager, 11 January 1939*, University of Glasgow Archives and Special Collections, ACC 2270/24/1, 52–3.

79 Frank J Donald 'Old Glamis Fabrics at the Empire Exhibition – Bellahouston, 1938 – article for The Furniture Trades' Organiser, Special Scottish Number for June', 8, Donald Bros Old Glamis Fabrics collection, Heriot-Watt University Textile Archive, Galashiels, DB 10/8/3.

80 Mary Fleming, 'Where Shall We Eat?', *SMT Magazine and Scottish Country Life*, May 1938, 108.

81 Captain S J Graham, *Empire Exhibition, Scotland – 1938, Bellahouston Park, Glasgow, 3rd May to 29th October 1938: Report to the Administrative Committee by the General Manager, 11 January 1939*, University of Glasgow Archives and Special Collections, ACC 2270/24/1, 118–19.

82 Richard Gray, 'The Cinemas of Alistair G MacDonald', *Picture House*, no. 19, 30–4.

83 'Empire Exhibition, Scotland – 1938 Administrative Committee', 8 November 1937, University of Glasgow Archives and Special Collections, ACCN2270/22/9.

84 'Pavilion for the Empire Exhibition', *Architects' Journal*, 23 December 1937, 1024.

85 Raymond Mortimer, 'If you go to Glasgow', *Vogue*, 8 June 1938, 98.

86 'Jubilee of the Pneumatic Tyre', *Scottish Field*, May 1938, 20.

87 'Scotland by Bus and Coach: The SMT and Associated Companies' Striking Information Pavilion at the Empire Exhibition', *SMT Magazine and Scottish Country Life*, June 1938, 63.

88 Mary Fleming, 'Where Shall We Eat?', *SMT Magazine and Scottish Country Life*, May 1938, 107.

89 As note 88, 108.

90 As note 88, 107.

91 As note 88, 107–8.

92 Thomas S Tait, 'Planning an Empire Exhibition' *SMT Magazine and Scottish Country Life*, May 1938, 89.

93 Mary Fleming, 'Where Shall We Eat?', *SMT Magazine and Scottish Country Life*, May 1938, 107.

94 'Customers injured by gale damage in Tree-Tops restaurant', *Glasgow Herald*, 14 October 1938, 6.

95 Captain S J Graham, *Empire Exhibition, Scotland – 1938, Bellahouston Park, Glasgow 3rd May to 29th October 1938: Report to the Administrative Committee by the General Manager, 11 January 1939*, University of Glasgow Archives and Special Collections, ACC 2270/24/1, 64.

96 Mary Fleming, 'Where Shall We Eat?', *SMT Magazine and Scottish Country Life*, May 1938, 108.

97 Alastair Borthwick, 'Introduction to Bellahouston', *SMT Magazine and Scottish Country Life*, May 1938, 39.

98 'Police – Addition of 50 men approved by Secretary of State', *Glasgow Herald*, 22 January 1938, 3. 'Arrests – Statement in High Court', *Glasgow Herald*, 13 July 1938, 8.

99 Captain S J Graham, *Empire Exhibition, Scotland – 1938, Bellahouston Park, Glasgow, 3rd May to 29th October 1938: Report to the Administrative Committee by the General Manager, 11 January 1939*, University of Glasgow Archives and Special Collections, ACC 2270/24/1, 151–5.

100 Charles Oakley, 'Summing Up the Exhibition', *SMT Magazine and Scottish Country Life*, October 1938, 73.

101 As note 100, 74.

102 As note 100, 74.

103 As note 100, 75.

104 As note 100, 75.

105 A G Macdonell, 'What 1938 Has Meant to Scotland', *SMT Magazine and Scottish Country Life*, October 1938, 35.

106 As note 105, 33.

107 As note 105.

CHAPTER 6

1   Ray McKenzie, *Sculpture in Glasgow: An Illustrated Handbook*, Glasgow: Foulis Archive Press with Neil Baxter Associates, 1999, 71.

2   'Commercial Bank of Scotland', *The Architect and Building News*, 10 August 1934, 171.

3   Ray McKenzie, *Sculpture in Glasgow: An Illustrated Handbook*, Glasgow: Foulis Archive Press with Neil Baxter Associates, 1999, 72.

4   Leslie Grahame Thomson, 'Concerning this Heritage', *Quarterly Illustrated of the Royal Incorporation of Architects in Scotland*, no. 38, 1932, 42–6.

5   'The Caledonian Insurance Company: New Building at Edinburgh, Architect: Leslie Grahame-Thomson, FRIBA', *The Architect and Building News*, 1 September 1939, 233–5.

6   Ray McKenzie, *Public Sculpture in Edinburgh Volume 2*, Liverpool: Liverpool University Press, 2018, 433–4.

7   'The National Bank of Scotland, Ltd, Temporary Head Offices, Edinburgh, Architects Thomas P Marwick and Son, FRIBA', *The Architect and Building News*, 6 March 1937, 302. 'Current Architecture: 1 Thomas P Marwick and Son', *Architectural Review*, March 1937, 179. 'Temporary Head Offices, National Bank of Scotland, Edinburgh', *Architects' Journal*, 25 February 1937, 341–3.

8   David Cottam, Stephen Rosenberg, Frank Newby, George Crabb and Gavin Stamp (ed), *Sir Owen Williams 1890–1969*, London: Architectural Association, 1986. Peter Hutchinson, *The Daily Express Offices* (1932–9), dissertation presented to the Mackintosh School of Architecture, University of Glasgow, for the Diploma in Architecture, 1984, Glasgow: Glasgow School of Art Library.

9   Robert Rennie, 'The Modern Shopfront', *Quarterly Illustrated of the Royal Incorporation of Architects in Scotland*, no. 44, autumn 1933, 11 and 13.

10 As note 9, 13.

11 As note 9, 11.

12 As note 9, 13.

13 As note 9, 15.

14 As note 9, 17.

15 Advertisements in the *Scottish Drapery Journal*, 1935–39.

16 Sir John Burnet, Thomas Tait and David Raeside, *The Architectural Work of Sir John Burnet and Partners with a Preface by A Trystan Edwards*, Geneva: Masters of Architecture, 1930, 107–13.

17 'Showrooms – Thomas P Marwick and Son', *Architectural Review*, October 1938, 182.

18 'Death of Noted Edinburgh Architect', *Edinburgh Evening News*, 4 August 1962, 7. 'Obituary: James Smith Richardson', *Proceedings of the Society of Antiquaries of Scotland*, vol 192, 1969–70, vii–x.

19 'Glasgow Polytechnic', *Scotsman*, 13 September 1929, 4.

20 'C&A Modes', *Daily Record*, 28 October 1931, 7.

21 Eric M Sigsworth, *Montague Burton: Tailor of Taste*, Manchester: Manchester University Press, 1990.

22 'Glasgow's New Trade Tonic – Prosperous Days Ahead', *Daily Record*, 26 September 1931, 9.

23 'Montague Burton Enterprise in Kirkcaldy', *Fife Free Press & Kirkcaldy Guardian*, 21 August 1937, 6.

24 Elain Harwood, *Art Deco Britain*, London: Batsford and Twentieth Century Society, 2019, 114 and 126.

25 Neil Gregory, 'Monro and Partners: Shopping in Scotland with Marks and Spencer', *Architectural Heritage*, vol 14, no. 1, November 2003, 67–73.

26 'Woolworth's New Premises at North Shore, Blackpool', *Architectural Design and Construction*, May 1938, 188–9.

27 'Addition of faience tiling at 164–168 Sauchiehall Street for F W Woolworth Ltd', Glasgow City Archives, Mitchell Library, Glasgow, Dean of Guild plans B4/12/1935/356.

28 F W Woolworth & Co Ltd, 168 Sauchiehall Street, July 1936, Glasgow City Archives, Mitchell Library, Glasgow, D-CA8/2887.

29 'Cooperative Society Opening of New Premises', *Leven Advertiser & Wemyss Gazette*, 3 August 1937, 2.

30 'Current Architecture: 1 Thomas P Marwick and Son', *Architectural Review*, August 1937, 65.

31 Glasgow Corporation Gas Department Showroom, March 1935, Glasgow City Archives, Mitchell Library, Glasgow, D-CA8/2953.

32 'Alloa Gas Extension', *Edinburgh Evening News*, 9 February 1938, 4.

33 'New Gas Showrooms at Dunfermline', *Scotsman*, 21 March 1939, 7.

34 Thomas Stephenson (ed), *Industrial Edinburgh*, Edinburgh: Edinburgh Society for the Promotion of Trade and Edinburgh Chamber of Commerce and Manufactures, 1921. See also Grant Westfield, 'History', www.grantwestfield.co.uk/about/timeline, accessed 31 January 2024.

35 'Histories of Edinburgh Companies no. 28: Heggie & Aitchison', HANDA, December 1963.

36 *Post Office Glasgow Directory 1869–1870*, 171.

37 *Post Office Glasgow Directory, 1889–1890*, 270.

38 'Archd. Hamilton (Shopfitters) Ltd', *Scottish Drapery Journal*, September 1935, 61.

39 *Post Office Glasgow Directory, 1903–1904*, 385.

40 'An Evening of Eloquence: Shop Fronts, Shop Fitting and Lighting', *Scottish Drapery Journal*, June 1935, 23.

41 'Whitney's', *Sunday Mail*, 20 November 1938, 5.

42 Joy Elizabeth Hunter, Art Deco Architecture in the Glasgow Area 1925–1940, dissertation presented to the Mackintosh School of Architecture, University of Glasgow, for the Diploma in Architecture, 1978, Figs. 55A-55C.

43 'Shop at Edinburgh by Rowand Anderson and Paul & Partner', *Architects' Journal*, 28 January 1937, 19–20.

CHAPTER 7

1   Jeffrey Richards, *The Age of the Dream Palace: Cinema and Society in Britain 1930–1939*, London: Routledge & Kegan Paul, 1984.

2   Robert Venturi, Denise Scott-Brown and Steven Izenour, *Learning from Las Vegas*, Cambridge: MIT Press, 1972.

3   Legislation.gov.uk, Cinematograph Act of 1909, www.legislation.gov.uk/ukpga/1909/30/pdfs/ukpga_19090030_en.pdf, accessed 31 January 2024.

4   Bruce Peter, *Scotland's Cinemas*, Ramsey: Lily Publications, 2011, 65–8.

5   As note 4, 71–82.

6   Philip Morton Shand, *The Architecture of Pleasure 1: Modern Theatres and Cinemas*, London: Batsford, 1930.

7   E Wamsley Lewis, 'E Wamsley Lewis and the New Victoria', *London Architect*, January 1972, 4–11.

8   Richard Gray, 'The Cinemas of Alistair G MacDonald', *Picture*

House, no. 19, 30–4.

9 'Five Openings This Month: Premier's Son Designs Elgin Playhouse', *Kinematograph Weekly*, 1 December 1932, 30.

10 'Two New Scottish Playhouses – Alister MacDonald's achievements – The Angus, Montrose, and Playhouse, Elgin', *The Ideal Kinema and Studio*, 15 December 1932, 12. 'The Playhouse, Montrose, Architect Alister G MacDonald, ARIBA', *The Architect and Building News*, 10 February 1933, 200–3.

11 'Two New Scottish Playhouses – Alister MacDonald's achievements – The Angus, Montrose, and Playhouse, Elgin', *The Ideal Kinema and Studio*,15 December 1932, 12. 'The Playhouse, Montrose, Architect Alister G MacDonald, ARIBA', *The Architect and Building News*, 10 February 1933, 200–3. 'Montrose's New Cinema Opened', *Dundee Evening Telegraph*, 17 November 1932, 2. 'Opening of Angus Playhouse, Montrose', *Forfar Herald*, 18 November 1932, 16.

12 'The Playhouse, Peebles', *Cinema and Theatre Construction*, October 1933, 12. 'The Lyceum, Dumfries', *Cinema and Theatre Construction*, November 1936, 55.

13 'Waterloo News Theatre', *Builder*, 14 September 1934, 426 and 434–5.

14 'The Playhouse, Perth – A remarkable ten-week job – black, red and gold interior', *The Ideal Kinema and Studio*, 11 January 1934, 40. 'New Cinemas: Playhouse, Perth', *Builder*, 11 August 1933, 240.

15 'New Cinema Opened at Perth', *Scotsman*, 22 December 1933, 7. 'Perth's New Cinema Opened', *Dundee Courier*, 22 December 1933, 10. 'Playhouse Opening Ceremony', *Perthshire Advertiser*, 23 December 1933, 14.

16 'Rothesay Plans', *Kinematograph Weekly*, 17 June 1937, 25. 'This Week in Scotland – Five Openings Scheduled', *Kinematograph Weekly*, 24 February 1938, 15.

17 'Opening of New Playhouse at Dunbar', *Edinburgh Evening News*, 25 June 1937, 3. 'Dunbar's New Kinema, The Playhouse, Opened Last Thursday Afternoon', *Kinematograph Weekly*, 1 July 1937, 27. 'Regal Lossiemouth', *Kinematograph Weekly*, 29 June 1939, 32. 'Anna Neagle to Visit Highlands for Opening of Regal, Lossiemouth', *Dundee Evening Telegraph*, 7 July 1939, 8. 'Fraserburgh Cinema', *Aberdeen Press and Journal*, 28 February 1939, 5. 'Fortunate in Our Kinema Proprietors: Provost's Tribute at Playhouse Fraserburgh Opening', *Kinematograph Weekly*, 9 March 1939, 50.

18 'Aberdeen's imposing super – Capitol's brilliant interior – lit by Holophane three-colour installation', *The Ideal Kinema and Studio*, 16 February 1933, 11 and 13.

19 'Granite Facade – "Granite City's" New 2,060 seater – Astoria, Aberdeen', *Cinema*, 2 January 1935, xviii.

20 'Paramount in Scotland: Architectural Quality of New Glasgow Super', *The Ideal Kinema and Studio*, 17 January 1935, 19. 'Paramount Glasgow', *Cinema and Theatre Construction*, February 1935, 14–16. 'Paramount Theatre, Glasgow', *Builder*, 1 February 1935, 230–3 and 235.

21 'Paramount in Scotland: Architectural Quality of New Glasgow Super', *The Ideal Kinema and Studio*, 17 January 1935, 19. 'Paramount Glasgow', *Cinema and Theatre Construction*, February 1935, 14–16.

22 'Green's Playhouse, Dundee', *Cinema and Theatre Construction*, April 1936, 32–4.

23 'Green's New Playhouse', *Dundee Evening Telegraph*, 3 March 1936, 6. 'Playhouse, Dundee, Opening Green's 4,000-seater

and its Tower of Babel', *Kinematograph Weekly*, 5 March 1936, 27.

24 'Congratulations M Alexander & Sons', *Newcastle Journal*, 18 May 1968, 10.

25 Toffolo Jackson – records of the company 1918–1989, Glasgow City Archives, Mitchell Library, Glasgow, TD1379.

26 'Seating Product Survey', *Ideal Kinema – Supplement to Kinematograph Weekly*, 13 September 1956, 11–16.

27 David King & Sons Ltd, Iron Founders 1873–c1968, Glasgow, Scotland, University of Glasgow Archives and Special Collections, Mitchell Library, Glasgow, GB 248 UGC 082. Walter Macfarlane & Co, Iron Founders c1850–c1965, Possilpark, Glasgow, Scotland, University of Glasgow Archives and Special Collections, GB 248 UGD 270.

28 'Roofed with grey "Turnall" Trafford Tiles – the "Astoria" Picture House, Possil Park Glasgow' *Cinema and Theatre Construction*, September 1932, 2. 'Astoria, Glasgow Opening', *Kinematograph Weekly*, 5 February 1931, 46.

29 'Orient Picture House, Glasgow – Three Thousand Seater Atmospheric', *Cinema and Theatre Construction*, June 1932, 16 and 36. 'Glasgow's new atmospheric – Orient PH A three thousand seater – novel note in proscenium arch decoration', *The Ideal Kinema and Studio*, 26 May 1932.

30 'Glasgow's Latest – The New Bedford – Two Thousand capacity, *The Ideal Kinema and Studio*, 5 January 1933, 31.

31 'Glasgow's latest 2,500 seater – Granada, Parkhead, added to Frutin Circuit – attractive stadium type theatre', *The Ideal Kinema and Studio*, 12 September 1935, 19–20. Designs for the interior of the Granada Cinema, Parkhead, Glasgow, Guthrie & Wells collection, Glasgow City Archives, Mitchell Library, Glasgow, TD655/2/13.

32 'Lady Weir Opens Tudor at Giffnock', *Kinematograph Weekly*, 10 December 1936, 19.

33 'New Kinema Schemes at their Progress', *Kinematograph Weekly*, 30 March 1939, 42. 'Newmilns: The Rex', *Kilmarnock Herald and North Ayrshire Gazette*, 19 September 1939, 5.

34 'The Mecca, Glasgow – James Welsh's new enterprise – attractive proscenium ornamentation', *The Ideal Kinema and Studio*, 14 September 1933, 36 and 53.

35 'The Commodore, Whiteinch – Dignified front elevation – Harmonious interior decoration', *The Ideal Kinema and Studio*, 16 March 1933, 21 and 25. 'The Vogue, Rutherglen', *Kinematograph Weekly*, 6 February 1936, 31. 'Gala Opening of the Vogue Strathmartine Road', *Dundee Evening Telegraph*, 21 September 1936, 10.

36 'Embassy, Shawlands', *Brick Builder*, September 37, No.47. 'Embassy, Glasgow', *Kinematograph Weekly*, 6 February 1936, 31.

37 Interview with George Singleton by Bruce Peter at his home in Edinburgh, spring 1994.

38 'The Caley Picture House', *Kinematograph Weekly*, 11 October 1928, 65.

39 'The New Tivoli', *Edinburgh Evening News*, 1 January 1934, 1.

40 'Luxury Kinema in Edinburgh Suburb – Embassy's modern treatment – Striking main facade', *The Ideal Kinema and Studio*, 9 September 1937, 31.

41 'Kirkcaldy's £20,000 Cinema Opened', *Dundee Courier*, 6 December 1938, 4. 'Embassy Troon Opening', *Kinematograph Weekly*, 4 March 1937, 23. 'Troon's New Kinema: Tributes to Blair's Enterprise', *Kinematograph Weekly*, 25 March 1937, 13.

42 'Singleton's Vogue at Govan Opening in June', *Kinematograph

Weekly, 26 May 1938, 21. 'Vogue Govan Opens – 2,500 Capacity', *Kinematograph Weekly*, 7 July 1938, 30.

43 Interview with George Singleton by Bruce Peter at his home in Edinburgh, spring 1994.

44 'The Riddrie Cinema', *Sunday Mail*, 6 February 1938, 4. 'Lord Provost Opens Riddrie PH – Tribute to James Welsh', *Kinematograph Weekly*, 10 February 1938, 21.

45 'Twelve New Theatres Install Western Electric Sound', *Kinematograph Weekly*, 4 May 1939, 38. 'The Latest Addition to Glasgow's Suburban Cinemas is the Aldwych', *Era*, 20 April 1939, 6.

46 Interview with George Singleton by Bruce Peter at his home in Edinburgh, spring 1994.

47 'Glasgow Repertory Cinema', *Scotsman*, 11 May 1939, 9. 'Glasgow's Cinema Adventure', *Daily Record*, 19 May 1939, 36.

48 Interview with Charles Oakley by Bruce Peter at the Glasgow Film Theatre, autumn 1992.

49 Letter from Robert Forsyth to the author entitled 'C J McNair & Elder, Architects', dated 25 February 1998.

50 Interview with Robert Forsyth by Bruce Peter at the Mitchell Library in Glasgow, 12 March 1995.

51 'Glasgow Regal – Today's Opening', *Kinematograph Weekly*, 14 November 1929, 46. 'Glasgow's Regal', *Kinematograph Weekly*, 21 November 1929, 64. 'The Regal, Glasgow', *Bioscope*, 27 November 1929, 47.

52 'The Front of the Regal, Hamilton, Recently Opened', *Kinematograph Weekly*, 3 September 1931, 74. 'Regal's Brilliant Opening', *Bioscope*, 26 August 1931, 41. 'ABC's new Riddrie House – Tower-like effect over main entrance', *The Ideal Kinema and Studio*, 17 December 1931, 30. 'The Regal, Stirling', *Cinema and Theatre Construction*, November 1932, 23. 'Falkirk's New Super Cinema', *Falkirk Herald*, 3 November 1934, 11. 'ABC's Fortieth Kinema in Scotland: Opening of the Regal, Falkirk, *Kinematograph Weekly*, 3 November 1934, 11. 'Scottish News of the Week: Paisley Regal Opened', *Kinematograph Weekly*, 29 November 1934, 43. 'Paisley's Regal Opened', *Kinematograph Weekly*, 6 December 1934, 21.

53 'The Regal, Coatbridge', *Airdrie & Coatbridge Advertiser*, 29 February 1936, 6. 'New Regal Cinema Opened', *Coatbridge Leader*, 22 February 1936, 2. 'Opening of Regal, Coatbridge', *Kinematograph Weekly*, 20 February 1936, 23. 'The Week in Scotland', *Kinematograph Weekly*, 24 December 1936, 33.

54 Interview with Robert Forsyth by Bruce Peter at the Mitchell Library in Glasgow, 12 March 1995.

55 'State, Glasgow Opened', *Kinematograph Weekly*, 17 June 1937, 25.

56 'Sir Alexander King', *Scotsman*, 29 June 1962, 7. 'Sir Alexander King Retires', *Scotsman*, 28 June 1968, 3.

57 'Lyceum, Govan, lavish new 2,600 seater', *Cinema*, 4 January 1939, xxix.

58 Interview with Robert Forsyth by Bruce Peter at the Mitchell Library in Glasgow, 12 March 1995. 'The Week in Glasgow: Ascot Opens', *Kinematograph Weekly*, 30 November 1939, 13. 'Alex King Opens the Ascot: Lord Provost's Tribute', *Kinematograph Weekly*, 14 December 1939, 28.

59 Interview with Robert Forsyth by Bruce Peter at the Mitchell Library in Glasgow, 12 March 1995.

60 'New Edinburgh Cinema: The Dominion at Morningside Opening on Monday', *Scotsman*, 28 January 1938, 14. 'New Cinema Opened at Morningside', *Edinburgh Evening News*, 31 January 1938, 9. 'The Dominion Opened: Edinburgh's Latest Cinema', *Scotsman*, 1 February 1938, 13.

61 'County Cinema, Portobello, Architect: T Bowhill Gibson, LRIBA', *The Architect and Building News*, 12 May 1939, 158–9.

62 Interview with Gari Todd by Bruce Peter at her home in London on 21 September 1997.

63 Allen Eyles, *ABC: The First Name in Entertainment*, London: Cinema Theatre Association and BFI Publishing, 1993, 28–49.

64 'ABC's Edinburgh Regal', *The Ideal Kinema and Studio*, 6 April 1939, page not numbered. 'The Regal, Edinburgh – Architects Stewart Kaye and Walls – Exterior designed to achieve harmony with surrounding buildings – Interior maintains the unpretentious note', *Cinema and Theatre Construction*, November 1938, 32.

65 'New Palace Arbroath', *Broughty Ferry Guide and Advertiser*, 18 May 1940, 12. 'Opening of the New Palace Theatre', *Arbroath Herald*, 10 May 1940, 3. 'Palace, Arbroath: New ABC 1,500 Seater', *Kinematograph Weekly*, 6 June 1940, 21.

66 'New Hamilton Cinema Opened', *Scotsman*, 15 November 1938, 12. '200th Odeon Opens at Motherwell', *Kinematograph Weekly*, 8 December 1938, 20.

67 'Odeon's First in Scotland: MP Opens Ayr', *Kinematograph Weekly*, 4 August 1938, 27.

68 'Fourteen Odeons for Scotland: F S Bates Forecast at Hamilton Opening', *Kinematograph Weekly*, 17 November 1938, 3.

69 Interview with Keith Roberts' son, Barry Roberts, by Bruce Peter and study of Roberts' drawings and photographs in St Albans on 4 September 1997.

70 'Clydebank Opening Shortly', *Kinematograph Weekly*, 13 January 1938, 15. 'Opening of La Scala', *Milngavie and Bearsden Herald*, 19 February 1938, 8. '2,600-seater at Clydebank for Alex King; David Kirkwood MP Opens La Scala', *Kinematograph Weekly*, 17 February 1938, 5.

71 'Regal Lanark Opening', *Kinematograph Weekly*, 23 July 1936, 19. 'MP Opens Regal, Lanark: A Grand Send-Off', *Kinematograph Weekly*, 3 September 1936, 12. 'Lanark's New Super Cinema', *Carluke and Lanark Gazette*, 21 August 1936, 3.

72 'Leven – Opening of the Troxy, Leven', *Leven Advertiser & Wemyss Gazette*, 16 July 1935, 4. 'Broxburn Regal', *West Lothian Courier*, 13 November 1936, 7.

73 'Armadale's New Theatre: Most Up-to-Date Features in Cinema Construction', *Linlithgowshire Gazette*, 10 December 1937, 6.

74 'Bathgate Regal Opening Wednesday First', *West Lothian Courier*, 22 July 1938, 1. 'New Cinema Opened at Bathgate', *Edinburgh Evening News*, 27 July 1938, 13. 'Description of Building', *West Lothian Courier*, 29 July 1938, 5.

75 'Opening of New Picture House', *Midlothian Advertiser*, 28 October 1938, 2. 'The Regal, Shotts', *Wishaw Press*, 9 June 1939, 6.

76 'This Week in Scotland: Five Openings Scheduled', *Kinematograph Weekly*, 24 February 1938, 15. 'Ideal Cinema', *Sunday Mail*, 27 February 1938, 27.

77 'Viking Opening at Largs Next Month', *Kinematograph Weekly*, 8 June 1939, 27. 'Provost's Tribute to Directors at Viking Opening', *Kinematograph Weekly*, 13 July 1939, 17.

78 Designs for the interior of the Radio Cinema, Kilbirnie, Guthrie & Wells collection, Glasgow City Archives,

Mitchell Library, Glasgow, TD655/2/20 and designs for the interior of the Viking Cinema, Largs, Guthrie & Wells collection, Glasgow City Archives, Mitchell Library, Glasgow, TD655/2/9.

79 'New Cinemas', *Builder*, 14 July 1933, 77 and 'New Cinemas', *Builder*, 28 July 1933, 159. 'Oban's new kinema theatre – Architectural features of the Playhouse – Highland scenes depicted on side walls', *The Ideal Kinema and Studio*, 17 August 1933, 26.

80 'New Oban Playhouse', *Kinematograph Weekly*, 25 May 1933, 21. 'Stornoway Playhouse', *Scotsman*, 31 January 1934, 9. 'New Cinema Opened at Anstruther', *Dundee Evening Telegraph*, 19 July 1934, 7. 'Anstruther's New Cinema', *Leven Advertiser & Wemyss Gazette*, 24 July 1934, 4.

81 *Kelly's Directory of Glasgow*, 1938, 1434.

82 'New Cinemas', *Builder*, 21 July 1933, 118 and 'New Cinemas', *Builder*, 30 November 1934, 955.

83 'New Cinemas', *Builder*, 20 May 1938, 1009 and 'New Cinemas', *Builder*, 9 September 1938, 495. 'Kinross – The County Cinema', *Perthshire Advertiser*, 23 March 1938, 10. 'Another Link in his Cinema Chain: Picture House, Peterhead', *Dundee Evening Telegraph*, 6 March 1939, 7. 'The Regal, Shotts', *Wishaw Press*, 9 June 1939, 6.

84 'New Cinemas', *Builder*, 24 June 1938, 1251. 'Denny Cinema De Luxe Opening Ceremony', *Falkirk Herald*, 25 February 1939, 11.

85 Interview with George Millar by Bruce Peter by telephone on 23 January 2008.

86 James Nott, *Going to the Palais: A Social and Cultural History of Dancing and Dance Halls in Britain 1918–1960*, Oxford University Press, 2015.

87 Designs for the interior of the F&F Palais, Partick, Guthrie & Wells collection, Glasgow City Archives, Mitchell Library, Glasgow, TD655/9/28.

88 Barrowland Ballroom, 228–244 Gallowgate, February 1935, Glasgow City Archives, Mitchell Library, Glasgow, D-CA8/1207.

89 'New Glasgow Ballroom to be Opened', *Sunday Mail*, 13 February 1938, 9.

90 'Beach Dance Hall, Restaurant and Tea Lounge', *Aberdeen Press and Journal*, 13 July 1929, 1.

91 'Dundee Ice Rink – Formal Opening by the Earl of Airlie', *Scotsman*, 1 October 1938, 18. 'Dundee Ice Rink Opening', *Dundee Courier*, 1 October 1938, 6. 'Kirkcaldy Ice Rink Open', *Leven Advertiser & Wemyss Gazette*, 11 October 1938, 8.

92 'Ayr Ice Rink', *Dumfries and Galloway Standard*, 15 March 1939, 8. 'Ayr Ice Rink: Scotland's Finest Ice Rink', *Dumfries and Galloway Standard*, 18 February 1939, 8.

93 'Murrayfield Ice Rink and Sports Stadium Limited', *Edinburgh Evening News*, 22 July 1938, 4. 'Murrayfield Ice Rink', *Edinburgh Evening News*, 11 February 1938. 'Murrayfield Ice Rink', *Midlothian Advertiser*, 31 December 1948.

94 Bruce Peter, *Form Follows Fun: Modernism and Modernity in British Pleasure Architecture 1925–1939*, Abingdon: Routledge, 2007, 43–5.

95 Shawfield Stadium boundary wall and gates, 1947, Glasgow City Archives, Mitchell Library, Glasgow, D-CA8/2983.

CHAPTER 8

1 Bruce Peter, *The Modern Hotel in Britain*, Ramsey: Lily Publications, 2016.

2 'Hotel that Looks Like a "Great White Ship"', *Caterer and Hotel Keeper*, 15 July 1933, 106. Rex Pope, 'Railway companies and resort hotels between the wars', *Journal of Transport History*, March 2001, 63–5. Barry Guise and Pam Brook, *The Midland Hotel: Morecambe's White Hope*, Lancaster: Palatine Books, 2007. Alan Powers, *Oliver Hill: Architect and Lover of Life*, London: Mouton Publications, 1989, 24–7.

3 'LMS Restaurant to "Go Overseas": From Gleneagles to South Africa', *Caterer and Hotel Keeper*, 15 November 1935, 15.

4 'Men! Live in Comfort at the Bellgrove Hotel', *Edinburgh Evening News*, 9 June 1937, 5.

5 Charles McKean, *The Scottish Thirties: An Architectural Introduction*, Edinburgh: Scottish Academic Press, 1987, 197.

6 'Plans Approved for Gourock Hotel', *Scotsman*, 16 January 1937, 14. 'Gourock's New Hotel', *Sunday Mail*, 27 March 1938, 4.

7 'Empire Exhibition, Scotland – 1938, Administrative Committee minute of thirtieth meeting, 4 August 1936', University of Glasgow Archives and Special Collections, ACC2207/22/7.

8 'Opening date for Beresford in Glasgow', *Caterer and Hotel Keeper*, 4 March 1938, 13.

9 'Glasgow's First "Skyscraper" Hotel', *Caterer and Hotel Keeper*, 29 April 1938, 13.

10 As note 9.

11 As note 9.

12 As note 9.

13 As note 9.

14 '50,000 Guests in Six Months', *Caterer and Hotel Keeper*, 14 October 1938, 26.

15 'Newhouse Hotel Opened', *Motherwell Times*, 15 July 1938, 2. 'Newhouse Hotel', *Coatbridge Leader*, 13 July 1938, 2.

16 'New £40,000 Scottish Hotel', *Caterer and Hotel Keeper*, 22 July 1938, 15.

17 As note 16.

18 As note 16.

19 'New Argyll Hotel', *Scotsman*, 19 April 1939, 17. 'New Kintyre Hotel', *Oban Times and Argyllshire Advertiser*, 22 April 1939, 8. 'Keil Hotel, Southend, Argyll', *Scotsman*, 18 August 1947, 6.

20 'Altered plans for £20,000 Highland hotel, *Scotsman*, 26 October 1938, 8.

21 I am grateful to Debbie Potter of Highland Archives for her assistance in researching the circumstances of the completion of the Drumossie Hotel.

22 Information provided by Shona Paterson, James Wilson Poe's daughter, in a telephone conversation with the author on 13 November 2024.

23 I am grateful to Colin Waller of Highland Archives for his assistance in researching the circumstances of the completion of the Grampian Hotel. Gavin Musgrove, editor of *The Strathspey and Badenoch Herald*, kindly enabled contact with Lesley Kettle, daughter of the hotel's subsequent owners, who provided additional information in an email received on 19 January 2024. The hotel features in a 1951 detective novel *Conquest in Scotland* by Berkeley Gray (a pseudonym of the London popular fiction writer Edwy Searles Brooks) who described the hotel as 'an oasis of modernity' with

'irreproachable' service and 'excellent' food.

24 'Grampian Hotel, Dalwhinnie (Completed 1941) Now Open', *Scotsman*, 29 July 1941, 1.

25 'Big Rush to Highlands Expected', *Inverness and Northern Counties People's Journal*, 24 May 1941, 1.

26 'Grampian Hotel Dalwhinnie Inverness-shire', *Scotsman*, 15 April 1941, 1.

27 'The Northern Hotel, Aberdeen', *Builder*, 7 May 1948, 548–51.

28 'Super Roadhouse Opening of "Maybury" in Edinburgh', *Edinburgh Evening News*, 20 November 1936, 3.

29 'Opening of a New Roadhouse, Craigmillar', *Edinburgh Evening News*, 17 October 1936, 2.

30 Charles McKean, *The Scottish Thirties: An Architectural Introduction*, Edinburgh: Scottish Academic Press, 1987, 80.

31 'Opening Announcement for Hilburn Roadhouse', *Edinburgh Evening News*, 17 August 1938, 1. 'Now Open Hilburn Roadhouse', *Edinburgh Evening News*, 19 August 1938, 1.

32 'Alterations to Edinburgh Properties', *Scotsman*, 2 March 1923, 9.

33 National Galleries Scotland, 'An Ornate Link to One of Edinburgh's Most Popular Tearooms', www.nationalgalleries.org/art-and-artists/features/ornate-link-one-edinburghs-most-popular-tearooms, accessed 31 January 2024.

34 'Scottish Legend in Picture: Decorative Panels for Wembley', *Scotsman*, 8 April 1924, 6.

35 'Crawford's New Premises 15–19 Hanover Street', Edinburgh, *Scotsman*, 26 March 1927, 9.

36 Ca'd'Oro, Guthrie & Wells collection, Glasgow City Archives, Mitchell Library, TD655/8/5 166/1027/A

37 Walter Hubbard Ltd, 510 Great Western Road, June 1931, Glasgow City Archives, Mitchell Library, Glasgow, D-CA8/1389.

38 City Bakeries, 276–280 St George's Road, August 1939, Glasgow City Archives, Mitchell Library, Glasgow, D-CA8/2758.

39 Ross's Dairies, 32 Bath Street, April 1930, Glasgow City Archives, Mitchell Library, Glasgow, D-CA8/2605.

40 'Fenton Barns', *Farming News and North British Agriculturalist*, 30 June 1939.

41 'The Moorings', *Daily Record*, 30 June 1936, 23.

42 'Co-op Tearooms and Restaurant Stonehaven', *Aberdeen Press and Journal*, 30 June 1937, 3.

43 Bay Horse, 964 Pollockshaws Road, 1934, Glasgow City Archives, Mitchell Library, Glasgow, D-CA8/2466.

44 Thornwood, Dumbarton Road, 1939, Glasgow City Archives, Mitchell Library, Glasgow, D-CA8/2887.

45 Variety Bar, 15 Cowcaddens Street, April 1938, Glasgow City Archives, Mitchell Library, Glasgow, D-CA8/764.

46 Graham Lironi, *Rogano: Glasgow's Favourite Restaurant*, Edinburgh: Black and White Publishing, 2009, 4–9.

47 Pub Heritage Group, 'Historic Pub Interiors: The Steps Bar', pubheritage.camra.org.uk/pubs/254, accessed 31 January 2024.

CHAPTER 9

1 Moritz Kahn, *The Design and Construction of Industrial Buildings*, London: Technical Journals Ltd, 1917.

2 Joan Skinner, *Form and Fancy: Factories and Factory Buildings by Wallis, Gilbert and Partners 1916–1939*, Liverpool: Liverpool University Press, 1997, 5–23.

3 As note 2, 114–28.

4 As note 2, 128–37.

5 'Dr Charles Oakley: devoted service to his adopted city of Glasgow', *Scotsman*, 13 April 1993, 12.

6 'Templeton Street Extension', *Templetonian*, no. 30, December 1935, 4.

7 'New Factory at Glasgow Green', *Templetonian*, no. 36, December 1938.

8 'This Arshetecture', *Architects' Journal*, 12 January 1939, 47.

9 'Michael Nairn and Greenwich', *Aberdeen Press and Journal*, 18 January 1938, 11.

10 Robert Bevan, 'A Beacon Is Re-Ignited; Original Architect (1930s): W Cornelius Armour, Architects for Conversion: Cornelius McClymont', *Building Design*, no. 29, 1997, 14–17. Cornelius McClymont, 'Glasgow: The Transformation of an Art Deco Factory', *Architecture Today*, March 1997, 14.

11 Hubert Fitchew, 'Literature: Co-Operative Architecture in Sweden', *Architects' Journal*, October 1935, 525–6.

12 '500 Will Come to See Opening: British Luma Factory, Shieldhall', *Daily Record*, 25 August 1939, 17.

13 Robert Bevan, 'A Beacon Is Re-Ignited; Original Architect (1930s): W Cornelius Armour, Architects for Conversion: Cornelius McClymont', *Building Design*, 1329, 1997, 14–17. Cornelius McClymont, 'Glasgow: The Transformation of an Art Deco Factory', *Architecture Today*, March 1997, 14.

14 E J Field, 'Inco in Scotland: introduction to Zenith', *Inco Triangle*, July 1948, 7.

15 Erection of offices, canteen at Thornliebank for Henry Wiggin & Co Ltd, Dean of Guild plans, Glasgow City Archives, Mitchell Library, Glasgow, B4/12/1937/519. The only RIBA-registered architect named Beckett at that time was Herbert Arthur Beckett, whose practice, Duncan Clark & Beckett, was located in Colchester. The firm, which still exists, has been unable to confirm whether he designed the Thornliebank project.

16 Roy H Campbell, 'The Scottish Office and the Special Areas in the 1930s', *Historical Journal*, vol 22, no. 1, 1979, 167–83.

17 Mary Fleming, 'Hillington Industrial Estate: A Romance of Modern Scotland', *SMT Magazine and Scottish Country Life*, June 1938, 49.

18 'Hillington Industrial Estate', *Builder*, February 1950, 214. 'Hillington Industrial Estate', *Builder*, October 1953, 561.

19 Mary Fleming, 'Hillington Industrial Estate: A Romance of Modern Scotland', *SMT Magazine and Scottish Country Life*, June 1938, 49.

20 As note 19.

21 As note 19, 51.

22 As note 19, 51

23 As note 19, 51.

24 As note 19, 51.

25 As note 19, 51.

26 As note 19, 51.

27 As note 19, 50.

28 As note 19, 50.

29 W Hudson and J K Hunter, 'The Galloway Hydro-electric Development with Special Reference to the Constructional Works', *Proceedings of the Institution of Civil Engineers*, April 1938, 323–75.

30 Historic Scotland, *Power to the People: The Built Heritage of Scotland's Hydroelectric Power*, Edinburgh: Historic Scotland, 2010, 17–19.

31 As note 30, 19.

32 As note 30, 19–23.

33 As note 30, 26–35.

34 As note 30, 37–48.

35 Georgina Allison, 'The Miners' Welfare Commission and Pithead Baths in Scotland', *Twentieth Century Architecture*, London: Twentieth Century Society, 1994, 55–64. Gareth Salway and Ceri Thompson, *The Pithead Baths Story*, Cardiff: National Museum of Wales Books, 2012.

36 J A Dempster, 'Modern Industrial Architecture in the Mining Industry', *Quarterly Illustrated of the Royal Incorporation of Architects in Scotland*, no. 53, 1936, 15–21.

37 'Manor Powis Colliery Baths', *Baths and Bath Engineering*, July 1934, 111. 'Pithead Baths, Cardowan, Lanarkshire, Architects: J H Forshaw, FRIBA, J A Dempster, ARIBA', *The Architect and Building News*, 9 August 1935, 165–9.

38 'Pithead Baths', *Architects' Journal*, 12 July 1934, 54. 'Arniston Colliery Baths', *Baths and Bath Engineering*, July 1934, 111.

39 'Pithead Baths', *Architects' Journal*, 19 July 1934, 92. 'Kames Pithead Baths', *Architects' Journal*, 12 July 1934, 54. 'Kames Colliery Baths', *Baths and Bath Engineering*, August 1934, 130.

40 'Polkemmet Pithead Baths, Lanarkshire, Scotland, Architect J A Dempster FRIBA', *The Architect and Building News*, 4 June 1937, 278–81.

CHAPTER 10

1 Barbara Tilson, 'The Modern Art Department, Waring & Gillow, 1928–1931', *Journal of the Decorative Arts Society*, No. 8, 1984, 40–3.

2 John Whitaker, *The Best: H H Martyn & Co, Specialists in Architectural Decoration and the Gloster Aircraft Co*, Cheltenham: John Whitaker, 1985.

3 'These Foolish Things', composed by Eric Maschwitz with lyrics by Jack Strachey, 1935, and 'A Fine Romance', composed by Jerome Kern with lyrics by Dorothy Fields, 1936.

4 Fritz August Breuhaus De Groot, *Der Ozean-Express: Bremen*, Munich: Verlag F Bruckmann, 1929. Anne-Marie Ericsson, *M/S Kungsholms Inredning*, Lund: Bogförlaget Signum, 2005.

5 Leslie Lewis, 'Modern Tendencies in Ship Furnishing', *Shipbuilding and Shipping Record*, January 1929, 9.

6 'Twin-screw Passenger Liner *Empress of Japan*', *Shipbuilding and Shipping Record*, September 1930, 349–53.

7 As note 6, 353–4.

8 As note 6, 353–4.

9 Canadian Pacific brochure for the *Empress of Britain*, 1931, author's collection.

10 As note 9.

11 As note 9.

12 '*Monarch of Bermuda*', *Shipbuilding and Shipping Record*, November 1931, 647–55.

13 As note 12, 648–9.

14 As note 12, 653–5.

15 As note 12, 655.

16 '*Queen of Bermuda*', *Shipbuilding and Shipping Record*, February 1933, 180–3.

17 Interview with David Henderson by Bruce Peter by telephone on 12 November 2020.

18 List of ship interior projects by McInnes Gardner Ltd courtesy of Jack MacIntyre, formerly of McInnes Gardner Ltd.

19 As note 18.

20 Documents relating to design submissions from decorative contractors, Cunard Archive, University of Liverpool Archives, D42/C3/1/6/97.

21 Correspondence between Thornton Smith, Cunard and Hill, Dickenson & Co, April 1931, Cunard Archive, University of Liverpool Archives, D42/C3/1/6/97.

22 Letter from Ashley Speaks to H J Flewitt, Cunard Company Secretary, 27 February 1931, Cunard Archive, University of Liverpool Archives, D42/C3/1/6/97.

23 Letter from J H Early to Sir Percy Bates, 4 June 1931, Cunard Archive, University of Liverpool Archives, D42/C3/1/6/97.

24 Suggestions as to general style of decoration, Cunard Archive, University of Liverpool Archives, D42/C3/1/6/97.

25 Letter from Benjamin Morris to Frederick Bates, 6 July 1931, Cunard Archive, University of Liverpool Archives, D42/C3/1/6/115.

26 'Suggested procedure assuming production of designs in New York and the acceptance thereof, as the basis of contracts and construction', 21 August 1931, Cunard Archive, University of Liverpool Archives, D42/C3/1/6/115.

27 'Memorandum: Design and lighting of the First Class dining saloon', Benjamin Morris to Cunard, 27 March 1934, Cunard Archive, University of Liverpool Archives, D42/C3/1/6/100.

28 As note 27.

29 Extract of minutes of Shipbuilding Committee, 4 June 1934, Cunard Archive, University of Liverpool Archives, D42/C3/1/6/100.

30 Minutes for report from S J Lister to the Cunard Shipbuilding Committee, 17 August 1934, Cunard Archive, University of Liverpool Archives, D42/C3/1/6/99.

31 'The Passenger Accommodation', *Shipbuilding and Shipping Record*, 28 May 1936, 737.

32 George Blake, *RMS Queen Mary*, London: Batsford, 1936, pages not numbered.

33 'The Passenger Accommodation', *Shipbuilding and Shipping Record*, 28 May 1936, 737.

34 As note 33.

35 As note 33.

36 E P Leigh-Bennett, 'A City goes to Sea', *RMS Queen Mary: A Noble Tribute to the Imagination of Man*, London: Cunard-White Star, 1936, pages not numbered.

37 'The Passenger Accommodation', *Shipbuilding and Shipping Record*, 28 May 1936, 737.

38 'Carpets for RMS *Queen Mary*', *Templetonian*, June 1936, 4–6.

39 'The Passenger Accommodation', *Shipbuilding and Shipping Record*, 28 May 1936, 737.

40 E P Leigh-Bennett, 'A City goes to Sea', *RMS Queen Mary: A Noble Tribute to the Imagination of Man*, London: Cunard-White Star, 1936, pages not numbered.

41 'Cabin Fittings and Decorative Flooring', *Shipbuilding and Shipping Record*, 28 May 1936, 716.

42 E P Leigh-Bennett, 'A City goes to Sea', *RMS Queen Mary: A Noble Tribute to the Imagination of Man*, London: Cunard-White Star, 1936, pages not numbered.

43 'Cabin Fittings and Decorative Flooring', *Shipbuilding and Shipping Record*, 28 May 1936, 716.

44 E P Leigh-Bennett, 'A City goes to Sea', *RMS Queen Mary: A Noble Tribute to the Imagination of Man*, London: Cunard-White Star, 1936, pages not numbered.

45 'The Passenger Accommodation', *Shipbuilding and Shipping Record*, 28 May 1936, 737.

46 As note 45.

47 E P Leigh-Bennett, 'A City goes to Sea', *RMS Queen Mary: A Noble Tribute to the Imagination of Man*, London: Cunard-White Star, 1936, pages not numbered.

48 'The Passenger Accommodation', *Shipbuilding and Shipping Record*, 28 May 1936, 737.

49 As note 48.

50 As note 48.

51 As note 48.

52 As note 48.

53 Letter from John Brown & Co to Sir Percy Bates, 10 October 1935, Cunard Archive, University of Liverpool Archives, D42/C3/1/6/100.

54 Letters and correspondence relating to the building of the *Queen Mary*, John Brown & Co archive, University of Glasgow Archives and Special Collections.

55 As note 54.

56 John Maxtone-Graham, *The Only Way to Cross*, Macmillan, New York, 1972, 293.

57 'RMS Queen Mary', *The Architect and Building News*, 29 May 1936, 240–3. Neil Potter and Jack Frost, *The Mary: The Inevitable Ship*, George G Harrap & Co, London, 1961, 122.

58 Oliver P Bernard, 'My Impressions of the *Queen Mary*', *Shipbuilding and Shipping Record*, 26 May 1936, 691.

59 As note 58, 692.

60 Martin Bellamy and Bill Spalding, *The Golden Years of the Anchor Line*, Ochiltree and Glasgow: Stenlake Publishing and Glasgow Museums, 2011, 29–30 and 39–43.

61 'The Anchor Line's First Motor Ship', *Motor Ship*, November 1937, 268.

62 As note 61.

63 'The *Mauretania*: The latest Cunard-White Star liner and the largest ship to have been built in England', *Shipbuilding and Shipping Record*, 15 June 1939, 755–64.

64 Letters and correspondence relating to the building of the *Queen Elizabeth*, John Brown & Co archive, University of Glasgow Archives and Special Collections, UCS 1/5/37.

65 Report by Sir Percy Bates on SS *Orion*, 14 September 1936, Cunard Archive, University of Liverpool Archives, D42/C3/1/5/25.

66 Letter from Sir Percy Bates to Professor Charles Reilly, 7 September 1936, Cunard Archive, University of Liverpool Archives, D42/C3/1/5/25.

67 Documents and correspondence between Cunard, Benjamin Morris and George Grey Wornum, Cunard Archive, University of Liverpool Archives, D42/C3/1/5/29.

68 Miriam Wornum, extract from an unpublished biography of George Grey Wornum to have been titled 'Grey Matter', reproduced in *Sea Lines: The Magazine of the Ocean Liner Society*, no. 78, spring 2015, 12–13.

69 Margaret Richardson, *66 Portland Place: The London Headquarters of the Royal Institute of British Architects*, RIBA Publications, London, 1984.

70 Letter, John Brown & Co to Cunard, 7 May 1938, University of Glasgow Archives and Special Collections, 8JP/AL/114.

THE ART DECO LEGACY

1 'Addition to King Circuit Opened: The Plaza, Port Glasgow', *Kinematograph Weekly*, 25 January 1951, 9. 'Bellshill Flocks to George Opening', *Motherwell Times*, 30 November 1951, 7. 'The George – Bellshill's Newest Cinema', *Motherwell Times*, 23 November 1951, 9. 'The George Opens', *Bellshill Speaker*, 30 November 1951, 3.

2 'New Girvan Station Buildings', *Paisley Daily Express*, 14 August 1951, 4. 'Ayrshire Coast Station has New Look', *Kilmarnock Herald and North Ayrshire Gazette*, 24 August 1951, 2.

3 'New £117,000 School at Longstone: Modern Yet Traditional', *Scotsman*, 22 February 1957, 5. 'Make Lives Bright and Modern, Like School', *Edinburgh Evening News*, 21 February 1957, 6.

4 Robert Bruce, *First Planning Report to the Highways and Planning Committee of the Corporation of the City of Glasgow*, Glasgow: Corporation of the City of Glasgow, 1945.

5 Miles Glendinning (ed.), *Rebuilding Scotland: The Postwar Vision 1945–1975*, East Linton: Tuckwell Press, 1997.

6 Joy Elizabeth Hunter, Art Deco Architecture in the Glasgow Area 1925–1940, dissertation presented to the Mackintosh School of Architecture, University of Glasgow, for the Diploma in Architecture, 1978, Glasgow: Glasgow School of Art Library. Chris Doak, Klondyke of the Kinema World: A Tale of Picture Houses in Glasgow, dissertation presented to the Mackintosh School of Architecture, University of Glasgow, for the Diploma in Architecture, 1979, Glasgow: Glasgow School of Art Library.

7 Alan Powers and Gavin Stamp, 'The Twentieth Century Society: A Brief History', *Twentieth Century Architecture Seven: The Heroic Period of Conservation*, London: Twentieth Century Society, 2004, 158–9.

8 Graham Lironi, *Rogano: Glasgow's Favourite Restaurant*, Edinburgh: Black and White Publishing, 2009, 9–17.

9 Miles Glendinning and Diane Watters (eds), *Home Builders Mactaggart & Mickel and the Scottish Housebuilding Industry: 1925–2015 Celebrating 90 Years*, Edinburgh: Royal Commission on the Ancient and Historic Monuments of Scotland, 2015, 95.

10 *Queen Mary*, 'History', queenmary.com/history, accessed 31 January 2024.

11 Miles Cowsill, *Queen Mary 2*, Ramsey: Ferry Publications, 2011.

12 Maurizio Eliseo, *Queen Elizabeth: More Than a Ship*, Greenwich: Carmania, 2011.

13 *Daily Record*, 'Open and Shut Case: Poirot film gave golf boss inspiration for Castle Stuart clubhouse design' (8 July 2011), www.dailyrecord.co.uk/news/scottish-news/open-and-shut-case-poirot-film-1107483, accessed January 2024.

BIBLIOGRAPHY

Interviews

Charles Oakley by Bruce Peter at the Glasgow Film Theatre, autumn 1992.

George Singleton by Bruce Peter at his home in Edinburgh, spring 1994.

Robert Forsyth by Bruce Peter at the Mitchell Library in Glasgow, 12 March 1995.

Keith Roberts' son, Barry Roberts, by Bruce Peter and study of Roberts' drawings and photographs in St Albans, 4 September 1997.

Gari Todd by Bruce Peter at her home in London, 21 September 1997.

George Millar by Bruce Peter by telephone, 23 January 2008.

David Henderson by Bruce Peter by telephone, 12 November 2020.

Shona Paterson by Bruce Peter by telephone, 13 November 2024.

Books

Bellamy, Martin and Spalding, Bill
The Golden Years of the Anchor Line, Ochiltree and Glasgow: Stenlake Publishing and Glasgow Museums, 2011.

Benton, Charlotte, Benton, Tim and Wood, Ghislaine
Art Deco 1910–1939, London: V&A Publications, 2003.

Billcliffe, Roger
Charles Rennie Mackintosh: The Complete Furniture, Furniture Drawings and Interior Designs, London: Taplinger, 1979.

Blake, George
RMS *Queen Mary*, London: Batsford, 1936.

Booth, Gavin
Alexander Coachbuilders, Glossop: The Transport Publishing Company, 1980.

Boulton, David
Jazz in Britain, London: W H Allen, 1958.

Breuhaus De Groot, Fritz August
Der Ozean-Express: Bremen, Munich: Verlag F Bruckmann, 1929.

Brown, Alison, Mckenzie, Ray and Proctor, Robert (eds)
The Flower and the Green Leaf: Glasgow School of Art in the Time of Charles Rennie Mackintosh, Edinburgh: Luath Press, 2009.

Brumfield, William Craft
The Origins of Modernism in Russian Architecture, Berkeley: University of California Press, 1991.

Burnet, Sir John, Tait, Thomas and Raeside, David
The Architectural Work of Sir John Burnet and Partners with a Preface by A Trystan Edwards, Geneva: Masters of Architecture, 1930.

Buxton, Neil K and Aldcroft, Derek H
British Industry between the Wars: Instability and Industrial Development 1919–1939, London: Scholar Press, 1979.

Carpenter, Robin
Mr Pink: The Architectural Legacy of Walter Francis Crittall (1887–1956), Chelmsford: Essex County Council and Braintree District Council, 2007.

Caughie, Pamela L (ed)
Disciplining Modernism, Basingstoke: Palgrave Macmillan, 2009.

Chalmers, Thomas
One Hundred Years of Guttapercha, Glasgow: R & J Dick Ltd, 1946.

Clifford, John
De Havilland and Hatfield 1910–1935, Stroud: Fonthill Media, 2015.

Cole, Beverly and Durack, Richard
Railway Posters 1923–1947 from the Collection of the National Railway Museum, York, London: Laurence King, 1992.

Constantine, Stephen
Social Conditions in Britain 1918–1939, Abingdon: Routledge, 2006.

Cottam, David, Rosenberg, Stephen, Newby, Frank, Crabb, George, and Stamp, Gavin (ed)
Sir Owen Williams 1890–1969, London: Architectural Association, 1986.

Cowsill, Miles
Queen Mary 2, Ramsey: Ferry Publications, 2011.
Crittall, Francis Henry, *Fifty Years of Work and Play*, London: Constable, 1934.

Cumming, Elizabeth
Hand, Heart and Soul: The Arts and Crafts Movement in Scotland, Edinburgh: Birlinn, 2006.

Denby, Elizabeth
Europe Re-housed, London: Allen & Unwin, 1944.

Donnelly, Max
Christopher Dresser: Design Pioneer, London: Thames & Hudson, 2021.

Dube, Wolf-Dieter
German Expressionism: Art and Society 1909–1923, London, Thames & Hudson, 1997.

Eliseo, Maurizio
Queen Elizabeth: More Than A Ship, Greenwich: Carmania, 2011.

Elliott, Bridget and Windover, Michael
The Routledge Companion to Art Deco, Abingdon: Routledge, 2019.

Elliott, Patrick and Llewellyn, Sacha
True to Life: British Realist Painting in the 1920s and 1930s, Edinburgh: National Galleries of Scotland, 2017.

Emmerson, Roger and Tilmouth, Mary
Matthew Steele Architect: A Biography, Edinburgh: RIAS Publishing, 2010.

Ericsson, Anne-Marie
M/S Kungsholms Inredning, Lund: Bogförlaget Signum, 2005.

Eyles, Allen
ABC: The First Name in Entertainment, London: Cinema Theatre Association and BFI Publishing, 1993.
Empire Exhibition 1938 Official Guide.

Farquharson, Lindsay
General Wade's Legacy: The Eighteenth Century Military Road System in Perthshire, Perth: Perth & Kinross Heritage Trust, 2011.

Ferguson, Hugh
Glasgow School of Art: The History, Glasgow: Glasgow School of Art, 1995.

Ferrari, Anna (ed)
Visions of Ancient Egypt, Norwich: Sainsbury Centre of the Arts, 2022.

Ferrier, Ronald W
The History of the British Petroleum Company Volume 1: The Developing Years 1901–1932, Cambridge: Cambridge University Press, 1982.

Frayling, Christopher
The Royal College of Art: One Hundred and Fifty Years of Art and Design, London: Hutchinson, 1987.

Fry, Maxwell
Autobiographical Sketches, London: Elkon Books, 1975.

Glen, Duncan
William Williamson: Kirkcaldy Architect, Kirkcaldy: Akros Publications, 2008.

Glendinning, Miles (ed)
Rebuilding Scotland: The Postwar Vision 1945–1975, East Linton: Tuckwell Press, 1997.

Glendinning, Miles and Watters, Diane (eds)
Home Builders Mactaggart & Mickel and the Scottish Housebuilding Industry: 1925–2015 Celebrating 90 Years, Edinburgh: Royal Commission on the Ancient and Historic Monuments of Scotland, 2015.

Glover, Julian
Thomas Telford: Man of Iron and the Building of Britain, London: Bloomsbury, 2018.

Gray, Berkeley
Conquest in Scotland, London: Collins, 1951.

Greenhalgh, Paul
Ephemeral Vistas: The Expositions Universelles, Great Exhibitions and World's Fairs, 1851–1939, Manchester: Manchester University Press, 1988.

Gronberg, Tag
Designs on Modernity: Exhibiting the City in 1920s Paris, Manchester: Manchester University Press, 1998.

Guise, Barry and Brook, Pam
The Midland Hotel: Morecambe's White Hope, Lancaster: Palatine Books, 2007.

Harwood, Elain
Art Deco Britain, London: Batsford and Twentieth Century Society, 2019

Hillier, Bevis
Art Deco of the 20s and 30s, London: Studio Vista, 1968.
Historic Scotland, *Power to the People: The Built Heritage of Scotland's Hydroelectric Power*, Edinburgh: Historic Scotland, 2010.

Hitchcock, Henry Russell and Johnson, Philip
The International Style, New York: Museum of Modern Art, 1933.

Hunter, Jack
A Flight Too Far: The Story of Lady Mackay of Glenapp, Stranraer: Stranraer & District Local History Trust, 2008.

Ionides, Basil
Colour and Interior Decoration, London: Country Life, 1926.

Jackson, Anthony
The Politics of Architecture, London: Architectural Press, 1970.

Jackson, Lesley
Alastair Morton and Edinburgh Weavers Ltd: Visionary Textiles and Modern Art, London: V&A Publications, 2012.

Jones, Owen
The Grammar of Ornament, London: Day & Son, 1856.

Kahn, Moritz

The Design and Construction of Industrial Buildings, London: Technical Journals Ltd, 1917.

Kelly's Directory of Glasgow, 1938.

Kenefick, William

Red Scotland! The Rise and Fall of the Radical Left, c1872 to 1932, Edinburgh: Edinburgh University Press, 2007.

Kinchin, Perilla and Kinchin, Juliet

Tea and Taste: Glasgow Tearooms 1875–1975, White Cockade Publishing, 1991.

Kopp, Anatole

Constructivist Architecture in the USSR, London: St Martin's Press 1986.

Lancaster, Osbert

Homes Sweet Homes, London: John Murray, 1939.

Leigh-Bennett, E P

'A City Goes to Sea', *RMS* Queen Mary: *A Noble Tribute to the Imagination of Man*, London: Cunard-White Star, 1936

Lironi, Graham

Rogano: Glasgow's Favourite Restaurant, Edinburgh: Black and White Publishing, 2009.

Logan, R

The James Templeton Story, Glasgow: James Templeton & Co, 1960.

Long, Philip and Thomas, Jane (eds)

Basil Spence Architect, Edinburgh: National Galleries of Scotland, 2008.

MacDonald, Catriona

Scotland and the Great War, Edinburgh: John Donald Publishing, 2014.

McDonald, John R H

Modern Housing: A Review of Present Housing Requirements in Gt. Britain, a Resume of Post-War Housing at Home and Abroad, and Some Practical Suggestions for Future Housing, London: John Tiranti & Co, 1931.

McKay, Stuart

Cabin Moths, Tonbridge: Air-Britain, 2024.

McKean, Charles

The Scottish Thirties: An Architectural Introduction, Edinburgh: Scottish Academic Press, 1987.

McKenzie, Ray

Public Sculpture in Edinburgh Volume 1, Liverpool: Liverpool University Press, 2018.

McKenzie, Ray

Public Sculpture in Edinburgh Volume 2, Liverpool: Liverpool University Press, 2018.

McKenzie, Ray

Sculpture in Glasgow: An Illustrated Handbook, Glasgow: Foulis Archive Press with Neil Baxter Associates, 1999.

McKinstry, Sam

Sure as the Sunrise: A History of Albion Motors, Edinburgh: John Donald, 1997.

Maxtone-Graham, John

The Only Way to Cross, New York: Macmillan, 1972.

Middlemas, Robert Keith

The Clydesiders: A Left-Wing Struggle for Parliamentary Power, London: Hutchinson & Co, 1965.

Muir, Augustus

Nairns of Kirkcaldy: A Short History 1847–1956, Cambridge: W Heffer & Sons, 1956.

Musée des Arts Décoratifs

Les Années "25" Art Déco/Bauhaus/Stijl/Esprit Nouveau, Paris: Musée des Arts Décoratifs, 1966.

Nash, Eric

Manhattan Skyscrapers, New York: Princeton Architectural Press, 2005.

Nock, O S

British Locomotives of the Twentieth Century Volume 2: 1930–1960, London: Guild Publishing, 1984.

Nott, James

Going to the Palais: A Social and Cultural History of Dancing and Dance Halls in Britain 1918–1960, Oxford: Oxford University Press, 2015.

Ovsyannikova, Elena and Vissiliev, Nikolai

Boris Velikovsky: Architect of the Russian Avant-Garde, Stuttgart: Arnoldsche, 2017.

Peter, Bruce

Form Follows Fun: Modernism and Modernity in British Pleasure Architecture 1925–1939, Abingdon: Routledge, 2007.

Peter, Bruce

Scotland's Cinemas, Ramsey: Lily Publications, 2011.

Peter, Bruce

The Modern Hotel in Britain, Ramsey: Lily Publications, 2016.

Peter, Bruce

Scottish Buses: A Global Success Story, Ramsey: Lily Publications, 2021.

Plumber, Raymond

Nothing Need Be Ugly: The First 70 Years of the Design and Industries Association, London: Design and Industries Association, 1985.

Post Office Glasgow Directory 1869–1870.

Post Office Glasgow Directory, 1889–1890.

Post Office Glasgow Directory, 1903–1904.

Potter, Neil and Frost, Jack
The Mary: The Inevitable Ship, London: George G Harrap & Co, 1961.

Powers, Alan
Oliver Hill: Architect and Lover of Life, London: Mouton Publications, 1989.

Rauhut, Christophe
Fragments of Metropolis in Berlin: Berlin's Expressionist Legacy, Berlin: Hirmer, 2016.

Reichow, Christopher
US Intentions with the Dawes-Plan toward Germany, Munich: GRIN Verlag, 2011.

Richards, Jeffrey
The Age of the Dream Palace: Cinema and Society in Britain 1930–1939, London: Routledge & Kegan Paul, 1984.

Richardson, Margaret
66 Portland Place: The London Headquarters of the Royal Institute of British Architects, London: RIBA Publications, 1984.

Rodger, Johnny (ed)
Gillespie, Kidd & Coia Architecture 1956–1987, Glasgow: The Lighthouse, 2007.

Roux-Spitz, Michel
Batiments et Jardins, Paris: Éditions Albert Lévy, 1928.

Rudberg, Eva
The Stockholm Exhibition 1930: Modernism's Breakthrough in Swedish Architecture, Stockholm: Stockholmia, 1999.

Salway, Gareth, and Thompson, Ceri
The Pithead Baths Story, Cardiff: National Museum of Wales Books, 2012.

Scott-Moncrieff, Anna and Davidson, C L
Aboard the Bulger, London: Methuen, 1935.

Shand, Philip Morton
The Architecture of Pleasure 1: Modern Theatres and Cinemas, London: Batsford, 1930.

Shand, Philip Morton
The New Architecture and the Bauhaus, London: Faber & Faber, 1935.

Shields, Rob
Places on the Margin: Alternative Geographies of Modernity, Abingdon: Routledge, 1991.

Sigsworth, Eric M
Montague Burton: Tailor of Taste, Manchester: Manchester University Press, 1990.

Simpson, Eric
Wish You Were Still Here: The Scottish Seaside Holiday, Stroud: Amberley, 2013.

Sir John Burnet, Tait & Lorne
The Information Book of Sir John Burnet, Tait & Lorne, London: Architectural Press, 1938.

Skinner, Joan
Form and Fancy: Factories and Factory Buildings by Wallis, Gilbert and Partners 1916–1939, Liverpool: Liverpool University Press, 1997.

Sontag, Susan
Against Interpretation, London: Penguin, 2009.

Stamp, Gavin
Alexander 'Greek' Thomson, London: Laurence King, 1999.

Stephan, Regina, Benton, Charlotte and Heinze-Greenberg, Ita
Erich Mendelsohn: Architect 1887–1953, New York: The Monacelli Press, 1999.

Stephenson, Thomas (ed)
Industrial Edinburgh: Edinburgh Society for the Promotion of Trade and Edinburgh Chamber of Commerce and Manufactures, 1921.

Stewart, Ian
The Glasgow Tramcar, Newton Mearns: Scottish Tramway Museum Society, 1983.

Sutherland, Thomas Scott
Life on One Leg, London: Christopher Johnson, 1957.

Van Bergeijk, Herman
W M Dudok, Rotterdam: Nai010, 2001.

Venturi, Robert, Scott-Brown, Denise, and Izenour, Steven
Learning from Las Vegas, Cambridge, MA: MIT Press, 1972.

Walker, David M
St Andrew's House: An Edinburgh Controversy 1912–1939, Edinburgh: Historic Scotland, 1989.

Walpole, Ken
Here Comes the Sun: Architecture and Public Space in Twentieth Century European Culture, London: Reaktion, 2000.

White, Michael
De Stijl and Dutch Modernism, Manchester: Manchester University Press, 2003.

Whitaker, John
The Best: H H Martyn & Co, Specialists in Architectural Decoration and the Gloster Aircraft Co, Cheltenham: John Whitaker, 1985.

Williams-Ellis, Clough
England and the Octopus, London: Geoffrey Bles, 1929.

Young, Fred H
A Century of Carpet-Making 1839–1939, Glasgow: Collins, 1943.

Reports

Report on (1) The Incorporation of Architectural Quality and Amenity in the Lay-out, Planning and External Treatment of Houses for the Working Classes; and (2) The Erection of High Tenements, London: His Majesty's Stationery Office, 1935.

Bruce, Robert, *First Planning Report to the Highways and Planning Committee of the Corporation of the City of Glasgow*, Glasgow: Corporation of the City of Glasgow, 1945.

Theses and Dissertations

Cleaver, Jonathan

The interrelationship of carpet weaving technologies and design in the work of James Templeton and Company, Glasgow, carpet manufacturer, 1890–1939, PhD thesis, Glasgow: University of Glasgow, 2021, University of Glasgow Library.

Doak, Chris

Klondyke of the Kinema World: A tale of picture houses in Glasgow, dissertation presented to the Mackintosh School of Architecture, University of Glasgow, for the Diploma in Architecture, 1979, Glasgow, Glasgow School of Art Library.

Fowle, Frances

Alex Reid in Context: collecting and dealing in Scotland in the late-19th and early-20th centuries, PhD thesis, Edinburgh: University of Edinburgh, 1994, University of Edinburgh Library.

Hunter, Joy Elizabeth

Art Deco Architecture in the Glasgow Area 1925–1940, dissertation presented to the Mackintosh School of Architecture, University of Glasgow, for the Diploma in Architecture, 1978.

Hutchinson, Peter

The Daily Express Offices (1932–1939), dissertation presented to the Mackintosh School of Architecture, University of Glasgow, for the Diploma in Architecture, 1984, Glasgow School of Art Library.

Jewison, Deborah

Policy and Practice: Design Education in England from 1837–1992, with particular reference to furniture courses at Birmingham, Leicester and the Royal College of Art, PhD thesis, Leicester: De Montfort University, 2015, De Montfort University Library.

Wyllie, Ann

Guthrie & Wells: Interior Decorators 1920–1930, MA Decorative Arts dissertation, Glasgow: University of Glasgow, 1988, University of Glasgow History of Art Department Dissertation Library, T0010.

Journals

Academy Architecture and Architectural Review

'Royal Masonic Hospital', January 1931, 10–13.

American Architect

'The Royal Masonic Hospital, London, England, Sir John Burnet, Tait and Lorne, Architects', January 1935, 58–64.

Apollo

Skipworth, Peyton, 'Rebels Against Commercial Ugliness', January 2008, 42–7.

The Architect and Building News

'The Playhouse, Montrose, Architect Alister G MacDonald, ARIBA', 10 February 1933, 200–3.

Yerbury, Francis R, 'Hilversum Town Hall, Architect: W M Dudok, 26 May 1933, 225–8.

'Inverness High School', 23 February 1934, 268.

'The Curzon Cinema, Mayfair, W, Architects: Sir John Burnet, Tait and Lorne, FRIBA', 9 March 1934, 307–11.

'Commercial Bank of Scotland', 10 August 1934, 171.

'Cragburn Pavilion', 15 February 1935, 237.

'A House in Scotland, Architect John R H McDonald, BSc', 21 June 1935, 344–5.

'Pithead Baths, Cardowan, Lanarkshire, Architects: J H Forshaw, FRIBA, J A Dempster, ARIBA', 9 August 1935, 165–169.

'House for Miss Reid at Murrayfield, Edinburgh', 9 August 1935, 179.

'House in Edinburgh: Basil Spence and William Kininmonth, Architects', 23 August 1935, 226–7.

'Edinburgh: Niddrie Marischal School', 27 September 1935, 374.

'A House in Edinburgh, Architects: Kininmonth and Spence, ARIBA', 11 October 1935, 40–1.

'Dunfermline Corporation Fire Station, Architect: James Shearer', 1 May 1936, 123–5.

'RMS *Queen Mary*', 29 May 1936, 240–5.

'Rothesay Pavilion Competition', 21 February 1936, 259.

'Portobello Swimming Pool, Edinburgh, W A McCartney, AM Inst CE, City Engineer', 1 January 1937, 13–15.

'Glasgow University Sports Pavilion, Architect: T Harold Hughes FRIBA', 29 January 1937, 158–9.

'The National Bank of Scotland, Ltd, Temporary Head Offices, Edinburgh, Architects Thomas P Marwick and Son, FRIBA', 6 March 1937, 302.

'Polkemmet Pithead Baths, Lanarkshire, Scotland, Architect J A Dempster FRIBA' 4 June 1937, 278–81.

'Showrooms – Thomas P Marwick and Son', October 1938, 182.

'County Cinema, Portobello, Architect: T Bowhill Gibson, LRIBA', 12 May 1939, 158–9.

'The Caledonian Insurance Company: New Building at Edinburgh, Architect: Leslie Grahame-Thomson, FRIBA', 1 September 1939, 233–5.

'New Government Offices, Edinburgh, Architect: T S Tait, FRIBA of Sir John Burnet, Tait & Lorne', 20 October 1939, 58–60.

Architects' Journal

'New Offices for the *Daily Telegraph*', February 1929, 239–42.

'New Offices for the *Daily Telegraph*: Details of the Main Front', February 1929, 243–5.

Burnet, Sir John, 'The New Entrance Loggia at Selfridge's: Graham, Anderson, Probst and White', May 1929, 751–8.

Fry, E Maxwell, 'At the Royal Academy: The Architecture Reviewed', May 1931, 644–50.

'Pithead Baths', 12 July 1934, 54.

'Kames Pithead Baths', 12 July 1934, 54.

'Pithead Baths', 19 July 1934, 92.

Noad, R Mervyn, 'New Club-House at Renfrew Aerodrome', September 1935, 369–71.

Fitchew, Hubert, 'Literature: Co-Operative Architecture in Sweden', October 1935, 525–6.

'A New Type of Railway', 2 January 1936, 32.

'Diving Stage at Edinburgh', 12 March 1936, 398.

'Suresnes, France by Beaudoin and Lods', 28 May 1936, 820–2.

'Hospital at Paisley by Sir John Burnet, Tait and Lorne', 3 September 1936, 295–8.

'Burlington School for Girls, Hammersmith Designed by Sir John Burnet, Tait and Lorne', 21 January 1937, 137–43.

'Shop at Edinburgh by Rowand Anderson and Paul & Partner', 28 January 1937, 19–20.

'Temporary Head Offices, National Bank of Scotland, Edinburgh', 25 February 1937, 341–3.

'Kensal House Flats and Nursery School in Ladbroke Grove', 18 March 1937, 466–8.

'Paisley Infectious Diseases Hospital – Sir John Burnet, Tait and Lorne', 24 June 1937, 1128–9.

'The New Flying Scotsman: London–Edinburgh in Six Hours', 8 July 1937, 45.

'Ravelston Garden, one of several blocks of flats at Craigleith, Edinburgh, by Neil and Hurd', 22 July 1937, 137.

'Pavilion for the Empire Exhibition', 23 December 1937, 1024.

'This Arshetecture', 12 January 1939, 47.

Architecture

'The Late Henry Pynor', January–March 1947, 279.

Architecture Heritage

Stamp, Gavin, 'An architect of the Entente Cordiale: Eugène Bourdon (1870–1916) Glasgow and Versailles', vol 15, no. 1, November 2004, 80–116.

Gregory, Neil, 'Monro and Partners: Shopping in Scotland with Marks and Spencer', vol 14, no. 1, November 2003, 67–73.

Architecture Today

McClymont, Cornelius, 'Glasgow: The Transformation of an Art Deco Factory', March 1997, 14.

Architectural Design and Construction

'Surbiton Southern Railway Station', April 1938, 137.

'Richmond Southern Railway Station', *Architectural Design and Construction*, April 1938, 138.

'Woolworth's New Premises at North Shore, Blackpool', May 1938, 188–9.

'Ravelston Garden, Edinburgh, by Neil and Hurd, Architects', October 1938, 381–2.

'Railway Stations: Modernisation on the Southern Railway', December 1938, 463.

Architectural History

Stevens, Russell and Willis, Peter, 'Earl De La Warr and the Competition for the Bexhill Pavilion, 1933–34', vol 33, 1990, 135–66

Architectural Review

Blake, V, 'Adelaide House, London', February 1925, 61–73.

'Trade and craft: Adelaide House, London Bridge', June 1925, lb, liib, livb.

'Infectious Diseases Hospital, Paisley: Sir John Burnet, Tait and Lorne, Architects', September 1936, 104–8.

'Current Architecture: 1 Thomas P Marwick and Son', March 1937, 179.

'Flats and Nursery School, Ladbroke Grove, Committee of Architects: Robert Atkinson, C H James, G Grey Wornum, E Maxwell Fry, Executant Architect', May 1937, 207–10.

'Current Architecture: 1 Thomas P Marwick and Son', August 1937, 65.

Richards, J M, 'Glasgow 1938: A Critical Survey', July 1938, 3–9.

Art and Industry

'A Study of Design Aboard the RMS *Caronia*', August *1949*, 62–3.

Bath and Bath Engineering

'Developments in the Baths World: Notes and News from All Quarters', January 1934.

'Stonehaven', June 1934, 92.

'Manor Powis Colliery Baths', July 1934, 111.

'Arniston Colliery Baths', July 1934, 111.

'Kames Colliery Baths', August 1934, 130.

'Arbroath', August 1934, 134.

'Burntisland', October 1934, 179.

'Gourock', January 1935, 21.

'Developments in the Baths World: Notes and News from All Quarters', December 1935.

Bioscope

'The Regal, Glasgow', 27 November 1929, 47.

'Regal's Brilliant Opening', 26 August 1931, 41.

Black Musical Research Journal

Rye, Howard, 'The Southern Syncopated Orchestra 1919–1922', vol 29, no. 2, fall 2009, 153–228.

Rye, Howard, 'Chronology of the Southern Syncopated Orchestra: 1919–1922', vol 30, no. 1, spring 2010, 5+.

Brick Builder

'Embassy, Shawlands', September 37, No. 47.

Builder

'Perspective view of new shops and flats, Oxford Street, W', 20 June 1933, 1044.

'New Cinemas', 14 July 1933, 77.

'New Cinemas', 21 July 1933, 118

'New Cinemas', 28 July 1933, 159.

'New Buildings in Scotland: Dunfermline Fire Station', 4 August 1933, 206.

'New Cinemas: Playhouse, Perth', 11 August 1933, 240.

'Kelso High School', 11 August 1933, 245.

'Freemasons' Hospital and Nursing Home, Ravenscourt Park, W.', 18 August 1933, 254, 255, 260 and 262–72.

'The Curzon Cinema, Curzon Street, W', 9 March 1934, 407, 418 and 426.

'Waterloo News Theatre', 14 September 1934, 426 and 434–5.

'New Cinemas', 30 November 1934, 955.

'Paramount Theatre, Glasgow', 1 February 1935, 230–3 and 235.

'Renfrew Aerodrome', 31 June 1935, 1152–3, 1158 and 1162.

'Glasgow Royal Infirmary Auxiliary Hospital and Convalescent Home, Canniesburn', 20 May 1938, 980.

'Mount Royal, Oxford Street, W', 2 November 1934, 764–5.

'New Government Building, Edinburgh', 8 May 1935, 920.

'A Model of the Empire Exhibition, Bellahouston Park, Glasgow by Sir John Burnet, Tait and Lorne, Architects', 26 February 1937, 462.

'Infectious Diseases Hospital, Hawkhead Road, Paisley,' 14 January 1938, 79–84.

'New Cinemas', 20 May 1938, 1009.

'New Cinemas', 24 June 1938, 1251.

'New Cinemas', 9 September 1938, 495.

'The Northern Hotel, Aberdeen', 7 May 1948, 548–51.

'Hillington Industrial Estate', February 1950, 214.

'Hillington Industrial Estate', October 1953, 561.

Building Design

Bevan, Robert, 'A Beacon Is Re-Ignited; Original Architect (1930s): W Cornelius Armour, Architects for Conversion: Cornelius McClymont', *Building Design*, no. 29, 1997, 14–17.

The Cabinet Maker and Complete House Furnisher

'The Scottish Furniture Industry', 27 April 1935, 117–18.

'The Scottish Furniture Industry: Its virtues, its achievements, the business outlook', 27 April 1935, 118.

'News of Scottish Retail Trade: The compromise between quality and quantity – fashion follows the south', 27 April 1935, 119.

Sneddon, D D, 'What Glasgow Buys: Outlook of the Scottish public', 4 May 1935, 184.

'Glasgow Exhibition – Good display by Wylie & Lochhead', 18 May 1935, 271.

'Glasgow Furnishing: Corporation's 1s-a-week scheme starts next week', 31 August 1935, 279.

'All-Scottish House – plans for Glasgow exhibition', 5 October 1935, 14.

'Success of the Scottish House', 12 October 1935, 44.

'Scottish Manufacturers Exhibition – prominent northern manufacturers well represented in Glasgow', 12 October 1935, 47.

'Three Views of the Modern Style – from Paris, London and Glasgow', 26 October 1935, 106.

'Scottish Strike Continues', 6 June 1936, 395.

'Scottish Trade's Recovery – prolonged strike of 1936 has not checked expanding markets', 24 April 1937, 125.

'West of Scotland Carpet Industry – 100,000 employed by continuous demand for Home and Empire markets', 24 April 1937, 128.

Home of Scottish Craftsmanship; Beith and Lochwinnoch manufacturers who have made Scottish traditions', 24 April 1937, 129.

'Furnishing Fabrics from Scotland – A comprehensive survey', 24 April 1937, 134.

'The Empire Exhibition: Scotland's elaborate plans for biggest exhibition since Wembley', 30 April 1938, 135–6.

Caterer and Hotel Keeper

'Hotel that Looks Like a 'Great White Ship', 15 July 1933, 106.

'£1,000,000 "Flatels" Scheme: Mount Royal nearly ready', 17 August 1934, 331.

'LMS Restaurant to "Go Overseas": From Gleneagles to South Africa', 15 November 1935, 15.

'Opening date for Beresford in Glasgow', 4 March 1938, 13.

'Glasgow's First "Skyscraper" Hotel', 29 April 1938, 13.

'New £40,000 Scottish Hotel', 22 July 1938, 15.

'50,000 Guests in Six Months', 14 October 1938, 26.

Cinema

'Granite Facade – "Granite City's" New 2,060 seater – Astoria, Aberdeen', 2 January 1935, xviii.

'Lyceum, Govan, lavish new 2,600 seater', 4 January 1939, xxix.

Cinema and Theatre Construction

'Orient Picture House, Glasgow – Three Thousand Seater Atmospheric', June 1932, 16 and 36.

'Roofed with grey 'Turnall' Trafford Tiles – the "Astoria" Picture House, Possil Park Glasgow', September 1932, 2.

'The Regal, Stirling', November 1932, 23.

'The Playhouse, Peebles', October 1933, 12.

'Paramount Glasgow', February 1935, 14–16.

'Green's Playhouse, Dundee', April 1936, 32–4.

'The Lyceum, Dumfries', November 1936, 55.

'The Regal, Edinburgh – Architects Stewart Kaye and Walls – Exterior designed to achieve harmony with surrounding buildings – Interior maintains the unpretentious note', November 1938, 32.

Commercial Motor

'Expedited daily SMT Scotland–London Services', 28 April 1931, 63.

'Modern Bodywork Features as revealed at the Scottish Show', 23 November 1934, 40.

'42 Years of Service to Scotland', 11 February 1949.

Country Life

Hussey, Christopher, 'New Bridges and Concrete Structure', 28 April 1928, 594.

Hussey, Christopher, 'The New Savoy Theatre', 16 November 1930, 18.

'A Modern House in Scotland', 8 June 1935, 604–5.

Oswald, Arthur, 'Gribloch, Kippen, Stirlingshire I: The home of Mr and Mrs J M Colville', 12 January 1951, 110–14.

Oswald, Arthur, 'Gribloch, Kippen, Stirlingshire II: The home of Mr and Mrs J M Colville', 19 January 1951, 182–6.

Era

'The Latest Addition to Glasgow's Suburban Cinemas is the Aldwych', 20 April 1939, 6.

Farming News and North British Agriculturalist

'Fenton Barns', 30 June 1939.

HANDA

'Histories of Edinburgh Companies No. 28: Heggie & Aitchison', December 1963.

Historical Journal

Campbell, Roy H, 'The Scottish Office and the Special Areas in the 1930s', vol 22, no. 1, 1979, 167–83.

HKIA Journal

Wai, Tony Lam Chung, 'From British Colonization to Japanese Invasion: 100 Years of Architects in Hong Kong 1841–1941', no. 45, 2006, 51.

The Ideal Kinema and Studio

'ABC's new Riddrie House – Tower-like effect over main entrance', 17 December 1931, 30.

'Glasgow's new atmospheric – Orient PH A three thousand seater – novel note in proscenium arch decoration', 26 May 1932.

'Two New Scottish Playhouses – Alister MacDonald's achievements – The Angus, Montrose, and Playhouse, Elgin', 15 December 1932, 12.

'Glasgow's Latest – The New Bedford – Two Thousand capacity, 5 January 1933, 31.

'Aberdeen's imposing super – Capitol's brilliant interior – lit by Holophane three-colour installation', 16 February 1933, 11 and 13.

'The Commodore, Whiteinch – Dignified front elevation – Harmonious interior decoration', 16 March 1933, 21 and 25.

'Oban's new kinema theatre – Architectural features of the Playhouse – Highland scenes depicted on side walls', 17 August 1933, 26.

'The Mecca, Glasgow – James Welsh's new enterprise – attractive proscenium ornamentation', 14 September 1933, 36 and 53.

'The Playhouse, Perth – A remarkable ten-week job – black, red and gold interior', 11 January 1934, 40.

'Paramount in Scotland: Architectural Quality of New Glasgow Super', 17 January 1935, 19.

'Glasgow's latest 2,500 seater – Granada, Parkhead, added to Frutin Circuit – attractive stadium type theatre', 12 September 1935, 19–20.

'Luxury Kinema in Edinburgh Suburb – Embassy's modern treatment – Striking main facade', 9 September 1937, 31.

'ABC's Edinburgh Regal', 6 April 1939, page not numbered.

'Seating Product Survey', 13 September 1956, 11–16.

Illustrated London News

'The New Russell Institute at Paisley opened by Princess Mary', 26 March 1927, 15.

Inco Triangle

Field, E J, 'Inco in Scotland: introduction to Zenith', July 1948, 7.

Journal of British Studies

Darling, Elizabeth, 'Finella, Mansfield Forbes, Raymond McGrath, and Modernist Architecture in Britain', no. 50, January 2011, 125–55.

Journal of Contemporary History

Richardson, Harry W, 'The Economic Significance of the Depression in Britain', vol 4, no. 4, 1970, 3–19.

Begg, Stewart H M, 'The Nationalist Movement in Scotland', vol 6, no. 1, 1971, 135–152.

Journal of Scottish Historical Studies

Barclay, Gordon, 'Duties in aid of the civil power: The deployment of the Army to Glasgow, 31 January to 17 February 1919', vol 38, no. 2, 261–92.

Journal of the Decorative Arts Society

Tilson, Barbara, 'The Modern Art Department, Waring & Gillow, 1928–1931', no. 8, 1984, 40–3.

Journal of Transport History

Pope, Rex, 'Railway companies and resort hotels between the wars', March 2001, 63–5.

Taylor, Lawrence D, 'The monorail "revolution" of the 1950s and 1960s and its legacy', November 2016, 236–7.

Kinematograph Weekly

'The Caley Picture House', 11 October 1928, 65.

'Glasgow Regal – Today's Opening', 14 November 1929, 46.

'Glasgow's Regal', 21 November 1929, 64.

'Astoria, Glasgow Opening', 5 February 1931, 46.

'The Front of the Regal, Hamilton, Recently Opened', 3 September 1931, 74.

'Five Openings this Month: Premier's Son Designs Elgin Playhouse', 1 December 1932, 30.

'New Oban Playhouse', 25 May 1933, 21.

'ABC's Fortieth Kinema in Scotland: Opening of the Regal, Falkirk, 3 November 1934, 11.

'Scottish News of the Week: Paisley Regal Opened', 29 November 1934, 43.

'Paisley's Regal Opened', 6 December 1934, 21.

'The Vogue, Rutherglen', 6 February 1936, 31.

'Embassy, Glasgow', 6 February 1936, 31.

'Playhouse, Dundee, Opening Green's 4,000-seater and its Tower of Babel', 5 March 1936, 27.

'Regal Lanark Opening', 23 July 1936, 19.

'MP Opens Regal, Lanark: A Grand Send-Off', 3 September 1936, 12.

Lady Weir Opens Tudor at Giffnock', 10 December 1936, 19.

'Embassy Troon Opening', 4 March 1937, 23.

'Troon's New Kinema: Tributes to Blair's Enterprise', 25 March 1937, 13.

'Rothesay Plans', 17 June 1937, 25.

'State, Glasgow Opened', 17 June 1937, 25.

'Dunbar's New Kinema, The Playhouse, Opened Last Thursday Afternoon', 1 July 1937, 27.

'Clydebank Opening Shortly', 13 January 1938, 15.

'Lord Provost Opens Riddrie PH – Tribute to James Welsh', 10 February 1938, 21.

'2,600-seater at Clydebank for Alex King; David Kirkwood MP Opens La Scala', 17 February 1938, 5.

'This Week in Scotland – Five Openings Scheduled', 24 February 1938, 15.

'Singleton's Vogue at Govan Opening in June', 26 May 1938, 21.

'Vogue Govan Opens – 2,500 Capacity', 7 July 1938, 30.

'Odeon's First in Scotland: MP Opens Ayr', 4 August 1938, 27.

'This Week in Scotland: Five Openings Scheduled', 24 February 1938, 15.

'Fourteen Odeons for Scotland: F S Bates Forecast at Hamilton Opening', 17 November 1938, 3.

'200th Odeon Opens at Motherwell', 8 December 1938, 20.

'Fortunate in Our Kinema Proprietors: Provost's Tribute at Playhouse Fraserburgh Opening', 9 March 1939, 50.

'New Kinema Schemes at their Progress', 30 March 1939, 42.

'Twelve New Theatres Install Western Electric Sound', 4 May 1939, 38.

'Viking Opening at Largs Next Month', 8 June 1939, 27.

'Regal Lossiemouth', 29 June 1939, 32.

'Provost's Tribute to Directors at Viking Opening', 13 July 1939, 17.

'The Week in Glasgow: Ascot Opens', 30 November 1939, 13.

'Alex King Opens the Ascot: Lord Provost's Tribute', 14 December 1939, 28.

'Palace, Arbroath: New ABC 1,500 Seater', 6 June 1940, 21.

'Addition to King Circuit Opened: The Plaza, Port Glasgow', 25 January 1951, 9.

L'Esprit Nouveau

Le Corbusier, 'L'art décoratif d'aujourd'hui', 1925 (English translation 1987).

London Architect

Wamsley Lewis, E, 'E Wamsley Lewis and the New Victoria', January 1972, 4–11.

Motor Ship

'The Anchor Line's First Motor Ship', November 1937, 268.

National Floorcoverings Review

'Where Carpets are Made: James Templeton & Company', April 1932.

Partisan Review

Greenberg, Clement, 'The Avant Garde and Kitsch', autumn 1939, 34–9.

Greenberg, Clement, 'Towards a Newer Laocoon', July–August 1940, 296–310.

Picture House

Gray, Richard, 'The Cinemas of Alister G MacDonald', no. 19, 30–4.

Proceedings of the Institution of Civil Engineers

Bruce, Robert, 'The Great North Road over the Grampians', January 1931, 121–2.

Brown, Guthrie, J 'Kincardine-on-Forth Bridge', April 1937, 748–59.

Hudson, W and Hunter, J K, 'The Galloway Hydro-electric Development with Special Reference to the Constructional Works', April 1938, 323–75.

McBeth, Douglas, 'François Hennebique (1842–1921) – Reinforced Concrete Pioneer', vol 126, no. 2, 1998, 86–95.

Proceedings of the Society of Antiquaries of Scotland

'Obituary: James Smith Richardson', vol 192, 1969–70, vii–x.

Quarterly Illustrated of the Royal Incorporation of Architects in Scotland

Schultz, Earle, 'The Quest of Maximum Efficiency', no. 19, autumn 1926, 88.

Templeton, Francis Orr, 'Notes on the Work of Contemporary French Architects', no. 30, summer 1929, 37–8.

Templeton, Francis Orr, 'Notes on the Work of Contemporary French Architects', no. 32, winter 1930, 104–7.

Templeton, Francis Orr, 'Notes on the Work of Contemporary French Architects', no. 33, spring 1930, 8–11.

Thomson, Leslie Grahame, 'Concerning this Heritage', no. 38, 1932, 42–6.

Brodie, Margaret, 'Omnibus', no. 41, 1932, 20–3.

Rennie, Robert, 'The Modern Shopfront', no. 44, autumn 1933, 11 and 13.

McManus, Jnr, Philip E J, 'The Town Hall, Hilversum, Holland', no. 45, 1933, 35–40.

Johnston, Ninian, 'Members' Column: The Brink – A Reply to Mr John N Graham', no. 47, 1934, 52.

Wilson, John, 'Continental Housing', no. 51, 1935, 18–24.

'Notes from the Chapters: Edinburgh', no. 51, 1935, 38.

Lindsay, Ian G, 'Editorial – The Death of Mansfield D Forbes', no. 52, 1936, 5.

Forbes, Mansfield D, 'Attention to Tradition', no. 52, 1936, 34–5.

Dempster, J A, 'Modern Industrial Architecture in the Mining Industry', no. 53, 1936, 15–21.

Hastie, Hamish P, 'Modern Methods in Dutch Architecture', no. 53, 1935, 22–6.

Scottish Journal of Historical Studies

Mackenzie, Angus, 'Self-Help and Propaganda: Scottish National Development Council 1931–1939', vol 30, no. 2, Edinburgh: Edinburgh University Press, 2010, 123–54.

Railway Magazine

'The Coronation Scot, LMSR', July 1937, 39–42.

'The LNER Coronation Express', August 1937, 79–81.

'The New LMS and LNER Speed Records', August 1937, 111–116.

Scottish Drapery Journal

'An Evening of Eloquence: Shop Fronts, Shop Fitting and Lighting', June 1935, 23.

'Archd Hamilton (Shopfitters) Ltd', September 1935, 61.

Scottish Field

'Modern Industry', April 1938, 7.

'Building an Exhibition', March 1938, 41.

'Symbol of Unity of the People', May 1938, 6.

'Jubilee of the Pneumatic Tyre', May 1938, 20.

Scott-Moncrieff, George, 'The Month in Scotland', June 1938, 13.

'The GPO at Work', September 1938, 52.

Shipbuilding and Shipping Record

Lewis, Leslie, 'Modern Tendencies in Ship Furnishing', January 1929, 9.

'Twin-screw Passenger Liner *Empress of Japan*', September 1930, 349–54.

'*Monarch of Bermuda*', November 1931, 647–55.

'*Queen of Bermuda*', February 1933, 180–3.

The direct-drive turbine steamer *Queen Mary*', 1 June 1933, 538.

'Clyde Paddle Steamer', 8 February 1934, 150.

'The New Clyde Paddle Steamers *Mercury* and *Caledonia*', 10 May 1934, 495.

Bernard, Oliver P, 'My Impressions of the *Queen Mary*', 26 May 1936, 691–2.

'Cabin Fittings and Decorative Flooring', 28 May 1936, 716.

'The Passenger Accommodation', 28 May 1936, 737.

'The *Mauretania*: The latest Cunard-White Star liner and the largest ship to have been built in England', 15 June 1939, 755–64.

'The *Empress of Britain*', April 1956, 267–71.

SMT Magazine and Scottish Country Life

Kininmonth, William, 'Architecture Which Mirrors Today's Thought', October 1937, 44–7.

Borthwick, Alastair, 'Introduction to Bellahouston', May 1938, 35–39.

Oakley, Charles, 'Scotland's Prowess in Engineering', May 1938, 79–82.

Tait, Thomas S, 'Planning an Empire Exhibition' May 1938, 88–9.

Shiels, T Drummond, 'How Scotland has Helped the Empire', May 1938, 84–7.

Reid, Alexander, 'Our Property among the state exhibits', May 1938, 96–7.

Fleming, Mary, 'Where Shall We Eat?', May 1938, 107–8.

Bruce, Ann, 'Women's Work at Bellahouston: The contributions from women of the Empire', May 1938, 117–18.

Fleming, Mary, 'Hillington Industrial Estate: A Romance of Modern Scotland', June 1938, 49–51.

'Scotland by Bus and Coach: The SMT and Associated Companies' Striking Information Pavilion at the Empire Exhibition', June 1938, 63.

Macdonell, A G, 'What 1938 Has Meant to Scotland', October 1938, 35.

Oakley, Charles, 'Summing Up the Exhibition', October 1938, 73–5.

Sphere

'The New Architecture of the Twentieth Century: Facade of the Russell Institute, Paisley', 31 March 1928, 32.

Templetonian

'Templeton Street Extension', no. 30, December 1935, 4.

'Carpets for RMS *Queen Mary*', June 1936, 4–6.

'New Factory at Glasgow Green', no. 36, December 1938.

'Retirals: James Kincaid', December 1939, 3.

'Obituary: James Kincaid', spring 1965, 19.

Thirties Society Journal

Gold, Susan, 'The Royal Masonic Hospital', no. 2, 1982, 29–34.

Transactions of the Newcomen Society

Thwaite, Malcolm, *The George Bennie Railplane and Hugh Fraser Air-rail Systems of Transport,* vol 75 (1), 2005, 37–84

Twentieth Century Architecture

Allison, Georgina, 'The Miners' Welfare Commission and Pithead Baths in Scotland', 1994, 55–64.

Powers, Alan and Stamp, Gavin, 'The Twentieth Century Society: A Brief History', 2004, 158–60.

Vogue

Defries, Amelia, 'These Exhibitions', 13 April 1938, 114–15.

Mortimer, Raymond, 'If you go to Glasgow', 8 June 1938, 57–98.

Newspapers

Aberdeen Press and Journal
Airdrie & Coatbridge Advertiser
Arbroath Guide
Arbroath Herald
Ayr Advertiser
Bellshill Speaker
Broughty Ferry Guide and Advertiser
Bulletin
Carluke and Lanark Gazette
Coatbridge Leader
Daily Record
Dumfries and Galloway Standard
Dundee Courier
Dundee Evening Telegraph
Edinburgh Evening News
Falkirk Herald
Fife Free Press and Kirkcaldy Guardian
Forfar Herald
Glasgow Herald
Hawick Express
Inverness and Northern Counties People's Journal
Kilmarnock Herald and North Ayrshire Gazette
Kilmarnock Standard
Leven Advertiser & Wemyss Gazette
Linlithgowshire Gazette
Midlothian Advertiser
Milngavie and Bearsden Herald
Motherwell Times
Musselburgh News
Newcastle Evening Chronicle
Newcastle Journal
Oban Times and Argyllshire Advertiser
Paisley Daily Express
Perthshire Advertiser
Scotsman
Scottish Daily Express
Sea Lines
Southern Reporter
Sunday Mail
Sunderland Daily Echo and Shipping Gazette
Times
West Lothian Courier
Wishaw Press

Archival Sources

Burns Monument Centre, Kilmarnock
R941-42KK

Glasgow City Archives, Mitchell Library, Glasgow
B4/12/1935/356, B4/12/1937/519, B4/12/1938/335,
D-CA8/2983, D-CA8/1207, D-CA8/1389, D-CA8/2063,
D-CA8/2466, D-CA8/2605, D-CA8/2758, D-CA8/2887,
D-CA8/2953, D-CA8/764, TD1379, TD153/31, TD655/2/13,
TD655/2/20, TD655/2/9, TD655/8/5 166/1027/A,
TD655/9/10, TD655/9/28

Glasgow School of Art Archives Stoddart-Templeton Collection
GB 248 STOD/201/1/9/1

Heriot-Watt University Textile Archive
DB 6/1/3/5 28–29, DB 6/1/3/9 33–38, DB 7/6/1/1, DB 7/6/1/2,
DB 10/8/3

Historic Environment Scotland Archives
MS/614/2, MS/614/11/1, MS/614/12/1–4, MS/614/14,
MS/614/18/1

National Records of Scotland
HH45/46, HH45/47, HH45/51, HH45/52, MW5/102,
MW5/106, MW5/135, MW5/180

**University of Glasgow Archives and Special Collections:
Empire Exhibition Archive**
ACC 2270/24/1, ACC 2270/24/2, ACC2207/22/7,
ACC2270/23/1, ACC2270/23/5, ACCN2270/22/7,
ACCN2270/22/9, ACCN2270/8/4/3, GB 248 UGC 082,
GB 248 UGD 270

**University of Glasgow Archives and Special Collections:
John Brown Archive**
UCS 1/5/30, UCS 1/5/37, 8JP/AL/114

University of Liverpool Archives: Cunard Archive
D42/C3/1/5/25, D42/C3/1/5/29, D42/C3/1/6/97,
D42/C3/1/6/99, D42/C3/1/6/100, D42/C3/1/6/115

GLOSSARY OF STYLES

Aestheticism (1870s–1910s)

A late Victorian movement that prioritised beauty and 'art for art's sake' rather than moral messages or the realism and ugliness of the industrial era. Key figures included the writer Oscar Wilde and the painter James McNeill Whistler. In the decorative arts, typically this included elements of Arts and Crafts, Art Nouveau and Japanese imagery, using coordinated colours and striking motifs such as peacock feathers.

Arts and Crafts Movement and Style (1870s–1910s)

A movement and style, initially encouraged by the socialist design entrepreneur William Morris, to re-assert the cultural value of skilled craft making as an antidote to mechanised production. Arts and Crafts architecture referenced the shape, features and materials of local, traditional buildings. In design, furniture and textiles featured simple flat patterns inspired by nature and medieval art, rather than the excessive decoration present in their mass-produced counterparts.

Art Nouveau (1890s–1920s)

A commercial and international style of art, design and architecture that took its name from a Parisian fashion boutique. It drew inspiration from the natural world, and its defining features include graceful tendrils, organic forms, curvilinear lines, and unconventional geometry.

Baroque (1700s–1920s)

An ornate and theatrical style originating in Italy, consisting of architectural compositions of sculpted, gilded and frescoed naturalistic decoration upon classical forms. The style was revived in the nineteenth century, when industrialised production enabled its cost-effective application in palatial commercial premises such as department stores, hotels and clubs.

Beaux Arts Style (in France, C18th–C20th; in Britain and USA latter C19th–early C20th)

The mode of neoclassicism initially taught in the École des Beaux Arts in Paris and admired for its use in French royal palaces and in the mid-nineteenth century rebuilding of Paris. The typical architectural format has repetitive compositions of pilasters and window bays with restrained baroque enrichment and steep Mansard roofs with elaborate inset windows. The later British and American versions of this style were often monumental in scale and often featured deep cornicing.

Constructivism (1917–1927)

Russian Constructivism was an influential art and architectural movement with a focus on abstract geometric forms. It was heavily influenced by earlier avant-garde movements such as Cubism and Futurism. In opposition to the glamour of mainstream Art Deco, Constructivists aspired to serve a social purpose, aligning with the Communist ideals of the Soviet Union. The movement extended beyond traditional art forms to include architecture, graphic design, theatre, and clothing.

Egyptian Revival (1800–1940)

An architectural style that arose in recurring waves, the first after Napoleon's conquest of Egypt at the end of the eighteenth century and subsequently from the 1920s, following the discovery of Tutankhamun's tomb. Key features, applied mainly to commercial buildings, include architectural elements and decorations from ancient Egypt, such as curved cornices with fluting, scarabs, papyrus leaves and lotus flowers.

Expressionism (1920–1933)

A variety of symbolist approaches to the representation of the modern which arose in 1920s Germany, inspired initially by the horrors of war and so characterised by distortion, fragmentation and exaggerated gothic-inspired forms. Later, the style attempted to capture the dynamism of modern life through repetitive elongated horizontals, verticals, curves and night-time illumination.

Jazz Moderne (1925–1940)

A popular variant of Art Deco, inspired by the rhythms and tones of jazz music, translated into zigzag and wave patterns, rendered in bright colours. It could be cheaply produced using basic materials and so was widely used by commercial providers of entertainment.

Glasgow Style (1890–1910)

The Glasgow Style mixed Art Nouveau elements with those of the Scottish vernacular and, later, with rectilinearity inspired by Japanese and emergent Germanic influences.

National Romanticism (1890s–1930s)

A movement in the Nordic countries that spread to the Baltic States and Russia, with comparable aims to the Arts and Crafts Movement. It promoted traditional decorative crafts and took inspiration from nature, medieval patterning, Norse mythologies and folklore.

Neoclassicism (1750s–1930s)

Art and architecture based on Ancient Greek and Roman models, inspired by archaeological discoveries and with particular importance placed upon simplicity and correctness.

Neo-Georgian (1890s–1930s)

A revival of the neoclassical style prevalent between 1714 and 1830, evoking a sense of order, particularly in the two decades after the First World War.

ACKNOWLEDGEMENTS

My wife, Elspeth Hough, my parents, Ann Glen and John Peter, and my family.

Alasdair Burns, Christine Wilson, Neil Gregory, Ranald MacInnes, Lesley Ferguson, Neil Fraser, Susan Hamilton and Kevin MacLean of Historic Environment Scotland. Ross McAuley, Stephen Bottomley, Jamie Brown, Jenny Brownrigg, Duncan Chappell, Charlotte Dunn, Alan Horn, Helen McCormack, Alastair Macdonald, Nicholas Oddy, Andy Robertson and Sarah Smith of The Glasgow School of Art. Frances Follin for proofreading and Linda Sutherland for the index.

Alan Ainsworth; Tim Baker; Lily Barnes; Clio Barr; Norman Barr; Will Barras; Janet Beattie; Jonathan Boonzaier; Gavin Booth; Elaine Boyle; Stewart J Brown; Jack Burnett-Stuart; Dugald Cameron; Loris Clements; Joy Crooks; Chris Doak; Elspeth Edelstein; Richard Ewing; Thelma Ewing; the Reverend Ian Forrester; Mary Forrester; Jean Fraser; Martin Fraser; Olivia Gecseg; Gordon Gibb; Faye Hammill; Owen Harrison; David Henderson; Everette Hoard; John Hume; Ian Johnson; Ian Johnston; Nikki Kane; Lesley Kettle; Juliet Kinchin; Kate Lapping; Lindsey Lennie; Andrew Lucas; John McCutcheon; Ken MacGregor; Jack MacIntyre; Stuart Mackay; Kenneth MacKenzie; Angela Courte MacKenzie; J Gregor McPherson; Roy Malcolm; Karen Marr; Frank Martin; John Messner; Moz Mohammad; James Munro; Gavin Musgrove; Barbara Neilson; Fionnag NicChoinnich; Irene O'Brien; Gary Painter; David Parry; Clive Polden; Debbie Potter; David Robertson; Ian Schiffman; Joseph Sharples; Julia Stephen; Sean Stitt; Martin Søberg; Helen Taylor; John Thomas; David Trevor-Jones; Nerys Tunnicliffe; Colin Waller; Amber Whitlock; Ghislaine Wood; Lesley Wood.

Arbroath Library; Ayr Carnegie Library Local History Department; Edinburgh Central Library; Fife Archives; Glasgow City Archives; Glasgow Life; Heriot-Watt University Cameron Smail Library; Highland Archive Service; Historic Environment Scotland; Inverness Library; Leeds Archive Service; The Mitchell Library; The National Archives; National Library of Scotland; National Records of Scotland; University of Edinburgh Library; University of Glasgow Scottish Business Archives.

The research for the chapter on ocean liner interiors was carried out with the assistance of a Royal Society of Edinburgh Small Research Grant.

INDEX

Page numbers in *italics* refer to captions.

Historic Environment Scotland

HISTORIC ENVIRONMENT SCOTLAND | ÀRAINNEACHD EACHDRAIDHEIL ALBA

We are the lead public body for Scotland's historic environment: a charity dedicated to the advancement of heritage, culture, education and environmental protection. Through our books we are telling the stories of Scotland – exploring ideas and starting conversations about the past, present and future of our nation's history and heritage.

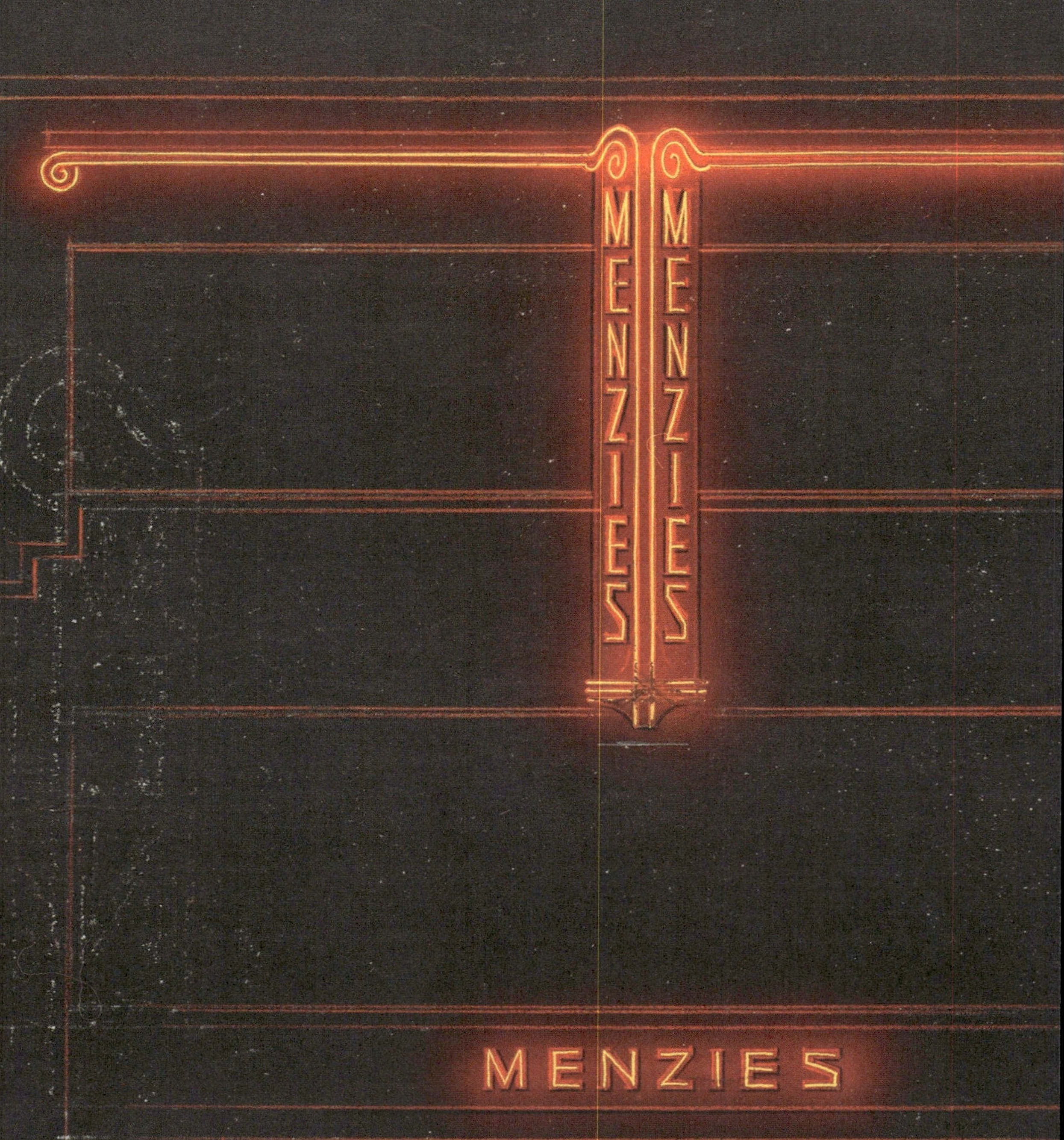
MENZIES
MENZIES
MENZIES